MARINE ISSUES

From a Scientific, Political and Legal Perspective

MARINE ISSUES

FROM A SCIENTIFIC, POLITICAL AND LEGAL PERSPECTIVE

Editors:

PETER EHLERS, ELISABETH MANN-BORGESE,
RÜDIGER WOLFRUM

Assistant Editor:

CRISTINA HOSS

KLUWER LAW INTERNATIONAL
THE HAGUE / LONDON / NEW YORK

Published by:
Kluwer Law International
P.O. Box 85889, 2508 CN The Hague, The Netherlands
sales@kli.wkap.nl
http://www.kluwerlaw.com

Sold and Distributed in North, Central and South America by:
Kluwer Law International
101 Philip Drive, Norwell, MA 02061, USA
kluwerlaw@wkap.com

Sold and Distributed in all other countries by:
Kluwer Law International
Distribution Centre, P.O. Box 322, 3300 AH Dordrecht, The Netherlands

Library of Congress Cataloging-in-Publication Data is available.

Printed on acid-free paper.

ISBN 90-411-1740-7

Kluwer Law International incorporates the imprint Martinus Nijhoff Publishers.

Printed and bound in Great Britain by MPG Books Limited, Bodmin, Cornwall.

Table of Contents

Foreword

A the reader may know, Professor Elisabeth Mann Borgese, died unexpectedly on February 9, 2002. However, she has worked until the end on the editing of the present book.

The remaining editors wish to express their deep regret for the loss of one of the most beloved masters of the helm of International Law.

Prof. Dr. Peter Ehlers
Prof. Dr. Dr. hc. Rüdger Wolfrum *Hamburg/Heidelburg, 10 February 2002*

List of Abbreviations

AEM	Applied Environmental Microbiology
AJIL	American Journal of International Law
AöR	Archiv des öffentlichen Rechts
B-BSH	Berichte des Bundesamtes für Seeschiffahrt und Hydrographie
BGBl	Bundesgesetzblatt
BSEP	Baltic Sea Environment Proceedings
BSMP	Baltic Sea Marine Proceedings
BWRS	Ballast Water Research Series
BYIL	British Yearbook of International Law
CEP	Contemporary Economic Policy
CJTNL	Columbia Journal of Transnational Law
EcoLQ	Ecology Law Quarterly
EELR	European Environmental Law Review
EL	Environmental Lawyer
EPIL	Encyclopedia of Public International Law
EPL	Environmental Policy and Law
GIELR	Georgia International Environmental Law Review
HZ	Historische Zeitschrift
ICES CRR	ICES Cooperative Research Report
IJIL	Indian Journal of International Law
IJMCL	The International Journal of Marine and Coastal Law
ILM	International Legal Materials
JfWG	Jahrbuch für Wirtschaftsgeschichte
JIR	Jahrbuch für internationales Recht
JMLC	Journal of Maritime Law and Commerce
JMS	Journal of Marine Systems
JZ	Juristenzeitung
MAP TRS	MAP Technical Reports Series
MarPol	Marine Policy
MPY UNL	Max-Planck Yearbook of United Nations Law
NuR	Natur und Recht
NYIL	Netherland Yearbook of International Law

OCLJ	Ocean and Coastal Law Journal
ODIL	Ocean Development and International Law
OJ	Official journal of the European Communities
PiO	Progress in Oceanography
RCADI	Recueil des Cours/Académie de Droit International de La Haye
RECIEL	Review of European Community and International Environmental Law
RGDIP	Revue Générale de Droit International Public
RSRS	Regional Seas Reports and Studies
TELJ	Tulane Environmental Law Journal
UoRLR	University of Richmond Law Review
WLLR	Washington and Lee Law Review
YIEL	Yearbook of International Environmental Law
ZaöRV	Zeitschrift für ausländisches öffentliches Recht und Völkerrecht = Heidelberg Journal of International Law
ZGHK	Zeitschrift für das Gesamte Handelsrecht und Konkursrecht

*Wolfgang Graf Vitzthum**

FROM THE RHODIAN SEA LAW TO UNCLOS III

Outlining the highly complex history of the law of the sea is like sailing in uncharted waters. We all know, however, that there is a captain on board the Pacem in Maribus ship, *Elisabeth Mann Borgese*, who will always save us, passengers, crew and stowaway, from being shipwrecked. Sometimes parts of the lading will have to be thrown overboard in stormy sea to lighten the ship. Way back in 1968, however, when the Pacem in Maribus ship set sail, our captain did the opposite: she took me on board as the ship boy. Having been present at the maiden voyage of the Pacem in Maribus ship,[1] it is an honour and a privilege for me to give an outline of the history of the law of the sea some 32 years after those humble beginnings. I can only hope that after my lecture neither our captain nor you will feel the need to throw me overboard in order to prevent the ship from getting into distress.

1. Lex Rhodia and UNCLOS III: Cornerstones of the History of the Law of the Sea

The land divides and the sea unites. Throughout history, the oceans have brought people together, mainly by enabling and facilitating maritime traffic and trade. In this respect, the starting point of my outline, the Lex Rhodia, is typical: This monument of Byzantine jurisprudence, of influence for more than 2000 years, is the codification of the customs of maritime trade in the Mediterranean Sea during Greek Antiquity.[2] It laid the foundation of modern maritime jurisprudence.

The main focus of my presentation, however, will be the public order of the oceans, that is to say the development of the law of the sea as a branch of public international law. In sketching these developments I will take you on a journey through history, relying, *inter alia*, upon the classic work of *Wilhelm Grewe*, *Epochen der*

* Prof. Dr., Professor, University of Tübingen.

1 *Wolfgang Graf Vitzthum*, Pacem in Maribus, in: *AöR* 94 (1969), 419–425.

2 *Walter Ashburner*, Nomos Rhodion Nautikos, The Rhodian Sea-Law (Oxford 1909) (reprinted Aalen 1976); *Dimitrios G. Letsios*, Nomos Rhodion Nautikos, Das Seegesetz der Rhodier (Rhodos, 1996); *Jean Rougé*, Recherches sur l'organisation du commerce maritime en Méditerranée sous l'Empire romain, pp. 397–413 (Paris 1966) ("Le jet et les problèmes de la loi Rhodienne"); *Hans Kreller*, Lex Rhodia, Untersuchungen zur Quellengeschichte des römischen Seerechtes, in: *ZGHK* 85 (1921), 257–367; *Philipp Heck*, Das Recht der Großen Haverei, pp. 592–627 (Berlin 1889).

P. Ehlers, E. Mann-Borgese and R. Wolfrum (eds.), Marine Issues, 1–17

Völkerrechtsgeschichte, which was recently translated into English by *Michael Byers*.[3] The last chapter of this book deals with the Third United Nations Conference on the Law of the Sea, UNCLOS III, the second topic mentioned in the title of my lecture. After nine years of negotiations, the United Nations Convention on the Law of the Sea was signed at Montego Bay, Jamaica, on 10 December 1982. Twelve years later, this instrument, probably the most important in the history of the law of the sea, entered into force,[4] after the cause for the fierce opposition to its Part XI on deep seabed mining had been removed by the adoption of the Agreement relating to the Implementation of Part XI of the United Nations Convention on the Law of the Sea on July 28, 1994 by the United Nations General Assembly. Today there are many law of the sea problems that call for new legal approaches.

My topic, "From the Rhodian Sea Law to UNCLOS III", thus stretches from the second century B.C. to the end of the second millennium, taking the two most noteworthy instruments of the law of the sea as its beginning and end. What are the changes that the law of the sea went through over the two millennia? Which principles, rules, and institutions have been thrown overboard during the journey in order to keep the law of the sea afloat? What has been saved, what has been made worse, what has been improved? What are the influences of those historical developments on today's law of the sea and on international law in general?

2. Rhodian Sea Law: Antiquity and Beyond

We do not know much about the ancient law of the sea. The Rhodian Sea Law, however, the *nómos Rodíon nautikós*, is well known. Why? Why is this collection of Eastern Mediterranean maritime law the starting point of any survey of the history of the law of the sea?

The Aegean island of Rhodos became a major centre of commerce in Greek Antiquity. Almost all trade between Europe and Asia was channelled through the island. The Rhodians were famous for their *eunomía*, their law-abiding character. Therefore, it does not come as a surprise that the paramount code on marine and commercial law was called the "Rhodian Law". Its body of rules can be traced only much later, to sources belonging to the Roman Empire and to the Byzantine (or "Eastern Roman") Empire. In the famous *Corpus Iuris Civilis* compiled by the

---

3 *Wilhelm Grewe*, The Epochs of International Law (Berlin/New York 2000). See also *Karl-Heinz Ziegler*, Völkerrechtsgeschichte (München 1994); *Wolfgang Preiser/Stephan Verosta/Hans-Ulrich Scupin*, History of the Law of Nations, in: *Rudolf Bernhardt* (ed.), *EPIL* vol. II (1995), 716–793.

4 See *UN (Division for Ocean Affairs and the Law of the Sea)*, The Law of the Sea, Official Texts, pp. 7–213 (New York 1997). – UNCLOS was not a widely accepted codification of existing legal rules. On the contrary, in parts it contained controversial norms not yet in force in 1982, as well as a draft for an entire sectoral world order for the deep sea bed and its resources. See also *Davor Vidas/Willy Østreng* (eds.), Order for the Oceans at the Turn of the Century (The Hague/London/Boston 1999).

Byzantine Emperor *Justinian* in the 6th century A.D. (the Code of Justinian), the Rhodian law is expressly mentioned.[5]

One example is the law of jettison, *Lex Rhodia de iactu*. Under the name of "general average" (the word *avaria* must have been latinized from Arabic)[6] or *Grosse Haverei* this classical *aequitas*-oriented rule can still be found in today's maritime law of many jurisdictions. With the York and Antwerp Rules (YAR), in their latest version of 1994, internationally agreed terms of contract are available that aim at unifying the law of general average.

The *Digests* explain what it is all about:

> "... [If] cargo has been jettisoned in order to lighten a ship, the sacrifice for the common good must be made good by common contribution".[7]

---

5 See *Franz Wieacker*, Römische Rechtsgeschichte, Quellenkunde, Rechtsbildung, Jurisprudenz und Rechtsliteratur, pp. 349–351 (München 1988). See also *K.M.T. Atkinson*, Rome and the Rhodian Sea-Law, in: *IURA* 25 (1974), 46–98; *Percy Thomas Fenn*, Justinian and the Freedom of the Sea, in: *AJIL* 19 (1925), 716–727; *Pitman B. Potter*, The Freedom of the Seas in History, Law, and Politics, pp. 25–35 (London 1924); *Kreller* (*supra* note 2), pp. 273–309, 337–347; *Coleman Phillipson*, The International Law and Custom of Ancient Greece and Rome, vol. II, pp. 366–384, 379–380 (London 1911); *Mauritius Müller-Jochmus*, Geschichte des Völkerrechts im Alterthum, pp. 223–266 (Leipzig 1848). – The content of the *Corpus Iuris* compilation dates back to classical Roman law and thus cannot be attributed to the period of transition from Antiquity to the Middle Ages. It had been developed by lawyers of the Roman Empire and put to new uses by Justinian. Thus, only Byzantium still made use of the sophisticated Roman law that elsewhere – and this is true also for Roman sea law – fell more and more into oblivion. See *Kreller* (*supra* note 2), pp. 347–362.

6 See *Hassan S. Khalilieh*, Islamic Maritime Law, pp. 100–105, 101 (Leiden/Boston/Köln 1998): The Muslims developed the laws of *general average* "further than what was found in the Latin sources of the late twelfth century." *Ibid*, p. 105: "When part of the shipment was jettisoned, the owners of jetsam became [under Islamic Law] partners, proportionately, in the goods that remained safe. The legal act is termed [...] as an 'involuntary partnership'." See also *Müller-Jochmus* (*supra* note 5), pp. 249–256; *Carsten Grau*, Havarie-grosse nach YAR und die Neuerungen durch Sydney 1994, in: *Transportrecht* 21 (1998), 279–280; *Donaldson/Staughton/Wilson*, The Law of General Average and the York-Antwerp Rules, p. 232 (10th ed., London 1975); *Gerard J. Mangone*, United States Admiralty Law (The Hague/London/Boston 1997); *Heinrich Honsell*, Ut omnium contributione sarciatur quod pro omnibus datum est, Die Kontribution nach der lex Rhodia de iactu, in: *Ars boni et aequi, Liber Amicorum W. Waldstein*, pp. 141–150 (Stuttgart 1993); *Herbert Wagner*, Die lex Rhodia de iactu, in: *RIDA* 44 (1997), 357–380; *Gunter Wesener*, Von der lex Rhodia de iactu zum § 1043 ABGB, in: *Recht und Wirtschaft in Geschichte und Gegenwart, Liber Amicorum J. Bärmann*, pp. 31–51 (München 1975); *C. John Colombos*, The International Law of the Sea, pp. 29–30 (4th ed., London 1959); Heck (*supra* note 2), pp. 628–640.

7 "Lege Rhodia cavetur, ut, si levandae navis gratia iactus mercium factus est, omnium contributione sarciatur quod pro omnibus datum est," Paulus libro secundo Sententiarum, Digests 14, 2, 1. See also Paulus libro 34 Ad edictum, Digests 14, 2, 2 pr. 1: "... aequissimum enim est commune detrimentum fieri eorum, qui propter amissas res aliorum consecuti sunt, ut merces suas salvas haberent" ("for it is only fair that the loss should be shared by all those whose property has been saved by means of the sacrifice of a property of others"). We also learn from the Digests (D. 14, 2, 9) that the Roman Emperor Antoninus [Pius], responding to a petition by a sea merchant who claimed to have been plundered by tax collectors, declared: "I am master of the world, but the law of the sea must be judged by the sea law of the Rhodians where our own law does not conflict with it." See *Corpus Iuris Civilis*, Text und Übersetzung, vol. III, Digesten 11–20, (*Okko Behrends et al.*, tr. (into German) and ed.)

Under "Rhodian Law" everything, which benefits from the sacrifice for the common safety in a common peril (*Seewurf* or *Notwurf*), is liable to contribute – but free man. This reminds us of the idea developed by the German philosopher Immanuel Kant (*Grundlegung zur Metaphysik der Sitten; Metaphysik der Sitten*) in the age of Enlightenment and which forms the basis of modern day human rights concepts: human beings as such are not liable to contribute merely because their lives have been saved, since the value of a human being cannot be assessed in monetary terms; in other words, human life and dignity carry no price tag, do not have a "Marktpreis".[8]

In Antiquity and in the early Middle Ages States were not particularly interested in extending their jurisdiction over the seas. The sea was left to the merchants and their trade (and, from time to time, to the warriors and their naval battles). We know of no legal doctrine at the time claiming sovereignty over the sea.[9] On the contrary, State practice supports the conclusion that "free seas" were regarded as a prerequisite for "free communication." Obviously, this was the underlying principle of the Rhodian Sea Law, which – with its contents restricted to the necessary regulation of maritime trade – shows that State influence was rather limited. This is also reflected by the way in which the rules of maritime law were formed. Being a veritable "merchant law" it derived from the customs of sea-faring merchants.[10]

Antiquity suffered, in a double sense, from an "oceanic plague" which, although to a lesser degree, is still haunting us today: piracy. Detailed reports are available of the crimes – robbery, kidnapping, etc. – committed by pirates. Rome, mainly interested in *terra firma*, in land territory, in the beginning did not recognize the importance of security on the seas. This law enforcement vacuum was used by pirates. They even kidnapped *Julius Caesar* in 75 B.C. and released him only after he had paid a

pp. 206–207, 212 (Heidelberg 1999); The Digest of Justinian, English translation (*Alan Watson* ed.), vol. I, pp. 419–421a (Philadelphia 1985).

8 See *Christoph Enders*, Die Menschenwürde in der Verfassungsordnung, pp. 189–201 (Tübingen 1997); *Wolfgang Graf Vitzthum*, Menschenwürde als Verfassungsbegriff, in: *JZ* 1985, 201–205. See also *Khalilieh* (*supra* note 6), p. 97: "Medieval European lawyers were less concerned (than Islamic jurists) about addressing the issue of human jettison.".

9 *Fenn* (*supra* note 5), pp. 721–723; *Peter Klose*, Die völkerrechtliche Ordnung der hellenistischen Staatenwelt in der Zeit von 280 bis 168 v. Chr., p. 168 (München 1972) (at p. 119 *Klose* notes a historical episode of 220 B.C.: When the city of Byzantium decided to levy tolls on goods being transported through the Bosporus, it was the Republic of Rhodes which therefore declared war upon the city, a war which was finally avoided by the city giving in).

10 *Leon E. Trakman*, The Evolution of the Law Merchant, in: *JMLC* 12 (1980), 1–24, 153–182. – The aforementioned York-Antwerps Rules (*supra* note 6) fit well into this general scheme since they, too, were fostered by merchant practice. Although using these rules in shipping contracts is common practice, it is not mandatory. Thus even today this area of merchant law shows a remarkable self-restraint by States which allows the YAR – if applied by the contracting parties – to take precedence over national legal regulations of general average.

considerable ransom.[11] When Rome realized the threat, the Empire fought back in a powerful, efficient way. In 67 B.C., *Pompeius* – acting under the *Lex Gabinia* – lead a successful war against the pirates in the Eastern Mediterranean. The pirates were not regarded as "regular enemies", *iusti hostes*. *Cicero*, in his *De Officiis* (3, 29/107), called them *communis hostis omnium*, the "common enemy of all". The definition by the great orator and distinguished lawyer is still valid today: *piratae hostes humani generis sunt*. According to Article 100 UNCLOS, all States are under a duty to cooperate in the repression of piracy.[12]

Roman law contained rules according to which the sea was free.[13] At the same time, however, it were the Romans who considered themselves to be masters of the whole Mediterranean – we see, double standards of super powers are not a new phenomenon. In Roman conception, the Mediterranean was their *mare nostrum*. This meant, above all, the obligation of preserving law and order as in the case of the fight against piracy.[14]

3. The Middle Ages and the Age of Discoveries: the Influence of the Cities and the Struggle for the Globe

From the period of transition from Antiquity to the Middle Ages (400–800 A.D.) I turn to the Middle Ages. It is not before this epoch that new developments in the

[11] *Karl-Heinz Ziegler*, Pirata communis hostis omnium, in: *Manfred Harder/Georg Thielmann* (eds.), *De iustitia et iure, Festgabe für Ulrich von Lübtow*, pp. 14–95 (Berlin 1980); *Alfred P. Rubin*, The Law of Piracy, pp. 6 *et seq.* (2nd ed., Irvington-on-Hudson, N.Y. 1998); *Phillipson* (*supra* note 5), pp. 371–375; *Raimund Schulz*, Caesar und das Meer, in: *HZ* 271 (2000), 281–309; *Rainer Lagoni*, Piraterie und widerrechtliche Handlungen gegen die Sicherheit der Seeschiffahrt, in: *Jörn Ipsen/Edzard Schmidt-Jortzig* (eds.), *Recht – Staat – Gemeinwohl, Festschrift für Dietrich Rauschning*, pp. 501–534, 501–502 (Köln/Berlin/Bonn/München 2001).

[12] See also Articles 101–107, 110 UNCLOS; *Lagoni* (*supra* note 11), pp. 512–520.

[13] As can be read in the Digests (D.1.8.2. pr), the seas were regarded to be *naturali iure communia omnium* (common to all by natural law), owned by no one, open freely to all men. "Et quidem naturali iure omnium communia sunt illa: aer, aqua profluens, et mare, et per hoc litora maris" ("And indeed by natural law the following belong in common to all men: air, flowing water, and the sea, and therewith the shores of the sea"). See Corpus Iuris Civilis (*supra* note 7), vol. II, p. 138 (1995); The Digest of Justinian (*supra* note 7), p. 24a; *Gutierrez-Masson*, Mare nostrum: imperium or dominium?, in: *RIDA*, 3re sér. 40 (1993), 293–315, 314/315.

[14] The exact scope and meaning of the *mare nostrum* concept are not totally clear today. *Hugo Grotius* argued that the capacity which the Romans claimed for themselves in this regard was restricted to policing the ocean in order to fight piracy and did not entail any propriety rights over the sea. See *Grotius*, Mare Liberum, ch. 5 (Leiden 1609); German translation by *Richard Boschan*, Hugo Grotius – Von der Freiheit der Meere (Leipzig, 1919). A slightly different approach also seems convincing. It argues that Rome merely claimed *imperium*, as a form of "political sovereignty", but strictly no *dominium* or property over the sea, thus leaving the uses of the sea as a common good open to all. See *Gutierrez-Masson* (*supra* note 13): "… celui d'imperium, la souveraineté politique de Rome sur la mer et le litus, ce qui permettrait une fonction de contrôle ou d'inspection sur eux, mais complètement étrangère à l'idée de dominium ou propriété, et celui de communem, qui, au contraire, se rapportait à l'usage pour tous les hommes de la mer…, ce qui exclurait toute forme d'appropriation de la part de Rome ou de tout autre peuple." See also *Fenn* (*supra* note 5), p. 724: *populi Romani esse* may indeed have merely meant "are subject to the guardianship of the Roman people.".

law of the sea can be traced. Characteristic of this era is the important role played by the cities of Venice and Genoa in the South and the Hanseatic League, an alliance of Northern European merchant cities, in the North. While Venice and Genoa made most of their riches trading in oriental spices and luxury articles, the Hanseatic merchants based their success on basic consumer goods, especially grain.[15]

The influence of the cities is reflected in the development of maritime law. While Antiquity was marked by a widespread uniformity of the applicable law – the *Lex Rhodia*, as we have seen, being the paramount set of rules –, the medieval merchant cities issued their own sea laws, although "Rhodian" influences on these new laws of the mercantile marine cannot be denied; after all, lawyers and lawmakers love to borrow from each other. Thus, we find the sea laws of Venice and Genoa and of other Mediterranean cities like Amalfi, Pisa and Marseilles.[16] Influential compilations of maritime laws emerged which systematically arranged, *inter alia*, the judgements of the maritime law tribunal on the Island of Oléron in the Bay of Biscay, the *Rôles d'Oléron* (Laws of Oleron), or summarized the decisions of "maritime consuls" in the great ports of the Western Mediterranean, the *Consolat del Mar* (Consulate of the Sea). In the Baltic Sea, merchants accepted the Laws of Wisby or the laws of the Hanseatic Cities of Lübeck (of 1586) and Hamburg (the latter, the "Hamburger Recht" of 1497 and 1603, was influenced, *inter alia*, by the Lex Rhodia).

The custom of sea merchants played a pivotal role in the formation of these maritime law codes. Thus, the *Tabula Amalfitana* – the maritime law of the Italian city of Amalfi dating from the 14th century – declares:

> "Lex est sanctio sancta, bona tamen consuetudo est sanctior, et quod ubi consuetodo loquitur, lex omnis taceat." (Law is a sacred sanction, the good custom, however, is more sacred, and therefore where custom speaks, the whole law should remain silent).

The freedom of the seas or, to be more precise, the Roman law principle that no one had dominion or supreme control over the seas – irrespective of whether this principle was a legal or only a factual one – was now facing a serious challenge. While the Hanseatic League considered the freedom of the seas beneficial to its interests in free trade,[17] others claimed sovereignty or exclusive power over sea areas adjacent to their coasts. This can be seen, for example, in England's claim over "its" *Narrow Seas* or in Denmark's efforts to exercise control over the Baltic.[18]

The most famous case in this respect is Venice. Relying on its superior fleet and having extended its territorial reach over the entire coast of the Adriatic, Venice was

---

15 *Zsigmond Pál Pach*, Zur Geschichte der internationalen Handelswege und des Handelskapitals vom 15. bis 17. Jahrhundert, in: *JfWG* 1969, 179.

16 *Karl-Friedrich Krieger*, Die Entwicklung des Seerechts im Mittelmeerraum von der Antike bis zum Consolat del Mar, in: *JIR* 16 (1973), 179–209; *Colombos* (*supra* note 6), pp. 30–34; *Potter* (*supra* note 5), pp. 36–56.

17 *Ernst Reibstein*, Das Völkerrecht der deutschen Hanse, in: *ZaöRV* 17 (1956/57), 38–68, 65.

18 See *Thomas W. Fulton*, The Sovereignty of the Sea (Edinburgh/London 1911).

in a position to exercise effective control in this part of the Mediterranean. Entry into the Adriatic Sea was made conditional upon the permission of Venice – and the payment of high fees. Symbol of these claims was an annual ceremony on Ascension Day – the "marriage with the sea." With the words "*Desponsamus te mare in signum veri perpetuique dominii*" (We marry you, the sea, as a sign of true and lasting governance) the Venetian Doge at this occasion threw a ring into the sea. However, Venice also guaranteed the safety in these waters. It kept the shipping lanes free from the depredations by pirates; Rhodes and Rome had also played the role of protectress and refuge of merchant shipping in the Mediterranean during their time. Rights over maritime zones were thus coupled from the outset with the duty to preserve law and order therein.

The Age of Discoveries saw the rise of other countries to sea power: Spain and Portugal came first, followed by the Dutch and the English. While earlier quests for sea dominance aimed at sea areas close by (like the Adriatic Sea in the case of Venice), the new sea powers began to struggle for the globe.

Spain and Portugal started the race for newly discovered territories, gaining supremacy over huge territories in South America and South-East Asia. Colonisation of these territories, which were rich in resources, began quickly – and unbelievably ruthless. Papal bulls granted or confirmed (*Inter caetera* [1493], *Ea quae pro bono* [1506]) exclusive rights over the respective discoveries. The existence of competing claims led to the conclusion of the Treaty of Tordesillas on 7 June 1494, by which the two Iberian Powers partitioned the Atlantic Ocean and parts of the New World by an inter-polar line of longitude lying 370 leagues west of the Cape Verde Islands. On this basis Spain and Portugal tried to exclude others from sailing to their colonies by denying them the right of navigation on the oceans covered by the Tordesillas regime.[19]

However, neither the French, nor the Dutch or the English accepted any regime dividing the world without them being part of it. Thus, when in 1580 (twenty-nine years prior to the appearance of *Grotius*' *Mare liberum*) Spain protested against the activities of English privateers (like *Sir Francis Drake*) in Western Atlantic areas which under the Tordesillas agreement came under Spanish dominion, *Queen Elizabeth* (1558–1603) declared that:

> "[…] she understood not, why hers and other Princes' subjects should be barred from the Indies, which she could not persuade herself the Spaniard had any rightful title to by the Byshop of Rome's donation … [The] use of the air is

[19] *Grewe* (*supra* note 3), p. 258. Spain was given the right to navigate in Portugal's portion provided Spanish ships followed the most direct route to their destination. See also *Gundolf Fahl*, Der Grundsatz der Freiheit der Meere in der Staatenpraxis von 1493 bis 1648, pp. 25–26 (Köln/Berlin/Bonn/München 1969); *Ziegler* (*supra* note 3), pp. 152–154, 159–160; *H. Vander Linden*, Alexander VI. and the Demarcation of the Maritime and Colonial Domains of Spain and Portugal, 1493–1494, in: *Am. Hist. Rev.* 22 (1916), 1–20. – At the time, defining "longitude" may have been technically impossible. The parameters were probably defined differently.

> common to all; neither can any title to the ocean belong to any people or private man, forasmuch as neither nature nor regard of the public use permitteth any possession thereof".[20]

The fervent defence of the freedom of the seas by the English declined at the beginning of the 17th century when England found itself in conflict over fishing rights in the North Sea. In 1609 King James I. (1603–1625) issued a decree making fishing in the disputed areas conditional upon a licence granted by the English authorities.[21]

This brings us to the well-known "battle of the books." It was no coincidence that the same year – 1609 – saw the publication of an anonymous study with the title *Mare liberum.* This book, which later turned out to be part of a larger work on the law of prize and booty (*De iure praedae*) by a brilliant young Dutch advocate, *Hugo Grotius* (1583–1645), had been written in 1604. It had served as a defence brief in a prize law case dealing with the Portuguese carack *Santa Catarina* captured by a Dutch vessel in the Moluccan Straits in 1603 – an area which was claimed at the time by the Portuguese. In his treatise *Grotius* denied any right over the sea. The sea, the Dutch Protestant argued, was a common good of all mankind. Neither the Holy Bible, nor Papal donations, natural law, occupation, discovery, or any title of prescription or custom could change the fact that the sea was – by its very nature and according to eternal law – free for the common use by all; by the law of nations, trade is free to all persons whatsoever – the Portuguese prohibition of trade had no foundation in equity.[22]

The publishing of *Mare liberum* was no longer directed against the Portuguese but was intended to serve the Low Countries in their disputes with England. The claims to the *Oceannus Britannicus*, i.e. to the exclusivity of certain fishing grounds adjacent to the coasts of England, were defended, *inter alia*, by the Englishman *John*

---

20 *Fulton* (*supra* note 18), p. 107. See also citation by *Camden*, The History of the Most Renowned and Victorious Princess Elizabeth, Late Queen of England (1688), p. 255: "... this [Papal] Donation of that which is another man's, which is of no validity in law, and this imaginary property, cannot hinder other Princes from trading into those countries and, without breach of the law of nations, from transporting colonies into those parts thereof where the Spaniards inhabit not; ...neither from freely navigating that vast ocean, seeing the use of the sea and air is common to all. Neither can a title to the ocean belong to any people or private persons; forasmuch as neither nature nor public use and custom permitteth any possession thereof." *Camden*, *ibid*, p. 309: "necnon Oceanum illum vastum libere navigent cum maris et aeris usus omnibus sit communis... Nec ius in Oceanum populo, aut privato cuipiam possit competere, cum nec natura, nec usus publici ratio occupationem permittat." – The activities of the privateers were authorized by *lettres de marque* or *lettres de représailles*.

21 See *Fulton* (*supra* note 18), pp. 116, 118–164, and annex F.

22 *Grewe* (*supra* note 3), p. 267. *Grotius* relied generally on poets (e.g. *Vergil*), historians, historical facts, pre-Christian authorities, the Bible, and similar sources to support his arguments and citations. See also *Daniel P. O'Connell*, The International Law of the Sea, vol. I (*I.A. Shearer* ed.), pp. 9–18 (Oxford 1982); *Lassa F. Oppenheim*, International Law, A Treatise (*H. Lauterpacht* ed.), pp. 593–594 (8th ed., London 1955); *Potter* (*supra* note 5), pp. 57–80; *Charles Ralph Boxer*, The Dutch Seaborne Empire 1600–1800, pp. 84–112 (London 1965); *Fahl* (*supra* note 19), pp. 106–116, 119–122; *Frans De Pauw*, Grotius and the Law of the Sea, pp. 46–61 (Brussels 1965); *Ziegler* (*supra* note 3), pp. 168–169; *Hans Klee*, Hugo Grotius und Johannes Selden, pp. 17–26 (Bern 1946).

Selden in his book *Mare Clausum*, published in 1635. *Selden* argued – in contrast to *Grotius* – that it was indeed possible to occupy the oceans; to that end it was only necessary to control them effectively by means of naval power.[23] Both scholars, *Grotius* and *Selden*, acted as advocates of commercial and other vested interests; at the same time they were inspired by patriotic motives.

Of course, it was the Grotian concept which in principle prevailed: the freedom of the seas has become a generally recognized principle of international law, even a norm of *ius cogens*. It is difficult to tell, however, whether this success was due to the fact that in these juridical controversies *Grotius* had put forward the more convincing arguments. The interests of the maritime powers developed in such a way that it was simply more beneficial to them to accept *Grotius*' pragmatic notion. The *Mare liberum* has become *the* classic of the international law of the sea. It may, indeed, have been the most influential formulation of the principle of the freedom of the seas – but it certainly was not the first one. *Grotius* relied on many sources from Antiquity to his days. Most prominent among these featured the writings of late Spanish scholasticism, especially by *Fernando Vásquez* and *Francisco de Vitoria*, and of the Italian jurist *Alberico Gentili*.[24]

Vásquez (about 1504–1566) in his study of 1559, *Controversiae Illustres (II, 89, § 34)*, defended the freedom of the seas at a time when Spain claimed sovereignty over the world oceans:[25]

> "Ergo in aequoribus et aquis nullum jus est aut esse potest humano generi, praeterquam quoad usum communem." (Consequently, there is or can be no right over the seas and the water for mankind, except for common use).

Vitoria (1483–1546) – in citing Roman and natural law – stated that "... iure naturali communia sunt omnium, et aqua profluens et mare ..." (the water and the seas are by natural law common to all). Therefore "neminem licet ab illis prohibere" (it is not permitted to exclude anyone from them).[26] The morality-based approach of the

---

23 See *Fulton* (*supra* note 18), pp. 366–377.

24 *Antonio Truyol y Serra*, Grotius dans ses rapports avec les classiques espagnols du droit des gens, in: *RCADI* 182 (1983), 431–446. See also *Oppenheim/Lauterpacht* (*supra* note 22), pp. 593–594: "The real reason for the freedom of the open sea is represented in the motive which led to the attack against maritime sovereignty, and in the purpose of which such attack was made – namely, the freedom of communication, and especially commerce, between the States which are separated by the sea. The sea being an international highway which connects distant lands, it is the common conviction that it should not be under the sway of any State whatever. It is the interest of free intercourse between the States that the principle of the freedom of the open sea has become universally recognized and will always be upheld.".

25 *Ernst Reibstein*, Die Anfänge des neueren Natur- und Völkerrechts, Studien zu den "Controversiae illustres" des Fernandus Vasquius (1559), pp. 226 *et seq.* (Bern 1949); *Georg Stadtmüller*, Geschichte des Völkerrechts, vol. I, pp. 95–115 (Hannover 1951); *Antonio-Enrique Pérez Luño*, Die klassische spanische Naturrechtslehre in 5 Jahrhunderten, pp. 51 *et seq.* (Berlin 1994).

26 De Indis recenter inventis et de jure belli hispanorum in barbaros. Relectiones (1539), III, 2 and III, 1, (*Walter Schätzel* ed.) (Tübingen 1952); *Rolf Grawert*, Francisco de Vitoria, Naturrecht – Herrschaftsordnung – Völkerrecht, in: *Der Staat* 39 (2000), 110–125, 118–122; *Ziegler* (*supra* note 3), pp. 163–164.

teacher of *Vásquez* founded the freedom of navigation on an eternal "human right" to communication, the *ius communicationis*:

> "... a principio orbis (cum omnia essent communia) licebat unicuique, in quamcumque regionem vellet, intendere et peregrinari. Non autem videtur hoc demptum per rerum divisionem; nunquem enim fuit intentio gentium per illam divisionem tollere hominum invicem communicationem ..." (Everyone could from the beginning of the world [when everything was common to all] head out for and travel in any region he wanted. This right does not seem to have been abolished by the partition of the world; as the peoples never had the intention to abolish the mutual communication between men by this partition).

Finally, *Alberico Gentili* (1552–1608) has to be mentioned among those who influenced *Grotius*. In his *De iure belli libri tres* of 1588/89 (lib. I, cap. XIX), the Italian attacked the view that Venice possessed the Adriatic – as a violation of the law of nature: "the sea is open to all because of its nature and its use is common to all, just as that of the air" (Elizabeth I was referring to air too).

The battle of the books also illustrates how closely the position of States on the question of the freedom of the seas depended upon their maritime interests. As long as "Britannia" was not powerful enough "to rule the waves," it was a fervent advocate of the freedom of the seas. However, with England becoming the pre-eminent sea power, its attitude changed, at least *de facto*. The same holds good for the Netherlands. Four decades after the publication of *Mare liberum*, the Dutch delegation to the peace negotiations of Münster and Osnabrück played a leading role among those favouring (in part) the idea of *Mare clausum*. This was hardly surprising in view of the fact that the Dutch in the meantime had become the leading seafaring nation which tried to bar others from participating in "its" transoceanic maritime traffic and trade. However, by supporting the freedom of the seas again in the 19th century (and all through the 20th century), the Netherlands and above all "Britannia" promoted the general acceptance of this principle.

4. The French and the British Epochs: Territorial Sea and "Visit and Search"

The following epochs may be referred to as the French and the British Age, the former dating from the Peace of Westphalia (1648) to the Congress of Vienna (1815) and the latter lasting until the Treaty of Versailles and the League of Nations (1919/1920).

The dominant land power after the Thirty Years' War, France, has never been able to establish an effective pre-eminent position on the oceans. In the development of the law of the sea, however, France played a leading role. In 1681 Louis XIV enacted the *Ordonnance de la marine*. This compilation of maritime laws drew heavily on precedents, especially on the *Rôles d'Oléron* and the *Consolat del Mar*.[27] With

[27] *William Tetley*, Maritime liens and claims, p. 24 (2nd ed., Toronto 1998); *Ziegler* (*supra* note 3), p. 191.

the *Ordonnance*, which later found its way into the *Code Napoléon*, the period which marked the development of maritime law by the adoption of private customary codes was over. The age of national legislation had begun.

In the French Age the principle of the freedom of the seas became widely accepted. *Emer de Vattel* (1714–1767), the Swiss authority and pupil and follower of the German philosopher *Christian Wolff* (*Ius Gentium*, 1749), stated in 1758 in *Le droit des gens*:

> "Since, then, the right of navigation and fishing on the high seas is common to all men, the Nation which undertakes to exclude another from that advantage does it an injury and gives just cause for war; ... [it] does an injury to all nations whose common right it violates".[28]

The phrase "an injury to all nations" reminds us of the *ius cogens* and *erga omnes* dimensions this principle of the law of the sea acquired some 200 years later.

The principle of the freedom of the seas underwent important modifications in the French Age. First of all, there was the distinction between the open or high seas on the one hand and the areas adjacent to the coast on the other, that is to say the marginal or territorial sea. The latter became subject to the control of the coastal State. Economic considerations, basically fishery and security interests, lay behind this development. *Cornelius van Bynkershoek* stated in 1703 in chapter II of his dissertation entitled *De Dominio Maris*:

> "Hence we do not concede ownership of a maritime belt any farther out than it can be ruled from the land, and yet we do concede it that far; for there can be no reason for saying that the sea which is under some man's command and control is any less his than a ditch in his territory."

A major problem, of course, was the delimitation of the breadth of the territorial sea. *Bynkershoek* supported the cannon shot rule:

> "... it seems a better rule that the control of the land [over the sea] extend as far as a cannon will carry; for that is as far as we seem to have both command and possession."

This principle of effective rule – *terrae dominium finitur ubi armorum vis* – became generally accepted, although it entailed some uncertainty with respect to the actual breadth of the territorial sea. Thus a more precise rule was sought and found in the three-mile limit. Its origins may be traced to Scandinavian State practice claiming – without any reference whatever to the cannon-shot rule – zones of the Scandinavian one-league or four nautical miles.[29] Cannons, in *Bynkershoek*'s times, had a range

---

28 *Emer de Vattel*, The Law of Nations or the Principles of Natural Law, vol. III, ch. XXIII §§ 282, 283 (1758) (*C.G. Fenwick* tr., *Classics of International Law*) (1902) (reprinted 1964); see also *Potter* (*supra* note 5), pp. 91–96, 104–117; *Ziegler* (*supra* note 3), pp. 198–199.

29 *Hunz S.K. Kent*, The Historical Origins of the Three-Mile Limit, in: *AJIL* 48 (1954), 537–553; *Thomas Baty*, The Three-Mile Limit, in: *AJIL* 22 (1928), 503–537, 515–517; *Thorsten Kalijarvi*, Scandinavian Claims to Jurisdiction over Territorial Waters, in: *AJIL* 26 (1932), 57–69, 59–60.

considerably less than three nautical miles.[30] The three-mile criterion is thus an early example of "creeping jurisdiction" which, perhaps not surprisingly, attracted coastal States strongly. In 1793, the U.S. in their Proclamation of Neutrality referred to it,[31] and British practice thereafter regularly relied on it.

The French Age also witnessed the emergence of what today is called the Contiguous Zone. In order to suppress smuggling, the British Hovering Acts, which were in force from 1736 until 1876, prohibited the hovering of foreign (smuggling) ships within distances of up to 24 nautical miles from the British coast. Justice *Scott* in the *Le Louis* case in 1817 considered such coastal state legislation to be permissible.[32]

In another new development, the principle of the freedom of the seas was linked to the rights of neutrals. France used the principle as a propaganda tool against Britain during their trade war. This was prompted by the highly restrictive British concepts relating to the trade of neutrals: *The Rule of War of 1756* and the *Doctrine of Continuous Voyage*. According to the first concept, a State was free to trade *with* the enemy but not *for* the enemy. This made reference to ships of neutrals which during the Anglo-French Seven Years War tried to transport goods from the French colonies to Europe when France, because of British sea power, was no longer able to do it on its own. The British claimed that they could legally seize such ships, as they ought to be considered French vessels in reality. The Continuous Voyage concept was directed against ships which were transporting goods ultimately to an enemy port. According to this doctrine, those ships could be seized as well. Thereby it was not important if the ultimate destination was reached by an intermediate transshipment through a neutral port.

Finally, a further feature of the French Age has to be mentioned: piracy and privateering. We find the continued application of the doctrine that pirates are denationalised, that they lose the protection of the flag under which they sail – a concept that dates back to the *Rôles d'Oléron*. It was therefore widely held that any State could seize pirate ships and prosecute them. On the other hand, States issued licences to privateers (*Kaperbriefe*). Privateers like *Sir Francis Drake* were thereby permitted and required to hunt for enemy ships on the oceans, seize them, and take them to the country that had issued the licence. Privateering, however, often turned into simple piracy, which in the end led States to effectively stop privateering at the end of the French Age.

Turning to the British Age, it has to be stressed that already before the Congress of Vienna in 1815 Britain had become the paramount sea power. The freedom of

---

30 *Wyndham L. Walker*, Territorial Waters: The Cannon Shot Rule, in: *BYIL* 22 (1945), 210–232, 230–231.

31 *John B. Moore*, A Digest of International Law, vol. I, pp. 703–707 (Washington D.C. 1906).

32 "... maritime states have claimed a right of visitation and enquiry within those parts of the ocean adjoining to their shores, which the common courtesy of nations has for their common convenience allowed to be considered as parts of their dominions for various domestic purposes, and particularly for fiscal or defensive regulations more immediately affecting their safety and welfare.... This has nothing in common with a right of visitation and search upon the unappropriated parts of the ocean.".

the seas now became an undisputed principle of international law. "Liberalism" and "free trade," the rallying ideas of the 19th century, could not have been reconciled easily with calls for *Mare clausum*. Britain with her strong interest in commerce and global trade considered open oceans beneficial to her national interest.

This, however, did not prevent Britain from making use of her dominant maritime position to gain certain advantages. This is shown by the fact that Britain claimed a right to visit and search foreign vessels on the open seas – in time of peace! Initially, such a right existed for combatting piracy. Every State was entitled to seize pirate ships. When the Congress of Vienna entrusted Britain with the fight against piracy, she willingly accepted, using this to legitimize her policing operations on the seas – thereby indirectly fostering her own national trade interests. In addition, Britain created the concept of quasi-piracy. This covered acts which were considered equivalent to piracy although they did not constitute pirate acts in the traditional understanding. Thus, ships engaged in slave trade, ships without nationality or sailing under the flag of an unrecognised government, ships whose crew had mutinied, or ships used for illegal privateering were treated as pirate ships.[33]

The abolition of the slave trade is of particular interest in this connection. The Vienna Congress had issued a *Déclaration des puissances sur l'abolition de la traite des nègres* in 1814 which was integrated into the General Act of the Congress in 1815. However, the signatories did no more than assuring that in the fight against slave trade

> "... they are animated with the sincere desire of concurring in the most prompt and effectual execution of this measure, by all the means at their disposal, and of acting in the employment of these means, with all the zeal and perseverance which is due to so great and noble a cause".[34]

Taking this weak rhetoric as a starting point, Britain established an efficient system of bilateral treaties which accorded the reciprocal right to visit and search ships sailing under the flag of the contracting parties. In other words: any ship which might attempt to carry on the slave trade lost, by that fact alone, all right to the protection of its flag. Upon decisive resistance by the USA, Britain, in the end, had to step back, declaring, in 1858, "that by international law we had no right of search, no right of visitation whatever, in time of peace."

The British Age witnessed important codification projects, especially concerning the law of maritime war. Thus, in 1907 the Second Hague Peace Conference adopted the Convention for the Establishment of an International Prize Court,[35] and the Convention Concerning the Rights and Duties of Neutral Powers in Maritime War[36] (neutral rights have traditionally been the hardcore of the freedom of the seas in

---

[33] See also Articles 102 and 110 UNCLOS.

[34] Fontes Historiae Iuris Gentium (*Wilhelm G. Grewe* ed.), vol. 3/1, pp. 376–377 (Berlin 1992). See also *Ziegler* (*supra* note 3), pp. 222–223.

[35] *Ibid*, p. 621.

[36] *Ibid*, p. 626.

times of war). Already in 1856, there was the Paris Declaration Respecting Maritime Law[37] and in 1909 the London Declaration Relative to the Law of Naval Warfare was reached.[38] Common to all these instruments was the aim to reduce – similar to the laws of land warfare – the terrors of naval warfare, and to improve the protection of neutrals. The London Declaration of 1909 was to be the cornerstone of these endeavours. However, Britain, the leading maritime power of the epoch, did not accept the London Declaration. Consequently, the Convention on the International Prize Court never entered into force as it had been made conditional upon the full material regulation of naval warfare.

5. The 20th Century and Beyond: Process of Terraneisation and Principle of Common Heritage

The history of the law of the sea in the 20th century, especially after World War II, is characterized by a process of terraneisation.[39] The discovery of vast reserves of natural resources under the seabed and the increasing importance of fisheries led to the perception of the seas as a supplier of resources. Coastal States started to claim exclusive rights over as much of the resource-rich maritime areas as possible. The Continental Shelf Proclamations from 1945 onwards were only the beginning. The 1958 Geneva Conventions on the Law of the Sea did not stop creeping jurisdiction.

These tendencies, together with the idea of establishing a New International Economic Order that should lead to a more equitable global distribution of wealth – including the wealth of the oceans – were behind the UNCLOS III project. One of its aims was to find a compromise between the interests of individual States on the one hand and those of the world community as a whole on the other. The deep-sea bed and its resources were declared – codifying *Arvid Pardo*'s slogan of 1967 –

[37] *Ibid*, p. 549.

[38] *Ibid*, p. 637; see also *Potter* (*supra* note 5), pp. 154–168; *Ziegler* (*supra* note 3), pp. 230–232; *Theodor Niemeyer*, Das Seekriegsrecht nach der Londoner Deklaration vom 26. Februar 1909, pp. 19–21, 27–34 (Berlin 1910).

[39] *Wolfgang Graf Vitzthum*, The Terraneisation of the Ocean, in: *Law and State* 15 (1977), 124–136. – UNCLOS III accelerated, channelled and sanctioned a practice which had gradually emerged during the 1970s: the enclosure of the resources of the landward third of the oceans by the coastal States, as well as their reaching-out for the enclosed, semi-enclosed and marginal seas. Even parts of the deep seabed have thus been "nationalised." According to UNCLOS, there are several functionally differentiated national offshore zones for the satisfaction of different interests. Due to the establishment of exclusive economic zones of a breadth of 200 nautical miles, e.g. nine-tenth of the world fish resources have become subject to the jurisdiction of coastal or island States. In order to "nationalise" the submarine "foreland" of the continents, the continental margin in the geo-morphological sense has been included in the normative definition of the continental shelf (see Art. 76 UNCLOS). The arguments of "natural law" put forth for this enormous extension of the continental "shelf" have been merely the curtains veiling vital oil, gas and strategic interests. See *Wolfgang Graf Vitzthum*, The Law of the Sea Development, in: *IJIL* 23 (1983), 161–197; *Ziegler* (*supra* note 3), pp. 274–275.

the common heritage of mankind.[40] The common heritage concept found acceptance in other areas of public international law, too.

State practice, the case law of the International Court of Justice and UNCLOS III considerably extended the rights of coastal States to the detriment of the global commons and the freedom of the seas. On the other hand, the 1982 Convention introduced a sophisticated system for the settlement of disputes. The establishment of the first international court dealing exclusively with law of the sea matters, the International Tribunal for the Law of the Sea (ITLOS) – on whose home turf we are playing today –, is especially noteworthy.[41] Of further importance are provisions improving the protection of the marine environment.[42]

In 1995, the Agreement Relating to the Conservation and Management of Straddling Fish Stocks and Highly Migratory Fish Stocks was concluded, aiming at the better management of fish stocks that cross borders of jurisdiction.[43] This Agreement supplemented the previous regime with a new approach for managing high seas fisheries, introducing, *inter alia*, the precautionary principle. But will it satisfy the needs of the international community as a whole? UNCLOS has left many related problems unsolved. Although their regulation is necessary in order to assure the sustainable development of such fish stocks, the 1995 Agreement, in implementing UNCLOS, meant a further increase of coastal states' rights – in relation to high seas fisheries, which is one of the uses guaranteed, in principle, to all States by the freedom of the high seas.

The International Tribunal for the Law of the Sea is beginning to play a major role. However, its jurisdiction is obligatory and exclusive only as far as the Sea-Bed Disputes Chamber is concerned (Art. 287 para. 2 UNCLOS). The Free and Hanseatic

---

40 *Harry N. Scheiber* (ed.), Law of the Sea, The Common Heritage and Emerging Challenges (The Hague/London/Boston 2000); *Wolfgang Graf Vitzthum*, New Economic World Order and New Maritime World Order, in: *Law and State* 19 (1979), 7–24; *Rüdiger Wolfrum*, The Principle of the Common Heritage of Mankind, in: *ZaöRV* 43 (1983), 312–337; *Michael C. Wood*, International Seabed Authority: The First Four Years, in: *MPY UNL* 3 (1999), 173–241. See also *UN, Division for Ocean Affairs and the Law of the Sea*, The Law of the Sea, A Select Bibliography 1998 (New York 1999). – The Pardo proposal to "internationalise" the deep seabed marked the dramatic starting point of the reform of the law of the sea in 1967. One result finally achieved was the highly controversial regime laid down by Part XI of UNCLOS, modified by the Agreement Relating to the Implementation of Part XI of UNCLOS, adopted by the UN General Assembly on 28 July 1994 (*supra* note 4), pp. 214–231. The 1994 Agreement established a new, somewhat different regime for seabed mining.

41 Article 287 UNCLOS in connection with Annex VI. The Tribunal's rules of procedure are laid down in *ITLOS*, Basic Texts, pp. 15 *et seq.* (1998). See *Gudmundur Eiriksson*, The International Tribunal for the Law of the Sea (The Hague/London/Boston 2000).

42 See Articles 192–237 UNCLOS. On a regional level, several conventions dealing with different aspects of the protection of the marine environment have been concluded, e.g. the Barcelona Convention for the Protection of the Mediterranean Sea (1976) and the 1992 Convention for the Protection of the Marine Environment of the North-East Atlantic (OSPAR Convention).

43 The Straddling Stocks Agreement (34 *ILM* 1542 (1995)) entered into force on 11 December 2001. See *Jonna Ziemer*, Das gemeinsame Interesse an einer Regelung der Hochseefischerei. Dargestellt am Beispiel des Fish Stocks Agreement (Berlin 2000).

City of Hamburg is undoubtedly a place most suitable to host this important interpreter of the law of the sea. As to the Tribunal's impact on the law of the sea, in particular on the principle of the freedom of the high seas, the second judgment in the *M/V Saiga* case[44] is in point. According to the Tribunal, Guinea, by applying its customs laws to a customs radius including parts of its exclusive economic zone, violated UNCLOS. The Tribunal emphasised the functionality of sovereign or exclusive rights in the exclusive economic zone, thereby setting limits to the process of "horizontal," "vertical" and "functional" creeping jurisdiction. In dealing with the right of hot pursuit under Art. 111 UNCLOS, the Tribunal denied in that case the existence of the preconditions of this right. Once more, the Tribunal indirectly stressed the principle of the freedom of the High Seas. Another aspect was touched upon in the *Camouco* case,[45] where the Tribunal had to decide whether the arrest of a Panamanian fishing vessel by a French frigate was in accordance with the "reasonableness of the bond." The future history of the law of the sea, it seems, will not be written without extensive reference to the work of the Hamburg Tribunal.

6. The European Challenge: Eurocentrism and Multiculturalism

An outline of the history of the law of the sea at a conference titled "The European Challenge" would be incomplete without referring to European developments, especially to the maritime activities of the European Community (EC). Europe has always been a centre for the development and the codification of the law of the sea. In this regard we may speak of a certain "Eurocentrism"[46] of the law of the sea. *Ram Prakash Anand* has shown in his book *Origin and Development of the Law of the Sea*[47] that in South-East Asia in the era of discoveries a kind of "freedom of the seas" was recognized which was derived from the freedom of trade. The law of the sea as it stands today is thus in some respects the result of multicultural influences. However, I am sure you will not blame me of "eurochauvinism" at a conference in Europe if I wind up my lecture by focusing on European law and thinking.

The EC Treaty authorizes the European Community to take legal steps *vis-à-vis* fisheries, protection of the marine environment and offshore-activities.[48] This results from the fact that the law of the sea – as we have seen from the Rhodian Sea Law example – is closely connected with questions of communication, commerce, and trade. Today, the EC exercises Member States' rights in all areas of the "European

---

44 38 *ILM* 1323 (1999).

45 39 *ILM* 666 (2000); see *Bernhard H. Oxman/Vincent P. Bantz*, The "Camouco" (Panama v. France), in: *AJIL* 94 (2000), 713–721.

46 See *Carl Schmitt*, Der Nomos der Erde im Völkerrecht des Jus Publicum Europaeum, p. 19 (Köln 1950).

47 *Ram Prakash Anand*, Origin and Development of the Law of the Sea (The Hague/London/Boston 1983).

48 Articles 37 para 2, 175, 49–55 EC-Treaty.

Sea".[49] The EC's ability to enact regulations and directives is of a flexible and functional nature. Thus the EC is able to create a suitable regime for each part of the "European Sea", differing from each other in aims and means. The EC can therefore serve as an example for an entity in which the universal framework obligations of UNCLOS are transformed and supplemented by more concrete norms on a regional level.[50]

In addition, we should not forget the extraordinary legal personality of the European Community. It is not only an international but a supranational entity. Legal actions undertaken by its organs have direct effect on member States and their citizens. This unprecedented supranational character served as a model for the International Seabed Authority (Art. 156 *et seq.* UNCLOS): the decisions of its Council, too, will be directly binding on member States and companies (Art. 162 UNCLOS).

All these "European" – meaning supranational – elements were already proposed by our captain, *Elisabeth Mann Borgese*, at the christening of the Pacem in Maribus ship in 1968. The proposals were set out in her famous booklet *The Ocean Regime*.[51] As I said at the outset, the history of the law of the sea is like an uncharted ocean – with this work, with the documents of almost 30 Pacem in Maribus convocations and with the programmes of the International Ocean Institute, she has provided us and the generations to come, like the great seafarers in the age of discoveries, with the necessary charts and plans and the indispensable volume of sailing instructions to pilot the Pacem in Maribus ship through the stormy sea of the future developments of the international law of the sea.

---

49 The "European Sea" consists – as far as geography is concerned – of all or the major parts of the Baltic Sea, the North Sea, the North East Atlantic and the Mediterranean Sea.

50 Each part of the "European Sea" is, e.g., subject to a regime of its own for the protection of the marine environment. See *inter alia Uwe Jenisch/John Booth*, Bibliographie des deutschen Schrifttums zum Internationalen Seerecht 1982–1996 (Baden-Baden 1998).

51 *Elisabeth Mann Borgese*, The Ocean Regime (Santa Barbara 1968). See also *Elisabeth Mann Borgese*, The Ocean Regime, in: *Shigeru Oda* (ed.), The International Law of the Ocean Development, pp. 280–293 (Leiden 1972), (not to forget her even more famous book, Drama of the Oceans, which was published in 1976 and has been translated into 13 languages, nor her equally influential study The Oceanic Circle, Governing the seas as a global resource (1998)); *Wolfgang Graf Vitzthum*, Pacem in Maribus, Selected Bibliography (Santa Barbara 1970).

*R.P. Anand**

NON-EUROPEAN SOURCES OF THE LAW OF THE SEA

LAW OF THE SEA: PRODUCT OF THE EUROPEAN CIVILIZATION

There is a wide-spread belief amongst Western, especially European, scholars that the law of the sea, like other rules of inter-state conduct of modern international law, is a product of Western European Christian civilization to which non-European countries have contributed practically little or nothing. It is asserted with a sense of pride that international law is a "product of the conscious activity of the European mind" and "European beliefs" and is based on European state practices which have been developed and consolidated during the last three centuries.[1] Thus, relating the story of the development of international law, Professor J.H.W. Verzijl states:

> The body of positive international law once called into being by the concordant practice and express agreement of European states, has since the end of the eighteenth century onwards, spread over the rest of the world as a modern *ratio scripta*, to which extra-European states have contributed extraordinarily little. International law as it now stands is essentially the product of the European mind and has practically been 'received'... lock, stock and barrel by American and Asiatic states.[2]

Relying entirely and almost exclusively on European history and European sources, with rare exceptions,[3] most of the Western scholars affirm or confirm this opinion. As Professor B.V.A. Roling asserts:

> There is no doubt about it: the traditional law of nations is a law of European lineage.[4]

Kunz confirms: "Our international law is a law of Christian Europe. It has its roots in the *Republica Christiana* of medieval Europe."[5] Practically every study on the

---

* Professor Emeritus of International Law, Jawaharlal Nehru University, New Delhi.

1 *J.H.W. Verzijl*, Western European Influence on the Foundations of International Law, in his *International Law in Historical Perspective*, pp. 435–36 (Leyden 1968).

2 *Ibid*, p. 442.

3 See *C.H. Alexandrowicz*, An Introduction to the History of the Law of Nations in the East Indies (16th, 17th and 18th Centuries) (Oxford 1967).

4 *B.V.A. Roling*, International law in an Expanded World, p. 10 (Amsterdam 1960).

5 *Josef L. Kunz*, Pluralism of legal and value systems and International Law, in his *The Changing Law of Nations*, p. 48 (Toledo, Ohio 1968).

P. Ehlers, E. Mann-Borgese and R. Wolfrum (eds.), Marine Issues, 19–35

history of international law in Europe expresses and confirms this opinion.[6] In fact it is noted "with a certain amount of amusement" how the Asian states grasp "as the highest and, indeed, as universal values certain fundamental ideas created and elaborated by the West". This offers curious but clear

> (E)vidence of the lasting dependence of non-western nations in the conduct of their international affairs upon fundamental concepts of the western world from which their political leaders nevertheless so ardently crave to liberate their states without, however, being able either to derive any different workable principle of international law from data of their own national history or to develop independent legal principles susceptible of replacing the traditional standard principles of existing international law.[7]

Although some of the ancient countries, like China, India, Egypt and Assyria, with quite advanced forms of civilizations, might have had certain generally accepted principles and rules of inter-state conduct, the western jurists feel that these practices "reveal little that could, even in the broader sense of the word, be considered as international law."[8]

Freedom of the Seas: The Paramount Principle

The bulk and essence of maritime law during the last more than two centuries can be summed up in the simple phrase, "*Freedom of the Seas*". What it meant was that beyond a limited area of territorial sea where the coastal state exercised sovereign jurisdiction, an area which was deemed essential for its security and protection of its other vital interests, the vast areas of the ocean were open and free, which could not be appropriated and must not be controlled by anyone. In these areas of what were called the 'high seas', all states enjoyed – or at least until recently were supposed to enjoy – as Article 2 of the 1958 Convention on the High Seas declared, freedoms of unobstructed navigation, uncontrolled fishing, right to lay down and maintain submarine cables and pipelines, and freedom to fly over, and such other undefined freedoms as they might like to exercise with due regard to the similar rights and freedoms of others.

History of the law of the sea is to a large extent the story of the development of the freedom of the seas doctrine and the vicissitudes through which it has passed through the centuries. For the last nearly 200 years, it had been accepted as an undisputed principle, almost a dogma, which no one could dare challenge. Recognized and referred to as *jus cogens*, it was supposed to be in the interests of all mankind. It expressed in a sense the essence and substance of the law of the sea. All other

---

6 See *Arthur Nussbaum*, A Concise History of the Law of Nations, p. 191 (New York 1962); see also several writers quoted in: *R.P. Anand*, New States and International Law, p. 7 (Delhi 1972).

7 *Verzijl* (*supra* note 1), p. 445.

8 *Nussbaum* (*supra* note 6), p. 10.

rules relating to inter-state conduct more or less revolved around this doctrine and their validity or otherwise was to be judged and depended on the touchstone of this incontrovertible principle. Thus, even when the coastal state's jurisdiction in a part of the sea close to its coastline came to be recognized as territorial sea for the protection of its security and other interests, its limits were always sought to be kept as narrow as absolutely essential to maintain this freedom in wide areas. In any case, beyond the narrow limits of the territorial sea, even limited jurisdiction for the protection of coastal fisheries was totally denied until the end of the Second World War. Contiguous zones for the protection of coastal economic, health and financial interests have been either refused or merely tolerated, in the name of the freedom of the seas, by the biggest maritime Power, Great Britain, which has ruled the waves for over 200 years.[9]

Origin of the Principle

It is generally assumed, without any question, and widely asserted that it was the seventeenth century Dutch jurist, Hugo de Groot or Hugo Grotius, who propounded the doctrine of the freedom of the seas for the first time in the modern period by elaborate argument. Although it is believed that the principle was clearly accepted under Roman law and had been reduced to a legal formula according to which the sea was recognized as "*commune omnium*", or common property of all, after the disintegration of the Roman Empire it had been lost and forgotten through the centuries.[10] The "reawakening" of the principle has been brought about by Hugo Grotius. As Meurer put it:

> Up to modern times the freedom of the seas slumbered the sleep of the Sleeping Beauty until there appeared from Netherlands the knight whose kiss awakened her once more.[11]

It is well-known that Grotius enunciated and elaborated his thesis relating to the freedom of the seas in his famous book *Mare Liberum or Free Seas* published anonymously in 1609.[12] Few works of such small size have gained such great reputation as the *Mare Liberum*. It is said to be "the first and the classic exposition of the doctrine of the freedom of the seas".[13] Grotius wrote this remarkable book,

---

9 See *Thomas W. Fulton*, The Sovereignty of the Sea, pp 593–603 (London 1911) (reprinted New York 1976); *J.L. Brierly*, The Law of Nations, pp. 205–06 (*Sir Humphery Waldock* 6th ed.) (Oxford 1963).

10 See *Christian Meurer*, The Program of the Freedom of the Sea, pp. 4–7 (*Leo J. Franchenberg* tr. from German) (Washington 1919).

11 *Meurer ibid*, p. 7.

12 *Hugo Grotius*, The Freedom of the Seas or The Right which belongs to the Dutch to take part in the East Indies Trade (*Ralph Van Deman Magoffin* tr., *James Brown Scott* ed. with an Introduction) (New York 1916).

13 *W.S. M. Knight*, Seraphin de Freitas: Critic of *Mare Liberum*, in: *Transactions of Grotius Society* 11 (1926), 1.

which has earned him the title of the 'founder' or 'father' of international law, in order to defend his country's right to navigate in the Indian Ocean and Eastern seas and to trade with India and the East Indies (Southeast Asian Islands), over which Spain and Portugal asserted a commercial monopoly as well as political domination. In fact, *Mare Liberum* was merely one chapter (Chapter XII) of a bigger work, *De Jure Praedae (On the Law of Spoils)* which Grotius, as advocate of the Dutch East India Company, had prepared as a legal brief but which he had refrained from publishing.[14]

This was a period of keenest international commercial rivalry between Spain, Portugal, Holland and England, all of whom were struggling to gather riches of the East. Ever since Rome made eastern products fashionable and her Egyptian subjects went out to seek them in the Indies, the European world had been possessed of the splendour of the East. Aromatic spices from India and the East Indies were in the greatest demand and yielded the largest profit. Spice trade with the East, especially pepper, then became a great motivating factor of history. As a recent writer points out: "Pepper may not mean much to us, but in that age it ranked with the precious stones. Men risked the perils of the deep and fought and died for pepper."[15] Spain and Portugal, the two Iberian Powers, who were the first to look for a sea route to India and the Spice Islands, claimed a legal title to half the non-Christian world each under a Papal Bull of May 4, 1493, by which Pope Alexander VI divided the world between the two and defined a line of demarcation running 100 leagues west of Azores and Cape Verde Islands and granted to Spain all lands west of it, and to Portugal all lands of its east. By a bilateral treaty of 1494 the two Powers fortified their title.[16]

Asian Traditions Ignored

It is submitted that the contribution of Asian, African and other extra-European countries towards the development of modern international law, or their attitude, outlook and behaviour toward its rules in their international relations, is more often than not based on ignorance of their history and lack of information or understanding of their cultures and cultural traditions. Europeans generally do not want to look beyond European history, written during the colonial period, to acknowledge that when European adventurers arrived in Asia in the fifteenth century, "they found themselves in the middle of a network of states and inter-state relations based on traditions which were more ancient than their own and in no way inferior to notions of European civilization."[17] These rules of inter-state conduct might have differed,

---

14 See *W.S. M. Knight*, The Life and Works of Hugo Grotius, p. 79 (London 1925).

15 *G.F. Hudson*, quoted by *K.M. Panikkar*, Asia and Western Dominance, p. 25 (1954).

16 See *Panikkar* (*supra* note 15), pp. 31–32.

17 *Alexandrowicz* (*supra* note 3), p. 224.

and in fact did differ, from the European state practice; but there is no doubt about their wide-spread acceptance amongst Asian States. Thanks to their liberal traditions of freedoms of peaceful navigation and international maritime trade, and permission to foreign merchants to establish themselves by their own laws, the Europeans got an easy foothold in Asia.[18] Whether expressed in the form of a doctrine or not, there is no doubt that the unobstructed freedoms of navigation and commercial shipping were accepted by all countries in the Indian Ocean and other Asian seas centuries before history was ever recorded, long before Grotius was ever heard of, or Europe emerged as a formidable force on the international stage. Besides historical records, numerous travelers' memoirs testify to this state of affairs.[19] Freedom of the seas was also a recognized rule in the Rhodian Maritime Code and was unequivocally adopted in Roman law. From the first century A.D., regular maritime commercial relations were established between Rome and several states in India and the Indian Ocean region, and they continued for nearly 300 years.[20]

On the eve of European penetration into the Indian Ocean, not only was the principle of freedom of the seas and trade well recognized in customary law of Asia, but also in some states this principle was codified and well-publicized. Examples include the maritime codes of Macassar and Malacca, which were compiled at the end of the thirteenth century, based on customary practices.[21] Resisting the Dutch attempts to monopolize the maritime trade of the Spice Islands, the ruler of Macassar is reported to have said in 1615 that the sea was common to all and that "it is a thing unheard of that any one should be forbidden to sail the seas."[22]

Freedom of the Seas: A Casualty in Europe

While the salutary practices of freedoms of navigation and unobstructed maritime trade continued to prevail and prosper in Asia, in Europe the Rhodian and Roman traditions of the freedom of the seas foundered in the turbulent waters of disputes and conflicts of numerous smaller states which emerged from the ruins of Rome, each vying with the other. Maritime commerce died in a "state of wild anarchy" in Europe, and even the memory of Rhodian law did not last beyond the thirteenth century. By this time, all European seas came to be more or less appropriated by

---

18 *Alexandrowicz ibid.*

19 See the Travels of Marco Polo (*William Marsden* tr. & ed. 1948); *Ibn Batutta*, Travels in Asia and Africa (1325–54) (*H.A.R. Gibb* tr.); Narrative and Journey of *Abd-er-Razak* [A Persian Traveler and Ambassador of Shah Rukh (1442)], India in the Fifteenth Century (*R.H. Major* tr. & ed.).

20 See *H.G. Rawlinson*, Intercourse between India and the Western World from the Earliest Times to the Fall of Rome, pp. 9–12 (1926); see also *E.H. Warmington*, The Commerce between the Roman Empire and India, pp. 35 *et seq.* (1974).

21 For a translation of both codes see *J.M. Pardessus*, Collection de Lois Maritimes, p. 6 (1895); see also *Sir Stanford Raffles*, The Maritime Code of the Malays, in: *Journal of the Royal Asiatic Society (Straits Branch)* 2 (Dec. 1879), 1–20.

22 Quoted in *G.J. Resink*, Indonesia: History between the Myths, p. 45 (1968).

European states, leading to numerous disputes and almost continuous warfare. Thus, in addition to the wide claims of Spain and Portugal, Venice claimed sovereignty over the Adriatic Sea, Genoa occupied the Liguarian Sea, England dominated the undefined British seas, and Denmark closed the Baltic by closing the Sound and extended control over the northern seas.[23]

Portugal Disturbs Peaceful Navigation in the Indian Ocean

When the Portuguese arrived in India by the end of the fifteenth century, they found no maritime Powers, no warships, and no arms in the sea. The Indian Ocean had never been a theatre of any serious naval conflicts. Asians were not peaceful peoples but felt no need to fight for the sea which was but of limited use for navigation, maritime trade, and catching small quantities of fish. They were essentially land powers. The hub of Asian activities and relations, their struggles and conflicts, related to the vast and fertile land on the largest continent of the world. The absence of armed shipping in the Indian Ocean helped tiny Portugal to control vast areas of the ocean. The Europeans were sea powers trained in the rough waters of the Atlantic and the North Sea, whose challenges hardened them into expert navigators and naval warriors. Portugal sought to apply European custom to control the vast Indian Ocean and enforce its control by its armed carracks and galleons against the unarmed Indian Ocean ships engaged in peaceful trade. Although Portugal was fairly successful in gaining a share of the Asian spice market and in disturbing peaceful navigation in the Indian Ocean, it could not wipe out the Asian maritime trade.[24] But the Portuguese monopoly of the Eastern spice trade and its huge profits aroused the jealousy of other European powers which began to challenge Portugal's authority in the late sixteenth century.

Contest of Wits and Arms in Europe

It was to contest the Portuguese monopoly, as we have noted earlier, that Grotius, taking his cue from the Asian maritime practices of free navigation and trade, propounded his doctrine in a brief he prepared for the Dutch East India Company. The company asked Grotius, who was associated with it as a lawyer, to defend the company's capture of a Portuguese vessel laden with Eastern spices in the Straits of Malacca in 1604. Learning as much as he could about India and the East Indies, their traditions of free trade and commerce throughout history, and the Portuguese attempts to stultify the traditional freedom of navigation to these countries, Grotius wrote *De Jure Pradae* in 1605 to defend the action. He tried to "show that war might rightly be waged against, and prize taken from the Portuguese, who had

---

[23] See *Fulton* (*supra* note 9), pp. 3–5; *Pitman B. Potter*, Freedom of the Seas in History, Law and Politics, pp. 36–38 (1924).

[24] See *Marie A.P. Meilink-Roelofsz*, Asian Trade and European Influence, pp. 136–72 (1962).

wrongfully tried to exclude the Dutch (and others) from trade with eastern countries".[25] His greatness lies in keenly observing the maritime customs of Asian countries, presenting them in the form of a doctrine supported by logical arguments, Christian theology, and the authority of the venerable Roman law, and recommending these views to European countries. This fact of history has been generally ignored by historians of international law. There is little doubt, as Professor Alexandrowicz said, "that Grotius either conceived or perfected his doctrine of the freedom of the seas under the influence of the maritime traditions of the East."[26]

Besides Asian traditions, Grotius relied on logic. He tried to establish two propositions: first, "that which cannot be occupied, or which never has been occupied cannot be the property of any one, because all property has arisen from occupation"; and second, "that which has been so constituted by nature that although serving some one person it still suffices for the use of all other persons, is today and ought in perpetuity to remain in the same condition as when it was first created by nature".[27] The air belongs to this class of things, and so does the sea. Therefore, argued Grotius with disarming logic of the time: "The seas is common to all because it is so limitless that it cannot become a possession of one, and because it is adapted for the use of all, whether we consider it from the point of view of navigation or of fisheries."[28]

It must be pointed out, however, that in spite of all this learning and logic, neither Grotius nor Holland were in favour of freedom of the seas as a principle. As the Dutch defeated the Portuguese and seized the profitable trade of the Spice Islands, they sought to create their own monopoly. Grotius conveniently forgot the freedom of the seas principle he had propounded with such fervour and went to England with a Dutch delegation four years later in 1613 to argue in favour of a Dutch monopoly of trade with the Spice Islands. In fact he was surprised to find that his won book, published anonymously, was being quoted by the British against him.[29] Successive attempts by each European state to demand freedom of the lucrative spice trade of the East Indies, and later attempts by each of them to try to create a monopoly for itself, along with a similar game being played in the Atlantic, led to a spate of books by numerous scholars in Europe. Most or all of these works were nothing more than apologies by these writers for their countries' policies and interests. In this *battle* of books and wits, which continued in the din of actual war, it was not Grotius, it must be pointed out, who won, as is generally assumed. The real victor was John Selden, British scholar and statesman, whose *Mare Clausum, sen de Domino Maris Libri Duo (The Closed Sea or Two books concerning the Rule over the Sea)* written at the behest of the English Crown, remained the most authoritative

[25] *Knight* (*supra* note 13), p. 80.

[26] *Alexandrowicz* (*supra* note 13), p. 229; see also *ibid*, p. 44.

[27] *Grotius* (*supra* note 12), pp. 28 *et seq.*

[28] *Ibid.*

[29] See *G.N. Clark*, Grotius' East India Mission to England, in: *Transactions of the Grotius Society* 20 (1934), 79; also *Knight* (*supra* note), pp. 136–43.

work on maritime law in Europe for the next 200 years.[30] Although several other publicists countered Selden's arguments, all the European countries continued to follow his prescription in controlling as much ocean as their power would permit. Selden won this protracted "battle" not by the brilliance of his arguments, but by the "louder language" of the powerful British navy.[31]

Resurgence of the Freedom of the Seas

It was only in the late 18th or really early 19th century that freedom of the seas came to be revived under the patronage of Great Britain which had emerged as the greatest power of the world. The needs and demands of the industrial revolution in Europe – larger markets, sources of raw material and surplus capital which could not be invested in Europe – led to huge colonial empires in Asia and Africa. As Europeans got more interested in commercial prosperity and free trade, and ever more Europeans started travelling to these wide-spread colonies, Selden's *Mare Clausum* became an anachronism which was no longer necessary. It was more useful for them to have open and free seas in order to exploit vast unexplored areas of the world which no one nation could reach alone. Pretensions to sovereignty over the sea and monopoly of trade slowly died their natural death and England became not only the strongest champion of the freedom of the seas, but its policeman.[32] Grotius, the dejected and rejected man in his life, and a false prophet for 200 years, was acclaimed and proclaimed a hero and his, in some respects illogical, arguments came to be accepted without any questions.

Law Vague and Uncertain

In any case, the freedom of the seas principle accepted by the Europeans had nothing in common with Asian maritime practices. Unlike Asians, who had maintained these freedoms for centuries for peaceful commercial relations, the chief purpose of their revival in the nineteenth century Europe was joint exploitation of Asia and Africa to satisfy the needs of their industries. It may also be mentioned that but for general agreement on vague freedom of the seas, implying freedom of peaceful navigation with a few agreed "rules of the road", which benefited all Europeans, there was little agreement on other rules. Freedom of fisheries, which England came to accept only after three wars with Holland and other conflicts with neighbours, continued to be a subject of serious disputes among Europeans. There was no agreement on a uniform limit of the territorial sea, or freedom of navigation through the maritime belt or straits, especially for warships. The same was true of the contiguous zone and England, ever since the repeal of its own Hovering Act in 1876, continued to

---

30 In England "*Mare Clausum* became in a sense law book." *Fulton* (*supra* note 9), p. 374.

31 See *Potter* (*supra*), p. 61.

32 See *Sir Geoffrey Butler/Simon Maccoby*, The Development of International Law, p. 53 (London, 1928).

question the legality of such jurisdiction exercised by other states.[33] Moreover, a large part of the law of the sea relating to war, contraband, blockade and rights of neutrals was always at the mercy of belligerents which stretched their rights according to their free will and contingencies of war. Thus, during the two World Wars, the belligerents outstretched their authority over the sea on the basis of controversial doctrines they propounded, like "ultimate enemy destination" and "long distance blockades", and enforced them over the strong protest of the neutrals through navicerts systems of their own.[34] Thus it is important to note that, apart from a few general principles, much of the maritime law, as it developed in the nineteenth and the first half of the twentieth centuries, was controversial, uncertain, and in several respects nothing more than a panorama of conflicting rules.

Legal Vacuum

Even more important is the fact that, beyond a limited maritime belt, the vast areas of the ocean – more than 70 per cent of the globe – remained a *legal vacuum*, an area of "no law" beyond what are referred to as a few "rules of the road". Freedom of the seas meant essentially non-regulation and *laissez faire* which was in the interests of the big maritime powers. This law, or rather lack of law under the freedom of the seas doctrine, was often used in the nineteenth century by European powers to threaten small states, to get concessions from them, or simply to subjugate them.[35] Even later, it gave them a license to use the freedom in furtherance of their immediate interests – whether for navigation, fisheries or military maneuvers – irrespective of the rights of others. The protracted and sometimes bitter fishery disputes between smaller European countries – Holland, Denmark, Norway and Iceland – on the one hand, and Great Britain, on the other, numerous such disputes on the American continent, and almost continuous protests by neutral states against violation of their freedoms of navigation and trade by belligerent maritime powers, were constant reminders of the dissatisfaction of the smaller coastal states. The situation became even more serious during and after the Second World War when the maritime powers took the liberty to further stretch this freedom and enclose even wider areas of the ocean either for defeating the enemy, or for conducting nuclear and missile tests, threatening the life and liberty of all peaceful users of the seas. Protests by smaller states to such uses of the sea were almost always rejected

---

33 See *Fulton* (*supra* note 9), pp. 593–603; *J.L. Brierly*, The doctrine of the contiguous zone and the dicta in *Croft vs. Dunphy*, in: *BYIL* XIV (1933), 156.

34 See *C. John Colombos*, International Law of the Sea, pp. 62, 748–52 (6th ed. London 1967); *Julius Stone*, Legal Controls of International Conflicts, pp. 484 *et seq.*, 500 *et seq.* (New York 1959).

35 There is no dearth of cases of trigger happy western naval commanders using naval ordnance against "backward" peoples of Asia and Africa on the smallest excuse, or no excuse at all. It was the classic age of punitive or minatory bombardments. See for details of numerous cases *R.R. Palmer/Joel Colton*, A History of the Modern World, pp. 548 *et seq.*, 615 *et seq.* (3rd ed. New York 1965).

on the ground that what was not prohibited in law was permitted, and that these were "reasonable" measures of security and self-defense.[36]

Most of the rules of modern maritime law were based on the practice of a few dominant maritime powers. Many a time their interest differed and their practices were not uniform. The situation was tolerated not only because of the over-bearing influence of the European maritime powers, especially Great Britain, along with France, Germany, and Russia, as well as extra-European powers like USA and Japan, which were all helped by this undefined and wide freedom of the seas, but also because the sea was of only limited importance and use. But the law even for these limited purposes was imprecise and not beyond doubt. An attempt was made to codify the law under the auspices of the League of Nations in 1930, but it failed because the big maritime powers, especially Great Britain, insisted on a narrow three-mile limit of the territorial sea, and the smaller states were deeply concerned about protecting their fisheries and other coastal interests in wider zones.[37]

Post-1945 Era: A New World

By the end of World War II, the whole balance of forces had changed. The West European powers, which had dominated the world scene for nearly 300 years, were no longer at the center of the world stage. Out of the ruins of the world holocaust emerged the United States and the Soviet Union with enough strength to dominate the world, and to challenge each other seriously. The world, divided into two power blocs, plunged into a bitter cold war that affected all aspects of international relations and law.

With the weakening of Europe, colonialism collapsed and there emerged numerous Asian and African states which for a long time had no status and no role in the formulation of international law. Comprising a majority of the newly extended world society, the Asian-African states, along with the thus far equally neglected and disgruntled Latin American states – called Third World as they came to be called – acquired a new influence in the divided post-war world society. Non-aligned to any of the power bloc as most of these countries were, they aligned themselves to take concerted action and play an important role in the international legal and political structure in pursuance of their interests.

There was another development. So far the uses of the sea were few and the coastal states were mostly concerned about their security, protection of their near-shore areas for fisheries, and their commercial fleets. The tremendous advances in marine technology after World War II revealed a new world with nine times as much vegetation available in the sea as was cultivated on land. Even more important, it came to be found that natural resources and minerals in quantities beyond anyone's

[36] See for such defense by both the US and British Governments, *Marjorie Whiteman*, Digest of International Law, vol. 4, pp. 585 *et seq.*, 600 *et seq.* (Washington D.C. 1965).

[37] See *Jesse S. Reeves*, The codification of the law of territorial waters, in: *AJIL* 24 (1930), 493.

imagination were present not only in the water of the sea but also on the ocean floor and in the underlying layers. By 1945, geologists had confirmed that huge quantities of sorely needed oil and gas resources lay buried under the seabed off the shores of various countries, outside the territorial sea, and technology was making them accessible. These invaluable resources could not be left there or risked to be exploited by other distant water states, as had been the case with fisheries for centuries.

The development of technology also revolutionized fishing mechanics. Significant technological breakthroughs in the ability to detect, concentrate, and harvest fish in the high seas increased the capacity of a few technologically advanced countries to indulge in overfishing, threatening entire fishery resources near the coasts of other states. The need to protect coastal resources – both living and non-living – had become all the more evident.

Freedom of the Seas not Immutable

Law could not remain unaffected by all these changes. Unlimited freedom of the seas, which had served the interests of a few maritime powers in an age with limited uses of the sea, could no longer remain unchallenged or unchanged. As Professor *Gidel* said as early as 1950:

> The expression 'freedom of the high seas' is in reality a purely negative, worn-out concept, nothing more; it has no meaning for us, except as the anti-thesis of another, a positive concept, which has long since disappeared.
>
> The idea of the freedom of the high seas is, paradoxically, a survival of the idea – long since dead – that the high seas are subject to dominion and sovereignty, just like any other territorial dominion.[38]

Europe had largely lost its control and hold over the law of the sea. It was no longer a law to be made by and for the European countries. Once it came to be realized that the sea was much more than a navigation route or a storehouse of fisheries which could be freely exploited under the old freedom of the seas doctrine, the old law lost its charm and sanctity. Most of the initiative and calls for change in the law came from extra-European countries. The first and most important challenge to the traditional freedom of the seas doctrine in the period following World War II came from the United States which had emerged as the strongest maritime power after the war. The twin proclamations by President Harry Truman on September 28, 1945, referred to developments in technology as necessitating the extension of US coastal jurisdiction to establish conservation zones in contiguous high seas areas to protect fisheries and the right to exclusive exploitation of the mineral resources of

[38] See United Nations' Memorandum on the Regime of the High Seas, pp. 2–3 (reputed to have been prepared by the French jurist *Gidel*) UN G.A. Doc. A/CN.4/38, 14 July 1950.

the continental shelf.[39] In both proclamations, the littoral state extended its limited jurisdiction to areas of the high seas close to its coasts, without any claim to an extension of territorial waters, and specifically declared unaffected the high seas character of the areas and the right to free and unimpeded navigation in those waters. In spite of this disclaimer, the Truman Proclamations were certainly novel claims that modified, if not grossly violated, the freedom of the seas doctrine.

The United States' proclamations led to numerous claims by other states not only for continental shelf jurisdiction but also for protection of their fisheries. By 1958, nearly a score of countries had made such continental shelf claims. Some Latin American countries went even further. Argentine, Chile, Peru, Ecuador, Costa Rica, El Salvador, and Honduras all extended their jurisdiction or sovereignty to 200 miles to protect their fisheries from depredations by outsiders. Practically every proclamation claiming special rights to the continental shelf or fisheries contained the statement that freedom of the high seas was fully recognized and maintained. But as the 1950 UN Memorandum on the Regime of the High Seas suggested, these disclaimers could not be taken seriously.[40]

Conflicting and Diverse Claims

There was a lot of confusion during this period about the legal validity or otherwise of all these claims about continental shelf and fisheries jurisdiction. The confusion was worse confounded by widening claims relating to territorial seas. By 1958, at least 27 of the 73 independent coastal states claimed specific breadths of territorial seas in excess of the so-called 'traditional' three-mile limit. These claims ranged between 5, 6, 12 and 200 miles. Six others, while rejecting the three-mile rule, did not specify their limits.[41]

Some countries sought to achieve the same purpose without extending their territorial waters or fisheries jurisdiction by adopting straight baselines for measuring the territorial sea joining outermost islands, islets, or rocks off their coasts. Thus, Norway essentially extended its territorial sea by redrawing its baselines and enclosing vast bodies of waters, large and small bays, and countless arms of the sea making them internal waters subject to the absolute sovereignty of Norway. This method for protection of coastal fisheries from outsiders was upheld by the International Court of Justice in the *Anglo-Norwegian Fisheries* case in 1951.[42]

UN Efforts to Codify the Law

The divergent standpoints adopted by different states since the Second World War on the territorial sea, fisheries jurisdiction, continental shelf, and other issues of the

39 See Proclamation No. 2667, in: 10 *Fed. Reg.* (1945) 12, 303.

40 See UN Memorandum (*supra* note 38), pp. 2–3.

41 See Draft of the synoptical table prepared by the UN Secretariat in pursuance of the Resolution of the First Committee (Territorial Sea and Contiguous Zone) at its 14th meeting (13 March 1958), UN Doc. A/Conf. 13/C.11; 20 March 1958; *ibid*, rev. 1, 1/3 April 1958; *ibid* rev. 1, corr. 2, 22 April 1958.

42 Fisheries (United Kingdom v. Norway), in: *I.C.J. Reports* (1951), 132.

law of the sea made the already ambiguous and uncertain situation "a confused medley of conflicting solutions."[43] To bring order in this confusing situation, the United Nations organized two conferences in 1958 and 1960 to develop and codify the law in a systematic manner. Four conventions[44] were concluded in 1958 which, on the whole, reasserted the traditional freedoms of the sea and accepted the coastal states' sovereign jurisdiction over its continental shelf and exclusive right to exploit its resources up to a depth of 200 meters or beyond that limit to wherever the depth of the superjacent waters admitted the exploitation of the natural resources. Although coastal states were permitted to extend maritime zones and adopt fish conservation measures over adjacent waters, no agreement could be reached on the extent of the territorial sea or fisheries jurisdiction, and the agreement on the definition of the continental shelf was vague and controversial. Another attempt was made in 1960 to reach an agreement on the territorial sea, but it also failed.[45]

Many coastal states still wished, and some claimed, wider territorial sea, but were unable to move the entrenched powers, or successfully challenge their historic 'rights' and change the traditional law. During the two conferences, there was a continuous struggle between numerically strong but poor, newly-independent Asian-African nations and their allies in Latin America, supported by the Soviet Group, on the one hand, and politically dominating, rich, satisfied, European and North American maritime powers, and some other small Asian-African countries under their influence, on the other.[46] While the maritime powers recounted and reassured the virtues of the freedom of the seas as a "time-honoured" principle, the dissatisfied states of the Third World thought that it was a "time-worn" old doctrine which could still serve and be useful but only if modified and adapted according to changed needs of the changed international society. Rejecting the three-mile rule for the territorial sea as a "fallen idol", the new members of the international community said that "agreement among maritime powers alone was not law" and that "rules should be based on general state practice, not on that of a handful of states that had repeatedly been challenged and now finally rejected."[47] The Western powers were still strong enough to enforce the traditional law of *laissez faire* which favoured them. The developing countries did not like this law, but could not help it.

---

43 UN Memorandum (*supra* note 38), p. 112.

44 Convention on the Territorial Sea; Convention on the High Seas; Convention on Fishing and Living Resources of the High Seas; and Convention on the Continental Shelf.

45 See *R.P. Anand*, Winds of Change in the Law of the Sea, in: *R.P. Anand* (ed.), *Law of the Sea: Caracas and Beyond*, pp. 41 *et seq.* (New Delhi, 1978).

46 See *Arthur H. Dean*, The Second Conference on the Law of the Sea: Fight for the Freedom of the Seas, in: *AJIL* 54 (1960), 752; *Robert L. Friedheim*, The Satisfied and Dissatisfied States negotiate International Law, in: *World Politics* 18, 20–41.

47 See *U Mya Sein* [Burma], *Shukairy* [Saudi Arabia] and *Hassan* [UAR], Second UN Conference on the Law of the Sea: Official Records, Summary Records of Plenary Meetings and Meetings of the Committee of the Whole, UN Doc. A/CONF. 1918, pp. 58, 74, 102, Geneva 17 March to 26 April 1960.

Renewed Challenge to the Freedom of the Seas

In a sense the 1958 Conventions had become outmoded by the time they were written. Since then the pressure to change the old freedom of the seas increased even more with a further widening of the international society. Moreover, technology soon made it feasible to exploit the vast resources of the seabed and ocean floor, especially oil and gas, at depths beyond the geological continental shelf. Indeed, exploitation became possible at any depth and countries started stretching their continental shelf jurisdiction to include the whole continental margin extending to a depth of 2,500 meters. It also came to be known that beyond the continental margin, generally referred to as the deep seabed, there lay extensive deposits of manganese nodules containing manganese, nickel, copper and cobalt, all metals essential for industrial economies.

In 1967, a perceptive representative of a very small country, *Arvid Pardo* of Malta, informed the UN General Assembly about the inadequacies of the current international law and freedom of the seas, which could and would encourage appropriation of vast areas of the sea which were suddenly found to contain untold wealth by those who had the technological competence to exploit them. To avoid a potentially disastrous scramble for sovereign rights over the seabed, he suggested the creation of an effective international regime for the seabed and ocean floor beyond a clearly defined national jurisdiction, and acceptance of that area as a "common heritage of mankind" that would not be "subject to national appropriation in any manner whatsoever, to be used and exploited for exclusive benefit of mankind as a whole."[48]

Pardo's essentially internationalist approach was heralded by many as an idea whose time had come. The General Assembly not only accepted *Pardo*'s suggestion but established a Seabed Committee to prepare for a third UN Conference on the Law of the Sea. In 1970, it unanimously adopted a Declaration of Principles Governing the Seabed and Ocean Floor. The Assembly declared that the seabed beyond the limits of national jurisdiction was not subject to national appropriation or sovereignty but was "the common heritage of mankind" and must be exploited for the benefit of humanity as a whole, "taking into particular consideration the interests and needs of the developing countries."[49]

Although the maritime powers sometimes denied the legal force of these declarations of the General Assembly, there was clear indication that the new majority had started asserting itself. At the third UN Conference, organized to regulate new uses of the sea for the vastly extended international society, the new states were determined to play a more vigorous role. Over the objections of "old guards" and defenders of the traditional law, who preferred a conference only for formulation of law for the exploitation of the seabed beyond the limits of national jurisdiction, these states wanted a comprehensive conference to review the whole international law of the sea.

---

48 *Arvid Pardo*, UN Doc. A/C.1/PV.1515, p. 6, 1 November 1967.

49 G.A. Res. 2749 (XXV) 25 UN GAOR Supp. No. 28, 24, UN Doc. A/8028 (1970).

They wanted to be able to "*analyze, question and remold, destroy if need be, and create a new equitable, and rational regime for the world's ocean and deep ocean*".[50]

FURTHER EROSION OF THE FREEDOM OF THE SEAS

In the meantime, the trend to curb the freedom of the seas by extending coastal state jurisdiction for the protection of security and economic interests of the coastal states continued or even increased after 1960. By the end of 1973, nearly 35 per cent of the ocean, an area equal to the land mass of the planet, was claimed by the coastal states. Deploring this trend, some well-meaning jurists regretfully felt that the era of *mare liberum* "may now be drawing to a close."[51] But others, like *Sir Hersch Lauterpacht*, pointed out that "in so far as the original conception of the freedom of the seas, as it came to full fruition in the nineteenth century, acquired a rigidity impervious to needs of the international community and to a regime of an effective order on the high seas, 'the loss of paramountcy' provides no occasion for anxiety."[52]

THIRD UN CONFERENCE ON THE LAW OF THE SEA

At the third UN Conference on the law of the sea, which met at its substantive session in Caracas, Venezuela, in 1974, the new majority of the developing countries made it clear that it was only the strong maritime powers "that profited from these undefined freedoms" of the traditional law.[53] The continuing *laissez faire* on the high seas had ceased to serve the interest of international justice.[54] In seeking to establish a new legal order, the developing countries said, they would be "seeking not charity but justice based on the equality of rights of sovereign countries with respect to the sea."[55] Only a new international law could establish this new order, because "between the strong and the weak, it is freedom which oppresses and law which protects."[56] The developing countries, in short, were determined, as the President of Venezuela said in opening the conference, that the sea could not be permitted to "be used in such a way that a few countries benefited from it while the rest lived in poverty, as had been done with the riches of the land."[57]

---

[50] *C.W. Pinto* [Sri Lanka], Problems of Developing States and their Effects on the Law of the Sea, in: *Lewis M. Alexander* (ed.), *Needs and Interests of the Developing Countries*, p. 4 (Kingston, R.I. 1973); see also Lusaka Declaration of the Third Conference of Heads of State or Government of Non-aligned Countries, September 1970, UN DOC. A/AC 134/34, p. 5, 30 April 1971.

[51] *Wolfgang Friedman*, Selden Redivivus: Towards a Partition of the Seas, in: *AJIL* (1971), 763.

[52] *Hersch Lauterpacht*, Sovereignty over submarine areas, in: *BYIL* XXVII (1950), 198, 403–407.

[53] See *Vratusa* [Yugoslavia], Third UN Conference on the Law of the Sea, Official Records, vol 1, p. 92, UN Sales No. E. 75, V.3 (1975).

[54] *Warioba* [United Republic of Tanzania] *ibid*, p. 92.

[55] *H.S. Amerasinghe* [Sri Lanka] *ibid*, p. 218.

[56] *Raharijaona* [Madagascar] *ibid*, p. 106.

[57] *Carlos Andres Peres ibid*, p. 36.

On April 30, 1982, after nine years of intense, arduous, sometimes bitter, and protracted negotiations, the UN Conference adopted "a comprehensive constitution for oceans",[58] a Convention that was said to be the most significant international agreement since the Charter of the United Nations. Without going into the details of this convention it may be pointed out that for the first time there was an agreement on a wide range of issues. For the first time in history there emerged a consensus in favour of agreed limits of the territorial sea of 12 nautical miles, 24 miles of the contiguous zone, a new exclusive economic zone (EEZ) extending up to 200 miles, and legal continental shelf extending to the end of the continental margin up to a depth of 2,500 meters or even beyond. An almost "revolutionary" effect of the acceptance of coastal state jurisdiction over a 200-mile EEZ has been the "elimination of the freedom of fishing and the substitution of coastal state sovereign rights over the exploration, exploitation, conservation, and management of living resources".[59] Moreover, the seabed beyond the limits of national jurisdiction came to be reaffirmed and accepted as the "common heritage of mankind". Although the exact meaning and content of "common heritage" might be somewhat vague, like numerous other concepts of international law, an international machinery for the exploitation of the oceans' resources has come to be devised and accepted by an overwhelming majority of states.

While in the beginning some of the Western Powers, led by the United States, refused to sign the 1982 Convention, and Chapter XI of the Convention relating to exploitation of the deep seabed resources had to be modified to accommodate their interests by an agreement concluded in 1994, practically all states have come around to accepting it in its modified form.[60] The basic premise of the consensus reached at the third UN Conference on the Law of the Sea is clear and beyond doubt, namely, that in future the sea must be used for the benefit of all and not merely for the interests of a few great powers.

For the first time in centuries freedom of the seas has lost its charm and stranglehold. It has come to be modified and adapted to fulfil new needs of the new international society. Although navigation is vitally important the sea is not merely a navigation route, as it has been for centuries, but is a new area of wealth, still largely unexplored, which will be the scene of the next adventure and expansion of humanity. While Europe is still extremely important, international law is no longer confined to Europe and must, therefore, serve the interests of the world-wide com-

---

58 *T.B. Koh*, [President of the UNCLOS III] quoted in: *R.P. Anand*, Odd Man Out: The United States and UN Convention on the Law of the Sea, in: *Jon M. Van Dyke*, *Consensus and Confrontation: The United States and the Law of the Sea Convention*, p. 73 (Honolulu 1985).

59 See *John Stevenson/B. Oxman*, Third United Nations Conference on the Law of the Sea: The 1975 Geneva Session, in: *AJIL* 69 (1975), 774–81.

60 See *Bernard Oxman*, Law of the Sea Forum: the 1994 Agreement on Implementation of the Seabed Provisions of the Convention on the Law of the Sea, in: *AJIL* 88 (1994), 687 *et seq.*; *Louis B. Sohn*, International Law Implications of the 1994 Agreement, in: *AJIL* 88 (1994), 696.

munity of states. Freedom of the seas will still be a relevant concept, but this freedom will not be unlimited. It will be the same kind of freedom that individuals enjoy in a national society, namely, freedom under generally agreed and widely accepted legal principles as adopted by the world-wide community of states.

*Doris König**

PORT STATE CONTROL: AN ASSESSMENT OF EUROPEAN PRACTICE

1. Introduction

Western and northern Europe was the area where, for the first time, a port State control (PSC)-regime was established. In reaction to several shipping disasters, *e.g.*, the grounding of the "Amoco Cadiz" off the coast of Brittany in March 1978, which led to severe pollution damage on the French coast, the need was felt to control and reduce substandard shipping in European waters. Eight port States, namely Belgium, Denmark, France, Germany, the Netherlands, Norway, Sweden and the United Kingdom, adopted in 1978 the Hague Memorandum of Understanding on Port State Control (in the following: The Hague MOU)[1] in order to improve the enforcement of internationally accepted minimum standards on construction, design, equipment, and manning (CDEM) of ships. In 1982 the Hague MOU was superseded by the Paris Memorandum of Understanding on Port State Control (in the following: the Paris MOU) which contained some more stringent provisions to render port State control measures more effective. In addition to the Paris MOU, the European Community in 1995 adopted a Directive on Port State Control. This directive is currently under review to improve the measures against substandard shipping once again.

In the following, an introduction will be given to the provisions of the 1982 UN Convention on the Law of the Sea (in the following: LOSC) concerning the rights and duties of flag States and port States (II), followed by an overview of the legal instruments the European port State control regime is based on (III). Finally, the new proposals for an improvement of that regime will be discussed which were introduced by the European Commission in the aftermath of the sinking of the oil tanker "Erika" off the French coast on 12 December 1999 (IV).

2. Flag State and Port State Jurisdiction in the 1982 UN Convention on the Law of the Sea

In customary international law of the sea only the flag State has been responsible for ensuring that ships comply with internationally accepted standards in respect of

* Prof. Dr., Bucerius Law School – Hochschule für Rechtswissenschaft – Hamburg.

[1] For an overview of the Hague MOU of 1978 see *G. Kasoulides*, Port State Control and Jurisdiction, pp. 142 *et seq.* (1993).

P. Ehlers, E. Mann-Borgese and R. Wolfrum (eds.), Marine Issues, 37–54

safety at sea and the protection of the marine environment. Accordingly, Art. 94 LOSC contains the duty of the flag State to effectively exercise its jurisdiction and control in administrative, technical and social matters over ships flying its flag. In particular, the flag State has to take all measures necessary to ensure that all its ships are regularly surveyed by a qualified surveyor of ships to guarantee their seaworthiness, that all necessary equipment and instruments for a safe navigation are on board, that the crew is sufficiently qualified and able to observe the international regulations concerning the safety at sea, the prevention of collisions, and the prevention, reduction and control of marine pollution. In order to prevent vessel-source pollution, flag States have the obligation to adopt appropriate laws and regulations that are *at least* as effective as those contained in generally accepted IMO conventions (Art. 211 para. 1 LOSC) and to effectively enforce them (Art. 217 LOSC).

Under the UN Convention, port States have the right to prescribe national rules and standards as a condition for the entry of foreign vessels into their ports, internal waters and offshore terminals (Art. 211 para. 3 LOSC). Since these areas are part of the port State's territory where the right of innocent passage does not apply, its prescriptive jurisdiction is, in contrast to regulations for the territorial sea (Art. 21 para. 2 LOSC), not restricted. The port *viz.* coastal State's CDEM standards do not have to comply with generally accepted international standards; they may be stricter. As far as enforcement jurisdiction is concerned, port States first of all have the right to enforce their national rules and standards against foreign vessels which are voluntarily within their ports, when a violation has occurred in their *own* internal waters, territorial sea or EEZ (Art. 220 para. 1 LOSC). In addition, port States have been entrusted with the right to enforce "applicable international rules and standards" against a foreign vessel in case of any illegal discharge (*e.g.* bilge water, oily residues, chemicals) in the internal waters, territorial sea or exclusive economic zone of *third States* or on the *high seas* (Art. 218 para. 1 LOSC).[2] To prevent severe pollution damage to the marine environment by substandard ships, they can also enforce "applicable international rules and standards relating to seaworthiness of vessels" (CDEM and operational standards). For this purpose they shall, as far as practicable, take measures to prevent the vessel from sailing or order it to proceed to the nearest repair yard (Art. 219 LOSC). By controlling ships that call at its ports, the port State does not serve its own interests alone. Inspections, investigations and criminal proceedings against violators also further the interests of all States in the region and the international community as a whole. The prevention of severe pollution damage to the marine environment is a means of protecting and preserving the oceans which are a common good of all mankind. From that perspective port States act not only

---

2 *T.L. McDorman*, Port State Enforcement: A Comment on Article 218 of the 1982 Law of the Sea Convention, in: *JMLC* 28 (1997), 305 *et seq.*

on their own behalf but also as some kind of "trustee" or "agent" for the international community.[3]

Unfortunately, several flag States do not fulfil their obligations under the UN Law of the Sea Convention. This problem is aggravated by so-called "flags of convenience" where less scrupulous operators register their ships under the flags of States which they know will not require full compliance with international standards. For this reason port States in various parts of the world have established a line of defence against substandard shipping through strengthened inspection under regional PSC regimes. Currently there exist eight regional port State control regimes worldwide (Paris MOU [1982]; Viña del Mar MOU [1992]; Tokyo MOU [1993]; Caribbean MOU [1996]; Mediterranean MOU [1997]; Indian Ocean MOU [1998]; Abuja (West and Central African) MOU 1999; Black Sea MOU [2000]).[4] Since the Paris MOU established the first regional port State control regime, it served as a model for the other regional arrangements.[5] These regimes have developed independently from the LOSC provisions mentioned above, but they are consistent with the Convention.[6] They support its approach of strengthening port State control in order to ensure safety at sea and protect the marine environment from dangers arising from substandard shipping.[7]

3. The Legal Framework in the European Union

In the European Union the port state control regime is based on the Paris MOU of 1982 and the EC Directive on Port State Control of 1995.

3.1. The Paris Memorandum of Understanding

The Paris MOU of 26 January 1982[8] is not an international treaty, but an administrative agreement between the maritime authorities of the participating States in order to effectively enforce international safety and environmental standards. It is,

3 *D. König*, Durchsetzung internationaler Bestands- und Umweltschutzvorschriften auf Hoher See im Interesse der Staatengemeinschaft, pp. 204 *et seq* (1989).

4 An overview of the different PSC-regimes is given by *H. Hoppe*, Port State Control – an update on IMO's work, in: *IMO News* 1/2000, 9 *et seq.*

5 *T.L. McDorman*, Regional Port State Control Agreements: Some Issues of International Law, in: *OCLJ* 5 (2000), 207 *et seq.*, 209.

6 *Ibid*, p. 224.

7 *T. Keselj*, Port State Jurisdiction in Respect of Pollution from Ships: The 1982 United Nations Convention on the Law of the Sea and the Memoranda of Understanding, in: *ODIL* 30 (1999), 127, 149.

8 Members are the maritime authorities of Belgium, Canada (1994), Croatia (1997), Denmark, Finland, France, Germany, Greece, Iceland (2000), Ireland, Italy, Netherlands, Norway, Poland (1992), Portugal, Russian Federation (1995/96), Spain, Sweden, and the UK. They cooperate with the International Labour Organisation (ILO), the International Maritime Organisation (IMO) and the United States Coast Guard. Other regional PSC regimes can be granted observer status, if they meet certain criteria.

therefore, an informal instrument of cooperation which is not legally binding. The participating States had no wish to create legal rights and obligations for themselves.

The Paris MOU was set up to meet the following objectives: protection of the marine environment and coastal areas, health and safety at sea, sound living and working conditions on board ships, and finally the prevention of adverse effects of substandard ships on fair competition in the maritime transport sector. These aims shall be reached by the elimination of substandard ships through similarly effective inspections in each port of the region. It has to be pointed out, however, that the members do not prescribe new regional or national standards, but concentrate on the harmonised and coordinated enforcement of existing internationally accepted standards. The legal basis for these standards and their enforcement is to be found in the national legislation of the participating States implementing the standards which are laid down in international conventions on safety at sea, the protection of the marine environment, and sound living and working conditions on board ships (sec. 2).[9] Consequently, a maritime authority can only apply and enforce those "relevant instruments" and amendments thereto to which its State has become a party. This leads to the result that the participating maritime authorities apply a different set of standards depending on the number of conventions and amendments thereto the State in question has accepted and transposed into national law.

In order to improve the enforcement of international standards the participating States have committed themselves (1) to maintain an effective system of port state control, (2) to achieve an annual total of inspections corresponding to 25% of all foreign merchant ships which entered their ports during a recent representative period of 12 months, and (3) to consult, cooperate and exchange information with the other authorities (sec. 1). In practice the 25% target results in an inspection density rate of approximately 90% of all ships calling at ports in the region.[10] Since the means of operation are basically the same as those contained in the EC Directive 95/21, they will be outlined below (III. 2). One of the main achievements of the Paris MOU is the introduction of innovative practices to support an effective enforcement of standards, namely (1) the practice of "targeting" certain types of ships with poor safety records (sec. 3.3) or ships flying flags with especially high

---

9 The so-called "relevant instruments" that have to be enforced are the following: the International Convention on Load Lines, 1966 (LL 66); the Protocol of 1988 relating to the International Convention on Load Lines (LL PROT 88); the International Convention for the Safety of Life at Sea, 1974 (SOLAS 74); the Protocol of 1978 relating to the International Convention for the Safety of Life at Sea (SOLAS PROT 78); the Protocol of 1988 relating to the International Convention for the Safety of Life at Sea (SOLAS PROT 88); the International Convention for the Prevention of Pollution from Ships, 1973, as modified by the Protocol of 1978 relating thereto (MARPOL 73/78); the International Convention on Standards of Training, Certification and Watchkeeping of Seafarers, 1978 (STCW 78); the Convention of the International Regulations for Preventing Collisions at Sea, 1972 (COLREG 72); the International Convention on Tonnage Measurement of Ships, 1969 (TONNAGE 69); the Merchant Shipping (Minimum Standards) Convention, 1976 (ILO No. 147).

10 *G. Kiehne*, Investigation, Detention and Release of Ships under the Paris Memorandum of Understanding on Port State Control: A View from Practice, in: *IJMCL* 11 (1996), 217, 219.

detention rates in order to give priority to their inspection, and (2) the publishing of "black lists" where flag states with high detention rates are listed. These practices proved to be effective as far as the selection of ships for inspection is concerned. The results of each inspection carried out in the region are gathered in the Sirenac[11] information system in Saint-Malo which is administered by the French Maritime Administration, the Centre Administratif des Affaires Maritimes (CAAM). This database enables the port authorities to find out which ships have been recently inspected in a previous port in the region and whether deficiencies have been reported. Ships which have been inspected within the previous six months and which were in a satisfactory condition shall not be inspected again, unless there are clear grounds for deficiencies. The limited man power for inspection shall thus be concentrated on high risk ships.

3.2. The EC Directive 95/21/EC of 19 June 1995 on Port State Control

In the European Community the Commission and the Council decided in the early nineties that the time was right to promote a "Common Policy on Safe Seas".[12] Accordingly, the Community enacted several directives in the fields of maritime safety and the prevention of marine pollution. Under Directive 93/75/EC vessels carrying dangerous or polluting goods to and from European ports were required to report details on their cargoes. Directive 94/57/EC established common rules and standards for the recognition of classification societies. In respect of port State control the Commission reacted to the inactivity of some more reluctant port authorities to fulfil their commitments under the Paris MOU by making a proposal for a directive to ensure compliance. In contrast to the Paris MOU, Directive 95/21/EC[13] on port State control (in the following: PSC-Directive) is legally binding for the EU Member States, *i.e.*, they had the obligation to transpose its provisions into national law by 30 June 1996. Non-compliance by certain Member States has given rise to several infringement procedures brought before the European Court of Justice (ECJ) by the Commission.[14]

The PSC-Directive's main objectives are: the prevention of shipping casualties and of pollution of the seas and coastlines, the improvement of on-board living and working conditions, and, from the economic perspective, the avoidance of distortions

11 Système d'Information Relatif aux Navires Contrôlés.

12 [1993] OJ C 271/1.

13 Council Directive 95/21/EC of 19 June 1995 concerning the enforcement, in respect of shipping using Community ports and sailing in the waters under the jurisdiction of the Member States, of international standards for ship safety, pollution prevention and shipboard living and working conditions (port State control), O.J. L 157 07.07.1995 p. 1, amendments in O.J. L 133 07.05.1998 p. 19, O.J. L 184 27.06.1998 p. 40, and O.J. L 331 23.12.1999 p. 67. For the political reasons for its adoption see *R. Salvarani*, The EC Directive on Port State Control: A Policy Statement, *IJMCL* 11 (1996), 225 *et seq.*

14 E.g., on 11 November 1999 the ECJ issued a judgment against Italy, because Italy had not fully implemented Directive 95/21/EC, Case C-315/98, *Commission v. Italian Republic* [1999], ECR I-8001.

of competition between the Member States (Preamble). These very broad objectives shall be reached by means of a more effective application and enforcement of adequate international maritime safety and environment protection standards. In more detail, the Directive aims at establishing common criteria for the control of ships and at harmonising inspection procedures and detention rules. Its purpose is to achieve a consistent effectiveness of inspections in *all* ports within the EU, thereby drastically reducing "the selective use of certain ports of destination to avoid the net of proper control". The international conventions establishing the rules and standards that are to be enforced are basically the same as those mentioned in the Paris MOU (Art. 2). Included are IMO codes of a mandatory status such as the International Safety Management Code (ISM Code) on operational requirements which came into force on 1 July 1998.

The Member States have to fulfil the following obligations: they have to carry out an annual total number of inspections corresponding to *at least* 25% of the number of ships which entered their ports in a given year of practice (Art. 5 para. 1). As under the Paris MOU, port authorities shall give priority to potential substandard ships (Art. 5 para. 2; criteria are listed in Annex I). It has to be stressed, however, that the selection criteria are not mandatory. Accordingly, each port authority remains free to decide which vessels it will inspect. In order to guarantee an effective control, Member States have to provide enough qualified professional inspectors to reach the 25% target. These inspectors have to fulfil certain qualification criteria to ensure that they have the required professional expertise to carry out inspections (Art. 12; qualification criteria are listed in Annex VII).

As far as the means of operation are concerned, the Directive largely reflects the terms of the Paris MOU, *i.e.*, the inspection does usually not include a full survey of the ship's condition but is largely document-based.[15] In order to avoid advantages for ships flying the flag of a State that has not ratified the international conventions mentioned above, both the Paris MOU (sec. 2.4) and the PSC-Directive (Art. 3 para. 3) contain a No More Favourable Treatment-clause. Since these ships cannot supply the relevant documents, they usually receive a detailed inspection.

The maritime authorities of all Member States have to follow a harmonised inspection procedure (procedures and guidelines in Annex IV): First, the Port State Control Officers (PSCOs) check the certificates and documents required by the international conventions mentioned above (the relevant certificates and documents are listed in Annex II), and they have to satisfy themselves of the overall condition of the ship, including the engine room, accommodation and hygienic conditions (Art. 6 para. 1, 2). Secondly, in the case of "clear grounds" for non-compliance, a more detailed inspection follows (Art. 6 para. 3). This is an in-depth inspection of the entire ship or parts thereof, covering the ship's construction, manning, living and working conditions and compliance with on-board operational procedures. "Clear

---

[15] For the similarities and differences between the EC Directive and the Paris MOU see *E.J. Molenaar*, The EC Directive on Port State Control in Context, in: *IJMCL* 11 (1996), 241 *et seq.*

grounds" for non-compliance are given, for instance, when ships have inaccurate certificates, when they have been reported by another Member State or by anyone with a legitimate interest in the safe operation of the ship, shipboard living and working conditions or the prevention of pollution (*e.g.*, trade unions, competent State agencies etc.), or when they have been accused of an alleged illegal discharge of harmful substances or effluents (Annex III). In the case of "clear grounds" for non-compliance by special ships that pose a high risk to safety at sea and the marine environment, a so-called expanded inspection has to be carried out. This includes, for example, a check of the emergency and the fire-fighting equipment, and a search for possible corrosion areas, possible cracks etc. (Art. 7; non-mandatory guidelines in Annex V. sec. B.). This provision applies to oil tankers of 20 and – in certain cases – 25 years of age, bulk carriers older than 12 years of age, gas and chemical tankers older than 10 years of age, and passenger ships (Annex V, sec. A).

As in the Paris MOU, there are three categories of standards which shall be enforced by port States: (1) CDEM standards, (2) standards for on-board living and working conditions, and (3) discharge and navigational standards. The PSC-Directive does not expressly cover the investigation of alleged discharge violations, whereas the Paris MOU provides for securing evidence for a violation of MARPOL 73/78 requirements on operational standards (sec. 5 and Annex 1a). But the provisions and selection criteria in the Annexes to the Directive show that ships having allegedly violated discharge standards usually receive a detailed, or in the case of the special ships mentioned above, an expanded inspection.

If deficiencies are revealed, the PSCO can take measures ranging from an order to rectify those deficiencies before departure to the detention of the ship (Art. 9). In the case of deficiencies that are "clearly hazardous" to safety, health or the marine environment, the ship shall be detained or a dangerous operation such as loading or unloading shall be stopped (Art. 9 para. 2; criteria for detention of a ship are listed in Annex VI). In the event that deficiencies give rise to detention, the flag administration has to be informed immediately to give it the opportunity of intervening in favour of the owner or operator. The detention order or stoppage of an operation shall not be lifted until the competent authority has satisfied itself that those deficiencies have been removed. In exceptional circumstances, the PSCO has the possibility to suspend the inspection, if the overall condition of a ship is obviously substandard, until this condition has been rectified by the "responsible parties", *e.g.*, the shipowner or the operator (Art. 9 para. 4). In the case of deficiencies all costs for inspection shall be covered by the shipowner or the operator (Art. 16 paras. 1, 2) which serves as a deterrent for economic reasons. The detention will not be lifted until full payment has been made or a sufficient guarantee has been given (Art. 16 para. 3). If the deficiencies cannot be removed in the port of inspection, the authority may allow the ship to proceed to the nearest repair yard available. If the ship does not comply with the conditions set for its departure, or if it does not call into the repair yard as required to, it shall be refused access to any port within the EU (Art. 11 para. 4). This banning of substandard ships from EU ports is the most rigorous sanction for shipowners or operators, because it means the loss of a substantial amount of money to them. In order to protect their interests, they are entitled to compensation in the case of undue detention or delay (Art. 9 para. 7). Furthermore, they have a right of appeal against a detention decision which will, however, not suspend the detention (Art. 10).

As far as the exchange of information is concerned, all Member States have the obligation to cooperate and to render information to the Sirenac information system in Saint-Malo (Art. 14 para. 2). To avoid unnecessary double work, ships inspected by any Member State during the previous six months shall not be inspected again provided that the ship is not listed in Annex I (priority inspection), no deficiencies have been reported following the previous inspection, and no clear grounds for inspection exist (Art. 5 para. 3). Furthermore, the PSC-Directive follows the Paris MOU practice of "black listing", *i.e.*, the maritime authorities have to publish quarterly information concerning ships detained during the previous three-month period and which have been detained more than once during the past 24 months (Art. 15). In addition, Member States have to supply information on the number of inspectors working on their behalf and the number of individual ships entering their ports in a representative calendar year to the Commission and the MOU Secretariat (Art. 17). This information enables the Commission to monitor the proper implementation of the Directive, and, in the case of non-implementation, to take appropriate measures against the Member State concerned.

3.3. Relationship between the Paris MOU and the EC-Directive 95/21

The relationship between the Paris MOU and the PSC-Directive is one of a mutual influence. The Paris MOU served as a model for the PSC-Directive which only tightened up the existing provisions. Where the Directive contained more stringent provisions than the Paris MOU, the MOU followed suit. The Paris MOU, for example, originally did not provide for the banning of ships from all ports of the region in certain cases of non-compliance. Now access to all ports of the participating States can be refused in two cases: (1) when the Document of Compliance or the Safety Management Certificate issued in accordance with the International Safety Management Code for the Safe Operation of Ships and for Pollution Prevention (ISM Code) are missing on board a ship, until the owner or operator has demonstrated that the ship has valid certificates (sec. 3.7.4.3), and (2) where a ship has been allowed to proceed – under certain conditions – to the nearest repair yard, if the ship leaves the port of inspection without complying with such conditions or does not call into the indicated repair yard (sec. 3.9.1).

The relationship between the two PSC regimes is also one of close cooperation. It is of great importance that both regimes use the same data base, namely Sirenac in Saint-Malo. Recently both started to cooperate with the new EQUASIS data base[16] which was initiated by the European Commission and the French Maritime

[16] *http://www.equasis.org.*

Adminstration (CAAM) last year. EQUASIS was set up to collect safety-related data on the world's merchant ships from both public and private sources such as shipowners, cargo owners, insurers, brokers or classification societies. In addition, the EU Member States have to supply data, as mentioned above, to monitor implementation of the Directive not only to the Commission but also to the MOU Secretariat. Finally, both regimes cooperate on an institutional level. In the Paris MOU Committee, for instance, the representative of the European Commission has the same status as the representatives of each of the participating maritime authorities (sec. 6).

4. New Proposals for Improvement of Port State Control in the EU

4.1. The "Erika" disaster as a starting-point

On 12 December 1999 the 25-year old, Maltese registered, single hull tanker "Erika" broke in two some 40 nm off the coast of Brittany. More than 10 000 tonnes of heavy fuel oil were spilt and, as a result, about 400 km of coastline were polluted. Because of these severe consequences, for the French tourism industry in particular, this disaster got a lot of public attention and generated political pressure to act. Once again it became clear that the normal regulatory framework on maritime safety and all efforts to increase port State control in the region had fallen short of what was needed to prevent such disasters effectively. The sinking of the "Erika" demonstrated that there was a need to tighten up the existing EU regulatory framework beyond the level of IMO standards. This is an approach the USA followed after the "Exxon Valdez" catastrophe in 1989 by enacting the Oil Pollution Act of 1990 which contains more rigorous standards than those of the international conventions mentioned above. The "Erika" incident also brought back to mind that several of the existing measures had not correctly been implemented by certain Member States thus creating "ports of convenience". The Sirenac database showed that the "Erika" had been subjected to four port State inspections since 1997 which only revealed certain minor deficiencies but no major structural problems. Nevertheless the French accident investigation came to the conclusion that the "Erika" suffered major structural failure. The hull completely fractured resulting in the ship breaking in two and sinking.

As a reaction to this accident the Commission presented two "packages" of measures containing three different proposals each. The first "package" which was adopted by the Commission on 21 March 2000[17] concentrated on new legislative measures strengthening the existing provisions. The Commission made proposals to amend the Directive 94/57/EC on classification societies (1) and the Directive 95/21/EC on port State control (2), and to enact a new Regulation on the accelerated

[17] COM (2000) 142 final; COD/2000/0065.

phasing-in of double hull or equivalent design requirements for single hull oil tankers (3). The second "package" contained a proposal on the establishment of a European Maritime Safety Agency which shall give technical support to the maritime authorities of the Member States, collect information on the implementation of Community legislation, and evaluate the effectiveness of existing measures. The second and third proposals aimed at the improvement of the international civil liability system for damage caused by oil pollution and stricter rules for the surveillance of maritime traffic in European waters. For a better understanding of the economic conditions in the oil transport sector which these new measures have to take into account some interesting facts and figures will be given first.

4.2. Economic Changes in the Oil Transport Market

An analysis of the economic situation in the oil transport market showed that this market has undergone changes over the past years which give rise to the necessity of more rigorous controls on the one hand and stronger economic incentives for quality-minded shipowners, charterers, classification societies and insurers on the other. About 90% of the total oil trade with the EU (intra- and extra-EU) is seaborne making the EU oil trade the largest in the world. Approximately 70% of tanker trade in the EU is concentrated off its Atlantic and northern coasts (with the remaining 30% in the Mediterranean). The largest EU oil ports are Rotterdam, Marseilles, Le Havre, Trieste, and Wilhelmshaven. Most of the crude oil from the Middle East is normally brought to European ports on Very Large Crude Carriers (VLCC).[18] Against this background it is of great concern for the region that 41% (approx. 3000 ships) of the total 1999 world tanker fleet are now over 20 years old. Statistics show that there is a general correlation between age and accidents to ships: 60 out of 77 tanker casualties between 1992 and 1999 were over 20 years of age.[19] In addition, PSCOs recorded a consistent increase in operational deficiencies related to safety and environmental procedures, *e.g.*, operational deficiencies have increased by 74% over the last 4 years.[20]

This situation is aggravated by the fact that the oil transport market has become highly competitive. Oil companies have largely disposed of their tanker fleets, and many small independent tanker owners have entered the market to fill in this gap. In addition, there is a trend towards "atomisation" among tanker owners. By splitting their fleet into several single-ship companies, *i.e.*, "brass-plate" companies registered in offshore locations, these owners reduce their financial risk. This practice makes it difficult to find out who are the financial owners and decision makers responsible for the safe operation of a ship. Charterers show a similar trend. While trying to find the cheapest tanker capacity available on the market, they shift from long term

18 COM (2000) 142 final of 21 March 2000, pp. 8 *et seq.*

19 *Ibid*, p. 12.

20 Paris MOU Annual Report 1999, 1.

contracts to short term charters (so-called "spot market"). Price competition on the spot market is fierce, and prices are often dictated by the cheapest, oldest tonnage available. As a result low-cost operators gain market shares at the expense of traditional companies with a decent safety record.[21] In a market where quality does not pay anymore the risk of a lack of maintenance and poor operational standards substantially increases. In the light of recent accidents these trends are alarming. Accordingly, measures to improve and effectively control maintenance and operational safety on-board ships are urgently needed.

4.3. Deficient Rule Enforcement

Instead of increasing their efforts some port States show little interest in improving inspection and control. An investigation of current PSC practice in the EU revealed that not all port States attain the 25% inspection target. Belgium (24.3%), Denmark (22.7%), France (14.1%) and Ireland (7.5%), for instance, do not fulfil their obligations properly.[22] Italy has, despite a judgment of the ECJ in an infringement procedure,[23] not yet transposed the PSC-Directive into national legislation. In addition, informal evidence from within the industry suggests a tendency in some ports to select ships which appear well maintained to minimise time loss and reach the 25% target.[24] There are also not enough qualified PSC inspectors in the Member States. According to a Commission's estimate currently there are 270 inspectors in the EU out of which 100 are carrying out inspections in one Member State alone.[25]

The deficient rule enforcement, however, is not only a problem of port State control. As inspections are carried out during port calls, normally involving loading and unloading operations, the ability of PSCOs to inspect cargo and ballast spaces is limited; inspection of the underwater hull structure is impossible. Ships' structures are inspected and monitored by classification societies. These specialised private organisations assess the condition of the ship against technical standards set by each society in order to issue the certificate of class. Often they are also authorised to act on behalf of the flag State to verify the ship's compliance with international safety and environmental protection standards and issue the relevant certificates. Classification societies, therefore, play a key role for the structural integrity of the world's merchant fleet. It is crucial that they keep up the highest possible quality standards in carrying out their regular surveys. In recent years, however, the increasing commercial pressure on classification societies has led to strong competition among these organisations in attracting clients. This problem is aggravated by the

21 COM (2000) 142 final, pp. 17 *et seq.*

22 Paris MOU Annual Report 1999, 16.

23 *Supra* note 14.

24 Doc. A5-0343/2000, Report of the Committee on Regional Policy, Transport and Tourism of 20 November 2000 on the Commission Proposal to amend Council Directive 95/21/EC (port State control), Explanatory Statement (*hereinafter* Committee Report).

25 *Ibid.*

emergence of second-class societies in the market and an increasing tendency for owners to switch class (so-called "class-hopping"). As a consequence, there is a general trend towards a decrease in the performance of classification societies.[26] For this reason the criteria for the recognition of classification societies and the control of their performance must be strengthened as well. Since the effectiveness of port State control and the application of high qualitiy standards by classification societes are closely related, the Commission wants to increase "cross fertilisation" between the directives on port State control and classification societies.[27]

4.4. Commission Proposal on Port State Control

Due to its subject this paper will focus on the proposed amendments to the PSC-Directive. These amendments aim at more stringent measures in respect of substandard shipping and a more effective control of the performance of the Member States by the Commission. The proposal concentrates on three areas where reform is needed:

(1) Tougher Measures against Substandard Ships

The Commission suggested to take tougher measures against manifestly substandard ships in order to discourage their use in European waters. It had become obvious that the targeting system established by the Directive and the Paris MOU did not function entirely satisfactorily. Ships with a high target factor were not always assigned the highest priority for inspection in practice. Member States, therefore, for the first time will not only have the option, but the obligation to inspect ships with a high "target factor", *i.e.*, ships posing a high risk because of their age, flag, or previous detentions.[28] In addition, the current provisions of the Directive relating to expanded inspection give the inspectors a wide margin of discretion to decide which ships to inspect and which parts are to be included in the inspection. Accordingly, oil tankers, gas and chemical tankers and bulk carriers of a certain age will be subject to *mandatory* expanded inspection, whenever one of these ships enters an EU port after a period of 12 months. These ships must notify their intention to enter a port some time before arrival in order to enable the port authorities to prepare inspections in advance. The non-mandatory guidelines for expanded inspection (Annex V. sec. B) will became mandatory. Furthermore, the age limit for high risk ships will be reduced. Oil tankers, for example, will be subject to mandatory inspection from the age of 15 years onwards, whereas under the current law they are recommended for expanded inspection when they are 20 or 25 years of age (depending

[26] COM (2000) 142 final, pp. 18 *et seq*. See also the Paris MOU Annual Report 1999, 1: In 24% (400) of the total number of detentions (1684) in 1999, classification societies were held responsible for one or more detainable deficiencies.

[27] COM (2000) 142 final, p. 21.

[28] *Ibid*, Art. 5 para. 2 of the Commission Proposal (2000/0065 (COD)), p. 57.

on the type of tanker).[29] Structural matters are currently addressed only in the form of a check of the survey report. Recent accidents have shown, however, that a check of the documents does not suffice to detect serious structural defects. Therefore it seems to be necessary that the structural inspection be based on a direct, visual examination of the ships structure by the inspector. In order to ensure a thorough inspection of risk areas of a tanker inspectors will have to examine at least one of the ballast tanks in order to detect any corrosion problems.[30]

The most important novelty is the banning of ships with a high risk potential (single-hull oil tankers, gas and chemical tankers, bulk carriers, passenger ships as listed in Annex V) from *all* Community ports under the following conditions: These ships are more than 15 years of age, they are "past offenders", *i.e.*, they have been detained more than twice in the preceding two years, *and* they fly the flag of a State that figures on the "black list" of flags with an above-average number of detentions.[31] This drastic measure serves as a sanction against "recidivist" shipowners, flag States that have persistently neglected their obligation to ensure compliance of ships under their flags with international standards,[32] and classification socities that have not kept up high quality standards. Port authorities will have to follow mandatory guidelines relating to refusal of access to Community ports.[33] The access refusal order may only be lifted if the owner or the operator of the ship can show to the satisfaction of the competent authority of the port of destination that the ship can be operated without danger to the safety of passengers or crew, or without presenting a risk to other ships or to the marine environment. In comparison to the current provisions the criteria for the banning of ships from EU ports will be widened considerably. Consequently, ships will be refused access to ports in the region more often. It should be mentioned that the banning of unsafe ships from regional ports is a measure which can already be imposed under U.S. law. Under the provisions of the Oil Pollution Act of 1990 vessels can be denied access to U.S. ports, if they do not comply with applicable CDEM and operational standards or if they have a history of accidents, pollution incidents or serious repair problems (U.S. Code, Title 33, sec. 1228).

The European Parliament made an even stricter proposal on banning. In the Preamble it wanted to add that high risk ships should not only be refused access to EU ports but also to the territorial waters of the Member States.[34] This suggestion

---

[29] *Ibid*, Art. 7 of the Commission Proposal (2000/0065 (COD)), p. 58, and Annex II (replacing Annex V), pp. 64 *et seq.*

[30] *Ibid*, Annex II, sec. C. 4, p. 66.

[31] *Ibid*, Art. 7a of the Commission Proposal (2000/0065 (COD)), p. 58.

[32] According to the Paris MOU Annual Report 1999, 9, these 6 flag states have been included in the "top ten" of the black list of flags with a persistent poor performance for four consecutive years: Belize, Honduras, Lebanon, Romania, Syria and Turkey.

[33] Annex II, sec. D of the Commission Proposal (2000/0065 (COD), in: COM (2000) 142 final, pp. 67 *et seq.*

[34] Committee Report (*supra* note 24), Amendment 1 (Recital 3).

violates the right of innocent passage in the territorial sea and exceeds the prescription and enforcement powers of coastal States under customary international law and the provisions of the UN Law of the Sea Convention mentioned above. It should, therefore, not be pursued. Furthermore, the European Parliament wanted to strengthen the criteria for the refusal of access to Community ports. Access shall be refused if a ship, irrespective of its age, has been detained more than twice in the course of the preceding 24 months in an EU port, *or* if a ship flies the flag of a "black listed" State for three consecutive years, *or* if a ship is not equipped with voyage data recorders (VDRs or "black boxes") for the purpose of providing information for use in an accident investigation. This suggestion aimed, *inter alia*, at discouraging the irresponsible use by shipowners of flags of convenience which do not respect and enforce international safety and environmental protection standards.[35]

(2) Increased Information Obligations

The follow-up of inspections between different ports is not satisfactory. It is, for instance, difficult to ascertain, from the information in the Sirenac database, which parts of the ship inspected were checked in previous ports already. This difficulty entails the risk of redundant inspections in the next ports of call and shows the need for improving the cost-effectiveness ratio of the European port State control regime. To achieve greater efficiency, inspectors in the next port of call have to obtain the necessary information on the ship to be inspected via mandatory consultation of the EQUASIS database on ship quality. They, in turn, will be required to state in their reports the nature of the inspection carried out, its results, details of any decisions taken by them and of the corrective action to be taken by the master, owner or operator.[36] The flag State and the classification society will be informed of the inspection results without delay, enabling them to intervene more rapidly in the case of a deterioration in the condition of the ship ("cross-fertilisation"). Under the current law the flag State and the classification societies are informed only of the detention of a ship. Information on the results of each inspection, however, could be useful in permitting the continuous monitoring of the evolution and possible deterioration of the condition of a ship by the flag administration or the classification society acting on its behalf. Finally, additional items will be added to the list of information to be published on inspections and detentions, including the name of the charterer and the type of charter, information on the most recent expanded inspection or special survey, and a list of measures taken following a detention (such as deadlines set for repairs etc.).[37]

(3) Improved Monitoring of the Application of the PSC-Directive

Member States will be required to provide detailed information to the Commission in order to enable it to evaluate better the effectiveness of the Directive and to verify

---

35 *Ibid*, Amendment 3 (Article 1 (5); Article 7a (Dir. 95/21/EC)).

36 COM (2000) 142 final, Art. 8 of the Commission Proposal (2000/0065 (COD)), p. 58.

37 *Ibid*, Art. 15 para. 2 of the Commission Proposal (2000/0065 (COD)), p. 59.

Member States' compliance with its provisions. A new Annex on data to be provided in the context of monitoring implementation will be added to the Directive. Information has to be given, for example, on the number of inspectors assigned to port State control and the number of individual ships entering the ports of a Member State in a representative calendar year.[38] This information will make it easier for the Commission to detect cases of non-compliance or lax practices in certain ports and to institute infringement proceedings against the Member States concerned (Art. 226 TEC).

4.5. Next Steps in the Legislative Proceedings

The Commission proposal, as amended by the Committee on Regional Policy, Transport and Tourism, was adopted by the European Parliament at first reading on 30 November 2000. The Council adopted a common position on that proposal (Art. 251 sec. 2 TEC) on 26 February 2001.[39] It did, for good reason, not follow the Parliament's proposal to extend the refusal of access to the territorial waters of the Member States.[40] The most significant amendments the Council proposed concerned the provisions on expanded mandatory inspections and on refusal of access to Community ports. Although the Member States were committed to stepping up port State controls, they were at the same time concerned about the prospect of an increased workload for their PSCOs and the need for rapid recruitment and training of additional personnel. For that reason the Council introduced several flexibility clauses that allow the Member States to exempt certain ships from the mandatory annual expanded inspection and to gradually reinforce their inspection services until 1 January 2003. With regard to the refusal of access to EU ports, the Council did not accept Parliament's proposal to refuse access to all ships, irrespective of their detention history, simply for flying the flag of a country on the Paris MOU black list or for failing to carry a VDR. Surprisingly, the Council's own proposal is more stringent than the Commission's initial proposal, as the age criterion of 15 years has been removed. Rather than simply taking account of a ship's age, the Council considered it appropriate to make a distinction between vessels flying the flags of States on the Paris MOU black list and to base the criteria for banning on the detention history of each individual vessel.[41] Accordingly, access to Community ports shall be refused, if the ship *either* flies the flag of a State appearing in the Paris MOU black list, *and* has been detained more than twice in the course of the preceding 24 months in a port of a State signatory of the MOU, *or* if the ship flies the flag of a State described as "very high risk" or "high risk" in the Paris MOU black list, *and* has been detained more than once in the course of the preceding 36 months in such a port (Art. 7 b). As far as the use of VDRs is concerned, the Council preferred to

[38] *Ibid*, p. 72.
[39] C5-0074/2001 of 28 February 2001.
[40] *Ibid*, p. 2.
[41] Statement of the Council's Reasons, Doc. 5179/1/01 REV 1 ADD 1 of 2 March 2001, p. 3.

continue its efforts in the context of the IMO in order to make it mandatory at the international level in five years for all cargo ships built before 1 July 2002 to carry such equipment and only in the case of failure to legislate to that effect at Community level.[42]

In general, some Member States such as Germany or the Netherlands were reluctant on more stringent standards of port State control in European ports and a firmer regional practice of banning. They feared that a particularly strict European practice might lead to competitive disadvantages for European ports and that it might trigger retaliatory measures against ships under the flags of the Member States by port States in other parts of the world. They, therefore, suggested to initiate a global harmonisation of inspection and banning practices within the IMO.[43]

The final legislative proposal on the amendments to the PSC-Directive will probably be adopted by the European Parliament before the summer break.

5. Conclusion

Since 1982 the number of inspections has largely increased. In the Paris MOU region the overall inspection rate was 27.6% in 1999, compared with 26.5% in 1998, 25.6% in 1997 and 24.5% in 1996.[44] Several improvements can be stated. Despite the increase in the overall number of inspections, the detention rate, for example, decreased from 11.21% in 1995 to 9.15% in 1999.[45] But the actual number of ships detained in 1999 of 1 684 is still high. Recent accidents like the breaking in two of the "Erika" have shown that there are still two key areas of concern in today's shipping operations, namely (1) the lack of maintenance leading to structural deficiencies such as corrosion, and (2) poor operational standards. These areas have been identified as "the weak link" in the safety chain of the shipping industry.[46] The sinking of the chemical tanker "Ievoli Sun" off the coast of Brittany on 31 October 2000 once again demonstrated that substandard ships still pose an acute danger to the European waters and coasts. To avoid such dangers in the future, more stringent rules and, above all, a more effective enforcement of these rules are needed.

For this reason, the European Commission must use all legal means including infringement proceedings to force certain EU Member States to fulfil their inspection obligations. It is extremely disconcerting that the 1999 inspection rates of France and Ireland were 14.1% and 7.5% instead of the minimum target of 25% and that Italy has still not transposed the PSC-Directive into national legislation, thus failing

[42] *Ibid*, p. 4.

[43] Critical on specific regional standards *H.-H. Nöll*, Europäisches Recht in der Seeschiffahrt, Die Rechtsetzung der Gemeinschaft und ihre Grenzen, in: *R. Lagoni/M. Paschke* (eds.), *FS für Rolf Herber*, pp. 463 *et seq.*, 474 (1999).

[44] Paris MOU, Annual Report 1999, p. 8.

[45] *Ibid*, pp. 9, 14.

[46] *Ibid*, p. 1.

to respect a judgment of the Court of Justice given in 1999.[47] In view of the EU enlargement process, it should be pointed out that Malta and Cyprus have detention rates about 10% and that both figure in the Paris MOU black list.[48] Both States will have to make substantial efforts to remedy this situation before the accession negotiations can be completed.

Not only the quantity but also the quality of inspections must be improved. Wide variations in inspection rates in the Paris MOU region, ranging from 7.5% (Ireland) to 53.3% (Russian Federation),[49] give rise to the question whether all inspections have been carried out with the same diligence and rigour. It, therefore, seems essential that PSCOs are well trained for their task and that, at least in the EU area where the PSC-Directive is legally binding on the Member States, compliance with the existing provisions is effectively monitored. With regard to the inspection procedure itself, it is of great importance that high risk ships get the highest priority when ships are selected for inspection. A first step in this direction are the so-called Concentrated Inspection Campaigns under the Paris MOU aimed at the inspection of structural safety of certain categories of ships such as bulk carriers and oil tankers. Another step in the right direction is the Commission proposal making the inspection of high risk ships mandatory for the EU Member States. The new sanction of banning manifestly substandard ships from all European ports also seems to be promising because of its severe economic consequences for the ship's owners or operators.

In addition, an investigation of the performance of classification societies that have been authorised to conduct surveys and issue certificates on behalf of the flag State has shown that a large number of detainable deficiencies fell within their responsibility.[50] The improvement of port State control must, therefore, be supplemented by more stringent qualitative criteria for the recognition of classification societies and a stricter control of their performance. The Commission proposal on amendments to the Directive 94/57/EC on classification societies has to be evaluated in this context and deserves strong support.

In the long run it might be prudent to establish a European structure for maritime safety which could support the action of Member States and the Commission in applying and monitoring EC legislation and in evaluating the effectiveness of the measures already in place. A European Maritime Safety Agency could be entrusted with tasks such as the assessment and audit of classification societies, on-the-spot inspection of the conditions under which Member States carry out port State control, the establishment of training courses for PSCOs and flag State inspectors, and information gathering and processing of statistics.[51] This proposal is, however, a politically sensitive issue, because it might result in the transfer of some of the

---

47 *Supra* note 14.

48 Committee Report (*supra* note), Explanatory Statement.

49 Paris MOU, Annual Report 1999, p. 16.

50 *Ibid*, p. 1.

51 COM (2000) 142 final, pp. 32 *et seq.*

remaining national competencies in the field of maritime safety to the Community level.

As far as the success of more stringent rules is concerned, one has to be cautious: It is vital that all Member States of the EU and all participating States of the Paris MOU devote sufficient resources to port State control in order to ensure an adequate enforcement of these rules. Success, therefore, depends first of all on the political will and the financial abilities of all port States in the region to increase the number of inspectors and to ensure that all of them are adequately trained and equipped. In this respect, the current practice is not entirely encouraging. Experience shows, nevertheless, that each disaster at sea has brought about more stringent rules and a more effective enforcement of these rules. This process in which the port States play a key role, has led to gradual improvements in the fields of safety at sea and the protection of the marine environment in the interest of the international community as a whole.

*Joachim Schwarz**

THE NORTHERN SEA ROUTE – CHANCE OF THREAT

In 1988 the former President Gorbatschov by his famous speech in Murmansk invited the western industry to participate in the exploitation of hydrocarbons in northern Russia and to develop and make use of the Northern Sea Route for shipping cargo between Europe and the Far East. Because of these political changes western companies and governments started to investigate the technical and economical feasibility of this new northern shipping corridor.

Norway, Japan and Russia collaborated within the project INSROP (International Northern Sea Route Project), while the European Union supported a project "Arctic Demonstration and Exploratory Voyage" and also national governments, industry and research organizations became interested in the development of new technologies to improve the economy and safety of such Arctic Transportation Systems.

A real breakthrough towards a commercial use of the NSR-transit, however, is expected, only after oil companies have started their operation of shipping oil from the western part of Siberia to the market in Europe.

1. Introduction

The political changes in the former USSR have caused the Northern Sea Route (NSR, s. Figure 1) to receive attention from countries in Western Europe, America and the Far East because of mainly two reasons:

- the 40% shorter seaway connection between Europe and the Far East and
- the huge natural resources, especially in northern Siberia.

From 1993 till 1999 Norway, Japan and Russia together with experts in 14 other countries worked on the INSROP-Project (International Northern Sea Route Programme) and produced 167 scientific publications.

In 1992 the German Ministry of Transport ordered the Hamburg Ship Model Basin (HSVA) to study the economic and technical feasibility of the Northern Sea Route.

Based on these studies by INSROP and HSVA the European Commission also became interested in the Northern Sea Route for reasons such as restoring the

* Dr.-Ing., Hamburgische Schiffbau-Versuchsanstalt GmbH.

P. Ehlers, E. Mann-Borgese and R. Wolfrum (eds.), Marine Issues, 55–62

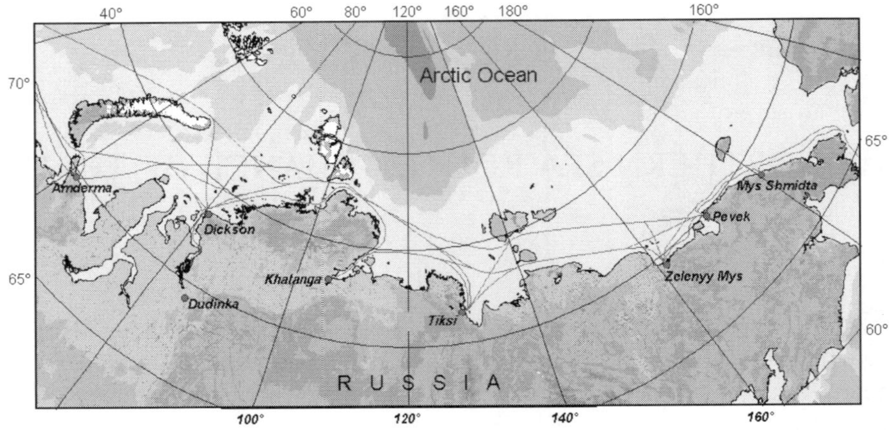

Figure 1.

marine Arctic transportation for transit between Europe and the Far East and for exporting oil from the huge hydrocarbon reserves in northern Siberia.

For this purpose the EU has financially supported the project "Arctic Demonstration and Exploratory Voyage" (ARCDEV) by which an oil tanker transported gas condensate from the Ob river to Rotterdam. Two Russian icebreakers escorted the tanker and 70 scientists mainly from Russia, Finland and Germany took part in this expedition, by which the technical and economical deficiencies were supposed to be identified for future research.

Further research programs on the development of a Marine Arctic Transportation System have meanwhile been submitted to the EU as well as to national research funding bodies.

2. The INSROP-Project

As we enter the 21st century, technological, political and even climatic developments are again making the NSR interesting to shipping companies for transit as well as for marine transportation of natural resources such as oil out of the Arctic to markets in western Europe.

Russia officially opened the NSR for foreign ships in 1991, and better and less costly ice-breaking technology is being developed. There are also indications that global warming may gradually improve the ice conditions of the NSR.

Nevertheless, the Northern Sea Route has so far not been utilized commercially to a significant degree by non-Russian vessels.

Acknowledging the need to establish an extensive NSR knowledge base, the multidisciplinary INSROP was created to investigate all aspects of potential, increased, international use of the NSR. The programme, which has primarily been a joint Norwegian-Japanese-Russian venture, has mobilized more than 450 researchers in 14 countries.

In all, 167 technical reports on a very broad spectra of subjects have been published, as well as several other end-products (INSROP's Integration Book, INSROP's Simulation Study, the INSROP GIS Database and the NSR Environmental Atlas) which have integrated the INSROP results in different ways. All products are made available to the public by internet – *www.fni.no/insrop*.

The most obvious obstacles to commercially viable shipping in the NSR are the harsh natural conditions, including ice for most of the year. Even though R + D can overcome such practical difficulties, the investments needed to build a fleet of adequate ice-classified cargo vessels are staggering. An equally big problem is for Russia to provide the political and economic strength needed to maintain a stable, well-functioning infrastructure along the NSR.

The main conclusion of INSROP's research is that a substantial increase in international commercial shipping *is* feasible – in economic, technological and environmental terms. INSROP's survey of the main cargo-generating regions at the western and eastern ends of the NSR (NW Europe, NE Asia and the North American West Coast) has identified a stable transit cargo potential, most notably for dry bulk. An even more obvious cargo potential is found in the huge oil and gas reserves in the Russian Arctic – both onshore and offshore. Calculations comparing the NSR with Suez have identified several scenarios in which the NSR will be the most profitable alternative, provided that Russia adopts a reasonable tariff policy for the route. The technology needed for building operationally and environmentally safe ice breaking cargo vessels is within reach, even though a development towards less costly technology and larger ship types is required. Ecologically vulnerable areas, as well as areas of special importance to local indigenous peoples, have been identified and mapped, and may largely be avoided. The main problems which will need to be solved before the NSR's potential can be fully utilized, are on the political level. Continuing economic and political turmoil makes it difficult for Russia to raise the necessary investments towards upgrading and maintaining an adequate infrastructure for the NSR. It has so far also prevented Russia from establishing a stable, competitive tariff regime.

The INSROP-Programme covered the following four project areas:

1. Natural Conditions
2. Environmental Factors
3. Trade and Commercial Shipping Aspects
4. Political, Legal and Strategic Factors

One should note that studies on environmental factors are of high value and show how serious the preservation of nature in the Arctic is taken.

3. Technical and Economical Evaluation of the Northern Sea Route

By the order of the German Ministry of Transport the author carried out a study to evaluate the technical and economical feasibility of the Northern Sea Route.[1]

This study concludes that the availability of 19 icebreakers with more than 16 MW propulsive power each – five of them with 56 MW – and the experience of several years of convoy trips along the NSR have proven that navigation even during the winter season is technically possible.

The commercial proposition of the NSR has been evaluated for three ship types (container, multi-purpose, bulk) in comparison with the Suez Canal Route (SSR) by the Required Freight Rate (RFR) method. The most difficult task was the determination of the convoy speeds in the various months of the year. The experience gained in Russian convoy trips was drawn upon here. The RFR-values were calculated for the current state of technology but also for conditions when research and development (R+D) results are implemented. The R+D would have to cover the entire transport system (ship design, communication, logistics, route advise etc.).

The RFR calculations show that, when conventional icebreaking technology is used, together with the assumptions made otherwise, year round shipping on the Northern Sea Route is only slightly cheaper than via the Suez Canal. If the sailing period is restricted to the summer months, the Northern Sea Route is already now an attractive proposition in economic terms.

Shipping via NSR would become more attractive economically, if the transport system were to be developed further in technological terms. If this is assumed, RFR-Values of 700 DM/TEU (6 months, summer) to 780 DM/TEU (entire year) can be counted upon, as opposed to 910 DM/TEU for the Suez Canal Route. Splitting of the route, i.e. 6 months NSR + 6 months SSR is not real beneficial, compared with operating the NSR year-round (Table 1). When operating the 1500 TEU Container Vessel between Hamburg and Yokohama year-round on NSR the profit compared with the Suez Canal Route would be almost 4 million DM/year, if R+D results are

Table 1. RFR-values for the 1500 TEU container vessel; SSR vs. NSR

Container Ship, Ice Class E4 (UL)	*RFR (DM/TEU)*	
Variant	*At today State of the art*	*With R+D*
SSR (Suez-Route)	910	
NSR 6 months (summer)	780	700
NSR 6 months plus SSR 6 months	840	790
NSR 12 months	890	780

1 *J. Schwarz*, Der Nördliche Seeweg, in: *HSVA-Report* 1994.

applied; without these developments the profit would only be marginal (755 TDM). Considering the risk involved in Arctic navigation the year-round navigation on the NSR with the present state of the art is not recommendable yet.

However, the commercial use of the Northern Sea Route could start with the 6 months summer operation. During this starting phase the technology could be improved by R + D which could lead step by step to a profitable year-round use of the Northern Sea Route.

The development of the trans-shipment from Europe to Japan/Korea would gain from the development of the oil tanker operation in the western part of the NSR which is supposed to start 2005.

The study resulted into the recommendation that a 3-phase RTD-programme should be established and carried out:

Phase 1. Demonstration of the existing status of Arctic Transportation with the aim to define the research needs.

Phase 2. Research and development on technical deficits with the aim of improving the economy and safety of the transport operations.

Phase 3. Implementation of research results into a transport system.

4. ARCDEV-Expedition

In April/May 1998 the EU sponsored Arctic Demonstration and Exploratory Voyage (ARCDEV) was carried out to demonstrate the technical feasibility of transporting oil/gas condensate from the Russian Arctic to Western Europe by icebreaking tankers and to evaluate the economical situation of such transport. A convoy of two ships – the icebreaking tanker UIKKO and the Russian icebreaker KAPITAN DRANITSYN – started at Murmansk for carrying gas condensate from Sabeta at the Ob-River to Western Europe (Figure 2).

The ARCDEV convoy made a record voyage, even though the ice conditions in the Kara Sea were severe. At the northern trip of Novaya Zemlya, where the ice conditions became too heavy for KAPITAN DRANITSYN, the most powerful atomic icebreaker ROSSIA took over the lead of the convoy (Figure 3).

Seventy scientists from seven countries in Europe – mainly from Russia, Finland and Germany – carried out investigations on the ship's performance in the Arctic ice. In spite of the overall success of the voyage a number of issues have been defined, where research would significantly improve the technical and economical performance of such a transport system.

According to the evaluation of the ARCDEV-results the following measures could improve the so far unsatisfactory economical situation of such marine transport system:

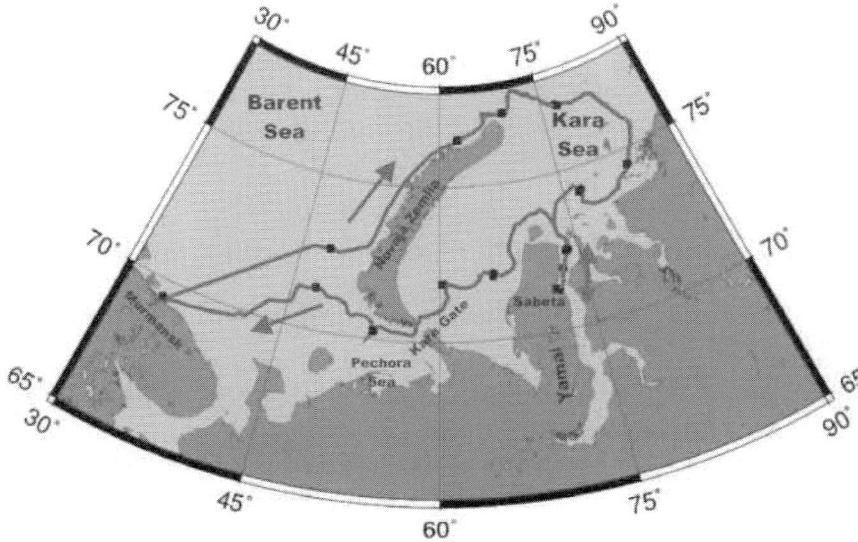

Figure 2.

1. The size of the tanker must be at least 60 000 tdw.
2. The average speed in ice should be improved by the development of sophisticated routing advice and of the icebreaking capability of the tanker.
3. The costs for the icebreaker assistance must be reduced. The calculation of the icebreaker fee should be based on the conditions of an operating tanker fleet and not on single voyage assistance.
4. Icebreaking tankers should be developed, which can and are allowed to navigate in moderate ice conditions without icebreaker assistance and which have also a good open water performance.
5. An offshore loading system should be developed, which provides environmentally safe oil loading operations in drifting ice with high efficiency in order to help reducing the transportation costs.
6. Development of combat techniques for oil spills in ice.
7. Development of ice routing advises.

All these items must be addressed by research and development in the years to come. The development of a competitive marine transport system for the Western Russian Arctic would contribute to the development of the Russian economy as well as in the long run to commercially using the Northern Sea Route from Europe to the Far East. More information on the ARCDEV-project can be obtained from *www.arcdev.neste.com*

Figure 3.

5. The MATRA-Project

Based on the Northern Sea Route study by HSVA in the early 90's and on the experience at the ARCDEV-Expedition, the author has organized the R + D-programme MATRA (Development of a Marine Transportation System for the Arctic). This cluster programme has been submitted to the German Ministry of Education and Research (BMBF) for funding. It consists of the following 6 sub-programs:

1. Icebreaking ship design
2. Environmental Protection
3. Harbor/Offshore Loading Terminal
4. Structures in Ice
5. Navigation in Ice
6. Route Optimization

Eighteen German companies and research institutions are partners in the project and cooperate with partners in Russia.

6. Outlook

The Northern Sea Route certainly has a chance also in view of the Global warming, the effect of which is expected to show up significantly along the coastal region of Siberia, i.e. the Northern Sea Route.

Commercial shipping will start with the year-round transportation of oil from the western part of the Russian Arctic. One can expect that such oil transport by icebreaking tankers will start within the next 5 to 10 years.

The technology for such tanker transportation is basically available, however, further studies are necessary to make this transport mode economical and safe.

Demonstration voyages along the NSR have indicated areas, where research could help to improve the Arctic Navigation.

Additional to the oil industry's projects Russia is planning commercial transit voyages between Europe and the Far East to demonstrate its feasibility; western shipping companies are invited to participate. These voyages will help the NSR to gain attention.

A real breakthrough of NSR-transit will have to wait for the technological developments presently underway in connection with the oil transport by icebreaking tanker.

Only if the technological achievements go together with environmentally safe operations the NSR has a CHANCE in a medium time frame.

A chance

- to export oil,
- to develop Northern Siberia and in the long run,
- to establish shipping routes between Europe and the Far East.

However, in spite of all possible precautions taken for a safe transport, one has to consider that human errors or technical failures can and will happen.

It is our responsibility to control the effect of accidents on the environment. Only then the navigation along the NSR – and elsewhere – does not need to be a THREAT.

*Uwe Jenisch**

THE DEVELOPMENT OF ENVIRONMENTAL STANDARDS FOR THE BALTIC SEA

1. The Legality of Regional Standards

The legal framework for the protection of the marine environment is generally governed by Part XII of the United Nations Convention on the Law of the Sea (UNCLOS).[1] International rules and standards represent essential elements of any international regime because they determine the scope of possible rights and obligations of states. The legal status of the jurisdictional zones is decisive for the Baltic Sea consists exclusively of territorial seas and economic zones of the nine riparian States.[2] There are no high seas "pockets" in the middle of the Baltic Sea.

The term "standards" may be found in different contexts throughout the whole UNCLOS Convention. For the purpose of this contribution on environmental standards in a regional sea the term "standards" is addressed incidentally in art. 197:

> Article 197
> Cooperation on a global or regional basis
>
> States shall cooperate on a global basis and, as appropriate, on a regional basis, directly or through competent international organizations, in formulating and elaborating international rules, standards and recommended practices and procedures consistent with this Convention, for the protection and preservation of the marine environment, taking into account characteristic regional features.

While this provision may be regarded as the "anchor" for regional conventions, a problem of definition arises as the drafting committee of UNCLOS has not found a clear and uniform terminology to distinguish between "rules, standards and recommended practices and procedures" often used in different combinations with the terms "international", "global", "applicable" or "generally accepted". The variety of terms has been discussed at some length.[3] While "rules" mean undoubtedly legal

---

* Kiel, Member of the Board, Ostseeinsitut für Seerecht und Umweltrecht (OSU), Rostock University.

1 UN Convention on the Law of the Sea, in force for 134 States, regulating the protection and preservation of the marine environment in Part XII, arts. 192–237.

2 Denmark, Sweden, Finland, Russian Federation, Estonia, Latvia, Lithuania, Poland and Germany.

3 *Budislav Vukas*, Generally Accepted International Rules and Standards, in: *23rd Annual Conference of the Law of the Sea Institute 1989*; *Georgios Timagenis*, International Control of Marine Pollution, vol. 2, note 44, p. 603 (New York 1980).

P. Ehlers, E. Mann-Borgese and R. Wolfrum (eds.), Marine Issues, 63–72

norms determining rights or duties, the term "standards" is more vague. Be this as it may. A brief analysis of IMO and the negotiating processes of UNCLOS lead *Budislav Vukas* to the right conclusion:

> "that the term "standards" should be understood as having an extra-legal meaning of a level of quality or achievement; it can be contained both in a convention (including its annexes) as well as in a non-treaty instrument – an instrument not having a binding force".[4]

Standards often contain technical norms intended to be binding, as "states should be allowed the freedom to make collective recommendations without their becoming instantly and directly a form of binding obligation".[5] Standards are often laid down in annexes or in mere recommendations (instead of in a convention itself) so as to make subsequent correction or adaptation easy.

According to art. 197, standards have to be fixed by "competent international organizations". The plural term "organizations" recognizes that in dealing with standards, no particular universal or regional organization has the exclusive competence.[6] Moreover, the double reference to "regional" interests and "characteristics" in art. 197 suggests that regional organizations like the Helsinki Commission (HELCOM) are indeed entitled to set standards. The combination of "competent international organizations and diplomatic conference" in art. 207.4 and in other articles,[7] covering different sources of pollution, allows for the necessary flexibility in the legislative machinery (which may be regional) through which States can establish harmonized rules and standards.[8]

Thus, the Baltic Sea cooperation through HELCOM – or through diplomatic conference which occasionally happens – are entitled to set environmental standards for the member states. This applies to most sources of pollution, e.g. pollution from land-based sources, from seabed activities or from dumping. The right to set standards for pollution from ships, however, is restricted in the interest of the integrity of global maritime navigation. As to the right of innocent passage through territorial seas in art. 21 and for vessel source pollution in general under art. 211 rules and standards may only be established by "the competent international organization" or through "*general* (emphasis added) diplomatic conference". Indeed the International Maritime Organization IMO, based in London, is "the only global institution with the mandate in this area, and all existing rules and standards on the design, construction, equipment and manning of vessels have in fact been established in or by IMO".[9] As a consequence HELCOM, as any regional body as well as a regional Baltic Sea

4 Budislav Vukas *ibid.*

5 *A.E. Boyle*, Marine Pollution Under the Law of the Sea Convention, in: *AJIL* 79, 357.

6 A different wording "the competent organization" (singular) may be found in arts. 21 and 211 dealing with pollution from ships.

7 Identical formulation in arts. 208.5, 210.4 and 212.3.

8 UNCLOS A Commentary, vol. IV, art. 207.7(d), p. 133.

9 UNCLOS A Commentary, vol. II, art. 21, p. 202.

diplomatic conference, are prevented from setting standards in the field of vessel source pollution, unless giving effect to generally accepted international rules and standards within the limits of arts. 21.2 and 211.5 and 211.6 (c). Due to the fact that the Baltic Sea consists entirely of EEZ zones the details of vessel source pollution like discharges or navigational practices (e.g. traffic separation schemes) can become compulsory only after being accepted by IMO under the procedures of art. 211.6.

It is within this international legal context that the new 1992 Helsinki-Convention[10] operates as the oldest and most comprehensive regional organization which encompasses pollution from all sources. The new Helsinki-Convention of 1992 builds upon the preceding one of 1974, leaving the institutional structure and the decision-making powers largely unchanged. Therefore, a brief outline of the machinery of the Helsinki Convention may be helpful to understand the processes of developing environmental standards, while it is most remarkable that the Baltic Sea cooperation now can fall back on more than 25 years of experience.

2. The Setting of Standards through the Helsinki-Convention

The Helsinki Commission (HELCOM) is the working body for the Convention.[11] The chairmanship changes every two years. Since 1999 there are now five working groups (committees), i.e.

- the Strategy Group,
- the Monitoring and Assessment Group (MONAS),
- the Sea-based Pollution Group,
- the Land-based Pollution Group and
- the Nature Conservation and Coastal Zone Management Group,

all of which may set up permanent or *ad hoc* working groups.

The working groups (committees) prepare matters for the Commission to decide upon. Furthermore, a Programme Implementation Task Force (PITF) was established[12] to enhance the implementation of the Baltic Sea Joint Comprehensive Environmental Action Programme which aims at the restoration of the Baltic Sea Area to a sound ecologically balanced region over a period of two decades.

The setting of standards is regulated in various stages and procedures like a layercake:

1. In the first stage, the Convention itself introduces in art. 3 – for the first time in a convention – important *environmental principles.* According to the Precautionary Principle, the Baltic States are obliged to implement protective measures, individually

---

[10] Convention on the Protection of the Marine Environment of the Baltic Sea Area, in force since 17 January 2000 for the nine riparian States (cf. *supra* note 2) and the European Commission. At the same date the "old" Helsinki-Convention of 1974 rescinded.

[11] Cf. Helsinki-Convention arts. 19–23.

[12] Established by the ministerial conference at Ronneby, September 1990.

or jointly, at an early date without waiting for conclusive scientific findings. At the same time, three other fundamental principles are stated in the Convention. The States shall promote the use of Best Environmental Practice for all pollution sources and Best Available Technology for point sources the criteria of which are layed down in Annex II of the Convention. Finally, the States shall apply the Polluter-Pays-System. Taken together, these principles constitute a certain "code of conduct" for all Baltic States which applies not only for the Baltic Sea itself but, as a rule, for all sources of pollution including those from land-based sources[13] far inside the country in the whole catchment area of the Baltic Sea. Whenever Baltic Sea States define or implement environmental standards they have to respond to these principles.

2. In the second stage, *direct bans* on pollution sources or polluting practices have to be observed which are either defined in substantive articles of the Convention or in amendable annexes, which update the former annexes and take account of legal and technical developments.[14] Two important sources of marine pollution are directly prohibited by the Convention. *Incineration* in the entire Baltic Sea Area including the territorial and internal waters is illegal.[15] The same applies for the prevention of *dumping of wastes* (with a few minor exceptions for dredged material).[16] The ban on dumping is extended to the deliberate disposal of ships and all "offshore-units".[17] Therefore, the Baltic Sea is the first regional sea where disused offshore constructions have to be entirely removed.

Other bans refer to a list of most "*harmful substances*" to be eliminated, which is addressed in the Convention itself[18] and in Annex I. The latter defines initially the necessary procedures such as the criteria for their identification and evaluation including a priority list of groups of harmful substances. In a second part, Annex I contains "banned substances" like DDT, PCB and PCT which are prohibited by the Contracting States. It is interesting to note that the bans on these substances were included in Annex I only in 1983 in an amendment process to the original texts of 1974.[19] In a third part of Annex I a list of pesticides is given which shall be minimized and, whenever possible, be banned.

Amendments to the Annexes, of which there are now seven, and their lists of banned substances may be "proposed" by a Contracting Party or "recommended" by the Commission.[20] Thus the Commission, too, may take legal steps apart from

---

13 Cf. art. 6.

14 *Patricia Birnie*, The New Helsinki Convention: Background and Commentary, in: *R. Platzöder/P. Verlaan, The Baltic Sea: New Developments in National Policies and International Cooperation*, p. 350, 353 (1996).

15 Cf. art. 10.

16 Cf. art. 11 and Annex V.

17 Cf. arts. 2 (4), 11 and Annex VI regulation 8.

18 Cf. art. 5.

19 *Malgorzata Fitzmaurice*, The Helsinki Convention on the Protection of the Marine Environment of the Baltic Sea Area, in: *R. Platzöder/P. Verlaan* (*supra* note 14), p. 313 (1996).

20 Cf. art. 32.

the Contracting States' right to do so. Such amendments shall be deemed to have been accepted at the end of a period determined by the Commission unless within that period anyone objects by a written notification. This "tacit acceptance" procedure allows for a swift, dynamic and cooperative development of standards with little administrative or diplomatic effort.

As to amendments to the articles of the Convention itself, the normal international process of written notification of acceptance from all Parties has to be observed.[21] To conclude this aspect, the Helsinki-Convention offers an amendable list of prohibited substances in the Convention itself and in its Annexes. The Annexes are binding for the individual Contracting State as no reservations are admitted although there is the right to suspend an Annex, however, not for more than one year.[22]

3. In a third stage, the standard setting role ("sensu strictu") of the HELCOM and its subsidiary bodies have to be analysed. Apart from normal administrative tasks,[23] HELCOM has *inter alia* the following main duties:[24]

- to make recommendations on measures relating to the purposes of this Convention;
- to keep under review the contents of this Convention and its Annexes... and to recommend amendments, including changes in the lists of substances...;
- to define pollution control criteria, objectives for the reduction of pollution, and objectives concerning measures...;

The main task of HELCOM in its duty to administer and improve the Baltic environmental regime is the elaboration and presentation of *recommendations* to the Contracting States in all fields of pollution control. Over the years, HELCOM has produced more than 200 recommendations in a step-by-step progress starting from general branch-wise instruments in the form of basic HELCOM recommendations and ending up in precise technical prescriptions. The list of recommendations is published on the internet.[25]

About 50 recommendations alone deal with the restriction of land-based sources of pollution. Many recommendations supersede previous ones and it is difficult to keep a record of valid recommendations. Here the BSEP-proceedings give updates from time to time and the working papers of the commissions publish topic-wise their status reports.[26] The very first recommendation (Rec 1/1) of May 1980 dealt with port reception facilities for oily residues.

The fixing of standards requires a solid amount of information. The acquisition of correct and reliable data about each and every aspect of the marine environment

---

21 Cf. art. 31 (3).

22 Cf. art. 33.

23 Cf. art. 21.

24 Cf. art. 20.

25 *http://www.helcom.fi.*

26 A status of HELCOM recommendations in the maritime field is contained in document Helcom/Sea 1/2000 of 2 May 2000.

in time and space is indispensable for the bodies of HELCOM in their task to set standards. Under the Helsinki Commission marine environmental data have been collected systematically since 1979 under the Baltic Monitoring Programme (BMP) which in turn produced periodic assessments of the status of the Baltic environment.[27] This task is performed by experts from all Baltic States as well as representatives of the International Council for the Exploration of the Seas (ICES).

This data collection procedure has been improved considerably over the last 20 years, for example to ensure comparability of different national data. The tools for this process are quality assurance in data collecting, data assessing and training of personnel. Moreover, there is a Baltic Marine Environmental Bibliography covering materials since the year 1970. Most recently a "Baltic Legal Manual"[28] has been published. Thus, HELCOM can be praised for its manifold efforts to make its rules and standards available to all partners.

The recommendations find their way into the agenda of HELCOM on its annual meetings on ministerial level. After consensus has been achieved, HELCOM decides. These "decisions" are regarded as recommendations to the governments concerned. The recommendations are published in the Baltic Sea Environment Proceedings.[29] Initial discussion in the various commissions and their subsidiary bodies may help to reduce the later risk of rejection. The final recommendations are not legally binding for the Contracting Parties and consequently the Commission has no direct power to enforce its decisions.[30] The implementation of recommendations is the sole responsibility of the States under their national jurisdiction. This involves the various national water and environmental laws and regulations at the level of state law, regional law or municipal law, as the case may be. In Germany, the annual HELCOM recommendations are published in German translation in "Bundesanzeiger", issued by the Federal Minister of Justice, before they become either directly applicable or serve as a basis for national legislation.

The Contracting Parties have to report on their national legal, regulatory or other measures taken in the implementation process.[31] Specific remarks about reasons for non-compliance and plans for future improvements are also requested. Non-observance can lead to political consequences and criticism from other members of HELCOM.

During the revision process of the Convention in the late '80s the question was raised whether the Commission should be given the authority to make binding

---

27 The Third Baltic Sea Pollution Load Compilation, in: *BSEP* No. 70 (1998); Third Periodic Assessment of the State of the Marine Environment, in: *BSEP* No. 64 A + B (1996).

28 *BSEP* No. 77, 2000; see also "Guidelines on ensuring successful convictions of offenders", in: *BSEP* No. 78, (2000).

29 BSEP Volumes 1–78 have been published since 1979.

30 *Eeva-Liisa Poutanen*, Activities of the Helsinki Commission, in: *R. Platzöder/P. Verlaan* (*supra* note 14), p. 337.

31 Cf. art. 16.

decisions, even by a qualified majority (instead of progressing by mere recommendations). All these proposals were rejected. The conclusion was that is was better to work by consensus. At that moment it became clear again that the Helsinki-Convention is not a supranational organization with its own legislative powers. Other than the European Union which partly works through binding "directives" and partly through non-binding "regulations" (requiring subsequent national legislation), HELCOM is confined to a permanent consensus system and to subsequent national legislation and implementation.

3. Example: Reception of Ship-Generated Waste

Pollution by ships is always a major public concern, although landbased pollution is undoubtedly by far the biggest source of marine pollution representing some 80% of all pollutants while shipping may be held responsible for the remaining part. From the wide scope of HELCOM activities ranging from landbased sources to radioactive residues, each being the subject of various standards, the problem of ship reception facilities in ports will be elaborated here in greater detail.

The Baltic Sea Region is one of the busiest transport markets in the world, representing 7,5% of world maritime transport or 340 mill. tons annually. Environmental protection of the Baltic Sea region is particularly well developed with regard to shipping.[32] The Helsinki Convention prohibits the release of oil, harmful substances other than oil and the discharge of sewage and garbage from ships.[33] These bans served as a model for the global MARPOL Convention of 1973/78. Both Conventions treat the Baltic Sea as a "special area" where these emissions are prohibited. But the advantage of the Helsinki Convention is that its bans and special areas were implemented earlier on a step-by-step basis. The "special area" status involves emission bans on:

- oily mixtures with a few exceptions (for smaller vessels/small quantities) (Marpol Annex I);
- other harmful substances (chemicals) that are transported as bulk cargo (emission ban from 1 January 1986); (Marpol Annex II);
- sewage water from ships unless mechanically treated (Marpol Annex V);
- ships' garbage.

Waste reception facilities have been set up in all ports, but under MARPOL there is still no legal obligation to discharge in port. The reception facilities are subject to regular reviews, and in some states as in Sweden, their use is largely free of charge.

Despite of these legal/administrative achievements, illegal discharges of oil by ships (500–700 cases annually) are a great concern as polluters are identified only in few

---

32 Approximately 300,000 vessel movements per year or 2,000 vessels per day illustrate the intensity of shipping. Estimate based on AMBIO vol. 9 No. 3 (April 1980).

33 Summary of all regulations in: Clean Seas Guide. The Baltic Sea Area, information for mariners from the Helsinki Commission issued by HELCOM (no date).

cases. Moreover, there is a need for a full and uniform implementation of the use of port reception facilities in all Baltic states. Therefore a work-programme, called the "*Baltic Strategy for Port Reception Facilities for Ship-generated Wastes and Associated Issues*" was adopted under the umbrella of HELCOM Recommendation 17/11 in March 1996 calling for *inter alia*:

- a control system of ships' discharges to reception facilities
- a harmonized fee system, the so-called "no-special-fee system" for the use and the financing of reception facilities (Rec. 19/8)
- mandatory discharge regulations before leaving port (Rec. 19/7)
- a recommendation in favour of garbage and toilet retention systems for new fishing vessels, working vessels and pleasure crafts (Rec. 19/9)
- a centralized authority in each state for the enforcement of the new system
- a harmonized system of fines (Rec. 19/14).

At the same time Recommendation 17/11 takes note of IMO/MEPC waste policy activities and agrees on the aim to develop uniform reception regimes with the North Sea area. Also an investment programme to improve reception facilities in the states in transition (Russia, Baltic Republics and Poland) has been elaborated.

After 2 years of deliberations the Baltic Strategy was formally adopted by the HELCOM Ministerial Conference of 23–27 March 1998 in Helsinki. The HELCOM recommendations have been published *inter alia* as IMO documents MEPC 43/INF and INF 4. The key element is the "no-special-fee system" which should be introduced according to Recommendation 19/8 as from 1 January 2000.

3.1. The No-Special-Fee System

According to the "guidelines", attached to Recommendation 19/8, the innovative no-special-fee is defined as a charging system where the costs of reception, handling and disposal of ship-generated wastes, originating from the normal operation of the ship, are included in the harbour fee or otherwise charged to the ship irrespective of whether wastes are delivered or not. The idea behind this concept is that ship operators may regard this as an incentive to discharge because they pay for it.

For practical reasons the new system covers initially only oily wastes from machinery spaces of ships, although its extension to sewage and garbage, i.e. MARPOL Annexes IV and V, is envisaged to be negotiated after 2001. As a principle, every ship calling at each port will be charged. But there are important exemptions. Ships engaged in "dedicated trade", such as ferry or liner services including feeder services are exempted on the condition that they have made disposal agreements with a competent company. "Dedicated trade" is defined as shipping in the Baltic Sea and North Sea Areas. A special procedure for issuing certificates of exemption has to be elaborated.[34]

[34] Procedures for Issuing Certificates on Exemption from Mandatory Delivery of Waste, proposal by the secretariat, in: *HELCOM SEA* 2/2001 2.2/4 of 17 November 2000.

The level of the fee based on the gross tonnage of the ship will be a standard fee to cover the running costs of the reception facilities. However, the quality of equipment for waste treatment on board a given ship may be taken into account when scaling the fee. Every ship obliged to pay the fee has the right to claim discharge of her oily wastes.

Little is prescribed regarding the quality of reception facilities.[35] The guidelines only advocate facilities adequate to meet the needs of the ships without causing undue delay. To fill this gap, HELCOM keeps a current record of the status of reception facilities in Eastern Baltic ports which are often subsidized by donor countries. A special joint IMO/HELCOM coordination group has been set up for this purpose[36] coordinating also the elaboration of Port Waste Management Plans for all ports. Under administrative aspects the Recommendation 19/8 requires a 24 hrs. advance notification, onboard inspections and documentation.

Finally, every possible effort shall be made to implement a harmonized fee system simultaneously in the North Sea. Consequently the Baltic Sea states that are EU-members (Finland, Sweden, Denmark, Germany) should pursue the "no-special-fee-system" also for the pending EU directive on "Port Reception Facilities for Ship-generated Waste and Cargo Residues".[37]

3.2. Mandatory Discharge Regulation

In order to make the no-special-fee-system viable all ships have to be obliged to discharge their residues. Under HELCOM Recommendation 19/7, also adopted by the Ministerial Conference on 26 March 1998, an important amendment to Annex IV of the Helsinki Convention is introduced, thus instituting a new and binding international legal obligation: The new Regulation "8 bis" calls for "Mandatory discharge of all wastes to a port facility", thereby obliging all ships to discharge all ship-generated wastes and all cargo residues to a port reception facility before leaving port. This rule applies theoretically to all ships visiting a Baltic port as of 1 July 2000.

A definition of "ship-generated waste" and "cargo residues" is part of the new legal instrument. A few exemptions from the mandatory discharge are offered for passenger ferries in short voyages, in cases of inadequate reception facilities or for "minor amounts" of waste.

As in the case of the no-special-fee system the new Regulation "8 bis" of the Helsinki Convention should also be consistent with the corresponding new EU Directive on Port Reception Facilities. Otherwise the shipowners of the Baltic Sea States would be discriminated against shipowners of non-contracting states which are not bound by the Helsinki Convention.

---

35 Guidelines for Ensuring the Adequacy of Port Waste Reception Facilities, proposal by the secretariat, in: *HELCOM SEA* 2/2001 2.2/1 of 17 November 2000.

36 Steering Group to coordinate the Implementation of the Project "Enhancement of Reception Facilities for Ships in Eastern Baltic Ports", latest status report of 13 October 2000, in: *REFAC STEER* 5/2000.

37 EU-directive to be published in 2001.

At present the no-special-fee-system and the mandatory discharge rule are implemented on a voluntary basis by many Baltic Sea States while national implementation legislation is still under way. Consequently there is a great task ahead for the state governments of the Baltic Sea Region to implement the new legislation, including the no-special-fee-system. The definition of the exemptions will play a major role.[38] Like in the case of the no-special-fee-system, the crucial issue is the harmonization of the Baltic reception-regime with the newly emerging EU-regime, which will in all probability need some time.

Troubled waters ahead! But the Baltic Sea States can be optimistic. The process of improving the HELCOM organization in general and the process of continually re-examining the standards and their proper implementation in particular, is well advanced. And what is even more important: There is widespread public support for HELCOM in all Baltic Sea States.

[38] *HELCOM SEA* 2/2001 2.2/2 of 17 November 2000 "unified interpretations ...".

*Malgosia Fitzmaurice-Lachs**

MONITORING COMPLIANCE AND ENFORCEMENT OF COMPLIANCE THROUGH THE HELSINKI CONVENTION

1. Introduction

1.1. Scope of the Paper

The subject-matter of my paper concerns one of the most complicated – and this not only within the framework of the Helsinki Convention[1] – problems of general environmental law, i.e., compliance and the enforcement of compliance. As a working definition of compliance one may give the following: "Compliance means that commitments entered into by a State are fully effectuated in practice."[2] As Professor *Wolfrum* observes, implementation and compliance are two different matters. In order to assess implementation by a state of binding treaty obligations it is enough to scrutinise the existing rules and regulations of that state. To assess compliance, however, is a more complicated matter, as it involves (apart from adopting relevant rules and regulations) the provision of the necessary administrative procedures for the enforcement of the respective rules on a national level. To ensure compliance, it is necessary to ascertain whether the factual situation or the State actions or policies are commensurate with international obligations. By "enforcement" may be understood all actions undertaken by States or other entities to induce or compel other States to achieve compliance with binding environmental obligations. There are several different procedures dealing with non-compliance, which include the following measures: co-operation, the possibility of compliance assessment, assistance in cases of non-compliance, settling of disputes and enforcement. Closely related to compliance is the monitoring system of activities of States-parties. The most widespread form of monitoring is a system of reports submitted by parties.[3]

---

* Professor of International Law, Queen Mary and Westfield College, London E1 4NS, United Kingdom.

1 All information on the Baltic Sea may be found on the Helsinki Commission website: *http://www.helcom.fi.*

2 *Rüdiger Wolfrum*, Means of Ensuring Compliance with and Enforcement of International Environmental Law, in: *RCADI* (1998), 29.

3 *Wolfrum ibid*, p. 30.

P. Ehlers, E. Mann-Borgese and R. Wolfrum (eds.), Marine Issues, 73–91

1.2. The Baltic Sea: A Brief Description

The area of the Baltic is about 370,000 square km and its volume about 21,000 cubic km. The Baltic Sea drainage area comprises more than 17,000 square km. The Baltic Sea is the largest body of brackish water in the world. Fresh water is discharged into the sea from hundreds of watercourses with the level of annual input at about 450 cubic km. Almost 80 million people live in the drainage area. The Baltic has very special geographical and hydrographical characteristics, in particular: the limitation of water exchange caused by the narrowness of the connections with the North Sea and by sills laying between the Baltic basins; the variable conditions between the different parts of the sea; the great difference in temperatures between winter and summer; and great variations in salinity.

All these factors contribute to the extreme sensitivity of the Baltic ecosystem. Taking into consideration the peculiar hydrographical conditions of the Baltic Sea, it has been said that even a "relatively small environmental change may cause severe unbalance to a whole ecosystem" and that "no doubt additional stress by pollution is of great importance to such an environment."[4] The Baltic Sea is a very polluted area. Some forms of pollution, such as increase in temperature and salinity in the deep and bottom waters of the Baltic Sea, are due to natural causes, and some are not entirely attributable to nature. (e.g., the oxygen content of the bottom water of the Baltic Sea), while others are the result of a mixture of causes (e.g., the phosphate concentration). Human-induced changes are those resulting from toxic or harmful systematic organic chemicals (such as e.g., PCBs, DDT, chlorinated terpens, and PCTs) and from organic wastes which are not organic in origin (e.g., lignin sulfonates). Natural substances causing pollution include nutrients, trace elements and hydrocarbons. The most serious problems have arisen from organochlorides, DDT and in particular PCBs. Thus the delicate ecological balance of the Baltic, otherwise strained by the unique features of that sea, has been further disturbed by a man.[5] The ecological conditions are worsened by the slow renewal of the Baltic Sea water which takes between 20 and 30 years. The Baltic Sea's only connection with the open sea is through the narrow and shallow Danish straits: the Sound and the Belts. Another ecologically aggravating factor is the extremely irregular oxygen exchange. In the surface layer, oxygen is replenished from the air. In the deep water, oxygen comes via the Danish Sounds. In the deepest parts there are two layers, the upper layer, and the stagnating layer in the bottom basins. In the bottom layer, the oxygen is not replenished for some years. In this layer there is a danger of complete deoxygenation due to constant consumption of oxygen through the respiration of organisms and the decomposition of organic materials.

---

4 The Baltic Sea, (*A. Voipio* ed.), p. 153, Institute of Marine Research, Helsinki, Finland (Amsterdam 1981).

5 *B. Boczek*, International Protection of the Baltic Sea Environment Against Pollution: A Study in Marine Regionalism, in: *AJIL*, 72 (1978), 782–814.

1.3. The Convention on the Protection of the Marine Environment of the Baltic Sea Area (the Helsinki Convention[6])

On the 17th January this year, the 1992 Helsinki Convention came into force. It replaced the 1974 Helsinki Convention. The situation was very complicated, due to the fact that the 1992 Convention was provisionally applied in an unofficial manner, for example in relation to such basic principles as environmental impact assessment, precautionary principle and polluter-pays-principle. These principles were of course unknown at the time of the conclusion of the 1974 Convention. The system was a labyrinth of various provisions: the two Helsinki Conventions were simultaneously applicable; also the relevant provisions of the International Maritime Organisation conventions and guidelines, in particular, the MARPOL 73/78 (by incorporation into the Annexes of both of the Helsinki Conventions); and finally the whole system of recommendations together with various manuals and guidelines, adopted by the HELCOM.

At present, however, the legal position is slightly less complicated because only the 1992 Convention is in force, (with Annexes), together with the relevant Annexes of the IMO; the provisions of the 1982 Law of the Sea Convention; and adopted recommendations of the HELCOM. However, since the majority of recommendations and manuals adopted on the basis of recommendations on implementation and compliance, were adopted before the year 2000, references to both Conventions were made.

The territorial application of the 1992 Helsinki Convention extends to internal waters of parties to the Convention (Article 4), and in that it differs from the 1974 Convention which excluded them. The subject-matter covers the protection of the marine environment of the Baltic Sea Area which includes living resources and other forms of marine life. The Convention is applicable to the water-body and the sea-bed.[7]

The provisions relating to implementation and compliance are contained in Articles 3 and 4 and 16, of the 1974 and 1992 Conventions respectively. Article 3 of the 1974 Helsinki Convention is very succinct in that it only refers to the obligation of the parties to the Convention to take all appropriate legislative, administrative and other relevant measures in order to prevent and abate pollution and to protect and enhance the marine environment of the Baltic Sea Area. Article 16 of the 1992 Convention is far more extensive in setting out the duties of the parties to implement

6 Adopted on 9 April 1992, entered into force on 17 December 2000.

7 Article 4 reads as follows: "1. This Convention shall apply to the protection of the marine environment of the Baltic Sea Area which comprises of the water-body and of the seabed including their living resources and other forms of marine life. 2. Without prejudice to its sovereignty each Contracting Party shall implement the provisions of this Convention within its territorial sea and its internal waters through national authorities. 3. This Convention shall not apply to any warship, naval auxiliary, military aircraft or other ship and aircraft owned by a State and used, for the time being, only on government non-commercial service. However, each Contracting Party shall ensure, by adoption of appropriate measures not impairing the operations or operational capabilities of such ships and aircraft to act in a manner consistent, so far as reasonable and practicable, with this Convention".

and to comply with the Convention. It imposes the following obligations on the Parties: Article 3 in paragraph 1 reads similarly to Article 4 of the 1974 Helsinki Convention and imposes on the Parties an obligation to implement the Convention though the enactment of relevant legislative, administrative, and other relevant measures. This provision, however, has to be read in conjunction with Article 16, which sets out the system for ensuring compliance through monitoring. It imposes on the Parties an absolute duty to submit reports on the following measures: 1. legal, regulatory, or other measures adopted for the implementation of the provisions of the Convention, of its Annexes and of recommendations adopted thereunder; 2. the effectiveness of the measures adopted to implement the above-referred to measures; and problems encountered in the implementation of the provisions mentioned above in point 1. Apart from this, on the request of any party or of the HELCOM, the parties to the Convention have a duty to provide information on discharge permits, emission or data on environmental quality, as far as available.

The new stricter approach to implementation and especially compliance, is a direct result of the change in the political climate, the collapse of communism, which has made possible the introduction of the principle of transparency in reporting. Although, the reporting system as such existed under the 1974 Convention, the information submitted by States was not always accurate or dependable. It has to be stressed that the recommendations and guidelines on implementation and compliance are not static. They change depending on the state of the Baltic environment as well as having to be updated and kept in line with those of the IMO.

2. Monitoring

2.1. *Introductory*

Monitoring under the 1992 Helsinki Convention concerns two different types of activities, which although related to each other are substantively different. The first type of monitoring is connected with national reports by parties on measures adopted to implement the provisions of the Convention and its Annexes, together with HELCOM recommendations accepted by States—and may be referred to as monitoring *sensu stricto*. The second type of monitoring related, at least at the early stages of the HELCOM, broadly speaking to marine scientific research, the purpose of which was "to follow the long-term (annual and long-term periods) change (trends) of selected determinants" (which are polluting substances, the level of which is to be determined in relation to selected species).[8] This type of monitoring has undergone the most radical change under the regime of the 1992 Helsinki Convention and this change is a continuing and ongoing process, since as of this year it has been subjected

---

8 Guidelines for the Baltic Sea Monitoring Programme for the Third Stage, in: *BSMP* Doc. No. 27 A (1988), 1.

to the most fundamental processes of revision, which combines elements of monitoring of marine scientific research with monitoring of compliance (see below). This form of monitoring may be referred to as monitoring *sensu largo*.

2.2. Monitoring sensu stricto

Monitoring *sensu stricto* belongs to the system developed under both Helsinki Conventions, in order to keep the following matters under review: the implementation by the parties of the provisions of the Convention (including its Annexes) and of the accepted recommendations of the HELCOM; the effectiveness of the measures taken; and the problems encountered in the course of implementation. This type of monitoring is governed by Article 16 of the 1992 Convention. Recommendations adopted by the HELCOM belong to the classical category of recommendations taken within the framework of international organisations, i.e., are non-binding. From this it follows that States are only bound by them if they are accepted by a decision adopted by a relevant organ at municipal level. Once they become a part of their domestic legal systems, States have the corresponding duty to implement them on a national level. Thus it is only *vis-à-vis* accepted recommendations that States have the statutory obligation to submit annual reports. The legal nature of recommendations of the HELCOM is not spelled out in the 1992 Convention which, in similar fashion to its predecessor, only states succinctly that one of the tasks of the Commission is to "... make recommendations on measures relating to the purposes of this Convention" (Article 20 paragraph a).

The scope of annual reports under the 1992 Convention is different from the reports which were submitted under the 1974 Convention. It is far more extensive and the subject-matter is not only the status of incorporation of these rules into national legal systems, but also how these rules work in practice in member States of the HELCOM. It may be thus said that the new system involves monitoring in contrast to the previous one. The national reports under the 1974 Convention included only legislative acts adopted in member States which reflected relevant provisions of the Convention and information concerning nationally accepted recommendations. There is a reason for this change. The system under the new Convention is an embodiment of the principle of transparency that involves the provision of all relevant information. The possibility of the adoption of this more extensive approach is a direct result of the change in political circumstances that arose after the collapse of communism. It must be said that under the regime of the previous Convention, not all information received from (then) Eastern European member States was accurate. It turned out that, due to lack of financial resources in the Eastern European States, the transformation of the recommendations into national and administrative systems by no means matched their implementation in practice.

It should also be stressed that national reports, under the current regime, include also reports on the status of implementation of relevant rules and regulations in internal waters. The annual national reports are also used for the compilation of reports on the periodic assessment of the state of the Baltic Sea and in this role they coincide with the monitoring techniques that are used in the realm of marine scientific research.

2.3. *Monitoring sensu largo*

Perhaps one of the most outstanding achievements under the 1974 Convention was the establishment of an effective monitoring programme – the Baltic Sea Monitoring Programme ("BMP") – under which the Baltic Sea environment and changes to it were constantly monitored and studied using modern techniques of marine scientific research. HELCOM, acting through the Scientific and Technological Committee (now defunct) established the Baltic Sea Monitoring Programme pursuant to its mandate under Article 16. The BMP was carried out in several stages. The first stage (1979–1983) was an experimental stage and served as a pilot programme for a limited number of stations and measurements, though, nevertheless, it provided basic coverage. The second stage (1984–1988) provided for more frequent, additional coverage of representative stations in the main sub-areas of the Baltic. The third stage (1989–1994) involved the most significant work performed under this programme to date. The BMP was supplemented by the national monitoring programmes. This was partly due to the exclusion from the scope of the 1974 Convention of territorial and internal waters. The solution adopted, although reflective of this period, was very unsatisfactory, since the status of coastal waters was supposed to be reported by States on a voluntary basis every fifth year, to enable preparation of periodic assessments. Although the BMP fulfilled a very positive role, nevertheless it had a major drawback in that it was almost impossible, in terms of joint or co-ordinated programmes, to obtain results which were comparable from country to country.

Similar in purpose to the BMP, are the Pollution Load Compilations ("PLCs"). According to Article 6 paragraph 1 of the 1992 Helsinki Convention, the Contracting Parties undertake to prevent and reduce pollution of the marine environment of the Baltic Sea Area from land-based sources by using, *inter alia*, "Best Environmental Practice" for all sources; and "Best Environmental Technology" for point sources. The relevant measures to this end are to be taken by each Party in the catchment area of the Baltic Sea without prejudice to its sovereignty. According to paragraph 1, Article 6 of the 1992 Helsinki Convention, the Parties undertake to co-operate in the development and adoption of specific programmes concerning emissions and inputs of harmful substances into the water.

For the purposes of implementation of the objectives of the Convention, HELCOM needs reliable data on inputs to the Baltic from land-based sources and in order to develop its environmental policy and to asses the effectiveness of measures taken to abate the pollution in the Baltic Sea catchment area. This data is required for the open seas and the coastal waters.[9]

---

9 The objectives of PLCs regarding pollution from land-based sources are as follows: 1. To compile information on the water-borne inputs of important pollutants entering the Baltic Sea from different

The greatest changes thus far in monitoring and assessment of the Baltic were introduced by the establishment of the Monitoring and Assessment Group (the HELCOM MONAS) in 1999 by the special meeting of HELCOM (HELCOM EXTRA 99) which re-structured the Commission to bring it more in line with the 1992 Helsinki Convention. The first meting of the HELCOM MONAS took place in Tallinn, 8–12 May 2000.[10] This meeting established the terms of reference for the MONAS. Generally speaking, the duties of the Group are to deal with the matters related to monitoring and assessment for the protection of the Baltic Sea Area, and, in particular, to advise the Commission in relation to the discharge of its duties under the Helsinki Convention arising from Articles 3, 6, 7, 11 and 16 as well as from Annex V of the Convention. From this, it appears that monitoring *sensu largo* has to a certain degree subsumed monitoring *sensu stricto* by referring explicitly to Article 16 (see above, the Article refers to reporting by States). Further, MONAS is set up to do the following tasks: to identify and quantify and assess the anthropocentric emissions/discharges/losses, including dredging, and assess their effects; to identify and quantify the changes in the environment as a result of regulatory actions; to take into consideration the implementation of new methods for monitoring and assessment as well as corresponding scientific research; to follow and co-operate with

---

sources in the Baltic Sea catchment area on the basis of harmonised monitoring methods; 2. To follow up the long-term changes in the pollution load from the various sources; 3. To determine the priority order of different sources of pollutants for the pollution of the Baltic Sea; 4. To assess the effectiveness of measures taken to reduce the load in the Baltic Sea catchment area; and 5. To provide information for assessment of long-term changes and the state of the marine environment in the open sea and the coastal waters. The system of PLCs was implemented in four stages. Firstly, the First Pollution Load Compilation, 1987, (PLC-1), of which the results were published in the BSEP, no. 20. The data and methods were very varied, thus it was recommended to use the findings with caution. Then the Second Pollution Load Compilation, 1990, (PLC-2), which was implemented as a pilot programme in the measuring year 1990, aiming at basic coverage of the major aspects concerned. The PLC-2 Guidelines defined the aim of the PLC and provided a harmonised methodological basis for collection and evaluation of data on a national level for evaluation of pollution sources, categories and parameters to be controlled. It also provided for uniform methodology for measurements, calculations and reporting. The results of the PCL-2 were published in BSEP no. 45. The Third Pollution Load Compilation (PLC-3) was carried out by the *ad hoc* Expert Group on Pollution Load to the Baltic Sea (TC POLO). The Guidelines for PLC-3 were prepared by the lead countries Estonia and Germany with the assistance of experts from all Contracting Parties and are based on the recommendations of the Seminar on Monitoring of Pollution Load, 1993. During this PLC a quality assurance system was established as well as a data-entry system closely connected to a database. The results of the PLC-3 were published in BSEP no. 70. Finally came the Fourth Pollution Load Compilation (PLC-4). HELCOM decided to carry out PLC-4 in 2000. The monitoring of the water borne pollution should be performed from 1 January 2000 to 31 December 2000 and should cover the point and non-point pollution sources of the drainage area of the Baltic Sea located within borders of the Contracting Parties. The data on pollution collected in the year 2000 should be submitted by all Contracting Parties to the Data manager in accordance with the agreed format, no later than 31 December 2000.

[10] *Monitoring and Assessment Group (HELCOM MONAS)*, Minutes of the First Meeting, Tallinn, Estonia, 8–12 May 2000, Baltic Sea Environment Protection Commission, in: *HELCOM MONAS* 1/2000, 13/2.

other international organisations dealing with relevant monitoring programmes; and to promote the development of environmental indicators for the Baltic Sea. To fulfil these duties the Group will pay particular attention to eutrophication and hazardous substances. In particular the Group will define, co-ordinate and keep under review the monitoring programmes for coastal waters and open seas as well as the monitoring of waterborne and airborne discharges, emissions and loads, and radioactive substances; will periodically compile discharge and emission inventories in co-operation with relevant parties (e.g. modelling centres as users of this data); will elaborate on relevant procedures and guidelines; will be responsible for quality assurance, including sampling, analytical methods, inter-comparisons, data processing and other matters needed to ensure satisfactory monitoring results; will prepare for publication assessments of the pollution load and the quality status of the marine environment, and assessments of the effectiveness of the measures adopted, the priorities and the need for any additional or different measures; will ensure harmonisation, initiation and co-ordination of research programmes required for the purposes of monitoring and assessment, and the promotion and development of the application of new and effective methods for monitoring and assessment, such as information systems, models, remote sensing and automatic recording systems.

The Group has observed that at present there are several drawbacks in relation to periodic assessments provided by the parties. In particular, the following points were raised: the reports on the state of and changes in the marine environment are not produced in a timely fashion; the requirements of HELCOM are not fully fulfilled; the national requirements are not fully fulfilled; other international requirements, such as those of the EEA, are not fully fulfilled. As we see, the shortcomings under the 1992 Convention are not unlike those under the previous one. Taking the above into consideration, MONAS stressed the need for a new assessment procedure. One of the major improvements will be to consider the new requirements from the EEA and the Parties on indicators, as an assessment tool. Future monitoring and the resulting Periodic Assessments should be governed by HELCOM regulations, requirements and needs; should be harmonised with the Parties; and should be harmonised with other European international organisations such as EEA and OSPAR. The new products should cover various temporal and spatial scales, including extreme events, and taking into account indicators as agreed upon HELCOM. It was proposed as well that the assessments should be submitted annually and thematically.

Finally, the HELCOM MONAS, will contribute, through monitoring and assessment, to furtherance of the concept of sustainable development as applied to the Baltic Sea. Taking into consideration three components of this concept (economic, social and environmental), MONAS in its implementation of the concept of sustainable development isolated the following elements: the identification, quantification, assessment and reporting of the state of, and of changes in, the environment; and the effects of anthropogenic emissions/discharges/inputs/activities, such as industry, agriculture, transport (including sea-based transport), fisheries, offshore installations, municipal waste water, tourism, dredging and sediment extraction. In order to achieve the goals spelled out above, MONAS put forward the following tasks to be developed and further improved: application of new and effective methods for monitoring and assessment of emissions, discharges and inputs as well as of the status of the marine environment; assessment tools such as indicators and causal change analyses of problems relating to the Baltic Sea marine environment; implementation of quality assurance of monitoring data, including sampling, analytical methods, inter-comparisons; data processing and other matters needed to ensure satisfactory monitoring results; new information products and procedures for wide and timely distribution of information about inputs and marine environment related monitoring using state of the art technologies; co-operation with other relevant international organisations; tools for prediction of the reaction of the Baltic Sea ecosystem to certain human activities; harmonisation, initiation and co-ordination of research programmes required for monitoring and assessment purposes.

Taking into account the short period of time during which the MONAS and its new monitoring/assessment programme has been in existence, it is, of course, very difficult to make any valid prediction as to the effectiveness of this new approach. It must be emphasised, however, that unlike the approach adopted by the 1974 Convention, this new one is based on the co-ordinated co-operation of States. Full State participation is expected and States will have the duty to submit full reports on implementation of the HELCOM recommendations and on the state of the Baltic Sea environment in their territorial and internal waters, on an annual basis. Another new feature is the close link and co-operation with other international organisations of a similar character, such as OSPARCOM, and with the EU. One should also stress the use of the new, state of art, assessment technologies. The new comprehensive structure of monitoring/assessment procedures in the Baltic Sea area, as already observed above, derives directly from a new climate of transparency. In environmental matters, this approach has been fully endorsed by the 1992 Rio Declaration and further confirmed by the Agenda 21.

The monitoring/assessment plays a fundamental role in the implementation of the Joint Comprehensive Environmental Action Programme (JCP).[11] The participants of the Conference in Ronneby presented a "shared vision" for the environmental management for the Baltic Sea through a programme of actions throughout the entire drainage basin. So-called "hot spots" were identified as requiring the most urgent attention. In order to co-ordinate the implementation of the JCP on a sustained basis, the Diplomatic Conference established the HELCOM Programme Implementation Task Force (HELCOM PITF). The task of the PITF is to provide

[11] The JCP provides an environmental framework for the long term restoration of the environment of the Baltic Sea, through a series of curative and preventive actions undertaken in a phased manner in this region. The JCP included all the countries of the drainage basin. The Programme was first established in Ronneby 1990, at the Baltic Sea Environment Conference. The participating parties at the conference included heads of States; high political representatives from the region; senior representatives of financial institutions; and observers from invited NGOs.

a broad-based structure which can facilitate and monitor on a pro-active basis the implementation of the JCP. This body was empowered with the function of strengthening and updating the programme which is by its nature a dynamic programme. The PITF has as participants all the Baltic basin countries, the EU, international financial institutions and some NGOs. What is of interest to this paper is the fact that one of the tasks before the PITF is the strengthening of monitoring and data collection. It was proposed that in order to achieve this, data collection has to be effected on the regional, national and local levels. An important area for support is the upgrading and standardisation of HELCOM environmental laboratories and training of staff in the eastern and southern parts of the region. This would influence favourably greater comparability of data assessments of transboundary environmental issues and improve environmental strategies and the evaluation of the effectiveness of measures adopted under the JCP.

In order to strengthen co-ordination on environmental data collection, reporting activities and assessment of impact on the Baltic Sea, the activities supported by the JCP in the area should be co-ordinated with the EU, EEA, and the OECD, so as to maximise the usefulness of information collected and to co-ordinate the reporting needs of these bodies. MONAS at its first meeting considered the basis for work, such as data access. It considered, for example, co-operation with the Baltic Online Geographical and Environmental Information Service (the BOING).

Furthermore, it must be noted that on 26 March 1998, the HELCOM has adopted a recommendation[12] of fundamental value in relation to monitoring – i.e. the Manual for Marine Monitoring in the Combined Programme of HELCOM. The recommendation was adopted on the basis of the Articles 4 and 16 of the 1974 Helsinki Convention and bearing in mind Articles 4[13] and 15[14] of the 1992 Helsinki Convention. This recommendation is of fundamental importance since it set the joint programme on monitoring and subsumed the work of the Commission under one organisational framework – i.e., Co-operative Monitoring in the Baltic Sea Environment, COMBINE. This Programme is of the utmost importance due to the fact that it harmonised the monitoring of the open seas with the monitoring of internal waters and the territorial sea. One of the Programme's tasks is to enhance the provision of reliable physical, chemical and biological data, that is necessary for the assessment of the state of the marine environment of the Baltic Sea. One of the main elements of accurate monitoring is to base all assessments on the previous decision of the Commission on adopting the Quality Assurance Policy. Another

---

12 HELCOM Recommendation 19/3.

13 Especially the applicability of this Convention to the territorial sea and internal waters.

14 Article 15 reads as follows: Nature Conservation and Biodiversity: "[t]he Contracting Parties shall individually and jointly take all appropriate measures with respect to the Baltic Sea Area and its coastal ecosystems influenced by the Baltic Sea to conserve natural habitats and biological diversity and to protect ecological processes. Such measures shall also be taken in order to ensure the sustainable use of natural resources within the Baltic Sea Area. To this end, the Contracting Parties shall aim at adopting subsequent instruments containing appropriate guidelines and criteria.".

decision which relates to this is that the participation in quality assurance exercises is mandatory for all laboratories providing monitoring data. In order to implement this recommendation, the Commission adopted an integrated programme of monitoring for coastal areas of the Baltic Sea. The Commission recommended to the Governments of the Parties to the Convention the following: a) that the monitoring of the state of the marine environment of the Baltic Sea should be performed from the 1st January 1998 onwards in accordance with the Manual for the Monitoring in the COMBINE Programme of the HELCOM adopted by the Environmental Committee of the Commission.; b) that the Manual should be applied also for monitoring the coastal waters covering also aspects of bio-diversity; c) that the annual monitoring data, as committed by the Parties in the Manual, should be made available for the Commission by the 1st of May of the following year for hydrographic and hydrochemical data, and by 1st September of the following year for biological data and harmful substances; and d) that the national data reports and other relevant additional information concerning monitoring and quality assurance should be submitted together with the data submission.

Finally it must be mentioned that the COMBINE Manual is going to be used by MONAS in relation to data collection and its processing This recommendation has been thus far only partly implemented. The Manual is to be updated once a year. Changes to be included in the Manual should be considered by the MONAS and after their endorsement submitted no later than 1st June. These changes will then be valid from 1 January the following year. The COMBINE monitoring has the following aims: to compare the level of contaminants in selected species of biota, from different geographical regions of the Baltic Sea in order to detect possible contamination patterns, including areas of special concern/hot spots; to measure levels of contaminants in selected species of biota at specific locations over time in order to detect whether levels are changing in response to the changes in inputs of contaminants in the Baltic Sea; to measure the levels of contaminants in selected species of biota in different locations within the Baltic Sea, particularly in areas of special concern, in order to assess whether the levels pose a threat to these species and/or to higher trophic levels, including marine mammals and seabirds.

Mention must also be made of HELCOM recommendation 12/8 adopted on 12 January 1991, on Airborne Surveillance with Remote Sensing Equipment in the Baltic Sea Area. This recommendation was adopted on the basis of Regulation 3 of Annex VI of the 1974 Helsinki Convention according to which the Parties shall develop and apply, individually and in co-operation, surveillance activities covering the Baltic Sea Area, in order to spot and monitor oil and other harmful substances released into the sea. The system was specially designed to provide a potential improvement in the ability to collect evidence for prosecution purposes in cases of illegal operational discharges from ships and their observance of relevant conventions. The HELCOM recommended the following to the Parties: to intensify their endeavour to cover the whole of the Baltic Sea Area with regular and efficient airborne surveillance by individual/joint action; to develop and improve the existing remote sensing system so that they can function efficiently also at night and in bad weather conditions; and to improve the possibility to use the information given by surveillance as evidence in court for the prosecution of offenders of oil discharges regulations. During the joint surveys a chosen traffic route is surveyed for a minimum of 24 hours by a number of aircraft from the Baltic States. A joint command post manages the surveillance in close co-operation with patrol vessels ready to take proper measures when offenders are detected.

The system which was developed within the framework of the Helsinki Convention in relation to combating pollution from ships is a hybrid of monitoring and enforcement. There are several HELCOM regulations and Manuals to this effect. Of great importance is recommendation 17/13 adopted on 12 March 1996. The subject-matter of this recommendation is the use of the Baltic States of the Manual on Co-operation in Combating Marine Pollution within the framework of the Convention on the Protection of the Marine Environment of the Baltic Sea. The recommendation was adopted on the basis of Article 11 and Annex VI of the 1974 Helsinki Convention; and Article 14 and Annex VII of the 1992 Helsinki Convention. This recommendation adopted a Manual for the use by the parties to the Convention when co-operating in combating marine pollution. As it is stressed below, in relation to reporting of incidents involving harmful substances and emergency dumping, the rules adopted for the Baltic Sea, incorporate, at times with certain modifications, the provisions of MARPOL 73/78 or other rules adopted by the IMO.

The best example of such a hybrid system is the HELCOM recommendation 19/16, adopted on 16 March 1998 on co-operation in investigation of violations and suspected violations of discharge and related regulations for ships, dumping and incineration. This recommendation is based on a variety of Articles from both Helsinki Conventions and the IMO's Assembly Resolutions and the MARPOL Convention. First of all, the recommendation recalled Regulation 2 of Annex IV of the 1974 Helsinki Convention stipulating that the Parties shall assist each other in investigating violations of the existing legislation on anti-pollution measures, which have occurred or are suspected to have occurred within the Baltic Sea by, *inter alia*, inspecting the record books, cargo record books, log books and engine log books, and taking examples for analytical identification purposes. Furthermore, this recommendation was based on the IMO Assembly Resolutions A787 (19) and A742 (18) and on Resolution MEPC 26 (23). Also taken into account was Regulation 3 of Annex VI of the 1974 Helsinki Convention and Regulation 3 of Annex VII of the 1992 Helsinki Convention which concerns surveillance activities and HELCOM recommendation 12/8 concerning airborne surveillance with remote sensing equipment in the Baltic Sea Area. Finally, also relevant are recommendations 17/13 concerning the use by the Baltic Sea States of the Manual on Co-operation in Combating Marine Pollution.

Among some important points of interest are the observations made by the HELCOM that effective implementation of the system in the entire Baltic Sea Area requires intensified co-operation and assistance in conducting investigations, exchanging and recognition of evidence in accordance with the national laws of the Parties;

and that according to Article 218 of the LOS Convention, such co-operation cannot be limited to the Parties to the Helsinki Convention but should be of concern also to other States and in particular the flag State of the investigated ship. To this recommendation are attached Guidelines for Co-operation in Investigating Violations or Suspected Violations of Discharge and Related Regulations for Dumping and Incineration Rules. It should be noted that these Guidelines make a distinction between general requirements laid down in anti-pollution regulations of the Helsinki Convention and MARPOL 73/78 and the prohibition of discharges under both instruments. The Guidelines are also applicable to ships flying the flag of State being parties to MARPOL 73/78 (except for Annex IV). As far as discharge provisions are concerned, the Guidelines are applicable to such ships if a violation has occurred or is believed to occur in internal waters, the territorial sea and exclusive economic zones of Parties (except for sewage discharge provisions of the Annex IV of the 1974 Helsinki Convention, which could be enforced in accordance with HELCOM Recommendation 11/9 in internal waters and the territorial sea and violations of Regulation 9B. of Annex IV of the 1974 Helsinki Convention concerning prohibition of incineration of ship-generated waste on board ship which concerns the territorial sea). The Guidelines are applicable to ships flying the flags of States not being parties to MARPOL 73/78, which violate or are believed to have violated the discharge provisions of Annexes I, II and V to MARPOL 73/78 in internal waters, territorial sea and exclusive economic zones of the Parties, as well as sewage discharge provisions and prohibitions of incineration of ship-generated wastes on board ships stipulated in Regulation 9B. of Annex IV of the 1974 Helsinki Convention in internal waters and territorial seas of the Parties. Moreover, on the conditions set in Article 218 of the LOS Convention, the Guidelines are applicable to any ship being voluntarily within a port or at an offshore terminal of a Party in case of any discharge from that ship made in contravention of Annexes I, II, and V to MARPOL 73/78 in waters beyond the jurisdiction of the Parties. Paragraph 9, Article 9 of the 1974 Helsinki Convention and Paragraph 6, Article 11 of the 1992 Helsinki Convention on the prohibition of dumping and Paragraph 3, Article 10 of the 1992 Helsinki Convention on the prohibition of incineration stipulate that in case of dumping or incineration which is suspected to be in contravention of the provisions of these Articles, the Parties shall co-operate in investigating the matter in accordance with Regulation 2 of the Annex IV of the Convention.

In cases of actual or suspected violations of the dumping or incineration provisions in the Baltic Sea Area, the Guidelines are also applicable to ships (or in case of dumping also to aircraft) not flying the flag of one of the Parties to the Helsinki Convention in the following circumstances: when loading, within territories or territorial seas of the Parties to the Helsinki Convention, matter which is to be dumped or incinerated; or if believed to be engaged in dumping or incineration within internal waters, territorial seas or exclusive economic zones of the parties to the Convention.

In fact, due to the combined regulation of the MARPOL and of the Helsinki Convention, monitoring of pollution from ships is very well developed. First of all the MARPOL and the Helsinki Conventions lay down a duty to keep Cargo, Oil and Garbage Record Books and specify the operations requiring entries in the appropriate Record Books. Accurate and timely entries in Cargo, Oil and Garbage Record Books are of fundamental importance to ensure compliance with the special discharge regulations. A copy of the relevant Record Book may be used in proceedings as evidence of facts stated in the entry. The Baltic Sea is also subjected to an extensive reporting system relating to spillages of oil and of other harmful substances. The master or other person in charge of any ship involved in an incident must report the particulars of the incident. Reports must be made by the fastest telecommunications channels available with the highest possible priority to the nearest coastal State. Additionally, the Baltic States agreed that by 1st January 2001 ships bound for or leaving a port of a Baltic Sea State and carrying dangerous or polluting goods, have the duty to report on the substances to the competent authority of that Baltic Sea State. Some States have already made this reporting requirement obligatory under their national laws.

According to the above-mentioned Guidelines, in cases when a Party to the Helsinki Convention, while investigating an incident, cannot obtain necessary information or evidence, it may request another Party to assist in obtaining it. When the other Party receives such an request, it then, in accordance with its own national laws, shall render legal or administrative assistance in order to produce the requested information or evidence to the extent possible and submit it to the requesting Party.[15] When communicating the results of actions requested by a Party, it should be borne in mind that the evidence provided should be presented in such way, as to facilitate legal proceedings against the offender by the flag State and/or by the Party under whose jurisdiction the offence has take place. All the evidence collected by aerial surveillance such as pollution observation log, pollution observation report, photographs, or video tapes, should be submitted to the State conducting an investigation.

[15] Requests for such legal or administrative assistance could include but are not limited to the following actions: search for a suspected ship; identification of the master and/or other possible persons; reporting of possible discharge; taking samples from ships and/or spillages; analyses of samples (if possible, the gas chromatography/mass spectometry (GC/MS) method should be used according to the Guidelines on Oil Sampling); inspection and/or copying of ship's documents (Oil Cargo, Garbage Record Books. Log books, engine log books. etc.); obtaining statements from ship's personnel; inspection of certain equipment on board ships; inspection of slop and oily-water collection tanks; inspection of cargo (dumping, incineration); verification of registration, owner of a ship, insurance, etc.; collection of other evidence.

3. Enforcement[16]

3.1. General Introduction

3.1.1. Implementation by the Baltic Sea States of the MARPOL73/78 and the 1992 Helsinki Convention

The International Convention for the Prevention of Pollution from Ships 73/78 and the 1974/1992 Helsinki Conventions form the basis of the marine environmental legislation in the Baltic Sea Area. These provisions are implemented through national legislation.

As a general principle, the actual enforcement of the relevant law concerning the protection of the Baltic Sea environment rests on the Baltic States. As observed, however, above, there is international co-operation established between the Baltic States which is aimed at facilitating the investigation of suspected violations of the laws. As has been described above, this co-operation includes reporting on pollution incidents and detected spillages, as well as collecting evidence and information about the suspected ships. The principles of co-operation are reflected in HELCOM recommendations 19/18 (see above) on "Reporting on Incidents Involving Harmful Substances and Emergency Dumping;" and HELCOM recommendation 19/16 on "Co-operation in Investigating Violations or Suspected Violations of Discharges and Related Regulations for Ships, Dumping, and Incineration Regulations."

These recommendations resulted in the establishment of relevant Guidelines (see above). These Guidelines are meant to act as a tool to further the co-operation between the Baltic States when investigating violations of anti-pollution regulations and prosecuting the offenders. They are aimed at operators and the police officers collecting evidence and bringing it before the courts to try suspected offenders. It has to be stressed that Recommendations are only binding for States if they are accepted within the domestic legal system and that not all Baltic States accept all HELCOM recommendations. On the other hand, the reporting system (for example, in relation to spillages of oil) is based on the provisions of MARPOL 73/78 (and its Annexes I–II, III–IV) which is in force for the Baltic States (see below, in detail).

The actual right of enforcement of anti-pollution regulations committed by foreign vessels in internal waters, territorial seas and the exclusive economic zones is the exclusive prerogative of the Baltic States individually.

3.1.2. What Vessels Have the Duty To Comply?

(a) Ships under the flag of a Party to a Helsinki Convention and or MARPOL 73/78. The regulations in the Helsinki Convention on discharge of oil, noxious liquid substances and garbage and the duty to keep the Cargo, Oil and Garbage Books

[16] The information in this part is derived from the *HELCOM 2000*, Baltic Sea Manual – Information on Anti-pollution Regulation at Sea and the Prosecution of Violations Thereof in the Baltic Sea Area, in: *BSEP* No. 77; and *HELCOM 2000*, Guidelines on Ensuring Convictions of Offenders of Anti-Pollution Regulations at Sea, in: *BSEP* No. 78.

correspond to the regulations in the MARPOL 73/78. From this it follows that ships flying the flag of a Baltic Sea State and ships flying the flag of a foreign State, parties to the MARPOL 73/78, have the duty to conform with its provisions in the Baltic Sea Area.

(b) All ships irrespective of the flag
Ships flying the flag of a State which is not a party to the MARPOL 73/78, have nevertheless the duty to comply, in internal waters, territorial seas and the EEZs of the Baltic States, with the regulations on the discharge of oil, of noxious substances and garbage and the duty to keep the Cargo, Oil and Garbage Record Book. All ships, irrespective of the flag, have the duty to comply within the internal waters and territorial seas of the Baltic States with the discharge regulations relating to ship-generated waste according to the 1992 Helsinki Convention. Moreover, they have to follow, in internal waters and territorial seas and the EEZs of the Baltic States, the prohibition of incineration and dumping, in accordance with the relevant provisions of the 1992 Helsinki Convention. Ships flying the flag of a Baltic Sea State have to comply with these provisions also on the high seas of the Baltic Sea.

3.1.3. The Laws to be Enforced
The anti-pollution laws which cover the Baltic Sea Are may be divided into three categories: discharge regulations as codified in MARPOL 73/78 and relating to the Baltic as a Special Area; regulations which concern the obligations to keep Cargo, Oil and garbage Record Books; other discharge and anti-pollution regulations.

3.2. Particular Matters

3.2.1. The Substances
(a) Oil[17]
By oil is understood any form of petroleum including crude oil, fuel, sludge, oil refuse, and refined products. There is a prohibition on the discharge of oil or oily mixtures in the Baltic Sea Area.

(b) Noxious Liquid Substances Carried in Bulk[18]
The categorisation A-D of noxious liquid substances carried in bulk is specified in the INO Bulk Chemical Code, Category A being the substances most harmful to the marine environment.

---

17 Regulated by Regulations 10, 11 and 16 paragraph 5 of Annex 1 of the MARPOL 73/78; Articles 8 and 9 and Regulation 4 of the Annex IV to the 1992 Helsinki Convention.

18 Regulation 5 paragraph, 4, 8 and 9 and Regulation of the Annex II of the MARPOL 73/78; Articles 8 and 9 and Regulation 4 of the Annex IV of the 1992 Helsinki Convention.

(c) Garbage[19]
Under the heading garbage is understood all kinds of victuals, domestic and operational waste excluding fresh fish and parts thereof; generated during the normal operation of the ship. The disposal of garbage is prohibited in the Baltic Sea Area. This prohibition also applies to pleasure craft. Food waste may be, however, discharged, but no less than 12 nautical miles from the nearest land.

3.2.2. Duty to Keep the Cargo, Oil and Garbage Record Books[20]

The duty to keep the Cargo, Oil and Garbage Record Books is of fundamental importance to ensure this compliance with all these rules and regulations. The specific duty to keep the book is specified in the Guidelines (see above), as well as in Appendix 1 of Annex 1 of the MARPOL 73/78, Appendix IV of Annex II of the MARPOL 73/78 and Appendix V of the MARPOL 73/78.

3.2.3. Other Discharges and Anti-Pollution Regulations

(a) Sewage[21]
It is prohibited to discharge sewage within a distance of 12 nautical miles from the nearest land. However, if comminuted and disinfected, using a system approved by the Administration, sewage may be discharged, provided that the distance is more than 4 nautical miles from the nearest land. Only if an approved sewage treatment plant is used, can discharge take place at any distance from the nearest land. For the ships flying the flag of the Baltic Sea States regulation on surveys and Sewage and Sewage Pollution Prevention Certificates also apply.

(b) Incineration[22]
Under the heading incineration is understood the deliberate combustion of wastes or other matter at sea for the purpose of their thermal destruction, excluding activities incidental to the normal operation of ships or other man-made structures. However, in the territorial waters of the Baltic Sea States, it is prohibited to incinerate also wastes deriving from the normal operation of the ship. As a general rule incineration is prohibited in the whole area of the Baltic Sea.

(c) Dumping[23]
Under dumping is understood any deliberate disposal at sea of wastes from ships, not covered by the above-mentioned disposal regulations. Dumping also means any

---

[19] Regulation 5 and 6 of Annex V of the MARPOL 73/78; Articles 8 and 9 Regulation 4 of the Annex IV to the 1992 Helsinki Convention.

[20] Regulation 20 of Annex 1, Regulation 9 of Annex II and Regulation 9 of Annex V of the MARPOL 73.78; Articles 8 and 9 and Regulation 4 of the Annex IV of the 1992 Helsinki Convention.

[21] Articles 8 and 9 and Regulation 5 of Annex IV to the 1992 Helsinki Convention; HELCOM Recommendation 19/7.

[22] The 1972 London Convention and the 1996 Protocol thereto; Article 10 of the 1992 Helsinki Convention.

[23] The 1972 London Convention and 1966 Protocol thereto; Article 11 of the 1992 Helsinki Convention.

deliberate disposal at sea of ships. As a general rule dumping is prohibited in the whole of the Baltic Sea area.

(d) Disposal of Dredged Material[24]
Disposal of dredged material is allowed in the Baltic Sea Area only under the condition of obtaining a prior special permit issued by the appropriate national authority. Additionally, in case of disposal outside the internal waters and the territorial seas, prior consultation in the HELCOM is required.

3.3. The General Duty of Enforcement

The Baltic Sea States have the duty, under international law, to enforce anti-pollution regulations up to 200 nautical miles from the baselines; in their internal waters; territorial sea; and the Exclusive Economic Zone. This duty applies to the ship flying the flag of all States, and is applied in a non-discriminatory manner, equally to all ships. As regards the ships flying the flag of the Baltic Sea States, they have an obligation to enforce anti-pollution laws on the High Seas.

Additionally, it has to be stressed that Germany has implemented Article 218 of the LOS Convention (the port State jurisdiction), which gives a port State the right to investigate and institute proceedings, when a ship is voluntarily within its ports, irrespective where an illegal discharge took place (on the high seas, or in the internal waters, territorial seas or exclusive economic zone of another State). In cases of illegal pollution in areas under jurisdiction of another State, investigation is conducted on request from the State concerned.

3.4.. Practice of the Baltic Sea States in Enforcing Anti-Pollution Regulations

The Baltic Sea States decided on a uniform interpretation and implementation of anti-pollution regulations by establishing criteria for the determination of the severity of a violation and the minimum level of the fine to be imposed. These can be found in the HELCOM Recommendation 19/14 "A Harmonised System of Fines in Case of Ship Violates Anti-pollution Regulations." In accordance with this recommendation, the breach of a duty to keep the Oil and Cargo Record Book is regarded as a continuing offence. It means that even if the duty to make entries in the record book arose on the High Seas, it can be enforced in a port of a Baltic Sea State.

3.5. Investigation and Prosecution

Investigations of (suspected) violations of anti-pollution regulations are carried out by different authorities in the Baltic Sea States. Some States bestow this task on specific Boards. The most common situation, however, involves co-operation between many varied authorities. Violations of anti-pollution regulations fall under two

---

24 Article 11 and Annex V of the 1992 Helsinki Convention.

different categories: administrative offences; and/or criminal offences based on civil or penal law. Except for Finland and Denmark, competent authorities can impose administrative fines for specified violations of anti-pollution regulations. The competent venue for the court proceedings is decided, *inter alia*, on the basis of the place of offence, or the residence of the defendant or suspect. Finland and Germany have centralised the competence at specific courts in case of (suspected) violations outside territorial waters. Various authorities can impose an administrative fine. HELCOM Recommendation 19/14 includes criteria for a common minimum level of fines in case a ship violates anti-pollution regulations.

4. Conclusions

The above presentation clearly indicates that the system of joint monitoring under the Helsinki Convention is very well developed. The initial stages of the system were already present under the 1974 Helsinki Convention. Due, however, to extra-legal factors its extensive development was impossible. It has been only the change in the political situation and the signing of the 1992 Helsinki Convention which brought about the present increase in the level of co-operation in monitoring. As shown above, the whole system is rather complicated and derives in part from the provisions of the MARPOL 73/78; in part from the provisions of the Helsinki Convention, which are perfected by the HELCOM Recommendations. The HELCOM, as observed above, issues so-called guidelines in the form of recommendations (not all of them are adopted by States) which contribute to the setting up of a uniform system of monitoring.

It has to be said, however, that at present, the entire system is undergoing a process of revision, due to the re-organisation of the HELCOM which took place in 1999. A special body, HELCOM MONAS (see above) has been set-up to establish a modern monitoring system which would especially focus on the monitoring of the state of ecology of the Baltic and which would reflect contemporary scientific approaches.

It may also be said that the HELCOM system is quite complicated and would benefit from a more uniform structure. As it is at present, it is rooted in many different sources; and therefore difficult to make coherent as a whole. It is probably a positive development that the HELCOM strives now to achieve a certain degree of coherency. The most important matter, in the view of the present author, is to strengthen the system of national reports which are the basis for the monitoring of the state of the Baltic environment. On the other hand, monitoring, which involves the compliance by ships with the provisions of the MARPOL 73/78 and the 1992 Helsinki Convention, is efficient and very well developed.

The enforcement of the relevant law rests on the individual States which have a duty to implement laws and regulations which are binding on them. Although there is a system in place which sets up a common assistance network, actual enforcement belongs to the domain of States parties to the Helsinki Convention. This reflects general international law as it stands at present.

*Peter Ehlers**

MARINE ENVIRONMENT PROTECTION – THE BALTIC SEA EXAMPLE

1. Introduction

The year 2000 is very appropriate – not only because of the beginning of a new millennium – to discuss the status of marine environment co-operation in the Baltic Sea Area. 20 years ago, in 1980, the Convention of the Protection of the Marine Environment of the Baltic Sea Area – the so-called Helsinki Convention – entered into force. Since the 70s, this Convention, which was already adopted by the Baltic Sea States in 1974, has become the regulatory frame for an intensive co-operation to protect the Baltic Sea environment. At the beginning of the year 2000 a new, revised Helsinki Convention entered into force and replaced the older one.

After more than two decades of co-operation, time has come to discuss whether or not the work done under the Helsinki Convention is a success and may serve as an example for other marine areas. Such an evaluation has to start by describing the ecological conditions and problems of the Baltic Sea. Following that it has to consider the Convention itself. Afterwards, particular attention has to be given to the process of co-operation, including present activities, main goals and priorities.

2. Ecological Conditions and Problems

Nine countries today share the coast line of the Baltic Sea. The coastal zone is inhabited by some 16 million people. In the whole catchment area, however, lives a population of about 85 million. Most of the countries in the catchment area have highly developed agricultural and industrial activities. So the Baltic Sea is subject to contamination from human activities by a substantial population. Its role as the final reservoir of pollution is particularly hazardous for the Baltic Sea which is a very sensitive marine area due to its natural conditions. It is a very shallow sea, the average depth is 55 m only. The Baltic Sea is a brackish water area receiving a large supply of fresh water from numerous rivers. Refreshment of waters of the Baltic Sea is achieved only through their exchange with saline water inflows from the North Sea through very narrow channels. The processes of exchange are irregular and depend mainly on the meteorological conditions. It is estimated that 25 to 30 years

* Dr., President and Professor of the German Bundesamt für Seeschiffahrt und Hydrographie (Federal Maritime and Hydrographic Agency) Hamburg/Rostock, Chairman of the Helsinki Commission.

P. Ehlers, E. Mann-Borgese and R. Wolfrum (eds.), Marine Issues, 93–104

are needed to entirely exchange the waters. Pollutants therefore remain in the sea for a long time. As a saline boundary layer is formed between the upper water layer and the deeper parts, the water in the deepest parts is only renewed very irregularly by inflows of sufficiently high salinity. When this does not occur, wide-spread areas of deep bottom water become "dead" as hydrogen sulphide concentrations build up.[1]

Polluting substances enter the Baltic Sea ecosystem via a number of pathways, inter alia:

- riverine run-off,
- atmospheric deposition
- direct discharges from land
- activities at sea.

The largest quantities come from land-based sources including cities and industrial areas and from the agrarian areas. The anthropogenic inputs consist of nutrients, heavy metals and organic substances including hydrocarbons and oil. Nutrients – namely nitrogen and phosphorus – are the inputs of greatest concern with respect to eutrophication in the Baltic Sea resulting in increased oxygen consumption and ultimately the formation of the toxic hydrogen sulphide. During the mid-90s a decrease of nutrients has been observed, but recent measurements do not show a continuation of this improvement. As concerns heavy metals traces of mercury, cadmium, zinc, copper and lead have been observed, but showing no significant difference to those found in the open North Sea and the Northeast Atlantic. Whereas in some areas a decrease of concentration values has been observed, there is however an upward trend in some other parts.

In the '70s, concentrations of toxic organic contaminants such as DDT and PCB were particularly high at the top of the food chain. Other examples of harmful substances detected in the Baltic Sea are halogenetic paraffins, polyaromatic hydrocarbons, PCT and pesticides. In the meantime a decline in concentrations of DDT and some other organic contaminants has been ascertained. However, due to the lack of long-term observations it is still very difficult to find significant trends especially with regard to the increasing number of "new contaminants" which are identified as potentially harmful to the marine environment.

The main sources of oil pollution in the Baltic Sea are emissions from land-based sources, shipping and offshore activities. Land-based sources are by far the largest contributor to oil inputs. However, the pollution caused by accidental and – above all – illegal oilspills through shipping and offshore activities is also a serious threat.[2]

---

1 See *Helsinki Commission*, The State of the Baltic Sea Marine Environment, p. 2 *et seq.*; *Helsinki Commission*, The Final Report on the Implementation of the 1988 Ministerial Declaration, in: *BSEP* No. 71, 6; cf. Bericht des Bundesministeriums für Umwelt, Naturschutz und Reaktorsicherheit zum Schutz der Meeresumwelt, insbesondere der Nord- und Ostsee, in: *Deutscher Bundestag, Ausschuss für Umwelt, Naturschutz und Reaktorsicherheit*, Protokoll 14/32, Attachment 1, p. 80.

2 See for an overview *Helsinki Commission*, Protection of the Baltic Sea – results and experiences.

3. The Helsinki Convention

The deterioration of the marine environment of the Baltic Sea has been a cause of growing concern in the late 60s. This led to the signing of the Helsinki Convention in March 1974 by the coastal States of the Baltic Sea area, marking an important political milestone in international ecopolitics. All sources of pollution were, for the first time for a sea area, made the subject of regulations in one Convention.[3] This Convention carried even greater weight as marine environment protection was one of the first areas in which the Baltic Sea States – in the times of cold war – showed any willingness to co-operate.

In the light of the political changes as well as of developments in international environmental law, law of the sea and experience gained, the Helsinki Convention was revised in 1992. After ratification by the now nine Baltic Sea coastal States and the European Commission the new Convention entered into force on 17th January 2000.[4] The Convention is in line with Section XII of UNCLOS[5] which obliges States to co-operate in formulating and elaborating international rules consistent with UNCLOS for the protection and preservation of the marine environment.

The purpose of the 1992 Helsinki Convention is two-fold.[6] On the one hand it formulates in 38 Articles and 7 Annexes regulations obliging Contracting Parties to undertake appropriate national implementation measures. Secondly it creates the legal basis for a close and permanent co-operation, in particular through the international Baltic Marine Environment Protection Commission.[7] The Convention covers the whole of the Baltic Sea including internal waters.[8] Where land-based inputs are concerned, necessary measures are to be taken in the whole of the catchment area.[9]

3.1. Fundamental principles and obligations

The Convention establishes fundamental ecopolitical principles which partly go beyond UNCLOS. The precautionary principle has to be applied so that preventive measures must be taken when there is reason to assume that substances introduced in the marine environment may create hazards, even when there is no conclusive

---

3 The Convention text is published e.g. in the German Law Bulletin *BGBl.* 1979 II p. 1229, for details see *Peter Ehlers*, 10 Jahre Helsinki-Übereinkommen – ein Bericht, in: *NuR* 1984, 138 *et seq.*

4 For the Convention text see *BGBl.* 1994 II p. 1355.

5 United Nations Convention on the Law of Sea, *BGBl.* 1994 II p. 1798. Cf. *Peter Ehlers*, Das Seerechtsübereinkommen im Verhältnis zum Helsinki-Übereinkommen, in: *B-BSH* 4 (1994), 41 *et seq.*

6 Cf. *Peter Ehlers*, The 1992 Helsinki Convention – an effective basis for environmental co-operation in the Baltic Sea Area, in: *Erkki J. Hollo/Kari Marttinen* (eds.), *North European Environmental Law, Publications of the Finnish Society of Environmental Law*, 25 (1995), 3 *et seq.*

7 *Hereinafter* Helsinki Commission.

8 Art. 1; unmarked articles refer to the 1992 Helsinki Convention.

9 Art. 6, para. 1, sentence 2.

evidence.[10] To prevent and eliminate pollution of the Baltic Sea the Contracting Parties shall promote the use of best environment practice and best available technology; the criteria are given in Annex II of the Convention.[11] Contracting Parties are further obliged to apply the polluter pays principle.[12] They shall ensure that measurements and calculations of inputs are carried out in a scientifically appropriate manner to assess the state of the marine environment.[13] Good neighbourly, international co-operation is established with regard to environmental impact assessments (EIA). If an EIA is required by international or supranational law the Convention creates notification and consultation obligations.[14]

The Convention states a general obligation for Contracting Parties to prevent and eliminate pollution caused by harmful substances by all sources. That means all substances which, if introduced into the sea, are liable to cause pollution.[15] Contracting Parties have to prohibit DDT, PCB and PCT. They shall endeavour to minimise, whenever possible to ban, those pesticides which are classed as hazardous substances.[16]

In addition to these fundamental obligations, the Convention regulates preventive measures for the different sources of pollution.

3.2. Pollution from Land-based Sources

To combat, prevent and eliminate pollution from land-based sources best environmental practice and best available technology are to be used. The Contracting Parties shall co-operate in the development and adoption of specific programmes, guidelines, standards or regulations concerning emissions and inputs to water and air, environmental quality and products containing harmful substances and materials.[17] The procedures and measures, described in Annex III cover municipal sewage water and industrial waste water as well as pollution from fishfarming and from diffuse sources, including agriculture. A prior special permit is required when harmful substances from point sources are to be introduced into the Baltic Sea area. In case of inputs from a water course flowing through the territories of two ore more Contracting Parties

---

10 Art. 3, para. 2; this principle is also reflected by the definition of "pollution" in Art. 2 No. 1. According to this definition pollution means "introduction of substances which are liable to create harmful effects", i.e. the potential risk is the decisive factor, not the proven effects.

11 Art. 3 para. 3, the criteria are laid down in Annex II.

12 Art. 3 para. 4.

13 Art. 3 para. 5.

14 Art. 7; although this article in its numerical order is part of the Convention's regulations for land-based pollution, it is one of the fundamental principles being of importance for all sources of pollution, as shows Regulation 3 of Annex VI requiring an EIA for offshore activities.

15 Art. 5, the term "harmful substances" is defined in Art. 2 No. 7.

16 Annex I sets out the necessary procedures and measures.

17 Art. 6, criteria and measures concerning the prevention of pollution from land-based sources are given in detail in Annex III.

or forming a boundary between them they shall jointly take appropriate measures.[18] On 1st July 2000 additional regulations to prevent pollution from agriculture which were agreed on in 1998, entered into force. They establish basic principles as a minimum basis for national legislation to reduce adverse environmental effects.[19]

3.3. Pollution from Ships

For the prevention of pollution from ships, regulations only at a regional level are inadequate due to the international nature of shipping. Such regulations, therefore, have primarily been done by the International Maritime Organisation (IMO) in which the main instrument against pollution from ships is MARPOL 73/78.[20] Considering this the Helsinki Commission obliges the Contracting Parties to apply MARPOL 73/78 and to co-operate within the IMO in promoting the development of additional international rules. Furthermore they have to co-operate in the effective and harmonised implementation of rules adopted by IMO.[21] This includes the investigation of violations of anti-pollution regulations.[22] As corresponding MARPOL regulations have not yet entered into force the Helsinki Convention still contains restrictions for the discharge of sewage from ships.[23] As an essential for preventing illegal discharges the Contracting Parties are obliged to provide reception facilities in ports applying uniform requirements.[24] They also shall take special measures to reduce harmful effects caused by pleasure craft activities.[25] On 1st July 2000 additional regulations entered into force requiring also pleasure craft, fishing and working vessels to comply with the sewage discharge restrictions. Moreover, all ships are now obliged to deliver their wastes to a reception facility before leaving port.[26]

3.4. Waste Disposal at Sea

As concerns the waste disposal at sea the Convention prohibits both incineration and dumping at sea.[27] Exemptions are possible for dumping dredged materials in compliance with guidelines following international standards and limit values.[28]

---

18 Art. 6 para. 6.

19 HELCOM Recommendation 19/6 amending the 1974 Convention, and HELCOM Recommendation 21/1 amending the new 1992 version of the Helsinki Convention, in force since 31 December 2000.

20 International Convention of 1973 for the Prevention of Marine Pollution from Ships, as amended by the Protocol of 1978, in: *BGBl.* 1982 II p. , 1996 II.p. 399.

21 Art. 8 para. 1, Regulation 1 of Annex IV.

22 Regulation 2 of Annex IV.

23 Regulation 5 of Annex IV, these regulations correspond to those of Annex IV of MARPOL 73/78.

24 Art. 8 para. 2.

25 Art. 9.

26 HELCOM Recommendation 19/7 amending the 1974 Convention, and HELCOM Recommendation 21/2 amending the new 1992 version of the Helsinki Convention, in force since 31 December 2000.

27 Art. 10, 11.

28 The details for exemptions are given in Annex V.

3.5. *Offshore Activities*

The Convention obliges Contracting Parties to undertake all measures to prevent pollution of the marine environment from the exploration or exploitation of the sea bed and the subsoil thereof. Adequate preparedness must be ensured for immediate response to pollution incidents.[29] The measures, set out in detail in Annex VI, include the application of the principles of best available technology and best environmental practice, EIAs and follow-up studies on the effects of offshore activities, restrictions to the use of oil-based drilling muds and prohibition of the discharge of drilling muds and cuttings.[30] Other regulations concern reporting procedures, contingency planning and the exchange of information.[31] In the light of discussions in other marine areas it is remarkable that Contracting Parties have to ensure that abandoned, disused offshore units are entirely removed and brought ashore under the responsibility of the owner.[32]

3.6. *Combating Marine Pollution Incidents*

The Convention lays the basis for an effective co-operation to combat pollution incidents. In case of an incident in the territory or adjacent maritime area of a Contracting Party such Contracting Parties whose interest could be affected have to be notified without delay and,. whenever necessary,consultations should take place. Individually or jointly the Contracting Parties have to take all appropriate measures to maintain an adequate ability to respond to pollution incidents.[33] Detailed principles for the co-operation are stipulated in Annex VII, dealing with adequate equipment, ships and manpower, regular surveillance outside the coast line including airborne surveillance, national contingency plans and bilateral or multilateral plans for response measures.[34] Ships have to report pollution events and must have an oil pollution emergency plan on board.[35] Mechanical means are to be used in any response to a pollution incident. Chemical agents may only be used in exceptional cases and after authorisation by the appropriate national authority.[36] When responding to a pollution incident at sea, a Contracting Party may request assistance from other Contracting Parties, but must bear the costs of the action.[37]

---

29 Art. 12.
30 Regulations 2–5 of Annex VI.
31 Regulations 6, 7 and 9 of Annex VI.
32 Regulation 8 of Annex VI.
33 Art. 13, 14.
34 Regulations 1–4 of Annex VII.
35 Regulations 5, 6 of Annex VII.
36 Regulation 7 of Annex VII.
37 Regulations 8, 9 of Annex VII.

3.7. Nature Conservation and Biodiversity

For international environmental law it is an important innovation that the 1992 Helsinki Convention no longer sees the protection of the marine environment only as a matter of reduction of inputs. Nature conservation and biodiversity are also included. Contracting Parties shall individually and jointly take all appropriate measures to conserve natural habitats and biological diversity. They further undertake to ensure sustainable use of natural resources within the Baltic Sea area.[38] This regulation presents a conceptional basis for concrete, well defined measures through appropriate guidelines and criteria.[39]

3.8. Reporting and Exchange of Information

The Convention requires the Contracting Parties to report regularly to the Commission on the legal and other measures taken to implement the Convention‘s provisions and the Recommendations adopted thereunder.[40] Making reporting binding under international law gives a valuable instrument to monitor the implementation of the Convention and the Commission’s decisions.

In the interest of transparency the Contracting Parties shall also ensure that information is made available to the public on the state of the Baltic Sea, measures taken or planned, permits issued, as well as the results of water sampling and water quality objectives.[41]

4. Co-operation

This very brief overview shows that protection of the environment cannot be gained only by establishing regulations which have to be implemented and applied nationally by the Contracting Parties. In addition an ongoing close co-operation is required to elaborate more detailed guidelines, standards and measures as well as new, additional regulations. For this purpose the Helsinki Commission has been established under the Convention, consisting of representatives of all Contracting Parties. Meetings are held at least once a year. The chairmanship is given to each Contracting Party for two years in alphabetical order.[42] The duties of the Commission are to continuously observe the implementation of the Convention, to make recommendations on measures relating to the purposes of the Convention, to define criteria and objectives,

---

38 Art. 15.

39 The Helsinki Commission has agreed on 10 Recommendations dealing with nature conservation, cf. HELCOM Recommendations 9/1, 15/1, 15/5, 16/3, 17/2, 17/3, 19/1, 19/2, 21/3 and 21/4; see also *BSEP* Nos. 63 (Coastal and Marine Protected Areas in the Baltic Sea Region) and 75 (Red List of Marine and Coastal Biotopes and Biotope Complexes of the Baltic Sea, Belt Sea and Kattegat).

40 Art. 16.

41 Art. 17; the Convention thus meets demands for greater involvement of the public and improved access to information.

42 Art. 19.

and to promote close co-operation with other bodies.[43] The Commission is supported by a permanent Secretariat located in Helsinki, consisting of the Executive Secretary as the chief official, additional Secretaries and the administration staff.[44] The Commission‘s budget is financed from contributions by the Contracting Parties.[45]

The work of the Commission is prepared by subordinate expert bodies, the organisation of which has several times changed since their first establishment in the late 70s. The Commission mainly takes decisions through Recommendations which have to be adopted unanimously.[46] Though legally the Recommendations have to be characterised as soft law, it is common understanding that through the need of unanimous decision Contracting Parties declare their firm political will to apply the Recommendations. Since 1980 the Commission has adopted 198 Recommendations on very different measures covering all purposes of the Convention.[47]

In addition to the regular Commission work the co-operation has further been enhanced by Ministerial Meetings and Conferences.[48] In 1988 the responsible Ministers of the Environment passed a Declaration on the Protection of the Marine Environment of the Baltic Sea Area deciding that the inputs of most harmful substances and nutrients have to be substantially reduced by 50% of the total discharges.[49] In 1990 a Conference on Prime Ministers' level ended with the Baltic Sea Declaration 1990 setting out principles and priority actions.[50] Following this conference the Ministers in 1992 decided on a Baltic Sea Joint Comprehensive Environmental Action Programme to drastically reduce emissions and restore the ecological balance.[51] This programme, which demands for investments in the order of 18 Billion ECU for a 20-year period in the meantime has become one of the corner stones of the environment co-operation.

Ministerial Meetings in 1994[52] and 1998 gave new incentives for the Commission‘s work. In 1998 the Ministers adopted additional regulations for agriculture[53] and a

---

43 Art 20.

44 Art. 21.

45 cf. Art. 22; for the budget year 2000/2001 the Commission adopted a budget of 10,132,000 FIM.

46 Art. 19 paragraph 5, Art. 23; as concerns amendments of the Convention and the Annexes see Art. 31, 32.

47 The Recommendations are published in the Annual Reports "Activities of the Commission", they are also available on the website of the Helsinki Commission: *http://www/helcom.fi*

48 Overviews on the activities and results in the framework of the Helsinki Convention are published in: *BSEP* Nos. 10 (Ten Years after the Signing of the Helsinki Convention), 56 (Intergovernmental Activities in the Framework of the Helsinki Convention 1974–1994).

49 For details see the Final Report (*supra* note 1).

50 See *BSEP* No. 56, 195.

51 The programme is published in *BSEP* Nos. 48 and 49; cf. also *BSEP* No. 72 (The Baltic Sea Joint Comprehensive Environmental Action Programme – Recommendations for Updating and Strengthening); for further details see the article by *Ulrich Kremser* in this publication, 105.

52 See Final Report (*supra* note 1), p. 10.

53 See *supra* note 19.

Baltic Strategy for Port Reception Facilities.[54] Furthermore they decided on a strategy to phase out hazardous substances by the year 2020.[55]

In 1999 an extraordinary Ministerial Meeting refocused the wide-spread activities of the Commission and its great number of subordinate bodies, leading to a new organisational structure and the definition of main goals and priorities.[56] The work of the Commission now is supported by 5 subordinate groups[57] and the Programme Implementation Task Force.[58] As far as necessary the activities of the groups may be assisted by projects. To steer, co-ordinate and accelerate the work, regular Heads of Delegation Meetings are to be held between the annual Commission meetings.

5. Present Activities, Main Goals and Priorities

Following well defined goals and given priorities, the activities of the Helsinki Commission and the newly established groups for the present and near future concentrate on the following:[59]

5.1. Review and Elaboration of Additional Recommendations

Many measures agreed on by Recommendations have to be seen only as a first step. This requires to review earlier decisions aiming at more stringent measures for the Baltic Sea, if necessary. Considering the European enlargement process and the work going on in other international environmental organisations,[60] existing and new Recommendations have to be harmonised with regulations elaborated within EU and other relevant international bodies. By that, adequacy for specific Baltic Sea requirements has to be safeguarded.

5.2. Implementation

The success of the work of the Commission does not depend on the elaboration of protective measures only, but in particular on the efficient implementation of the

54 See *supra* note 26, for more details cf. *Peter Ehlers*, The HELCOM Approach – A Baltic Strategy for Port Reception Facilities, in: *Hans-Joachim Koch/Rainer Lagoni* (eds.), *The Reception of Oily Waste from Ships in European Ports* (Forum Umweltrecht, vol. 23), pp. 141 *et seq.*

55 HELCOM Recommendation 19/5.

56 See Decision HELCOM 99 EXTRA, Minutes of the Meeting, Attachment 3.

57 Those groups are HELCOM STRATEGY, HELCOM MONAS, HELCOM LAND, HELCOM SEA and HELCOM HABITAT.

58 HELCOM PITF is an additional body composed not only of Contracting Parties of the Helsinki Convention, but also of other Governments, NGOs and financial institutions who are willing to contribute to the programme.

59 See HELCOM 99 EXTRA, Minutes of the Meeting, Attachment 3, Annex 2–4; a brief overview on recent actitivites is given in: Bericht des Bundesministeriums für Umwelt, Naturschutz und Reaktorsicherheit (*supra* note 1), pp. 45 *et seq.*

60 Closer co-operation and harmonization is especially necessary with the OSPAR Commission responsible for the protection of the marine environment of the North-East-Atlantic Area.

Convention itself and the Recommendations by the Contracting Parties. More than in the past the Commission therefore has to monitor and assess the implementation process. A first step is the request for more detailed reporting on the implementation by the Contracting Parties.

As concerns the efficient implementation of protection measures the Joint Comprehensive Environment Action Programme plays an outstanding role. This task is co-ordinated and assisted by HELCOM PITF. Particular attention is given to investment activities to reduce pollution from point and non-point sources in the whole catchment area.

5.3. Private/Public Partnership

As the implementation of many protection measures strongly depends on investments – and that means financial funding capacity – another important strategic issue is to improve the involvement and support from the business communities and financial institutions in both the private and the public sector.[61]

5.4. Sustainable Development

In the light of the achievements of the Rio Conference, the concept of sustainable development becomes more and more important also for environment protection strategies. Though sustainable development is not expressly highlighted as a fundamental principle in the Convention, it may already be identified as a basis for numerous activities.[62] The HELCOM STRATEGY Group is working on a Recommendation, operationalising the concept of sustainable development within areas of key importance.

5.5. Environmental Status

A pre-condition for efficient protection measures is a good knowledge of the environmental situation. For that reason the Convention obliges Contracting Parties to closely co-operate in the scientific and technological fields.[63] At a very early stage HELCOM established scientific monitoring programmes[64] and started to elaborate

---

[61] This task is also to be dealt with by the HELCOM STRATEGY group.

[62] For further details cf. the Document on Sustainable Development in the Baltic Sea Area, adopted by the 21st Commission Meeting in 2000, HELCOM 21/2000, Annex 3; see also *BSEP* No. 74 (Sustainable Development of the Agricultural Sector in the Baltic Region) and HELCOM Recommendation 21/3 concerning sustainable and environmentally friendly tourism in the coastal zones of the Baltic Sea Area.

[63] Art. 24.

[64] For further details see *BSEP* Nos. 12, 19, 27 A, B, C, D.

regular quality status assessments.[65] This was accompanied by pollution load compilations.[66] As a consequence the HELCOM MONAS Group is entrusted with the task to identify and quantify the anthropogenic discharges and activities, their effects in the Baltic Sea Area and the changes in the marine environment. The results have to serve as a sound basis for the evaluation of the need for additional measures.[67]

5.6. *Land-based Pollution*

Measures to reduce pollution from land-based sources are to be prepared by the HELCOM LAND Group. The goal given to this group is to identify current and emerging issues related to point and diffuse sources of land-based pollution, propose actions and promote investment activities. Recent priority areas are eutrophication, especially the contribution of agriculture, the phasing-out of hazardous substances[68] and relevant issues from the land transport sector.[69]

5.7. *Sea-based Pollution*

Identifying current and emerging sea-based sources of pollution and proposing actions to limit emissions and discharges is the task of the HELCOM SEA Group. This group also has to ensure a swift national and transnational response to marine pollution incidents. Its main priorities cover issues from the maritime transport sector, including the implementation of the Baltic Strategy on Port Reception Facilities as a prerequisite to eliminate illegal discharges.[70]

5.8. *Nature conservation*

Nature conservation is dealt with by the HELCOM HABITAT Group. The measures aim at conserving natural habitats and marine and coastal biodiversity and protecting ecological processes. The group's work also has to focus on the promotion of ecosystem approaches for the sustainable use and management of coastal and marine natural resources. This includes the promotion and development of coastal zone

---

65 The Helsinki Commission has elaborated quality status assessments in 1981 (*BSEP* No. 5 A, B), 1986 (*BSEP* No. 17 A, B), 1990 (*BSEP* No. 35 A, B) and 1994 (*BSEP* No. 64 A, B).

66 See the pollution load compilations elaborated by the Helsinki Commission, *BSEP* Nos. 20, 45, 70, as well as airborne pollution load compilations, *BSEP* Nos. 32, 39, 69.

67 A new quality status assessment for the period 1994–1998 will be adopted by the 22nd Commission meeting in March 2001.

68 The Helsinki Commission has established a project on hazardous substances with the objective to phase out emissions and losses of hazardous substances by the year 2020.

69 See *BSEP* No. 67 (Workshop on the Reduction of Emissions from Traffic in the Baltic Sea Area).

70 To intensify the co-operation of the Contracting Parties in investigating and prosecuting violations, the Helsinki Commission has published a Baltic Legal Manual (*BSEP* No. 77) and Guidelines on Ensuring Successful Convictions of Offenders of Anti-Pollution Regulations at Sea (*BSEP* No. 78).

management plans. One of the still unsolved priority issues, dealt with by this group, are the environmental impacts of fishery management and practices.

6. Conclusions

What are the conclusions? May HELCOM serve as an example for other marine areas? The Helsinki Commission, based on the Helsinki Convention as a most modern legal instrument, has developed an efficient and close network for environmental co-operation within in the Baltic Sea region. It covers all aspects starting from monitoring and assessing the marine environment, elaborating protective measures for all relevant issues and focussing on the implementation including far-reaching investment programmes. Whereas marine environment protection in the traditional sense was mainly understood as combating and reduction of pollution HELCOM has widened the scope by incorporating nature conservation issues, coastal zone management and impacts from fishery. The work is more and more guided additionally by the concept of sustainable development and by this is becoming part of the Agenda 21 activities.[71]

However, a co-operation network is not an end in itself. The outcome is decisive. The environmental situation of the Baltic Sea is no longer deteriorating, but has improved in some fields. That is an encouraging result confirming that the endeavours already made were not in vain. But by no means the work is going to be finalized in the near future. There still remains a heavy work load. This includes further reduction measures with regard to eutrophication, coastal zone management, an even more effective implementation of measures agreed on, and above all the fulfilment of the Joint Comprehensive Environment Action Programme.

Taken all in all the co-operation in the Baltic Sea Area can serve as an example for environment protection in other marine areas. However, that does in no way mean that the Baltic Sea States reciprocally cannot benefit from the experience gained in other parts of the world. Marine protection is a global issue where regional approaches hopefully will lead to a fruitful complement in conserving the world's largest ecosystems as a common heritage of mankind.

[71] The co-operation of the Baltic Sea States in implementing Agenda 21 of the United Nations Conference on Environment and Development, called Baltic 21, requires a close involvement of the Helsinki Commission.

*Ulrich Kremser**

THE BALTIC SEA JOINT COMPREHENSIVE ENVIRONMENTAL ACTION PROGRAMME

1. Introduction

This paper deals with the Baltic Sea Joint Comprehensive Environmental Action Programme (JCP), which is implemented within the framework of the Helsinki Commission. For the deeper understanding of the reasons why the Programme was created in 1992 in the Baltic Sea region, a short introduction is given. This introduction will cover some characteristics of the Baltic Sea, the way to the signing of the Helsinki Convention as well as the restricting political environment between 1974 and 1989/90. More detailed information on the Baltic Sea and on the Helsinki Commission is given by *P. Ehlers*[1] as well as by *Lozan*,[2] *Rheinheimer*[3] and HELCOM.[4]

The Baltic Sea is a semi-enclosed brackish water basin with only narrow connections to the ocean. The hydrological basin comprises 1.72 million km^2 and is shared by 15 countries with a population of about 85 million inhabitants and mostly developed industry and agriculture. Main polluting substances are nutrients, heavy metals and halogenated hydrocarbons which remain in the Baltic Sea for a long time (residence time about 25–30 years). The pollution affects adversely the use of Baltic Sea resources like fish and recreation and is threatening the ecosystem.

After World War II the industrial and agricultural production increased rapidly worldwide and also in the Baltic Sea Region. It took some years to learn that the carrying capacity of the sea does not any more correspond to the amount of polluting substances released in the course of the production processes. Environmental catastrophes on different continents accelerated the increase of public awareness and generated investigations on the state of the marine environment in several seas, including the Baltic Sea.[5] The findings resulted in a wave of regional agreements on protecting seas and oceans in the 1970's and in the signing of the Convention on

* Helsinki Commission.

1 *P. Ehlers*, Marine Environment Protection – The Baltic Sea Example; this publication.

2 *J.L. Lozan et al.* (eds.), Warnsignale aus der Ostsee (Berlin 1996).

3 *G. Rheinheimer* (ed.), Meereskunde der Ostsee (Berlin 1996).

4 *HELCOM*, Fourth Periodic Assessment of the State of the Marine Environment of the Baltic Sea, 1994–1998 (to be published in April/May 2001).

5 *ICES* (ed.), Report of the ICES Working Group on Pollution in the Baltic Sea, Cooperative Research Report, Series A No. 15 (Charlottenlund 1970).

P. Ehlers, E. Mann-Borgese and R. Wolfrum (eds.), Marine Issues, 105–119

the Protection of the Marine Environment of the Baltic Sea Area (Helsinki Convention) in 1974.

The Contracting Parties to the Helsinki Convention were divided by the iron curtain into two blocks. The Western block consisted of NATO and militarily neutral countries (Finland, Sweden), the countries of the Eastern block all belonged to the Warsaw Treaty Organization. Given the political climate prevailing at that time, the signing of the Helsinki Convention was quite a remarkable event. However, big differences on both sides regarding environmental legislation and the political will, combined with the economic means, reduced the room for actions. It resulted in opposite developments in East and West. In the Eastern countries the emissions and discharges of pollutants increased, whereas in the Western countries the amount of pollution dropped. Nevertheless, the Contracting Parties adopted many HELCOM Recommendations regarding limits on emissions of harmful substances and specific restrictions on agriculture and other activities of major environmental consequences.

The liberation process in Eastern Europe, accompanied by the breakdown of the Berlin Wall (1989) and the disintegration of the Soviet Union, led to stronger political contacts across the Baltic Sea. The chance was taken by Sweden and Poland who invited to the Ronneby Conference (Ronneby, Sweden, 1990). The "Baltic Sea Declaration", adopted by the Prime Ministers of the Baltic Sea States, was a cornerstone for further environmental cooperation in the region. This document proclaimed the ecological restoration of the Baltic Sea and it was determined to urgently prepare a Baltic Sea Joint Comprehensive Environmental Action Programme (JCP) for reduction of emissions.

At the Diplomatic Conference in 1992 in Helsinki, Finland, the Environment Ministers of the countries concerned approved the approach and the principles reflected in the JCP. The Programme Implementation Task Force (PITF) was established in order to initiate, facilitate and monitor the coordination of the implementation of the JCP and to periodically update the Programme.

2. Structure of the Programme

After the Ronneby Conference pre-feasibility studies were carried out in most of the main river basins of the catchment area of the Baltic Sea. Significant environmental issues were reviewed and their impact with regard to ecological systems, public health and the economy was evaluated. Topical studies additionally dealt with agricultural runoff and air quality impacts.

The key principles of the Programme constitute a framework for specific actions and approaches. It has to be recognised that planning and implementation can only take place over a long term. Natural factors have to be taken into account, economic and environmental objectives have to be harmonised. The Programme strategy encompasses both preventive and curative actions but emphasis should be placed on pollution prevention through policy, regulatory, and technical interventions, etc.

The strategy involves a long-term series of coordinated actions by each government concerned to promote and carry out policy and regulatory reforms, capacity building, capital investments for controlling pollution from point and non-point sources, to eliminate or reduce the generation of waste and to conserve environmentally sensitive and economically valuable areas, support applied research and to promote public awareness and environmental education.

The long-term Programme of specific actions is grouped into six components (Table 1) and should be implemented in a time span of 20 years. The investments needed for the preventive and curative actions, as estimated in 1991/92, amount to 18 billion ECU.

Table 1. JCP Elements and Estimated Total Costs

Programme element		*Total million ECU (1993–2012)*
1	Policies, Laws and Regulations	10
2	Institutional Strengthening and Human Resources Development	210
3	Investment Activities	
3A	*Point Source Pollution*	14,010
	– Combined Municipal and Industrial Wastewater Treatment	
	– Industrial Pollution Control	
3B	*Non-Point Source Pollution*	3,500
	– Agriculture	
	– Transport	
4	Management Programmes for Coastal Lagoons and Wetlands	220
5	Applied Research	30
6	Public Awareness and Environmental Education	20
	TOTAL	18,000

3. Identification of Investment Priorities – The Hot Spots Approach

The Programme focuses on investment activities regarding point and non-point pollution sources, *i.e.* on element 3. The other elements are to be seen as complementary but by no means as insignificant.

Investment priorities were identified by conducting pre-feasibility studies, elaborating national reports and initiating studies on special issues.

Pre-feasibility studies were carried out in the basins of main rivers (Daugava, Nemudas, Pregel, Vistula, Odra), in the coastal areas of the catchment area (Estonia, Lithuania, Poland and Northern Germany) as well as in the cities of St. Petersburg and Kaliningrad, in their respective regions, and in the Gulf of Riga.

National reports have been elaborated by the Contracting Parties to the Helsinki Convention (except the European Union), the Czech and Slovak Federal Republic,

Norway and the Union of Soviet Socialist Republics who – at that time – also presented Belarus and the Ukraine.

The topical studies highlighted fields of special interest as regards the environmental situation in limited areas (*e.g.* in the Leningrad Region, Estonia, Latvia, Lithuania, Poland) and agricultural runoff, atmospheric deposition of pollutants and wetlands.[6]

In the absence of any decision on how to screen priority projects, considerations have been given to[7]

- the size of the polluter
- the cost-efficiency of the action towards upgrading and reconstruction
- the impact of pollution on environment (in particular on the Baltic Sea), health, economy, etc.

Areas and sites of high emissions or discharges from one or more point and non-point sources were classified as Hot Spots and after approval by the countries concerned set on the List of Hot Spots. The absence of agreed criteria for inclusion of Hot Spots into the List certainly speed up the process at that time but became a burden later on when starting considerations on the deletion of Hot Spots from the List.

At the end of this exercise 132 Hot Spots had been identified, most of them in the countries in transition to market economy (99), but also in Denmark (3), Finland (10), Germany (9) and Sweden (12) (one of the Hot Spots is counted twice because it covers Germany and Poland). Figure 1 gives an overview on the geographical distribution of the Hot Spots as well as on the status. More detailed information on the status of Hot Spots is available on the HELCOM website (*http://www.helcom.fi*), in the Annual Reports of PITF (Annual Report 1999 is on the HELCOM website) and on the website of UNEP/Grid Arendal at *http://maps.grida.no/baltic*.

4. Status of Implementation of the JCP

4.1. Broad Partnership for Implementing the JCP

When telling about the implementation of the JCP the broad partnership should be mentioned which is – based on our experience – considered as one of the preconditions for successful work. Table 2 lists the partners.

The International Financial Institutions (IFIs) have already participated in the Ronneby Conference, played an important role in the elaboration of the JCP,

---

6 *HELCOM*, The Baltic Sea Joint Comprehensive Environmental Action Programme, in: *BSEP* No. 48 (1993).

7 *Sweco, COWIconsult, VKI in association with Hydroproject and Stolica*, Pre-feasibility study of the Vistula River Basin and Baltic Coast of Poland, Part I, Synthesis Report, Prepared for the World Bank with support from the Governments of Poland, Denmark and Sweden (1992).

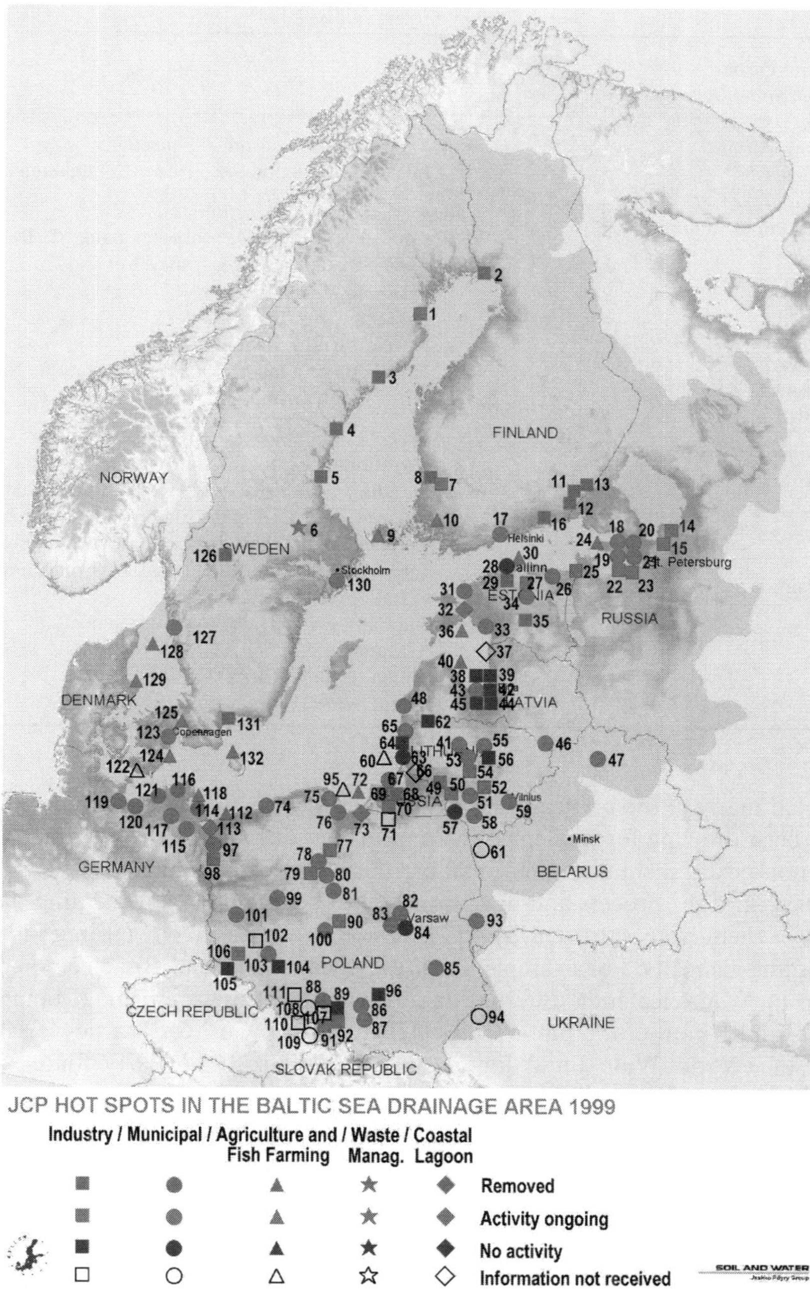
NORWAY
SWEDEN
FINLAND
RUSSIA
DENMARK
GERMANY
POLAND
BELARUS
UKRAINE
CZECH REPUBLIC
SLOVAK REPUBLIC
LATVIA
Helsinki
Stockholm
St. Petersburg
Copenhagen
Vilnius
Minsk
Warsaw
JCP HOT SPOTS IN THE BALTIC SEA DRAINAGE AREA 1999
Industry / Municipal / Agriculture and Fish Farming / Waste Manag. / Coastal Lagoon
Removed
Activity ongoing
No activity
Information not received
SOIL AND WATER

Figure 1.

Table 2. Participants in the Programme Implementation Task Force (HELCOM PITF)

Contracting Parties and Co-operating Governments	*Other Parties*
Contracting Parties: – Denmark – Estonia – European Community – Finland – Germany – Latvia – Lithuania – Poland – Russian Federation – Sweden *Co-operating Governments:* – Belarus – Czech Republic – Norway – Slovak Republic – Ukraine	*Regional Intergovernmental Organizations:* – International Baltic Sea Fishery Commission (IBSFC) *International Financial Institutions:* – Council of Europe Development Bank (CEB) – European Bank for Reconstruction and Development (EBRD) – European Investment Bank (EIB) – Nordic Investment Bank (NIB) – Nordic Environment Finance Corporation (NEFCO) – World Bank Group *Non-governmental Organizations:* – Coalition Clean Baltic (CCB) – Standing Conference of Rectors, Presidents and Vice-Chancellors of the European Universities (CRE) – European Union for Coastal Conservation (EUCC) – International Council for Local Environmental Initiatives (ICLEI) – International Network for Environment Management (INEM) – Union of Baltic Cities (UBC) – World Wide Fund for Nature (WWF)

conducted many of the pre-feasibility studies for identifying the Hot Spots and have always been drawing for implementing and further developing the programme.

The non-governmental international organisations (NGOs) include other parts of the society into the process and have expertise to be used for implementing the JCP. Several of them were entrusted by PITF to act as Lead Party regarding individual Programme elements. For example Coalition Clean Baltic (CCB) acted some years as Lead Party for element 6, International Network for Environmental Management (INEM) and Union of the Baltic Cities (UBC) still are Co-Lead Parties for element 2, and the World Wide Fund for Nature (WWF) is Lead Party for element 4 since 1993.

Another pillar for success, which is not reflected in this table, is the internal cooperation with the Working Groups under HELCOM.[8] The Groups are very supportive in different areas of the JCP, *e.g.* in conducting the compliance checks against technical requirements after a country has applied for deletion of a Hot Spot from the List, as well as in monitoring and assessing the response of the Baltic Sea to the measures on land regarding reduction of emissions and discharges, etc.

8 See *Ehlers* (*supra* note 1), figure 4.

4.2. Status of implementation of the elements 1, 2, 4, 5 and 6

The status of implementation is measured against the targets of the elements. Therefore, the aim of the component is described shortly at the beginning followed by the status of implementation.

Element 1: Policy, Laws and Regulations
This element of the Programme has been intended to focus on policy and regulatory activities, aiming at the establishment of a long-term environmental framework in all Baltic Sea States. One of the major aspects concerns legal arrangements as a background for investment activities in the environmental sector.

In most of the countries concerned a legal framework for environmental protection has been elaborated. Harmonization with the EU-legislation can be observed as a clear tendency. The background for investment activities seem to be prepared in almost all countries. By that, the main purpose of the implementation of that Programme element has been achieved. The remaining aspects can be dealt with in the future by cooperation between Observer Organisations to HELCOM and the Secretariat. Germany maintains its responsibility for this element and continues acting as Lead Party.

Element 2: Institutional Strengthening and Human Resources Development
This element of the Programme aims at building the organisational and human capacity to develop and implement effective environmental management systems, and to plan, design, and operate pollution control measures. The importance of this component can hardly be over-estimated. Any support from outside the country has to be channelled via institutions and persons who have the network, working methods, knowledge and capacity available. If not developed, any support is melting away.

The Programme activities were designed to help to define and strengthen the role of both central and local government authorities in the new and involving legal framework. A large variety of contacts and networks has been established around the Baltic Sea, *e.g.* by twinning arrangements between cities and regional administrations, networks between organisations, contacts between schools etc. Supported by the efforts to prepare for accession to the European Union the necessary arrangements have been finalised in most of the countries concerned, and this element of the Programme does no longer need to be dealt with permanently by the PITF. The remaining aspects will be observed and followed up by Observer Organisations to HELCOM, and the Lead Parties Germany, UBC and INEM are still prepared to assist.

Element 4: Management Programmes for Coastal Lagoons and Wetlands
This component aims at preserving wetlands and coastal lagoons as environmentally sensitive and economically valuable areas. They serve as important buffers in the transport of contaminants to the Baltic Sea by acting as natural traps and providing variable levels of treatment of biodegradable wastes, especially with respect to nutrients. They also provide critical habitats for a variety of fauna and flora including migratory birds.

The Programme activities focussed on elaborating and implementing Integrated Coastal Zone Management Plans (ICZMPs) in areas of the Baltic Sea coast. Five ICZMPs have been finalised, covering areas in Estonia, Latvia, Lithuania, Russia (Kaliningrad Region), Poland and Germany. An interim phase has been used for carefully preparing the implementation of the plans. The implementation needs close cooperation with the national authorities of the countries concerned, including the spatial planning sector. The implementation has started in most of the countries. The Lead Party WWF reports regularly to PITF on these activities.

Element 5: Applied Research
This element aims at building the knowledge base needed to develop solutions and widen and deepen the understanding of critical problems. The research tasks to which priority is applied include, *inter alia*, environmental trends, special issues of system ecology, evaluation of critical loads, environmental health problems, and are, of course, dealing with issues which could help to solve problems arising under element 3, in particular regarding agriculture and transport.

The Lead Parties Sweden and Latvia have tried to strengthen the cooperation with the HELCOM Working Groups, in particular with the Group responsible for monitoring and assessment of the state of the Baltic Sea (HELCOM MONAS). An overview on already ongoing research activities or planned projects in the Baltic Sea region has been elaborated, and the links between them and HELCOM needs and activities are described. The Fourth Periodic Assessment of the State of the Marine Environment of the Baltic Sea reflects environmental trends regarding nutrients and harmful substances in the water body, biota and the sediment. It also shows the response to measures taken within the catchment area targeted to reducing the pollution load into the Baltic Sea. For example, the sanitary conditions in many of the coastal waters have been improving for years, mainly due to new or updated wastewater treatment plants.

Element 6: Public Awareness and Environmental Education
This component focuses on developing a broad and sustainable base of support for the implementation of the JCP by localities, municipalities and national governments. The participation of non-governmental organisations and the development of effective environmental education programmes will be important in supporting both public awareness and political commitment.

Due to the importance of this issue, a Working Group has been established to raise public awareness and to inform decision makers and politicians. Efforts were mainly directed on establishing and implementing projects, which included most of the countries concerned and integrated the most active NGOs in this field. The results, however, did not meet the expectations. The Working Group was dissolved, and since January 2001 an Information Officer is employed at the HELCOM Secretariat. On the agenda is the development of an HELCOM information strategy, which should serve the implementation of the Helsinki Convention and of the JCP by, *inter alia*, rising awareness and preparing tailored information to attract decision makers and politicians.

4.3. Status of implementation of element 3: Investment Activities

4.3.1. General remarks

This component focuses on investments in measures to control point and non-point source pollution.

Regarding point source pollution control the investments should originally be used for

- emergency support and warning systems
- municipal wastewater treatment
- combined municipal and industrial waste water treatment
- pulp and paper industry environmental control
- environmental control in other industries
- solid and hazardous waste management
- air quality management.

Investments to control diffuse or non-point source pollution should deal with

- runoff from agriculture, forestry, live stock operations and rural settlements
- pollution from fish-farming
- air pollution from mobile sources of emissions
- air pollution from area sources of emissions.

Due to the development in the countries after the implementation of the JCP started in 1992, some items became obsolete or at least less urgent. Emergency problems have been solved and warning systems have been installed to a great extent, and twelve pulp and paper factories identified as Hot Spots were deleted from the List. Pollution from fish farming has been reduced mainly due to new methods and restrictive rules and regulations, including a HELCOM Recommendation. Emissions from power plants have been decreased decisively, too, by using Best Available Technology (BAT). Transport emerged instead as an item with a trend to increasing emissions, in particular as regards nitrogen.

Therefore, during the last years the focus of PITF has changed and is now on

- municipal and industrial wastewater treatment
- industrial pollution control;

as well as on

- agriculture
- transport.

Transport is considered as an issue to be dealt with by the respective Ministries in the countries and by the European Union. PITF tries to support the efforts and elaborated a HELCOM Recommendation for integrating environmental considerations into transportation planning and policy, implementation of the Polluter Pays Principle, and introduction of BAT for vehicles and fuels. Another project just finalised dealt with environmentally sustainable transportation investment decision-making in the Baltic Sea region. The guidelines extracted and concluded will be condensed into a HELCOM Recommendation which is presently under preparation. However, it is not anticipated that PITF will initiate investment activities to address issues related to pollution from transportation.

The implementation of the Programme in the areas indicated above might be reflected best by using the number of Hot Spots deleted, the investments carried out and/or allocated, and the reduction of emissions and discharges from the Hot Spots as indicators. This will be described in the following sub-chapters.

4.3.2. Deletion of Hot Spots

Of the 132 Hot Spots originally identified 19 have been deleted so far. They belong to municipal and industrial wastewater treatment (4) and to industrial Hot Spots (14). The Gulf of Riga Hot Spot was deleted from the List in the year 2000.

The twelve industrial Hot Spots deleted so far are pulp and paper mills located in Finland, Sweden, Estonia and Russia (Kaliningrad Region). The mills of Finland and Sweden have been upgraded and reconstructed in order to meet the technical standards required, the mills of Estonia (1) and Russia (1) have been closed down.

The procedure for deletion of Hot Spots from the List can be described as follows:

After the decision on the planned future under market conditions is made by the owner of the Hot Spot, preparations regarding upgrading and reconstruction or closing down will be taken. If the target of reduced pollution is assumed to be met as result of accomplishing measures or by closing down, the country will apply to PITF for deletion of the Hot Spot from the List.

Within HELCOM the HELCOM LAND Group,[9] which has the expertise to deal with technical requirements, will check the compliance and give advice to PITF on how to handle the case, *i.e.* whether to delete the Hot Spot from the List and if not, indicate why.

The compliance check has to be done against clear criteria for deletion of Hot Spots from the List. As mentioned in chapter 3 of this paper, these criteria had not been available when originally defining the Hot Spots in the years 1990–1992. The missing criteria resulted in a rather substantive political influence regarding the agreement at national level about the specific sites to be set on the List of Hot Spots also because of expectations on financial aid for reconstruction and upgrading.

It took several years to develop these criteria, which eventually were adopted by PITF in May 1999 (the criteria for deletion and inclusion of Hot Spots can be found on the HELCOM website under PITF; Hot Spots, Criteria). However, the experience has shown that special demands formulated by the criteria are difficult to meet in practice, and therefore the criteria are also anticipated to be subject to changes in the years to come.

As indicated above, the 19 Hot Spots deleted from the List are mostly located in

---

[9] See structure of HELCOM and the tasks of the groups in: *P. Ehlers* (*supra* note 1).

the western countries. Only three are within the countries in transition to market economy and they have been closed down. In the year 2001 the deletion of at least three more Hot Spots is anticipated, one in Latvia (industry), one Hot Spot and a sub-Hot Spot in Poland (municipal and industrial) and one in Germany (agriculture). Several applications (four) for deletion from Lithuania (with good chances to be deleted) are under preparation.

If only the number of deleted Hot Spots is used as an indicator for progress in the implementation of the JCP, the percentage (actually 19 of 132 = 14.4%) is disappointing, of course, after eight years of implementation. It is assumed to be improved up to 26/132 = 19.7% in 2001 after about half the time for implementing the JCP has elapsed. But there is a wide span of possible measures to be taken on the way towards deletion. A ranking system better able of showing the status of implementation measures at the Hot Spots will be developed. Additional indicators, such as on-going investments and the reduction of emissions, are described in the next sub-chapters.

4.3.3. Investments carried out and/or allocated

The upgrading and reconstruction of Hot Spots needs investments. The PITF does not have the money but is a kind of mediator and provides a platform for discussion and sharing of information. The loan agreements are negotiated between the Hot Spot owners, the governments, the donors, national banks, private sector and the IFIs. A "lion's share" of the investments have to come from domestic sources.

The costs for investments in all the 132 Hot Spots estimated in 1992 mounted to 9.43 billion ECU. A new estimate done in 1999 states 7.35 billion ECU, mainly due to investments carried out in the years from 1992 to 1999 and deletion of several Hot Spots. The new estimate regards only the Hot Spots still existing and revealed therefore higher costs, which might be explained by changed technical resolutions, increased prices and more precise information available, as was the case shortly after the political change in 1989/90. The municipal sector looks best, *i.e.* despite big investments needed the percentage of allocated resources is quite high.

Regarding agriculture the figure does not reflect reality. In most of the countries concerned management programmes are ongoing. Due to unidentified reasons the information does not go the right way for being collected. There are 17 agricultural Hot Spots and information on seven of them was not received in 1999. The first agricultural Hot Spot (Germany) is going to be deleted in the weeks to come.

The objective of the Programme is to restore the Baltic Sea to a sound ecological balance by reducing the pollution load into the Baltic Sea. It concerns both nutrients and harmful substances which are transported via rivers, direct discharges, ground water, the atmosphere and by inflow and mixing from the North Sea through the Danish Straits into the Baltic Sea. The net transport through the Straits varies with the pollutants themselves, but seems to be small in comparison with input via rivers and atmosphere. Eutrophication is considered as the biggest problem the ecosystem of the Baltic Sea is faced with. Other problem areas are connected to heavy metals and halogenated hydrocarbons.[10]

The reduction of emissions and discharges from Hot Spots achieved from 1991 to 1998 is considerably high (Annual Report 1999):

P-tot	by	39%
N-tot	by	28%
BOD_5	by	60%
AOX	by	69%
SOx	by	33%

Only NOX has increased by about 5%, mainly due to increasing numbers of cars and transportation in the countries concerned. Other sources of nitrogen are agriculture, municipalities, industry and power plants.[11] It is estimated that about 300,000 tonnes of nitrogen annually is deposited to the Baltic Sea, about one third of the total load.

The annual total phosphorus input into the Baltic Sea is estimated at about 50,000 tonnes. Main sources are agriculture, municipalities and industry.

The reduction of both nitrogen and phosphorus emissions from Hot Spots is important. The Third Pollution Load Compilation (PLC-3), carried out in 1995 by HELCOM, estimated a total nitrogen load of 760,000 tonnes and phosphorus load of 38,000 tonnes annually. The amount discharged from the Hot Spots' wastewater sector counts for about 100,000 tonnes nitrogen and 10,000 tonnes phosphorus, *i.e.* is about 13% or 28% respectively.[12]

The reductions as indicated by the figures above are also reflected in the improvement of the water quality in the coastal waters of the Baltic Sea. The interpretation mainly points to achievements in the wastewater treatment sector also in connection with industry. This is confirmed when having a look at the Hot Spots already deleted (Table 5 of the Annual Report 1999). High discharge of nutrients has often been indicated as the reason for being a Hot Spot.

The expectations regarding decreasing nutrient concentration in the open waters of the Baltic Sea after some years, however, should not be too high. The time which indicates the average turnover of the water of the Baltic Sea is estimated to be about 25–30 years. Additionally, large amounts of nutrients are stored in the sediments and a strong interaction with the water body takes place.

5. Conclusions

Eight years after inauguration the JCP is on the way to successful implementation.

The reasons are that

---

10 *HELCOM*, Third Periodic Assessment of the State of the Marine Environment of the Baltic Sea, 1989–1993, Executive Summary, in: *BSEP* No. 64 A (1996); *HELCOM* (*supra* note 4).

11 *U. Kremser*, Agriculture within the context of HELCOM's mandate and activities, in: *AMBIO* 26 No. 7 (1997), 415–417.

12 *HELCOM*, The Third Baltic Sea Pollution Load Compilation, in: *BSEP* No. 70.

- the JCP
  - is targeted towards a convincing goal: The restoration of the Baltic Sea
  - is adjusted to the specific regional environmental problems
  - is structured in order to safeguard a long-lasting progress
  - has been updated from time to time in order to adjust to the changed political, social, economic, environmental etc. conditions;

and

- the partnership does include the governments, national authorities on local, regional and national level, the IFIs, donors, the private sector and the NGOs;
- the implementation of the JCP is directly related to a sustained political commitment and broad-based public support in the region.

The JCP with its Hot Spots approach is recommended to be used as a model worldwide. Based on clear criteria the Hot Spots are easy to be identified. They attract attention by the people who know the Hot Spots and the problems connected to them. Upgrading and reconstruction towards deletion from the List of Hot Spots can be checked by the authorities and followed by the public. The problems and progress at the Hot Spots could be used for rising public awareness.

In order to accelerate the pace of implementation of the JCP, HELCOM PITF Regional Workshops have been arranged for re-assessing the Hot Spots in a region with similar characteristics, identifying and removing gaps and obstacles in the country, and for defining actions towards deletion from the List. First results became apparent in form of seven applications for deletion of Hot Spots from the List in the year 2001.

Literature

Ehlers, P., 2001 Marine Environment Protection – The Baltic Sea Example; this publication.

HELCOM, 1993a. The Baltic Sea Joint Comprehensive Environmental Action Programme. Balt. Sea Environ. Proc. No. 48.

HELCOM, 1993b.The Baltic Sea Joint Comprehensive Environmental Action Programme; Opportunities and Constraints in Programme Implementation. Balt. Sea Environ. Proc. No. 49.

HELCOM, 1996. Third Periodic Assessment of the State of the Marine Environment of the Baltic Sea, 1989–1993; Executive Summary. Balt. Sea Environ. Proc. No. 64A.

HELCOM, 1998a. The Third Baltic Sea Pollution Load Compilation. Balt. Sea Environ. Proc. No. 70.

HELCOM, 1998b. The Baltic Sea Joint Comprehensive Environmental Action Programme: Recommendations for Updating and Strengthening. Balt. Sea Environ. Proc. No. 72.

HELCOM, 2000. HELCOM Programme Implementation Task Force (HELCOM PITF), The Baltic Sea Joint Comprehensive Environmental Action Programme (JCP). Annual Report 1999. Helsinki Commission. Helsinki 2000.

HELCOM, 2001. Fourth Periodic Assessment of the State of the Marine Environment of the Baltic Sea, 1994–1998; to be published in April/May 2001.

ICES (Edit.), 1970. Report of the ICES Working Group on Pollution in the Baltic Sea. Cooperative Research Report. Series A, No. 15. Charlottenlund.

Kremser, U., 1997. Agriculture within the context of HELCOM«s mandate and activities. Ambio, Vol. 26, No. 7, pp. 415–417.
Lozan.J.L. *et.al.* (Edit.), 1996. Warnsignale aus der Ostsee. Berlin.
Rheinheimer, G. (Edit.), 1996. Meereskunde der Ostsee. Berlin.
Svenson, G., 1997. New approaches in environmental cooperation. BEI/EIB Forum, 23–24 October 1997 in Stockholm, Sweden. Proceedings: Bridging the Seas in Northern Europe, pp. 55–57.
Svenson, G., 1998. What is PITF – and why? HELCOM News No. 4, December 1998, HELCOM.
Sweco, COWIconsult, VKI in association with Hydroproject and Stolica, 1992. Pre-feasibility study of the Vistula River Basin and Baltic Coast of Poland, Part I, Synthesis Report. Prepared for the World Bank with support from the Governments of Poland, Denmark and Sweden.

*Roland Salchow**

THE QUALITY STATUS REPORT (QSR 2000) FOR THE NORTH EAST ATLANTIC

1. Introduction

The first comprehensive quality environmental status report for the OSLO-PARIS ('OSPAR') convention area, the QSR 2000,[1] has been prepared for the North East Atlantic.

Quality Status Reports are an important interface between science (assessment) and politics (measures), but also are necessary to strengthen the maritime awareness.[2]

The QSR shows that in the OSPAR area the worsening trends in pollution have been reversed. Many significant sources of pollution have been stopped. Fisheries management systems have been established. Already 10 years ago, incineration and dumping *at sea* were terminated – now we see the positive results of measures taken *on land*, by OSPAR or the EU.

But the picture is not all positive. The QSR shows that in spite of the reversed trends the marine environment is still under threat. Fisheries continue to affect fragile ecosystems. A substantial number of contaminant concentrations are too high, predominantly in the coastal regions. Important actions have to be taken.

The OSLO-PARIS convention sets the international framework for marine environmental politics for the North East Atlantic (including the North Sea). For such a huge area the QSR is the world-wide first such comprehensive presentation of the physical conditions, the wide variety of human activities (at sea and on land), as well as the chemical and biological effects in the marine environment.

2. The OSPAR Framework

In northern Europe marine environmental politics are organized within an international framework. Since the '70s the HELSINKI Convention for the Baltic Sea, as

* Director and Professor, General Federal Maritime and Hydrographic Agency, Chairman, ASMO Commission for Assessment and Monitoring of OSPAR.

1 Website for downloading the Quality Status Report: *http://www.ospar.org.*

2 *P. Ehlers*, Das internationale Jahr des Ozeans – ein Beitrag zur Stärkung des maritimen Bewußtseins (The international year of the ocean – a contribution to strengthen maritime awareness) (UNESCO 1–1999).

P. Ehlers, E. Mann-Borgese and R. Wolfrum (eds.), Marine Issues, 119–134

well as the OSLO-PARIS convention, now "OSPAR", for the NE Atlantic (incl. the North Sea) (Figure 1) have come into force.[3]

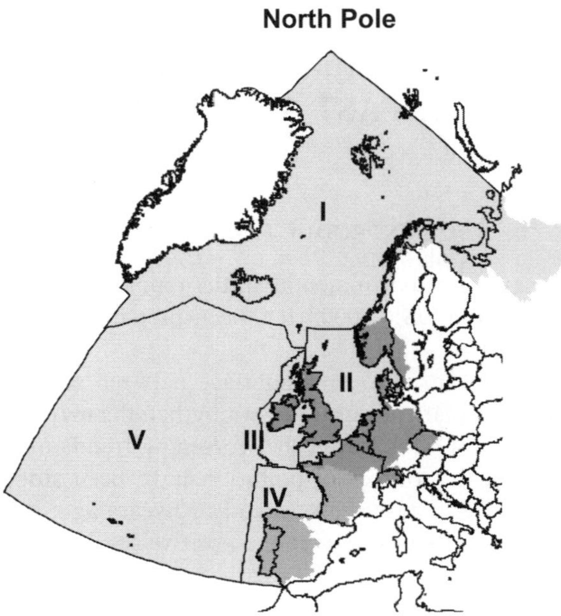

Figure 1. Catchment areas of the OSPAR Regions.

A wide variety of human activities takes place in the OSPAR area: fishing, offshore industries and shipping, as well as land-based industrial, agricultural and domestic activities. As a consequence the area is affected by the inputs of harmful substances and nutrients and the impacts of fishing or dredging.

The convention has been signed by 12 European governments and by the EU, and it aims at preventing and eliminating pollution. Information where steps are necessary is given by assessments of the quality status. As a result of our six years work the first convention-wide Quality Status Report 2000 was launched in June 2000 to ministers and the public.

OSPAR work is implemented within a structure that has four layers. On the first level is the Commission which meets once a year and is the ruling body; every few years there is a ministerial meeting of the Commission where ministers represent their countries. On the second level are "Strategy Committees" that undertake work on e.g. hazardous substances, offshore industry, eutrophication. On the second level, also, the ASMO Committee manages assessment and monitoring. The Quality Status

[3] *R. Salchow*, European Co-operation in the environment, in: *ASEAN Regional Cooperation, Perspectives* (Manila 1999).

Report has been prepared by this ASMO committee assisted by its working groups on the third and fourth levels.

3. The QSR

The QSR is based upon 5 regional reports for the five OSPAR regions (Figure 1):

Arctic, North Sea, Celtic Sea, Bay of Biscay and Iberian Coast, and the Wider Atlantic.

The degree of human impact varies between the different regions. The much higher densities of human population in catchments draining into Region II (the North Sea and the English Channel) produce significantly different pressures from those affecting Region V (the Wider Atlantic). Nevertheless, common types of pressure exist, particularly from intensive (and sometimes conflicting) uses of the coastal zone.

The QSR identifies the following important pressures:

1. most important issues: *fisheries* and *hazardous substances* (particularly organotin antifouling treatments and concerns about endocrine disrupters);
2. other generally important issues, (in order of priority):
   (a) Marine Biodiversity and Ecosystems, Radioactive Substances and Eutrophication,
   (b) oil spills and discharges of ballast water from shipping;
3. other issues with great significance in specific regions include:
   (a) North Sea: the hazardous substances organochlorine pesticides and polychlorinated biphenyls (PCBs);
   (b) in the North Sea and Celtic Seas, offshore activities and mariculture; and
   (c) in Celtic Seas, Biscay and the Iberian coast the impacts of coastal development.

A number of the important issues are described below.

3.1. Fisheries

In all five regions of the OSPAR area fisheries have been identified as an important issue. An investigation made by the ICES on the status of commercially exploited fish stocks demonstrates that 40 of the 60 major stocks were outside 'safe biological limits'[4] in their respective regions (table in the annex); the QSR believes fisheries for those stocks to be unsustainable.

The QSR describes the problems resulting from fisheries – roughly:

---

[4] *ICES*, Report of the Advisory Committee on Fishery Management, Part I and II, in: *ICES CRR* 229 (1999); *ICES*, Report of the Advisory Committee on Fishery Management, in: *ICES CRR* 236 (1999).

- Increased *efficiency* in fishing has increased the exploitation, e.g. in the North Sea 30–40% of the biomass of commercial fish species is caught each year.
- *By-catch* of undersized fish or non-target species including marine mammals with high levels of discards is a continuing problem in many areas. In certain flatfish fisheries half of the weight of the fish caught may be discarded.
- Physical disturbance of the *sea bottom* through demersal fishing gear affects benthic (bottom) habitats and communities living there. Otter trawl boards penetrate into soft sediment sea beds up to 20 cm. In certain areas with long term bottom trawling there has been a shift in benthic composition from larger more long-lived species to smaller more opportunistic species.

One of two main regulatory measures is the yearly setting of Total Allowable Catches (TACs) or Transferable Quotas. But for so-called socio-economic reasons, TACs are often set (by the EU) above scientifically recommended limits. Illegal landings and unrecorded discards of by-catch undermine the accuracy of stock assessments and thus the TACs. In Icelandic and Norwegian waters, discarding of commercially important fish is not permitted. Fleets subject to EU regulation are obliged to discard undersized fish.

Although effective in some fisheries, overall the measures to reduce fishing pressure have had only limited effectiveness, given the existing over-capacity of some fishing fleets. A sufficient decrease in fishing pressure was not achieved. An EU programme to reduce fishing fleets and engine power, up to 1997, has not been implemented fully by all member states. Even *if* a reduction in tonnage was achieved, it was balanced by a *more efficient use* of the remaining fleet. Now another EU reduction programme is running, trying to reduce the fishing effort by up to 30%.

3.2. Hazardous Substances

Apart from their intrinsic properties of toxicity, persistence, and liability to bioaccumulate, there is clear evidence that a diverse range of natural and man-made substances (including tributyltin (TBT) and various other organo-metallic compounds, PCBs, dioxins, and certain pesticides, pharmaceuticals and industrial chemicals) have potential to impair the reproductive process in aquatic organisms, for example through interference with their endocrine (hormonal) systems. Studies have shown that these endocrine-disrupting effects can occur even at very low ambient concentrations, considerably less than concentrations that are either mutagenic or acutely toxic.

Furthermore, high concentrations of these substances in marine seafood may pose problems to the consumer; in some areas high levels of mercury and PCBs in seafood have been detected.

In sediments or coastal waters concentrations in some areas exceed the reference values. To help assess the concentrations measured, ASMO has introduced as a tool two sets of values, the background concentrations BRC and the ecotoxicological criteria EAC. These assessment values are important for comparison; but we need to invest more work into getting clearer values. Concentration of a contaminant

Table 1. Some examples of anthropogenic sources of contaminants

Group	*Contaminant*	*Main anthropogenic sources*
Heavy Metals	Cadmium	Metallurgic processes, fossil fuel, fertiliser
	Mercury	Fossil fuel, incineration, metallurgic industry
	Lead	Mining, petrol
	Copper	Mining, antifoulants
Persistent Organic Pollutants	PCBs	Industrial products, oils
	TBT	Antifoulants
	PAHs	oil production, fossil fuel
	DDT, HCH, toxaphene, dieldrin, chlordane	Pesticides
	HCB	Industrial processes
	dioxins and furans	Incineration
Nutrients	nitrate, ammonia, phosphate	Agriculture, mariculture, sewage
Radionuclides	caesium, polonium, technetium	Reprocessing plants, phosphate production

below its EAC does not guarantee a safe situation. On the other hand, it is not compelling that biological effects occur where an EAC is exceeded.

OSPAR is striving to achieve its objective of continuously reducing inputs of these hazardous substances towards the target of cessation of inputs by 2020. In the list of chemicals for priority action a number of substances[5] are already included – these are the metals mercury, lead, cadmium, and the organic substances – chlorinated or not – PAHs, PCBs, organotin compounds, lindane (and isomers), nonyl-phenols, dioxins. Others are being considered.

A number of the substances are already under regulation (OSPAR, EC), mostly for point sources. Challenges are now diffuse inputs from the *use* of products containing the substances and the consequent run-off into rivers and the sea.

3.3. *Organic Pollutants*

TBT

Organotin compounds as TBT are used as antifouling agents, so in ship paint.[6] They result in endocrine disruption or in shell thickening in oyster and snail species as well as in converting sex characteristics of organisms (imposex).

TBT values are documented from Svalbard down to Portugal, preferably in harbours, estuaries and coastal waters. TBT in sediments is a long-lasting source.

[5] *OSPAR Commission*, Briefing Document on the work of DYNAMEC and the DYNAMEC mechanism for the Selection and Priorisation of Hazardous Substances (London 2000).

[6] *OSPAR Commission*, Point and Diffuse Sources: Background Document on Organic Tin Compounds (London 2000).

The prohibition of TBT in 1990 for the application on smaller ships resulted in biological recovery – in countries with effective regulations. Now it is necessary that IMO implements its plans for measures.

Polychlorinated biphenyls (PCB)

Synthetic PCBs are used extensively for electrical equipment, hydraulic fluids, and as plasticiser. Despite a ban on the production, PCBs are still a diffuse source of pollution, as Figure 2 shows for sediments:

In the open sea we found the PCBs to be clearly below ecotoxic reference criteria, but in coastal areas sometimes above, in harbours and estuaries they mostly exceed by far these criteria.

PCB concentrations in biota are not generally decreasing. Only a small number of significant downward trends have been observed at the coast of Norway, the southern North Sea and in the Celtic Seas. On the other hand, there are areas with no clear downward trend; e.g. along the Swedish Skagerrak coast concentrations of PCB in fish are still too high. High concentrations in mussels have been reported in all regions, except Region V.

Organochlorine pesticides

The organochlorine pesticides enter the marine environment mainly through diffuse inputs from agriculture (Figure 3, source Eurostat 1998), amenity areas and through transboundary pollution. Levels are generally decreasing. But some organochlorine pesticides are detected in biota at levels which may give rise for concern, e.g. in the North Sea.

The problem with persistence is seen at the example of DDT. Although it has been phased out since 1979, concentrations of DDE, resulting from DDT, still exceed EACs in mussels and fish in some areas.

Other substances

We can find persistent chlorinated paraffins even in the Arctic (200 to 800 μg/kg wet weight). They accumulate in marine mammals (seals, beluga, walrus). These paraffins are used as plasticisers, flame retardants and additives. Action had been started in the EU, but with limited success. OSPAR did in 1995 for the more difficult part of the paraffins. Some states implemented that, others did not.

Alkylphenols and related substances can also be found and these have been shown potentially to cause toxic effects in estuaries, and some are known to be endocrine disruptors.

We can also find PAHs, non-chlorinated aromatic hydrocarbons, sources of which include domestic and industrial combustion or direct oil spills. Sediments can act as a resevoir for PAHs where concentrations often exceed the EACs, especially in some estuaries in Region II.

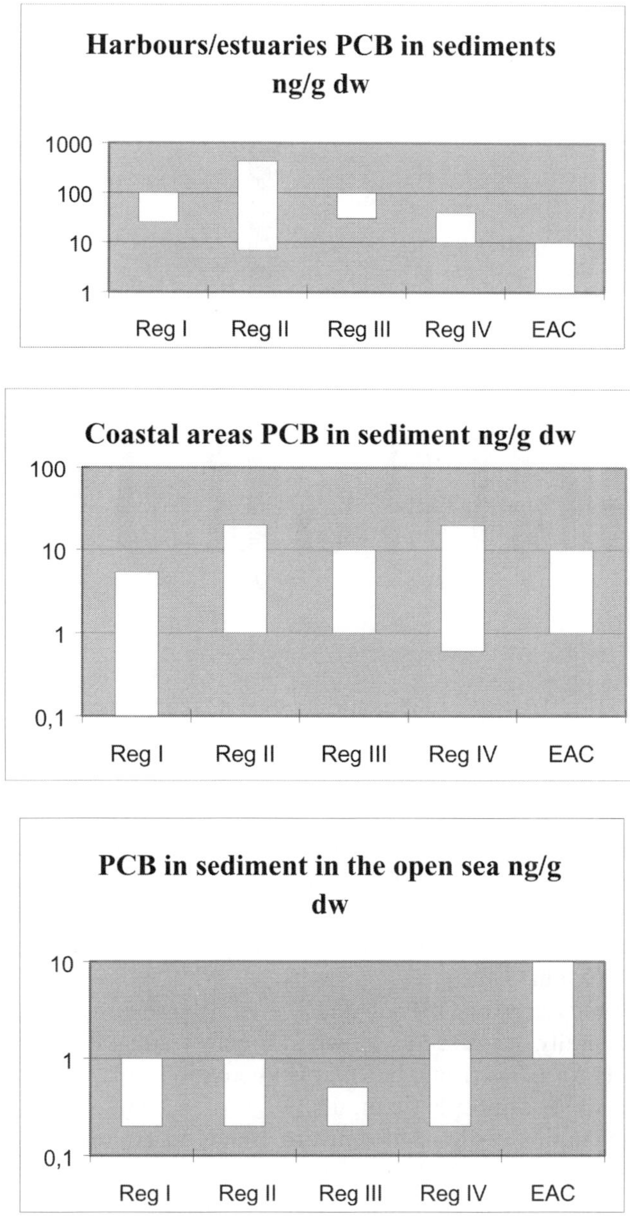

Figure 2. Sum of seven congeners ($\sum PCB_7$) *in sediment.*

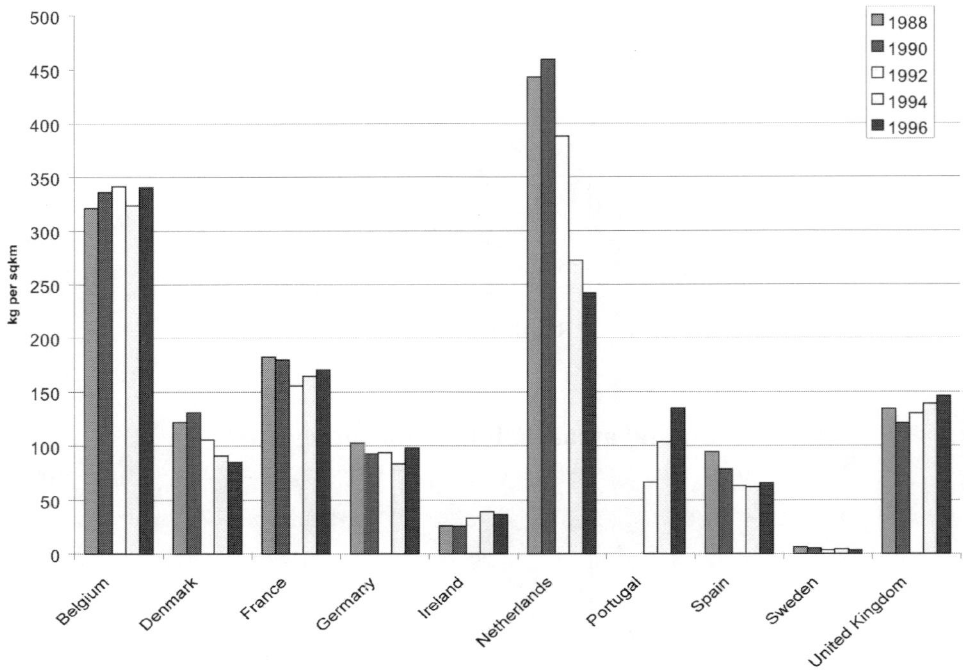

Figure 3. Total pesticides used in agriculture.

3.4. Metals

Heavy metals can pose a risk in a number of ways. Some metals, such as cadmium and mercury, can accumulate in fish and other biota. Mercury can damage the nervous system and the digestion machinery, while cadmium may influence the liver and kidneys and the development. Dissolved copper can affect lower trophic levels such as phytoplankton.

As a result of measures in OSPAR and the EU riverine inputs of cadmium and mercury have generally decreased as shown in Figure 4, suggesting that only mercury input in Region I (Arctic) is rising, but that is fluctuation on a very low scale. Trends are downward also for atmospheric inputs.

Reduced metal inputs result in downward trends in concentrations; there is no widespread contamination. Cadmium and mercury concentrations in seawater in different areas are shown in Figure 5, a result of the JAMP, the joint Monitoring and Assessment Programme organised in OSPAR, under ASMO.

But the picture is not all positive, as Figure 5 demonstrates. It shows that in seawater in estuaries and in the coastal zone, metal concentrations can exceed the ecotoxicological criteria indicating concern regarding their effects on biota; for example this is the case for cadmium in some estuaries in the North Sea and the

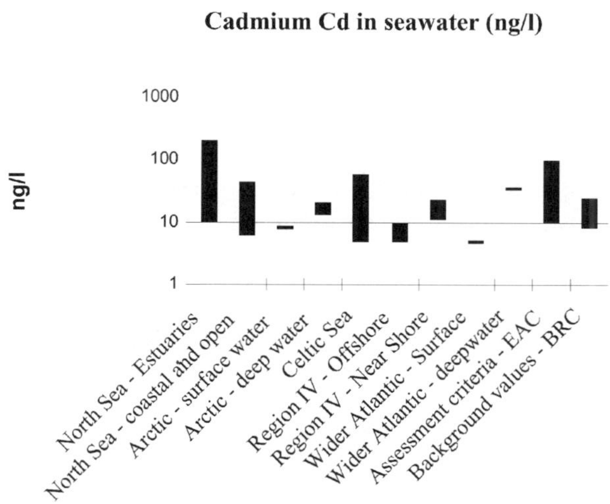

Figure 4. Downward trends in direct and riverine inputs of cadmium and mercury. Data for Region I cover the Norwegian and Barents Sea areas only. Mercury values in Region I are fluctuating on a low scale.

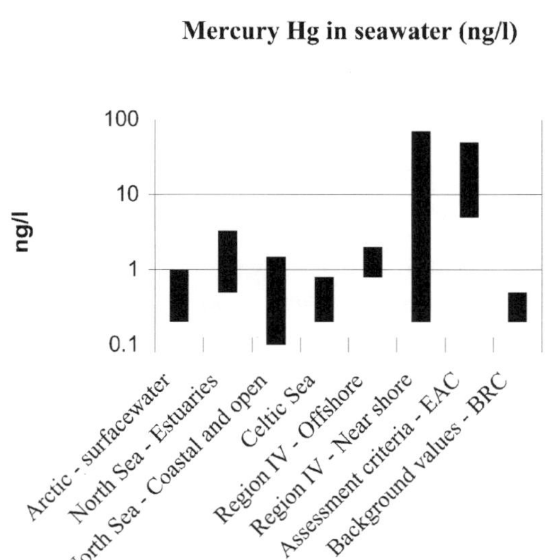

Figure 5. Concentration of metals in seawater. There are *ranges* of values because of differing concentrations already inside the areas. For comparison with assessment tools the figures show the ranges of EACs and BRCs. Region IV includes the Bay of Biscay and the Iberian Coast.

Celtic Sea as well as mercury in near-shore areas in Region IV, the Bay of Biscay and Iberian Region.

Cadmium, lead, mercury and copper in sediments have been found to exceed the EACs in specific areas close to current or past inputs, so in some parts of the North Sea and Irish Coast, as well as at Spanish and Portuguese coasts.

Furthermore, several heavy metals have been observed to travel long distances in the atmosphere, causing transboundary pollution in pristine areas such as the Arctic.

3.5. Other Generally Important Issues

Radioactivity

The issue of radioactivity has in none of the five regions been ranked as of high importance. Individual radiation exposures are generally very low and well within international dose limits.

Biodiversity

OSPAR's attention is now progressively drawn to matters of the protection of species, habitats and biodiversity. It is important to underline that the QSRs have identified strong pressures on the marine ecosystem that are not due to "pollution". These come from e.g. fisheries or mariculture. This QSR assesses the effects of a range of human activities on the ecosystem throughout the Regions. This information will assist OSPAR in implementing the new Annex of the Convention which we expect to enter into force in the near future.

Eutrophication

Eutrophication refers to undesirable effects resulting from enrichment by nutrients such as nitrogen and phosphorus from sewage or agricultural input. It results in increased phytoplankton and macro algae production and biomass – they may be toxic, remember the fish kills 10 years ago. Eutrophication also includes changes in species composition (including the occurrence of harmful algae and short-lived benthic algae in shallow waters as well as changes in the animal communities) and increased oxygen consumption in water and sediments, in some cases leading to detrimental effects on benthic fauna.

OSPAR is on the way to characterise the eutrophication status of the maritime area. Parts of the OSPAR maritime area to which the Comprehensive Procedure will be applied to determine their status with regard to eutrophication. Areas to which the Comprehensive Procedure will not be applied have been classified as non-problem areas with regard to eutrophication as a result of applying the Screening Procedure. A result of a screening in four regions is given in the QSR and shown in

Figure 6. Obviously eutrophication is confined to larger parts of the North Sea and to some coastal embayments and estuaries within Regions III and IV.

Oil

Oil results from riverine input and from shipping, as well as from oil and gas offshore activities (800 offshore platforms are operating in OSPAR waters, the majority located in the North Sea). Inputs of oil through rivers and sewage discharges are less significant, but continue on a steady level.

Inputs of oil from the offshore sector were reduced by 60% in the period 1985–1997

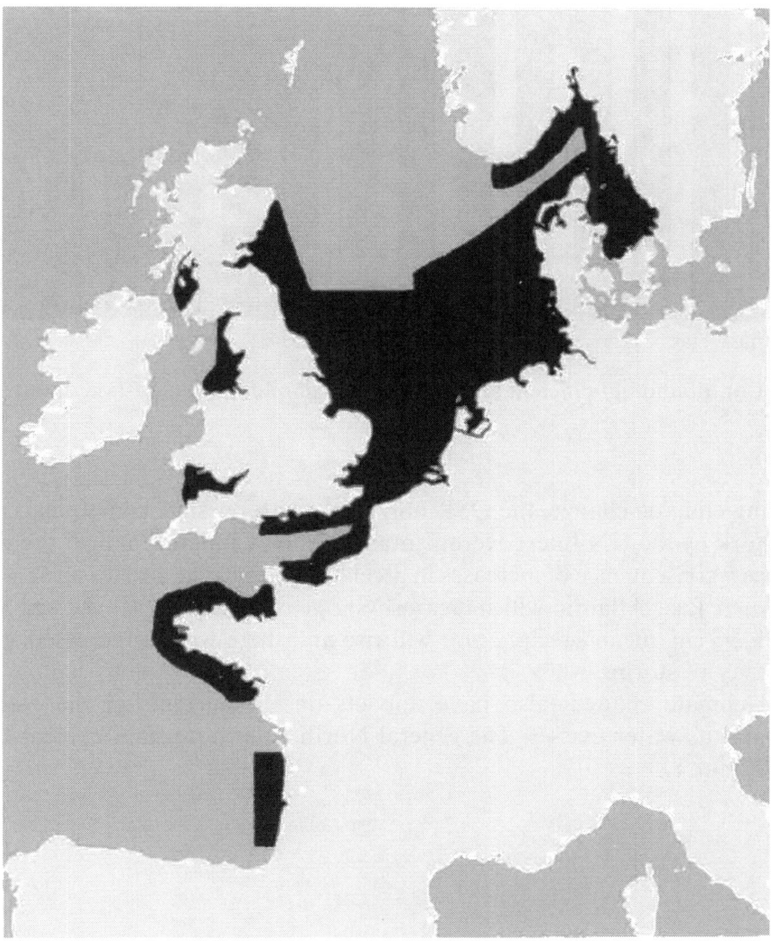

Figure 6. Problem or potential problem areas with regard to eutrophication to which the Comprehensive Procedure will be applied (it will also be applied to a number of Irish estuaries as well as some local areas of possible concern).

by decreasing oil discharges from cuttings for drilling. On the other hand, inputs from produced water from operating offshore installations have increased progressively with the number of installations and as oil fields have matured. These inputs now constitute the largest source of oil for the oil and gas sector. Heavy metals, PAHs and production chemicals are, together with oil, discharged via produced water. Changes of offshore oil discharges are shown in Figure 7.[7]

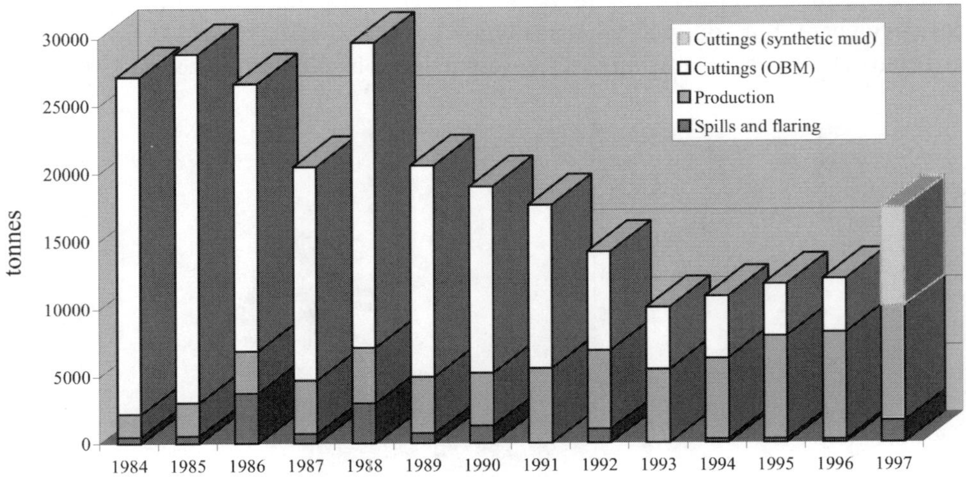

Figure 7. Contribution of different sources of inputs of oil from the offshore installations.

Climate

Concerning climatic change, the QSR only deals with possible consequences for our region. Work by the UN Intergovernmental Panel on Climate Change[8] predicts that, by 2100, as a consequence of increases in greenhouse gases the surface air temperature of the North East Atlantic will increase by approximately 1.5°C, the sea level will rise by 25–95 cm, mean precipitation will rise and there will be increased frequency and intensity of storms.

Global climate changes also have impacts on the currents in the North East Atlantic and its water masses. The general North Atlantic surface current system is given in Figure 8.

7 *OSPAR Commission*, Discharges, waste handling and air emissions from offshore installations, 1996–1997 (London 1999).

8 *IPCC*, Summary for policy-makers, The regional impacts of climate change: an assessment of vulnerability, A special report of Working Group II (*R.T. Watson et al.* eds.) (1997).

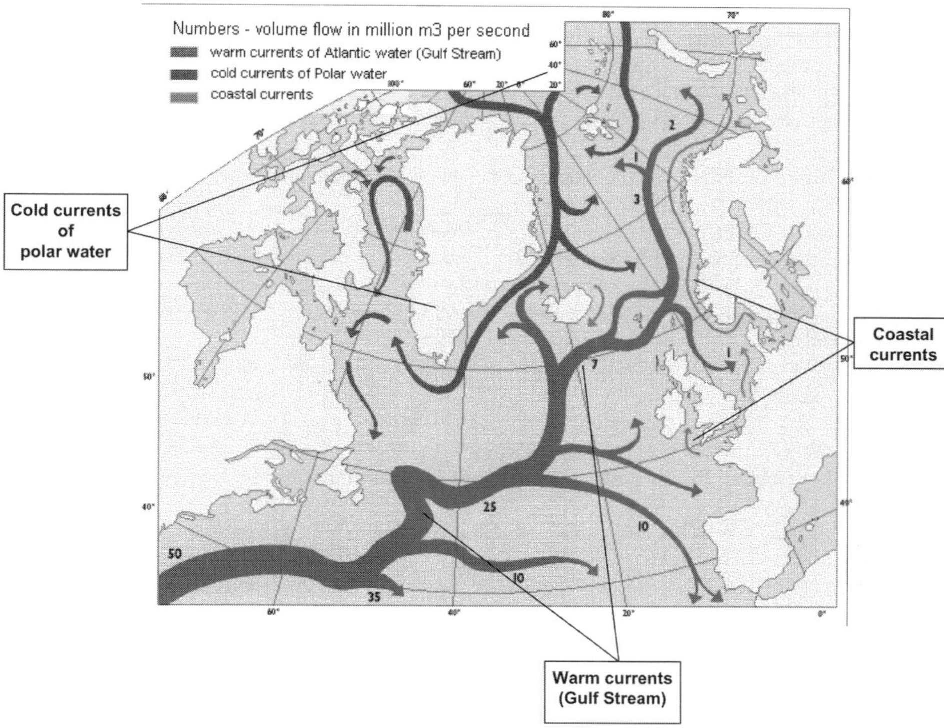

Figure 8. Mean surface currents.

4. RÉSUMÉ

We need assessments such as the QSR because – to use the words of Jeanette Winterson, the English writer – "some things are better explored than ignored". Quality Status Reports are an important interface between science (assessment) and politics (measures). Implementing measures without taking account of the scientific background could create further problems. At present OSPAR, HELCOM and the EU are deliberating upon which hazardous substances should be more strictly controlled so as to prevent them reaching the marine environment. According to a decision reached by OSPAR in 1998, concentrations in the marine environment of these substances should, within 20 years, be close to zero if they are man-made and close to background concentrations if they occur naturally.

REFERENCES

5th North Sea Conference (5NSC) 1997. *Assessment Report on Fisheries and Fisheries Related Species and Habitat Issues.* Ed. by M. Svelle *et al.* Intermediate Ministerial Meeting on the Integration of Fisheries and Environmental Issues, 1997, Bergen, Norway. Ministry of Environment.

Dolzer R. and T. Buß, 2000. International Marine Environmental Protection – The Legal Framework. In: Protecting our Environment. Ed. by R. Dolzer and J. Thesing. Konrad-Adenauer-Stiftung, Sankt Augustin.
Ehlers, P., 1999. Das internationale Jahr des Ozeans – ein Beitrag zur Stärkung des maritimen Bewußtseins (The international year of the ocean – a contribution to strengthen maritime awareness). UNESCO 1–1999.
ICES 1999a. Report of the Advisory Committee on Fishery Management, 1998.International Council for the Exploration of the Sea. Part I and II. ICES Coop. Res. Rep. 229.
ICES 1999b. Report of the Advisory Committee on Fishery Management, 1999. International Council for the Exploration of the Sea. ICES Coop. Res. Rep. 236.
IPCC 1997. *Summary for policymakers. The regional impacts of climate change: an assessment of vulnerability.* Ed. by R.T. Watson et al.. A special report of Working Group II, UN Intergovernmental Panel on Climate change.
OSPAR 1999. Discharges, waste handling and air emissions from offshore installations, 1996–1997. OSPAR Commission, London.
OSPAR 2000a. Briefing Document on the Work of DYNAMEC and the DYNAMEC mechanism for the Selection and Prioritisation of Hazardous Substances. OSPAR Commission, London.
OSPAR 2000b. Point and Diffuse Sources: Background Document on Organic Tin Compounds. OSPAR Commission, London.
Salchow R., 1999. European Co-operation in the environment. In: Perspectives. ASEAN Regional Cooperation, Manila.
Salchow R., 2000. Protecting Oceans and the Sea. In: Protecting our Environment. Ed. by R. Dolzer and J. Thesing. Konrad-Adenauer-Stiftung, Sankt Augustin.
Website for downloading the Quality Status Report: *www.ospar.org*

Annex

Table. Landings and spawning stock biomass of the commercially important fish species, and status of the stock according to whether it is within "safe biological limits"*

Ospar region	*Ices division of stock description*	*Landings 1997*	*Spawning stock biomass 1998*	*Status*
REGION I				
Cod	Northeast Arctic	755,000 t	419,000 t	Outside safe B/L
	Norwegian coastal	36,000 t	Uncertain	Uncertain
	Iceland	204,000 t	529,000 t	Within safe B/L
	Faeroe Plateau	34,000 t	68,000 t	Close to or within safe B/L
Herring	Norwegian (spring spawning)	1,427,000 t	9,800,000 t	Within safe B/L
	Icelandic (summer spawning)	64,000 t	486,000 t	Within safe B/L
Capelin	Barents Sea	Closed in 1997	254,000 t	Within safe B/L from 1998
	Greenland/ Iceland	1,245,000 t	490,000 t	Within safe B/L

Ospar region	*Ices division of stock description*	*Landings 1997*	*Spawning stock biomass 1998*	*Status*
Saithe	*Northeast Arctic*	*143,000 t*	*211,000 t*	*Outside safe B/L*
	Iceland	*37,000 t*	*90,000 t*	*Outside safe B/L*
	Faeroes	*22,000 t*	*50,000 t*	*Outside safe B/L*
Haddock	*Northeast Arctic*	*146,000 t*	*219,000 t*	*Outside safe B/L*
	Iceland (from ACFM 1999)	*44,000 t*	*67,000 t*	*Harvested outside safe B/L*
	Faeroes	*18,000 t*	*50,000 t*	*Close to safe B/L*
REGION II				
Cod	North Sea	124,000 t	136,000 t	Outside safe B/L
Whiting	North Sea	59,000 t	172,000 t	Outside safe B/L
Haddock	North Sea	142,000 t	213,000 t	Close to safe B/L
Saithe	North Sea	103,000 t	132,000 t	Outside safe B/L
Plaice	North Sea	83,000 t	274,000 t	Outside safe B/L
Sole	North Sea	15,000 t	26,000 t	Outside safe B/L
Herring	North Sea	248,000 t	1,145,000 t	Outside safe B/L
REGION III				
Herring	Irish Sea (VIIa)	6,600 t	10,300 t	Harvested outside safe B/L
	Celtic Sea and VIIj	18,800 t	70,000 t	Harvested outside safe B/L
	Via, VIIb-c	27,000 t	57,000 t	Harvested outside safe B/L
Cod	Via	7,000 t	15,100 t	Outside safe B/L
	Irish Sea (VIIa)	5,700 t	8,750 t	Outside safe B/L
	VIIe-k	11,800 t	12,800 t	Outside safe B/L
Haddock	Via	19,500 t	44,300 t	Outside safe B/L
	Vib (Rockall)	5,200 t	8,400 t	Outside safe B/L
Whiting	Via	10,900 t	17,200 t	Outside safe B/L
	Irish Sea (VIIa)	4,200 t	8,100 t	Outside safe B/L
	VIIe-k	18,100 t	31,800 t	Within safe B/L
Saithe	VI	9,400 t	11,900 t	Outside safe B/L
Plaice	Irish Sea (VIIa)	1,900 t	5,600 t	Within safe B/L
	Celtic Sea (VIIf and g)	1,200 t	1,540 t	Outside safe B/L
Sole	Irish Sea (VIIa)	1,000 t	3,000 t	Outside safe B/L
	Celtic Sea (VIIf and g)	900 t	2,000 t	Outside safe B/L
Megrim	VI	3,600 t	NA	Within safe B/L
Anglerfish	VI	12,800 t	NA	Outside safe B/L
REGION III–IV				
Megrim	VII and VIIIa,b,d,e	17,300 t	65,000 t	Within safe B/L
Anglerfish	VIIb-k and VIIIa,b	28,900 t	73,700 t	Within safe B/L

Ospar region	*Ices division of stock description*	*Landings 1997*	*Spawning stock biomass 1998*	*Status*
REGION IV				
Sardine	VIIIc and IXa	115,000 t	253,000 t	Outside safe B/L
Anchovy	VIII and IXa	27,500 t	NA	Within safe B/L
Horse mackerel	VIIIc and IXa	57,000 t	256,000 t	Close to safe B/L
Hake	VIIIc and IXa	7 600 t	13 200 t	Outside safe B/L
Sole	Bay of Biscay (VIIIa,b)	6,900 t	13,600 t	Outside safe B/L
Megrim (*Lepidorhombus boscii*)	VIIIc and IXa	900 t	5,300 t	Outside safe B/L
Megrim (*L. whiffiagonis*)	VIIIc and IXa	360 t	1,400 t	Outside safe B/L
Anglerfish (*Lophius budegassa*)	VIIIc and IXa	1,800 t	NA	Outside safe B/L
Anglerfish (*L. piscatorius*)	VIIIc and IXa	3,700 t	NA	Outside safe B/L
REGION I, II, III, IV, V				
Species highly migratory				
Mackerel	Combined stock	570,000t	2,650,000t	Outside safe B/L
Blue whiting	Combined stock	634,000 t	2,718,000 t	Within safe B/L
Western horse mackerel	Combined stock	443,000 t	1,000,000 t	Outside safe B/L
Northern	IIIa, IV, VI, VII and VIIIa,b	44,200 t	127,000 t	Outside safe B/L

*Extract taken from *ICES* (*supra* note 4).

*Wolff Heintschel v. Heinegg**

THE DEVELOPMENT OF ENVIRONMENTAL STANDARDS FOR THE NORTH-EAST ATLANTIC, INCLUDING THE NORTH SEA

The development of environmental standards for the North-East Atlantic, including the North Sea, is marked by three dates: 1972, 1974 and 1992. As is well known, these dates stand for:

- the Convention for the Prevention of Marine Pollution by Dumping from Ships, signed in Oslo on 15 February 1972;[1]
- the Convention for the Prevention of Marine Pollution from Land-Based Sources, signed in Paris on 4 June 1974;[2] and
- the Convention for the Protection of the Marine Environment of the North-East Atlantic signed in Paris on 22 September 1992.[3]

The latter, generally called OSPAR Convention, entered into force on 25 March 1998 and has, according to its Article 31 para. 1, replaced the Oslo and Paris Conventions. As regards the reasons for this replacement it suffices to refer to the preamble of the OSPAR Convention which at the end states that:

> "the present Oslo and Paris Conventions do not adequately control some of the many sources of pollution, and that it is therefore justifiable to replace them with the present Convention, which addresses all sources of pollution of the

* Prof. Dr. iur., Europa-Universität Viadrina Frankfurt (Oder).

1 11 *ILM* 262 (1972); entry into force 7 April 1984. An evaluation of the achievements of the OSLO Convention is given by *J.B. Skjærseth*, Towards the End of Dumping in the North Sea, in: *MarPol* 1992, pp. 130–140, 131 *et seq.*

2 13 *ILM* 352 (1974); entry into force 6 May 1978. See also Protocol Amending the Convention for the Prevention of Marine Pollution from Land-Based Sources, done at Paris 26 March 1986, 27 *ILM* 625 (1988). For an overview of the provisions of the Paris Convention see *M. Gavouneli*, Pollution from Offshore Installations, pp. 52 *et seq.* (London *et al.* 1995); *Th. Cron*, Das Umweltregime der Nordsee: völker- und europarechtliche Aspekte, pp. 131 *et seq.* (Baden-Baden 1995).

3 The text of the Convention is available at *http://www.OSPAR.org*. A general overview is given by, *inter alia*, *J. Juste*, La convention pour la protection du milieu de l'Atlantique Nord-Est, in: *RGDIP* 1993, 365–393; *L. de La Fayette*, The OSPAR Convention Comes into Force: Continuity and Progress, in: *IJMCL* 14 (1999), 247–297; *J. Hilf*, The Convention for the Protection of the Marine Environment of the North-East Atlantic – New Approaches to an Old Problem?, in: *ZaöRV* 55 (1995); 580–603.

P. Ehlers, E. Mann-Borgese and R. Wolfrum (eds.), Marine Issues, 135–153

> marine environment and the adverse effects of human activities upon it, takes into account the precautionary principle and strengthens regional cooperation".

It would certainly be overambitious to take the title of the subject the author has been entrusted with literally. The time frame would cover a period of nearly 30 years and even the activities of the OSPAR Commission,[4] including its subsidiary bodies, though in existence for a relatively short time, are that manifold and have already resulted in such detailed measures that it would certainly exceed the time and space available if one endeavoured to deal with all the aspects involved. Hence, the first part of this presentation will merely give a short overview over the scope of application, the aims and the general principles of the OSPAR Convention as well as a brief comparison with the Oslo and Paris Conventions. The second part will be devoted to a more detailed overview of the Convention and of its Annexes and Appendices. Thus, the ground will be prepared for an analysis, in the third part, of the OSPAR Commission's activities with regard to environmental standards.

1. OSPAR – Scope of Application, Objectives and General Principles

OSPAR – as this denomination reveals – is, on the one hand, simply a merger of the 1972 Oslo and of the 1974 Paris Conventions. On the other hand, it goes beyond its predecessors for its purpose is not merely the creation of a single but of a comprehensive instrument regulating the protection of the marine environment of the North-East Atlantic.[5] In other words, the parties have not just remedied unnecessary redundances. The Convention is not restricted to the protection of the marine environment against pollution from sources covered by its predecessors. It is also designed as protection against other adverse effects of human activities, thus going beyond prevention of pollution. As laid down in the preamble and in Article 2 para. 1 lit. (a) the parties are prepared and obliged to

> "take all possible steps to prevent and eliminate pollution and shall take the necessary measures to protect the maritime area against the adverse effects of human activities so as to safeguard human health and to conserve marine ecosystems and, when practicable, restore marine areas which have been adversely affected."

Moreover, the Convention contains provisions on modern environmental principles and practices, including transparency and participation of the civil society, thus

---

4 For the structure and competences as well as for the work of the Commission see *J. Juste* (*supra* note 3), p. 375.

5 *R. Lagoni*, Das OSPAR-Übereinkommen von 1992 und der Schutz der Nordsee: Einwirkungen auf das deutsche Umweltrecht, in: *H.-J. Koch*/*R. Lagoni* (eds.), *Zum Zusammenspiel von Völkerrecht und nationalem Umweltrecht*, pp. 79 *et seq.* (Baden-Baden 1996).

giving them legally binding force.[6] Finally it incorporates important achievements arrived at on the secondary level of the Oslo and Paris Conventions, like the precautionary principle or Best Available Techniques (BAT) and Best Environmental Practices (BEP), thus, by transferring them to the primary level, underlining their overall importance. It should be added that the Convention also provides for the Commission to adopt binding decisions and to supervise and to enforce compliance.[7]

It has to be kept in mind, however, that despite the widened scope of application now also covering "pollution from other sources", the Commission and its subsidiary bodies may not deal with any kind of pollution affecting the North-East Atlantic. First of all, Article 7 itself makes it clear that measures against pollution from sources not originally covered by the Oslo and Paris Conventions may be adopted only if such pollution is not already the subject of effective measures agreed by other international organisations or prescribed by other international conventions. Hence, ship-source pollution as well as pollution through atmospheric depositions are not covered by OSPAR because – at least at present – measures taken within the frameworks of IMO or the 1979 Convention on Long-Range Transboundary Air Pollution respectively, are considered more appropriate and effective.[8] Finally, as expressly stated in the preamble, the Convention does not deal with fishing. It is the parties' belief that "questions relating to the management of fisheries are appropriately regulated under international and regional agreements dealing specifically with such questions".

Of course, this brief introduction cannot but give a first impression as to the state of the development of environmental standards.[9] Even if such standards may be understood as a certain level of quality in the sense of a description of a value yet to be reached, such a restrictive understanding would neither conform to reality nor be of much worth – be it from the practical, be it from the legal perspective. The core issue here are the yardsticks to be applied when evaluating the quality of and hazards to the marine environment and, even more importantly, the means to be applied in order to achieve the overall result – the protection and improvement of the marine environment. It is in this wider sense that the notion of environmental standards is applied here.

2. OSPAR – The Primary Level

Let us now turn to the primary level, i.e. to the operative part of the Convention, its Annexes and Appendices, in order to verify if and to what extent they have contributed to a true development of environmental standards.

---

6 *T. Stoll*, Meeresschutz im Küsten- und Offshore-Bereich im Hinblick auf nicht-stoffliche Einflüsse, in: *NuR* 12 (1999), pp. 666–674, 671.

7 *R. Lagoni* (*supra* note 5), pp. 86 *et seq.*

8 Cf. *L. de La Fayette* (*supra* note 3), p. 252.

9 It is interesting to note that in the legal literature there exists no definition of that notion. Still, "environmental standards" are regularly being referred to.

2.1. Principle of Precaution

For many the most important achievement of the OSPAR Convention is the explicit incorporation of the principle of precaution, in Article 2 para. 2 lit. (a), thus beyond any doubt acknowledging its legally binding character.[10] This certainly is an improvement. Moreover, as the formulation clearly indicates, the obligations resulting from its application go much further than those according to other conventions that – either on the primary or on the secondary level – also pledge allegiance to the precautionary principle.[11] One must, however, not lose out of sight that, since the formulation in the beginning is identical with that of Article 1 lit. (d), it only applies to pollution and not to "other human activities" in the sense of Article 7. In the context of Annex V we will see, however, that the practical effects of that relatively narrow scope of application are less worrying than some might think.[12]

2.2. BAT and BEP

According to Article 2 para. 3 lit. (a) the contracting parties, in implementing he Convention, shall adopt programmes and measures which, inter alia, "[...] take full account of the use of the latest technological developments and practices designed to prevent and eliminate pollution fully". To this end, they shall, by lit. (b),

(i) taking into account the criteria set forth in Appendix 1, define with respect to programmes and measures the application of, *inter alia*,
  – best available techniques
  – best environmental practice
  including, where appropriate, clean technology;
(ii) in carrying out such programmes and measures, ensure the application of best available techniques and best environmental practice as so defined, including, where appropriate, clean technology.

Again, the mandatory prescription of these concepts formerly only defined and applied on the secondary level of the Oslo and Paris Conventions is in itself an important achievement. Moreover, despite of the parties' wide discretion in actually determining what constitutes BAT and BEP and the lack of prioritisation of the criteria set out in Appendix 1 it cannot be denied that the Commission and its subsidiary bodies have succeeded in working out quite impressive catalogues of BAT and BEP for specific industrial sectors and hazardous processes and, especially, for

---

10 It is still not settled whether the precautionary principle can be considered part of customary international law. See, *inter alia*, *U. Beyerlin*, Umweltvölkerrecht, pp. 60 *et seq.* (Munich 2000). For an analysis of the precautionary principle in the context of the OSPAR Convention see *R. Lagoni* (*supra* note 5), pp. 91 *et seq.*; *J. Hilf* (*supra* note 3), pp. 585 *et seq.*

11 See the references given by *L. de La Fayette* (*supra* note 3), pp. 254 *et seq.*

12 See, e.g., *J. Hilf* (*supra* note 3), p. 587; *J. Juste* (*supra* note 3), p. 381.

hazardous substances. In addition, Appendix 1 contains a progressive element thus preventing the parties to rely upon criteria and concepts that cannot be considered as still reflecting the latest technological developments. According to paras. 3 and 8 of Appendix 1, it follows from the respective preceding paragraphs that what is BAT and BEP for a particular source "will change with the time in the light of technological advances, economic and social factors, as well as changes in scientific knowledge and understanding."

Paras. 4 and 9 of Appendix 1 reveal that the application of BAT and BEP may not lead to environmentally acceptable results. In that case additional measures have to be applied. Here the reference to clean technology "where appropriate" does not imply that such technology might not always be appropriate. Rather, clean technology comes into play when the application of BAT and BEP leads to environmentally unacceptable results.[13]

2.3. Polluter Pays Principle

By Article 2 para. 2 lit. (b) the parties are obliged to apply the polluter pays principle "by virtue of which the costs of pollution prevention, control and reduction measures are to be borne by the polluter". In view of the fact that the precise content of that principle – under general international environmental law – is not yet settled or even generally agreed and in view of the lack of a further definition or clarifiation in the Convention and in its Annexes or Appendices it may well be that it can be regarded as only a very general principle and unqualified guideline.[14] The more so since its relationship to BAT and BEP has to be taken into consideraton, because, according to Appendix 1, the criteria to be applied in ascertaining BAT and BEP include "economic feasibility" and "social and economic implications".

2.4. Compliance Procedure, Access to Information, Participation of NGOs

(a) Reports and Compliance Procedure

Without going into further details[15] it must suffice to merely mention that, according to Article 23 the Commission shall

(a) on the basis of the periodical reports referred to in Article 22 and any other report submitted by the Contracting Parties, assess their compliance with the Convention and the decisions and recommendations adopted thereunder;

(b) when appropriate, decide upon and call for steps to bring about full compliance with the Convention, and decisions adopted thereunder, and promote the

---

13 Cf. *L. de La Fayette* (*supra* note 3), pp. 255 *et seq.*

14 See, e.g., *U. Beyerlin* (*supra* note 10), p. 61.

15 For a detailed description see *J. Hilf* (*supra* note 3), pp. 591 *et seq.*; *L. de La Fayette* (*supra* note 3), pp. 258 *et seq.*; *J. Juste* (*supra* note 3), p. 376/7.

> implementation of recommendations, including measures to assist a Contracting Party to carry out its obligations.

Hence, the Commission is entitled to review the reports the contracting parties are obliged to submit according to Article 22 and the well-elaborated reporting system and – this is quite rare in international environmental law – to take measures to ensure compliance. This may, however, not be misunderstood as the conference of a competence upon the Commission to take enforcement measures or sanctions.[16]

(b) Access to Information and Participation of NGOs

Finally, before turning to the Annexes and Appendices, a brief reference to access to information and to participation of NGOs.

According to Article 9 para. 1 the contracting parties are obliged to

> "ensure that their competent authorities are required to make available the information described in paragraph 2 of this Article to any natural or legal person, in response to any reasonable request, without that person's having to prove an interest, without unreasonable charges, as soon as possible and at the latest within two months".

The information referred to in this paragraph is defined in para. 2 as comprising "any available information in written, visual, aural or data-base form on the state of the maritime area, on activities or measures adversely affecting or likely to affect it and on activities or measures introduced in accordance with the Convention". However, access to information may be denied if one of the exceptions of para. 3 applies, e.g. for reason of public security, commercial and industrial confidentiality, and confidentiality of personal data and/or files.[17]

Article 11 provides:

1. The Commission may, by unanimous vote of the Contracting Parties, decide to admit as an observer:
   (a) any State which is not a Contracting Party to the Convention;
   (b) any international governmental or any non-governmental organisation the activities of which are related to the Convention.
2. Such observers may participate in meetings of the Commission but without the right to vote and may present to the Commission any information or reports relevant to the objectives of the Convention.
3. The conditions for the admission and the participation of observers shall be set in the Rules of Procedure of the Commission.

[16] See *R. Lagoni* (*supra* note 5), p. 86.

[17] Wherever access to information is granted in international environmental instruments, the confidentiality of personal data and files as well as of commercial and industrial secrets is provided for.

The Criteria and Procedures Governing Observership of Non-Governmental Organisations at Meetings within the framework of the OSPAR Commission are laid dowen in Annex II of the Commission's Rules of Procedure that were adopted at the meeting in Sintra.[18] At present, 19 NGOs have the status of general observers and 15 NGOs have the status of sepcialised observers.[19]

5. *Annexes and Appendices, especially Annex V and Appendix III*

In view of the fact that Annexes I to IV and Appendices 1 and 2 were adopted together with the Convention and have, consequently, been dealt with elsewhere,[20] it must suffice to merely mention them. The more so because we have in part already referred to them or will return to them later in the context of the secondary level.

The original Annexes and Appendices deal with:

- the Prevention and Elimination of Pollution from Land-based Sources (Annex I);
- the Prevention and Elimination of Pollution by Dumping or Incineration (Annex II);
- the Prevention and Elimination of Pollution from Offshore Sources (Annex III);
- the Assessment of the Quality of the Marine Environment (Annex IV);
- Criteria for the Definition of Practices and Techniques mentioned in Paragraph 3(b)(i) of Article 2 of the Convention (Appendix 1 on BAT and BEP); and
- Criteria mentioned in Paragraph 2 of Article 1 of Annex I and in Paragraph 2 of Article 2 of Annex III (Appendix 2 on Criteria to be applied when setting priorities).

At the meeting in Sintra a new Annex V[21] and Appendix 3[22] were adopted. Especially by these the Convention was moved beyond prevention of pollution, now also covering the protection and conservation of the ecosystems and biological diversity of the marine area.[23]

---

18 Reference number: 2000–15.

19 The difference between general and specialised observers relates to participation in the meetings of the Commission. According to para. 4.1 lit. a of Annex II, two seats per delegation will be allocated to general NGO observers, and a total number of six seats will be available for specialised NGO observers. Specialised observers may apply to attend the meetings of the Commission for one or more points of the agenda.

20 See, *inter alia, L. de La Fayette* (*supra* note 3), pp. 248 *et seq.*

21 Annex V on the Protection and Conservation of the Ecosystems and Biological Diversity of the Maritime Area. See also OSPAR Agreement on the Meaning of certain concepts in Annex V to the OSPAR Convention (Reference number: 1998–15.2).

22 Criteria for Identifying Human Activities for the Purpose of Annex V.

23 It should be added that, by Annex V and Appendix 3, the comparatively narrow scope of application of the precautionary principle is, thus, widened to "other human activities" than pollution.

Annex V and Appendix 3 are amendments of the Convention and have not yet entered into force.[24] They are supplemented by the Strategy on the Protection and Conservation of the Ecosystems and Biological Diversity, and by the OSPAR Action Plan. Pursuant to Article 2 of Annex V the parties commit themselves to

(a) take the necessary measures to protect and conserve the ecosystems and the biological diversity of the maritime area, and to restore, where practicable, marine areas which have been adversely affected; and
(b) cooperate in adopting programmes and measures for those purposes for the control of the human activities identified by the application of the criteria in Appendix 3.

According to Article 3, besides collecting and analysing relevant information, the Commission is, *inter alia*, required to develop programmes and measures, aiming at the application of an integrated ecosystem approach for the control of human activities identified as having adverse effects on ecosystems and biodiversity.[25] In view of the fact that almost any human activity might have such effects, in view of the nearly insurmountable problem of controlling such activities, and in view of the commitment also to restore damaged ecosystems and threatened biodiversity Annex V stands for quite ambitious goals.[26] It has to be taken into account, however, that the competence of the Commission in this field is rather limited since, according to the Convention's preamble and Article 4 para. 1 of Annex V "no programme or measure concerning a question relating to the management of fisheries shall be adopted under this Annex." Rather, according to Article 4 para. 1, where the Commission considers that action is desirable in relation to such a question, it is limited to draw that question to the attention of the authority or international body competent for that question. Agreement 1998–15.2[27] also adopted at Sintra lists the following instruments under which action may be taken:

(a) the Common Fisheries Policy of the European Community;
(b) the corresponding legislation of Contracting Parties which are not Member States of the European Union; or

24 In accordance with Article 15 of the OSPAR Convention, for those Parties who have ratified it, Annex V will enter into force on the thirtieth day after receipt by the Depository Government of notification of its ratification by at least seven Contracting Parties. At the time of writing, only Finland and Spain have notified their ratification of Annex V.

25 See, e.g., OSPAR Strategy on the Protection and Conservation of the Ecosystems and Biological Diversity of the Maritime Area (Reference number: 1998–19).

26 Hence, according to OSPAR Strategy 1998–19, the Commission will start with assessing which species and habitats need to be protected and those human activities that are likely to have an actual or potential adverse effect on these species and habitats or on ecological processes. See also Guideline 2000–03 on Criteria for the Selection of Species and Habitats; Annex 1 of the OSPAR Action Plan 1998–2003 on "Human activities to be assessed with regard to their impact on the marine environment, its species, habitats and biological diversity".

27 Meaning of certain concepts in Annex V to the 1992 OSPAR Convention (*supra* note 21).

(c) the corresponding legislation in force in the Faroe Islands, Greenland, the Channel Islands and the Isle of Man.
(d) the North East Atlantic Fisheries Commission and the North Atlantic Salmon Commission

Similarly, where the Commission considers that action under Annex V is desirable in relation to a question concerning maritime transport, it shall draw that question to the attention of the International Maritime Organisation.

As regards the remaining human activities having adverse effects on ecosystems and biodiversity, Appendix 3 contains a non-exhaustive list of criteria for identifying such activities. OSPAR Strategy on the Protection and Conservation of the Ecosystems and Biological Diversity of the Maritime Area (reference number: 1998–19)[28] contains a list of activities which the Commission is already assessing for the likely potential adverse effect on species which need to be protected, as:

(i) sand and gravel extraction;
(ii) dredging for navigational purposes, other than within harbours;
(iii) the exploration for oil, gas and solid minerals;
(iv) the placement of structures for the exploitation of oil and gas;
(v) the construction or placement of artificial islands, artificial reefs, installations and structures;
(vi) the placement of cables and pipelines. This assessment will include an assessment of the scope for action under other international laws;
(vii) the introduction of alien or genetically modified species, whether deliberately or unintentionally;
(viii) land reclamation.

3. OSPAR – The Secondary Level

As seen, the relatively general principles and obligations contained in the operative part of the Convention have, to a certain extent, been defined and clarified by its Annexes and Appendices. Thus, already the primary level allows for first conclusions as to the development of environmental standards by that Convention. This, however, is only the case if the yardsticks to be applied when evaluating the quality of the marine environment and when assessing potential hazards to it, and if the means to be applied in order to achieve the overall result are left out of consideration. Moreover, OSPAR remains what it was intended to be: a framework convention.[29] It is, thus, the secondary level which in view of the already impressive activities of

[28] Cf. *L. de La Fayette* (*supra* note 3), pp. 265 *et seq.*

[29] For a general evaluation of the framework approach see *U. Beyerlin* (*supra* note 10), pp. 41 *et seq.*; in the context of the OSPAR Convention see *J. Hilf* (*supra* note 3), pp. 583 *et seq.*; *L. de La Fayette* (*supra* note 3), p. 253.

the Commission and of its subsidiary bodies has to be focussed upon when it comes to environmental standards.

Although strategies do belong to the secondary level in many cases their provisions are rather general and vague. We will see, however, that when it comes to certain substances those strategies, too, have to be taken into account. Still, the real substance regarding environmental standards is contained in the decisions and recommendations.

It is important to note that the activities of the secondary level have not just begun in July 1998. As laid down in Article 31 para. 2, despite the replacement of the Oslo and Paris Conventions, decisions, recommendations and all other agreements adopted under those Conventions "shall continue to be applicable, unaltered in their legal nature.[30] Accordingly, 74 decisions and recommendations under OSPAR's predecessors, beginning from 1977, remain applicable within its framework. They cover value lists for certain substances, quality standards, reduction aims, control measures, in other words the whole spectrum of possible measures designed to reduce pollution of the marine environment by all kind of substances and by those activities falling within the scope of the Oslo and Paris Conventions. Moreover 39 agreements[31] regarding, *inter alia*, monitoring and guidelines for discharges, also remain applicable.

The emphasis, however, will have to be laid upon the activities within the OSPAR framework, i.e. on the period beginning in 1998. To this end it seems to be adequate to first give an overview of the decisions, recommendations, guidelines, strategies, and other agreements adopted in the period from 1998 to the present (see Table).[32] Presumably, it would not be a pleasant task to look at all these measures at the present occasion. Therefore, we will concentrate upon those decisions and recommendations of either a general interest or of high significance for the question we are concerned with here. Nevertheless, it needs to be stressed that, while e.g. eutrophication is not an issue of concern for Region I (Arctic Waters), it is a first priority class concern for Region II (Greater North Sea).[33] Hence, the Commission is prepared to implement its Strategy 1998–18 to Combat Eutrophication progressively by making every effort to combat eutrophication in the maritime area, in order to achieve, by the year 2010, a healthy marine environment where eutrophication does not occur.

---

[30] See OSPAR Decision 98/1 Concerning the Status of Decisions and Recommendations and Other Agreements Adopted under the Former Oslo Convention and Paris Convention within the Framework of the OSPAR Convention.

[31] *Ibid.*

[32] Source: summary record OSPAR 99/15/1, Annex 11. Any subsequent changes are indicated in the 'Note Memoire' as at Annex 2.

[33] Region III covers the Celtic Seas, Region IV the Bay of Biscay and Iberian Coast, Region V the Wider Atlantic. For the different threats in the different areas and for the action to be taken see the "Regional Quality Status Reports" of the OSPAR Commission.

Ref.-No.	*Category*	*Title/Subject*
98/1	Decision	Concerning the Status of Decisions and Recommendations and Other Agreements Adopted under the Former Oslo Convention and Paris Convention within the Framework of the OSPAR Convention
98/2	Decision	Dumping of Radioactive Waste
98/3	Decision	Disposal of Disused Offshore Installations
98/4	Decision	Emission and Discharge Limit Values for the Manufacture of Vinyl Chloride Monomer (VCM) including the Manufacture of 1,2-dichloroethane (EDC)
98/5	Decision	Emission and Discharge Limit Values for the Vinyl Chloride Sector, Applying to the Manufacture of Suspension-PVC (s-PVC) from Vinyl Chloride Monomer (VCM)
98/1	Recommendation	Best Available Techniques and Best Environmental Practice for the Primary Non-Ferrous Metal Industry (Zinc, Copper, Lead and Nickel Works)
98/2	Recommendation	Emission and Discharge Limit Values for Existing Aluminium Electrolysis Plants
99/1	Recommendation	Best Available Techniques for the Manufacture of Emulsion PVC (e-PVC)
2000/1	Decision	Substantial Reductions and Elimination of Discharges, Emissions and Losses of Radioactive Substances, with Special Emphasis on Nuclear Reprocessing
2000/2	Decision	Harmonised Mandatory Control System for the Use and Reduction of the Discharge of Offshore Chemicals
2000/3	Decision	Use of Organic-phase Drilling Fluids (OPF) and the Discharge of OPF-contaminated Cuttings
2000/1	Recommendation	Best Environmental Practice (BEP) for the Reduction of Inputs of Agricultural Pesticides to the Environment through the Use of Integrated Crop Management Techniques
2000/2	Recommendation	Best Environmental Practice (BEP) for the Use of Pesticides on Amenity Areas
2000/3	Recommendation	Emission and Discharge Limit Values for the Manufacture of Emulsion PVC (e-PVC) from Vinyl Chloride Monomer
2000/4	Recommendation	Harmonised Pre-Screening Scheme for Offshore Chemicals
2000/5	Recommendation	Harmonised Offshore Chemical Notification Format (HOCNF)
1998–3	JAMP Guidelines	Contaminant-specific Biological Effects Monitoring
1998–5	Principles	Comprehensive Study on Riverine Inputs and Direct Discharges (RID)
1998–6	Principles	Comprehensive Atmospheric Monitoring Programme (CAMP)
1998–11	Other	Working Procedures for the Group of Jurists/Linguists
1998–15.1	Other	The Protection and Conservation of the Ecosystems and Biological Diversity of the Maritime Area (cf. Annex 31 of OSPAR 98/14/1)
1998–15.2	Other	Meaning of certain concepts in Annex V to the 1992 OSPAR Convention
1998–16	OSPAR Strategy	Hazardous Substances
1998–17	OSPAR Strategy	Radioactive Substances
1998–18	OSPAR Strategy	Combat Eutrophication
1998–19	OSPAR Strategy	Protection and Conservation of the Ecosystems and Biological Diversity of the Maritime Area
1998–20	Guidelines	Management of Dredged Material

Ref.-No.	*Category*	*Title/Subject*
1998–21	Guidelines	Dumping of Fish Waste from Land-Based Industrial Fish Processing Operations
1999–1	JAMP Guidelines	Monitoring Contaminants in Sediments
1999–2	JAMP Guidelines	Monitoring Contaminants in Biota
1999–3	Other	Format and procedures for reporting basic information on national monitoring programmes in the maritime area
1999–4	Other	Structure of the QSRs
1999–5	Other	PRAM Procedure for the Collection and Assessment of Data and Information
1999–8	Guidelines	Preparation of Draft OSPAR Background Documents and Draft OSPAR Measures
1999–9	Other	List of Substances/Preparations Used and Discharged Offshore, which Pose Little or No Risk to the Environment (PLONOR)
1999–11	Guidelines	Submission of Information about, and the Assessment of, the Application of BAT in Nuclear Facilities
1999–12	Strategy	Environmental Goals and Management Mechanisms for Offshore Activities
1999–13	Guidelines	Artificial Reefs in relation to Living Marine Resources
1999–14	Other	Terms of Reference of, and Arrangements for the Coordination Committee
1999–15	Other	Agreement of Cooperation between IMO and OSPAR
2000–1	Other	OSPAR Coordinated Environmental Monitoring Programme (CEMP)
2000–2	Other	JAMP Guidance note on methods and criteria for harmonised sampling and analysis of PAHs in air and precipitation
2000–3	Other	Criteria for the selection of species and habitats
2000–4	Other	Reporting Formats on Mercury Losses from the Chlor Alkali Industry
2000–5	Guidelines	Completing the HOCNF
2000–6	Guidelines	Toxicity Testing of Substances and Preparations Used and Discharged Offshore
2000–7	Other	OSPAR List of Substances Liable to Cause Taint
2000–8	Other	Standard Implementation Reporting and Assessment Procedure
2000–9	Other	Timetable of Activities for the Review of BAT/BEP Measures Applicable under the OSPAR Convention
2000–10	Other	OSPAR List of Chemicals for Priority Action (Up-date 2000)
2000–11	Other	Programme for the More Detailed Implementation of the OSPAR Strategy with regard to Radioactive Substance
2000–12	Guidelines	Harmonised Quantification and Reporting Procedures for Nutrients (HARP-NUT)
2000–13	Other	Terms of Reference of OSPAR Committees
2000–14	Other	Staff Regulations of the Secretariat of the OSPAR Commission
2000–15	Other	Rules of Procedure of the OSPAR Commission
2000–16	Other	Procedure for publication of OSPAR reports
2000–17	Other	Procedure for Committees to decide on issues of a technical or scientific nature and to adopt "other agreements" that have no budgetary consequences for OSPAR

3.1. Offshore Installations

For the general public, of course, OSPAR Decision 98/3 on the Disposal of Disused Offshore Installations was of considerable importance in view of the *Greenpeace* camapaign surrounding the planned disposal of *Brent Spar*.[34] Today, according to para. 2 of that Decision the "dumping, and the leaving wholly or partly in place, of disused offshore installations within the maritime area is prohibited". However, para. 3 contains the following derogations which can be made for environmental or technical reasons:

(a) all or part of the footings of a steel installation in a category listed in Annex 1, placed in the maritime area before 9 February 1999, to be left in place;
(b) a concrete installation in a category listed in Annex 1 or constituting a concrete anchor base, to be dumped or left wholly or partly in place;
(c) any other disused offshore installation to be dumped or left wholly or partly in place, when exceptional and unforeseen circumstances resulting from structural damage or deterioration, or from some other cause presenting equivalent difficulties, can be demonstrated.

This is not the last word. According to para. 7 the Commission shall, in the light of experience in decommissioning offshore installations, in particular those in categories listed in Annex 1,[35] and in the light of relevant research and exchange of information, endeavour to achieve unanimous support for amendments to that Annex in order to reduce the scope of possible derogations under paragraph 3. The preparation of such amendments shall be considered by the Commission at its meeting in 2003 and at regular intervals thereafter.

The spectacular events to a certain extent overshadow the more persistent problem of preventing marine pollution from the operation of offshore installations.[36] In this regard Article 5 of the Convention provides:

> "The Contracting Parties shall take, individually and jointly, all possible steps to prevent and eliminate pollution from offshore sources in accordance with the provisions of the Convention, in particular as provided for in Annex III."

This provision is supplemented by Annex III.[37] However, that Annex in most of its parts relates to the dumping of offshore installations and is, thus, superseded by

---

34 For an analysis and for further references see *L. de La Fayette* (*supra* note 3), pp. 270 *et seq.*

35 Annex 1 on Categories of Disused Offshore Installations where Derogations may be considered lists: steel installations weighing more than ten thousand tons in air; gravity based concrete installations; floating concrete installations; and any concrete anchor-base which results, or is likely to result, in interference with other legitimate uses of the sea.

36 For an evaluation of the hazards see OSPAR Quality Status Report 2000, chapter 6.7.

37 Annex III on the Prevention and Elimination of Pollution from Offshore Sources.

Decision 98/3.[38] The remaining provisions are as general and vague as Article 5. In the time following the Sintra meeting the question was addressed by the Working Group on Sea-Based Activities (SEBA) whose efforts have resulted in the adoption of Strategy 1999–12 on Environmental Goals and Management Mechanisms for Offshore Activities. Pursuant to para. 3.1 of that Strategy the Commission will

> "carry forward the development of programmes and measures in respect of all phases of offshore activities in accordance with the provisions of the OSPAR Convention. This means that the Commission will address the programmes and measures:
> (a) needed to prevent, control and eliminate pollution under Annex III of the OSPAR Convention;
> (b) to be adopted under Annex V of the OSPAR Convention, once it has entered into force, following the identification of relevant human activities[39] by the application of the criteria in Appendix 3 of the OSPAR Convention;
> and, to these ends, will undertake activities as set out in the following paragraphs."

In June 2000 the following decisions were adopted at the meeting of the OSPAR Commission held in Copenhagen:

- Decision 2000/2 on a Harmonised Mandatory Control System for the Use and Reduction of the Discharge of Offshore Chemicals[40]
- Decision 2000/3 on the Use of Organic-Phase Drilling Fluids (OPF) and the Discharge of OPF-Contaminated Cuttings[41]

3.2. Radioactive Substances and Wastes

Pursuant to Article 3 para. 3 lit. (a) of Annex II on the Prevention and Elimination of Pollution by Dumping or Incineration dumping of low and intermediate level radioactive substances, including wastes, is prohibited. However, because of the French and British insistence upon an exception,[42] lit. (b) of that paragraph provided

38 As to former criticism see *L. de La Fayette* (*supra* note 3), pp. 274 *et seq.*

39 The first candidate list of human activities given in § 2.2 (c) of the OSPAR Strategy on the Protection and Conservation of the Ecosystems and Biological Diversity of the Maritime Area, which needs to be assessed in accordance with the criteria of Appendix 3 of the OSPAR Convention, includes, *inter alia*, the exploration for oil and gas and the placement of structures for the exploitation of oil and gas.

40 Entry into force: 16 January 2001. The purpose of this Decision is that by application of the management mechanisms set out in this Decision, authorities shall ensure and actively promote the continued shift towards the use of less hazardous substances (or preferably non-hazardous substances) and, as a result, the reduction of the overall environmental impact resulting from the use and discharge of offshore chemicals.

41 Entry into force: 16 January 2001. The purpose of this Decision is to prevent and eliminate pollution of the maritime area by the use and discharge of OPF and OPF-contaminated cuttings.

42 Cf. *L. de La Fayette* (*supra* note 3), p. 275.

that "those Contracting Parties, the United Kingdom and France, who wish to retain the option of an exception to subparagraph 3(a) in any case not before the expiry of a period of 15 years from 1st January 1993, shall report to the meeting of the Commission at ministerial level in 1997 on the steps taken to explore alternative land-based options".

France and the UK then accepted a ban on the dumping of radioactive waste under the 1972 London Dumping Convention.[43] Thus, at Sintra the ground was paved for adoption of OSPAR Decision 98/2 on Dumping of Radioactive Waste[44] which merely states that:

> "The exception, provided in subparagraph (b) of paragraph 3 of Article 3 of Annex II to the OSPAR Convention, to the prohibition, in subparagraph (a) of that paragraph, on the dumping of low and intermediate level radioactive substances, including wastes, shall not be continued."

Still, the problem of radioactive contamination of the marine environment remained unsolved because of the continuing introduction of radioactive substances from nuclear reprocessing facilities.[45] For this reason the Commission adopted Strategy 1998–17 with Regard to Radioactive Substances[46] that, in June 2000, was supplemented by a Programme for the More Detailed Implementation of the OSPAR Strategy with regard to Radioactive Substances[47] and by Decision 2000/1 on Substantial Reductions and Elimination of Discharges and Losses of Radioactive Substances, with Special Emphasis on Nuclear Reprocessing.[48] With the exception of France and the UK, who abstained from voting, the contracting parties have decided to review the current authorisations for discharges or releases of radioactive substances from nuclear reprocessing facilities as a matter of priority by their competent national authorities, with a view to, *inter alia*:

- implementing the non-reprocessing option (for example dry storage) for spent nuclear fuel management at appropriate facilities;
- taking preventive measures to minimise the risk of pollution by accidents.

---

43 In 1993, Annex 1 of the 1972 London Convention on the Prevention of Marine Pollution by the Dumping of Wastes and Other Matter (26 *UST* 2403, *TIAS* 8165) was amended by resolution LC 51(16), to also apply to radioactive wastes and other radioactive matter. That amendment entered into force in February 1994.

44 Entry into force: 9 February 1999.

45 Cf. *L. de La Fayette* (*supra* note 3), pp. 277 *et seq.*

46 That Strategy is "to prevent pollution of the maritime area from ionising radiation through progressive and substantial reductions of discharges, emissions and losses of radioactive substances, with the ultimate aim of concentrations in the environment near background values for naturally occurring radioactive substances and close to zero for artificial radioactive substances. In achieving this objective, the following issues should, *inter alia*, be taken into account: a. legitimate uses of the sea; b. technical feasibility; c. radiological impacts to man and biota.".

47 Reference number: 2000–11.

48 Entry into force: 16 January 2001.

It needs to be stressed that according to the Strategy, the Commission, by the year 2020, will ensure that discharges, emissions and losses of radioactive substances are reduced to levels where the additional concentrations in the marine environment above historic levels, resulting from such discharges, emissions and losses, are close to zero. This goal is being approached gradually, beginning with the collection of information and data and with the development of technical tools for assessing the impact of radioactive substances on the marine environment. The Working Group on Radioactive Substances (RAD), at its meeting in Luxembourg, 18–21 January 2000, has agreed on a long-term strategy[49] that

- is intended to give an overall overview and guidance on the issues and projects to be carried out under RAD. More detailed arrangements will be given e.g. in the annual update of the OSPAR Action Plan or in the agreed annual work programme for RAD;
- shall be updated at future meetings of RAD in accordance with the progress achieved and the necessary planning of RAD's future work;
- can be used as an indicator of progress made in implementing the OSPAR Strategy with regard to Radioactive Substances.

3.3. Hazardous Substances

In the Sintra Statement[50] ministers (and the member of the European Commission) have enunciated a very ambitious objective:

> "We agree to prevent pollution of the maritime area by continuously reducing discharges, emissions and losses of hazardous substances (that is, substances which are toxic, persistent and liable to bioaccumulate or which give rise to an equivalent level of concern), with the ultimate aim of achieving concentrations in the environment near background values for naturally occurring substances and close to zero for man-made synthetic substances. We shall make every endeavour to move towards the target of cessation of discharges, emissions and losses of hazardous substances by the year 2020."

Still, work on the subject is far from being characterised a success story.[51] Although Appendix 2 lists the criteria mentioned in paragraph 2 of Article 1 of Annex I and in paragraph 2 of Article 2 of Annex III and, in general terms, describes the substances which shall be subject to programmes and measures, not much progress has been made. In order to effectively protect the marine environment against hazardous substances it is necessary to develop programmes and measures to identify, prioritise,

---

49 Annex 6 (Ref. § 2.4c).

50 Ministerial Meeting of the OSPAR Commission, Sintra, 22–23 July 1998; Annex 45 (Ref. § B-10.2).

51 See, e.g., the Summary Record adopted at the Meeting of the Working Group on Radioactive Substances in Luxembourg, 18–21 January 2000.

monitor and control (i.e., to prevent and/or reduce and/or eliminate) the emissions, discharges and losses of hazardous substances which reach, or could reach, the marine environment. Because not all substances can be eliminated simultaneously and because at least for an interim period substitutes for hazardous substances have to be identified, a gradual approach has to be adopted that presupposes a system of prioritisation and risk management. This was agreed upon in the Strategy 1998–16 with regard to Hazardous Substances.[52] Of course, according to that Strategy the Commission will

> "apply the selection mechanism to substances and groups of substances of concern including those substances and groups of substances set out in the OSPAR 1998 List of Candidate Substances at Annex 3 in order to review the OSPAR List of Chemicals for Priority Action (cf. Annex 2) and to apply the prioritisation mechanism to rank these substances in order of priority."

The List of Chemicals for Priority Action[53] referred to contains the following substances:

Polychlorinated dibenzodioxins (PCDDs)
Polychlorinated dibenzofurans (PCDFs)
Polychlorinated biphenyls (PCBs)
Polyaromatic hydrocarbons (PAHs)
Pentachlorophenol (PCP)
Short chained chlorinated paraffins (SCCP)
Hexachlorocyclohexane isomers (HCH)
Mercury and organic mercury compounds
Cadmium
Lead and organic lead compounds
Organic tin compounds
Nonylphenol/ethoxylates (NP/NPEs) and related substances
Musk xylene
Brominated flame retardants
Certain Phthalates – Dibutylphthalate and Diethylhexylphthalate

It must be added that, in 1999, a further list was adopted, that enumerates

---

52 The list of activities to reach the objective comprises: 1. the selection and prioritisation of hazardous substances requiring elimination; 2. the identification of less-hazardous or non-hazardous substances to substitute for hazardous substances; 3. the development of programmes and measures (including BAT and BEP) to combat pollution; 4. monitoring; and 5. the assessment of implementation and effectiveness.

53 Annex 2 of the Strategy; see also Activities of OSPAR, July 1998 – June 1999, Implementation of the OSPAR Action Plan 1998–2003.

Substances/Preparations Used and Discharged Offshore, which Pose Little or No Risk to the Environment (PLONOR).[54]

The Commission has also established a Working Group on Priority Substances (SPS) and an *ad hoc* working group on the development of a dynamic selection and prioritisation mechanism (DYNAMEC) whose task is to update, where appropriate, the List of Chemicals for Priority Action by substances found in the List of Candidate Substances. In its meeting of November 2000 SPS has not only reported on a substantial progress of its work but has also stated that the application of the DYNAMEC mechanism is intended as a regular task, in particular with a view to giving expert advice to the Commission regarding the selection and identification of new hazardous substances for addition to the OSPAR List of Chemicals for Priority Action.[55]

Conclusion

The 1992 OSPAR Convention together with its Annexes and Appendices has, on the primary level, contributed to the development of environmental standards by

- giving legally binding force to a number of concepts and principles that until 1992 were merely applied on the secondary level of its predecessors and, if at all, of other international instruments;
- obliging its parties not merely to take measures to control and reduce certain sources of pollution but to take effective measures in order to protect ecosystems and biodiversity; thus
- taking a holistic approach to the problem of the degradation of the marine environment by human activities.

On the secondary level, on the basis of the OSPAR Action Plan 1998–2003, an impressive number of decisions, recommendations and agreements have been adopted that have truly developed – in a surprisingly ambitious and progressive manner – numerous environmental standards, especially on BAT and BEP, applicable criteria, and on certain substances, that are relevant not only for pollution control and reduction but also for the enlarged scope of application. The Quality Status Report 2000 gives evidence of the remarkable progress made so far – remarkable because OSPAR, though continuing the work done within the framework of the Oslo and Paris Conventions, is operative for less than 2 years only. Still, in view of the ambitious tasks there do remain some doubts whether the Convention's objectives

[54] Reference number: 1999–9. This list contains substances/preparations whose use and discharge off-shore: a. is subject to expert judgement by the competent national authority of Contracting Parties; or b. does not need to be strongly regulated as, from experience of their discharge the OSPAR Commission considers that they pose little or no risk to the environment.

[55] See, *inter alia*, the List of Actions Arising from the Meeting to be Undertaken by Contracting Parties Intersessionally adopted by the Working Group on Priority Substances at its meeting on 6–8 November 2000; (Ref. § 1.1).

will be achieved within the relatively short period of time available.[56] The more so since OSPAR is not but a regional approach whose success to a very large extent will depend on the efforts in other regions of the world aiming at a sustainable improvement of the marine environment.

56 See the OSPAR Action Plan 1998–2003.

*Rainer Lagoni**

MONITORING COMPLIANCE AND ENFORCEMENT OF COMPLIANCE THROUGH THE OSPAR COMMISSION

INTRODUCTION

The OSPAR Commission established by the Convention for the Protection of the Marine Environment of the North-East Atlantic (OSPAR Convention)[1] has several powers and functions under the Convention. Most important is its power to adopt decisions and recommendations by unanimous vote of the Contracting Parties. Under Art. 13 of the Convention, decisions of the OSPAR Commission become binding on the expiry of a period of two hundred days for the Contracting Parties that have voted for them unless they have not notified the Executive Secretary that they are unable to accept the binding effect.[2]

The OSPAR Commission undertakes and publishes at regular intervals quality status reports (QSRs) of the marine environment and of its development in the Convention area.[3] Such quality status reports[4] are being prepared under Art. 6 by the Commission on the basis of information provided by the Contracting Parties. Although the QSRs are not the subject matter of my paper, I mention them here because they are an important aspect of the reporting system under the OSPAR Convention.

Besides the QSRs the OSPAR Commission issues so-called implementation reports which are based on reports given by the Contracting Parties pursuant to Art. 22 OSPAR Convention. This article is the legal basis of the whole reporting system under the Convention.

And finally, under Art. 23 the OSPAR Commission shall, on the basis of the periodical reports of the Contracting Parties, assess their compliance with the Convention and the decisions and recommendations.

Hence, talking about "monitoring" the compliance of the Contracting Parties with the OSPAR Convention and about the enforcement of this compliance through the

* Professor Dr. iur., University of Hamburg.

1 *BGBl.* 1994 II 1360.

2 Art. 13(2) OSPAR Convention.

3 Art. 6 OSPAR Convention and Annex IV.

4 The OSPAR Commission published in December 2000 the Convention-wide Quality Status Report 2000 together with five regional reports for the regions I Arctic Waters, II the Greater North Sea, III the Celtic Seas, IV the Bay of Biscay and Iberian Coast, and V the Wider Atlantic.

P. Ehlers, E. Mann-Borgese and R. Wolfrum (eds.), Marine Issues, 155–163

OSPAR Commission – these are the two topics of my paper – means talking about Art. 23 of the OSPAR Convention.[5] But before turning to this article, I will give a brief overview first over the Convention and then over the reporting practice under Art. 22 of the Convention, because the compliance assessment of the OSPAR Commission pursuant to Art. 23 is closely linked to the reporting obligation of the Contracting Parties under Art. 22 of the Convention.

The OSPAR Convention

Signed in Paris on 22 September 1992 the OSPAR Convention entered into force on 25 March 1998 for 15 Western European States and the European Union. Contracting Parties are all States bordering the North-East Atlantic or the North Sea and Switzerland as an upstream State.[6] Finland, which is not bordering the Convention area,[7] is for traditional reasons also a Contracting Party.[8] The Convention relates to the maritime area between the east coast of Greenland and the European continent except the Mediterranean Sea and the Baltic Sea to which the Barcelona Convention and the Helsinki Convention apply. The area extends north of 36° north latitude (which is the latitude of Gibraltar) up to the North Pole, and between 42° west longitude and 51° east longitude. The "maritime area" under the Convention includes the internal waters (up to the freshwater limit) and the territorial seas of the Contracting Parties as well as their exclusive economic zones (or fisheries zones) and the High Seas.[9]

The OSPAR Convention was drafted to merge the preceding Oslo Convention for the Prevention of Marine Pollution by Dumping from Ships and Aircraft of 1972 and the Paris Convention for the Prevention of marine Pollution from Land-based Sources of 1974. The Oslo Convention was amended by Protocols in 1983 and 1989 and the Paris Convention by a Protocol in 1986. Both conventions had established their own Commissions. These Oslo and Paris Commissions have worked already as one entity since the signature of the OSPAR Convention in 1992.

The OSPAR Convention[10] has improved and modernised the preceding

[5] See the text of the articles in the annex to this paper.

[6] Upstream States that are no Contracting Parties are the Czech Republic and Luxembourg.

[7] Art. 1(a)(i) OSPAR Convention.

[8] Finland was already a Contracting Party of the Oslo Convention.

[9] Art. 1(a) OSPAR Convention.

[10] Generally to the Convention, see *E. Hey/T. Ijlstra/A. Nollkaemper*, The 1992 Paris Convention for the Protection of the Marine Environment of the North Sea, in: *IJMCL* 8 (1993), 1; *A. Gosseries*, Marine Pollution in the North Sea: The Position in International Law, in: *EELR* 3 (1994), 53; *J. Hilf*, The Convention for the Protection of the Marine Environment of the Northeast Atlantic, in: *ZaöRV* 55 (1995), 581; *R. Lagoni*, Das OSPAR-Übereinkommen von 1992 und der Schutz der Nordsee: Einwirkungen auf das deutsche Umweltrecht, in: *Koch/Lagoni* (eds.), *Meeresumweltschutz in Nord- und Ostsee*, pp. 79–101 (1996); *R. Salchow*, Protecting Oceans and Seas, in: *Dolzer/Thesing* (eds.), *Protecting our Environment*, pp. 131, 167–174.

Conventions of Oslo and Paris: It requires, *inter alia*, the application of the precautionary principle, the polluter pays principle, the best available technology and the best environmental practice, including clean technology.[11] It provides the OSPAR Commission with the power to adopt binding decisions,[12] allows the participation of observers (including NGOs), and establishes the right of access to information about the maritime area of the Convention.[13] Although it is replacing the Oslo and Paris Conventions, the decisions, recommendations and other agreements adopted under these conventions continue to be applicable under the OSPAR Convention until they are terminated.[14] This means, OSPAR is a continuation of the regional attempts made under the preceding Conventions of 1972 and 1974 including, however, the new environmental principles which have been developed since then.

The OSPAR Convention was still drafted as a classical instrument for the prevention and elimination of pollution of the marine environment in the region. For this purpose it deals, like its predecessors, with three different sources of pollution. These are pollution by dumping or incineration;[15] pollution from land-based sources;[16] and pollution from offshore sources.[17] Pollution by dumping or incineration, the subject matter of the former Oslo Convention, is of no relevance today, since dumping or incineration are no longer allowed in the Convention area. Pollution from land-based sources, however, remains the biggest source of marine pollution, whereas pollution from offshore sources is a regional factor in the areas of offshore activities in the North Sea. The Paris Convention dealt both with pollution from land-based and from offshore sources.[18] The OSPAR Convention does not regulate pollution from vessels,[19] which is the domain of the International Maritime Organisation (IMO).

But the OSPAR Convention is not limited to pollution prevention. The OSPAR strategies[20] regarding (a) the protection and conservation of ecosystems and biological diversity; (b) hazardous substances; (c) radioactive substances; (d) euthrophication; and (e) environmental goals and improved management mechanisms for the offshore oil and gas industry characterise it as a "Convention for the Protection of the Marine Environment" instead of a traditional pollution prevention

---

11 Art. 2 OSPAR Convention.

12 Art. 10(3) and 13(2) OSPAR Convention.

13 Art. 9 OSPAR Convention. See *www.ospar.org/eng/html/cp/welcome.html.*

14 Art. 31(2) OSPAR Convention.; see OSPAR Decision 98/1 of 23 July 1998, in: *BGBl.* 1999 II, 663, concerning the status of these decisions, recommendations and other agreements.

15 Art. 4 and Annex II OSPAR Convention.

16 Art. 3 and Annex I OSPAR Convention.

17 Art. 5 and Annex III OSPAR Convention.

18 According to Art. 3(c)(iii) Paris Convention, pollution from man-made structures under the jurisdiction of a Contracting Party in the Convention area was not considered a separate source of pollution, but a form of land-based pollution.

19 See the International Convention on the Prevention of Pollution from Ships 1973, as modified by the Protocol of 1978 (MARPOL 73/78), in: *BGBl.* 1982 II, 2.

20 See OSPAR Action Plan 1998 –2003, Update 2000, para. 33.

convention. OSPAR shall also protect the "maritime area against the adverse effects of human activities so as to safeguard human health, and to conserve marine ecosystems and, when practicable, restore marine areas which have been adversely affected".[21] This means, OSPAR is also an ecosystem protection Convention.[22] Annex V to the Convention, which entered into force on 30 August 2000,[23] contains detailed regulations for this purpose. Future decisions of the OSPAR Commission based on this Annex V "On the Protection and Conservation of the Ecosystems and Biological Diversity of the Maritime Area" will also provide for reporting under Art. 22 of the Convention.

Reporting to the Commission under Art. 22

Why is reporting essential for the prevention and elimination of marine pollution from land-based sources? It seems to me that there are two different reasons for this. First, such a goal can only be reached by co-ordinated action over a period of time. For technical and economic reasons the industrial sectors need time, before they can comply with the new legal requirements. Hence, already the Paris Convention and again the OSPAR Convention are legal instruments that follow certain strategies through a step by step approach aiming at a progressive development. Both Conventions state in their preambles that international action should be taken without delay "as part of progressive and coherent measures".[24] Accordingly the Paris Convention envisaged the elimination of even the most dangerous pollutants "if necessary by stages".[25] Implementation of the OSPAR Convention is a process, in which the Contracting Parties pursuant to Art. 2(3)(a) shall adopt programmes and measures, which contain, where appropriate, "time-limits for their completion". And when the Contracting Parties are bound thereby to "take full account of the use of the latest technological developments and practices", this involves a dynamic element of the implementation. We find the same gradual approach in the PARCOM and OSPAR decisions. They shall specify the timetable by which each decision shall be implemented, and they provide phasing-out periods for existing plants before such plants are to be included in the implementation reports.[26]

The second reason why reporting is essential for a regional convention on land-based pollution is supervision and control. Under Art. 10(2)(a) OSPAR Convention the Commission shall supervise the implementation of the Convention. Reporting

---

21 Art. 2(1)(a) OSPAR Convention.

22 Questions relating to the management of fisheries, however, are out of the scope of the Convention, see Preamble penultimate recital OSPAR Convention.

23 30 days after the ratification by 7 Contracting Parties; in Germany the ratification is still pending in the parliament.

24 Paris Convention 5th recital; OSPAR Convention 10th recital; however the Paris Convention aimed in its Preamble only at controlling this kind of pollution, whereas under OSPAR it shall be "prevented and eliminated".

25 Art. 4(1)(a) Paris Convention.

26 Art. 13(4) OSPAR Convention.

is, no doubt, the most appropriate means to control whether each party undertakes to ensure compliance with the provisions of a convention. Therefore already Art. 12(2) of the Paris Convention stipulated that the Contracting Parties "shall inform the Commission of the legislative and administrative measures they have taken to implement" their respective obligation to take such measures in their territories.[27] Accordingly the Paris Commission adopted in 1987 a practice to identify in its decisions the specific reporting obligations of the Contracting Parties with respect to the implementation of the specific measures envisaged in that decision.

The OSPAR Convention has added in Art. 22(1) several details to this obligation: The Contracting Parties shall report "at regular intervals" to the Commission. The reports shall not be limited to legal and regulatory measures, but shall also be on "other measures" taken by them in order to implement the Convention itself as well as the "decisions and recommendations" adopted under the Convention. Furthermore, the Contracting Parties shall report on the effectiveness of their implementing measures and on problems encountered in the implementation of the Convention or the decisions and recommendations of the Commission.

On the basis of Art. 22 the OSPAR Commission adopted a reporting procedure[28] according to which it prescribes in its decisions a standard format for the purpose of the implementation reports. This format determines the dates and periods when the reporting shall commence for new plants and existing plants.[29] In case of earlier PARCOM decisions, which did not identify the details of the implementation reports, reporting takes place on the basis of the standard procedure in an interval of 4 years.

The regular implementation reports consist of two sections. In the section on compliance, the Contracting Party shall report whether a reservation applies to the decision and whether the measure envisaged in the decision, as for example the introduction of emission and discharge limit values for certain chemicals, is applicable in the country. This may not be the case, for example, if there is no relevant chemical plant in its territory. The Contracting Party shall also report on the means of implementation, *i.e.* legislation, administrative action or negotiated agreement, and it shall give information on further details such as specific measures to give effect to the decision or special difficulties encountered in the implementation. In the other section on the effectiveness of the implementation, the Contracting Parties should endeavour to report on annual average emissions into the atmosphere and discharges into the waters on the basis of statistical information.

The double purpose of reporting – on the one hand, to facilitate the co-ordination of measures for the prevention of land-based pollution and, on the other hand, to enable the Commission to supervise and control the implementation measures of the Contracting Parties – explains why reporting under Art. 22 OSPAR Convention

---

27 In addition they had, in accordance with a standard procedure, to transmit to the Commission the results of monitoring and information on dangerous substances, Art. 17 Paris Convention.

28 OSPAR's Standard Implementation Reporting and Assessment Procedure.

29 See for example OSPAR Decision 98/4 para. 5 and Appendix, in: *BGBl.* 1999 II, 630; OSPAR Decision 98/5 para. 5 and Appendix, in: *BGBl.* 1999 II, 640.

includes also recommendations adopted by the Commission. Although they are not binding, their implementation is subject to control. Such recommendations can provide the basis for voluntary measures undertaken by the Contracting Parties under the Convention, and therefore they form an integral part of the whole implementation process which shall be supervised by the Commission. This is obviously meant when some authors write that the recommendations "shall be taken seriously"[30] by the Contracting Parties.

Assessment of Compliance through the Commission

The implementation reports form also the basis for an assessment of the compliance with the Convention and the decisions and recommendations adopted thereunder. The OSPAR Commission shall undertake such an assessment pursuant to Art. 23 lit. (a) of the Convention. Assessing the compliance through the Commission was still unknown to the Oslo and Paris Conventions or to other conventions on the protection of the marine environment, even to the Helsinki Convention of 1992.[31] There was only one example of compliance assessment in international law by then, which was the Montreal Protocol on Substances that Deplete the Ozone Layer of 1987.[32]

However, Art. 23 lit. (a) does not determine the procedure of assessing the compliance.[33] Nevertheless, it seems that any such assessment on the basis of the implementation reports would itself necessarily end up in a separate "compliance report" (unless it would be included in the quality status reports mentioned earlier). But according to the available information, the OSPAR Commission has not published any such report as yet. This can be explained with the short time of less than two years, since the OSPAR Convention has entered into force.

As the monitoring of the Contracting Parties' activities with respect to the individual decisions and recommendations is achieved in detail through the implementation reports, the compliance assessment under Art. 23 lit. (a) must apparently have other purposes as well. The assessment by the Commission of the compliance with the Convention and its decisions and recommendations provides a comprehensive overview over the relevant practice of the Contracting Parties under the OSPAR Convention. In the first line this enables the Commission "generally to review the effectiveness of the measures being adopted, the priorities and the need for any additional or different measures", as it is its obligation under Art. 10(2)(b) OSPAR Convention. Besides this, the compliance assessment under Art. 23 lit. (a) must also be considered in the context of the OSPAR's information policy. A compliance report

---

30 *Hey/Ijlstra/Nollkaemper* (*supra* note 10), p. 45.

31 Convention on the Protection of the Marine Environment of the Baltic Sea Area of 9 April 1992, in: *BGBl.* 1994 II, 139.

32 Of 16 September 1987, 26 *ILM* 1541 (1987) with amendments of 1990 and 1993. As to the differences see *Hilf* (*supra* note 10), p. 593.

33 Neither do the Rules of Procedure of the OSPAR Commission.

would also be an instrument of information of the general public rather than of controlling the individual Contracting Parties. Pursuant to Art. 9(2) of the Convention, any natural or legal person has a right of information "on the state of the maritime area, on activities or measures adversely affecting or likely to affect it and activities or measures introduced in accordance with the Convention."

Enforcement of Compliance through the Commission

However, assessing compliance through the OSPAR Commission would remain after all a dog without teeth, if the Commission would not have any power *vis á vis* a Contracting Party or Contracting Parties that do not comply with their obligations under the Convention or the decisions. This power, which is provided in Art. 23 lit. (b), makes the Commission the guardian of the Convention. It can, "when appropriate", decide upon and call for steps to bring about full compliance with the Convention and decisions adopted thereunder. Whether or not it is "appropriate" to decide upon steps and the nature of such steps depend upon the circumstances of the particular situation as, *e.g.*, the particular reasons for the non-compliance, its gravity or scope. The usual means would be consultations with the Contracting Party concerned. Accordingly, the standard implementation rules of individual decisions require the Contracting Parties also to provide information on the reasons for not having fully implemented the measure concerned and to spell out clearly plans for the implementation. But Art. 23 lit. (b) mentions also "measures" of the Commission "to assist a Contracting Party to carry out its obligations". It does not indicate, however, the nature of such measures. They could certainly be of an administrative nature, such as postponing an implementation date for a Contracting Party. Or they could include technical or scientific help or even economic assistance, although the Commission is hardly the appropriate forum for the latter, as it has rightly been observed.[34]

In accordance with the obligation of the Contracting Parties to report on their implementation, the OSPAR Commission shall also "promote the implementation of recommendations" under Art. 23 lit. (b). Yet, because the decision to implement a recommendation is of a purely political nature, measures taken by the Commission for this purpose could merely assist the Contracting Parties concerned, but in no way bind them.

An interesting legal, however hardly practical, question is whether the power of the OSPAR Commission under Art. 23 lit. (b) would also include enforcement measures against a Contracting Party. According to the text of Art. 23 lit. (b), the Commission shall "decide upon ... steps to bring about full compliance". Notwithstanding this, the answer is obviously to the negative,[35] because the decision

[34] *Hey/Ijlstra/Nollkaemper* (*supra* note 10), p. 45.

[35] *Hey/Ijlstra/Nollkaemper* (*supra* note 10), p. 45, regard it as "highly unlikely than anything other than orthodox political power will be used" in this context. *Hilf* (*supra* note), p. 593, considers it as "doubtful whether sanctions would be included hereby.".

would not be unanimous and therefore it would not become binding under Art. 13 OSPAR Convention for the Contracting Party concerned. Moreover the Commission has no particular powers with respect to enforcement measures against a non-complying party,[36] such a suspension of membership of the right to vote under Art. 20.

This view is further underlined by the role of the OSPAR Commission in dispute settlement. The binding settlement of disputes relating to the interpretation or application of the Convention by way of arbitration is reserved in Art. 32(1) to the Contracting Parties, whereas the Commission is only the forum within which non-binding dispute settlement, such as "inquiry or conciliation" can take place between the Contracting Parties. This means, the Commission itself cannot be a party to the procedures.

Conclusions

The obligation of member States to report to a commission at regular intervals on the measures they have taken with respect to the implementation of a treaty or a convention is nowadays not new in international law, and we know it also from EU directives. In case of a regional convention for the protection of the marine environment against land-based pollution and for the preservation of ecosystems, reporting is essential for the effectiveness of long term strategies under the convention.

Reporting under Art. 22 OSPAR Convention relates to compliance with OSCOM and OSPAR decisions and recommendations and on the effectiveness of the measures taken. As the implementation reports are linked to the individual decisions and recommendations, the whole reporting system under the Convention is a dynamic procedure.

The assessment of compliance through a commission, however, is a recent development in international law, unlike in EU law. Under the OSPAR Convention implementation assessment is closely linked to the reporting system. It enables the Commission to request information and to assist in the implementation by way of technical or administrative measures. But it does not give the OSPAR Commission the power to take any enforcement measures *vis á vis* a Contracting Party.

Annex: OSPAR Convention

Article 22 – Reporting to the Commission

The Contracting Parties shall report to the Commission at regular intervals on:

(a) the legal, regulatory, or other measures taken by them for the implementation

36 The only exceptions are rules 55, 56 of the OSPAR Rules of Procedure in case of arrears with the contribution to the budget. But again, the Commission shall decide, when a Contracting Party is in arrears for more than 12 months (rule 56).

of the provisions of the Convention and of decisions and recommendations adopted thereunder, including in particular measures taken to prevent and punish conduct in contravention of those provisions;
(b) the effectiveness of the measures referred to in subparagraph (a) of this Article;
(c) problems encountered in the implementation of the provisions referred to in subparagraph (a) of this Article.

Article 23 – Compliance

The Commission shall:
(a) on the basis of the periodical reports referred to in Article 22 and any other report submitted by the Contracting Parties, assess their compliance with the Convention and the decisions and recommendations adopted thereunder;
(b) when appropriate, decide upon and call for steps to bring about full compliance with the Convention, and decisions adopted thereunder, and promote the implementation of recommendations, including measures to assist a Contracting Party to carry out its obligations.

*Francesco Saverio Civili**

THE MEDITERRANEAN MARINE ENVIRONMENT: PRESSURES, STATE OF POLLUTION AND MEASURES TAKEN (THE BARCELONA CONVENTION AND THE MEDITERRANEAN ACTION PLAN)

THE PRESSURES

The resident population of the Mediterranean coastal states almost doubled in the last 40 years, reaching 450 million in 1997. Although the current mean rate of population growth of 1.3% per year is already showing signs of a decreasing trend, the population of the coastal states of the Mediterranean is expected to reach approximately 600 million in 2050 and possibly 700 million by the end of the 21st century. At present, one third of the Mediterranean population, around 145 million people, is concentrated on the narrow coast.

The pressure exerted on the Mediterranean coast from the heavy resident population load, is dramatically amplified by the intensive seasonal increase in the population from tourism. Owing to its mild climate, its extraordinary natural beauty and its rich cultural heritage, the Mediterranean has become one of the prime tourist destinations in the world. At least 50% of the tourists arriving in the Mediterranean are concentrated on the coast, while in some countries coastal tourism represents up to 90% of the total.

The dense human settlements established along the Mediterranean coast produce large amounts of municipal wastewater. Residences, hotels, other tourist facilities and businesses are usually, though not always, connected to municipal sewer systems. These systems may, or may not (as is the case for a large number of small and medium size communities in the Mediterranean) be connected to wastewater treatment facilities so that wastewater is discharged into the sea either untreated or after various degrees of treatment. It enters the sea through outfalls, or by seepage resulting from leaks or other faults in the sewerage system. Wastewater treatment plants today serve around 55% of 545 coastal cities with more than 10,000 inhabitants, in 19 Mediterranean countries reviewed by WHO/EURO as part of the MED POL Programme.[1]

---

* Dr. Senior Environmental Affairs Officer, MED POL Programme Coordinator, UNEP/MAP, Athens, Greece, *fscivili@unepmap.gr*.

1 *UNEP/WHO*, Municipal Wastewater Treatment Plants in Mediterranean Coastal Cities, in: *MAP TRS* 128, 63 *et seq*. (UNEP Athens 2000).

P. Ehlers, E. Mann-Borgese and R. Wolfrum (eds.), Marine Issues, 165–176

The Mediterranean drainage basin has from the earliest of times been subjected to exhaustive farming, grazing and the destruction of its forests to meet the food demand of a growing population.

In most Mediterranean countries all agricultural practices and land use including cultivation, irrigation, dairy farming, pastures and animal feedlots are considered as non-point sources of pollution. Agriculture may be only one of a number of non-point sources of pollution through run-off water, sediment transport and leaching, carrying phosphorus, nitrogen, pesticides, metals, pathogens, salts and trace elements, but has become the largest non-point contributor of pollutants to the Mediterranean. These pollutants gradually find their way, through groundwater, wetlands and rivers to the sea in the form of sediment and chemical loads. In particular, with the intensification of agriculture, the use of pesticides has greatly increased in the Mediterranean in the last twenty years, threatening the quality of ground and surface waters, human health and ecosystems.

More than 200 petrochemical and energy installations, basic chemical industries and chlorine plants are located along the narrow Mediterranean coast and catchment basins of rivers, including at least 40 major oil refineries, in addition to cement plants, steel mills, tanneries, food processing plants, textile mills and pulp and paper mills.

The activity of these industries exerts pressure in a number of ways on the Mediterranean environment. Owing to the narrowness of the coastal zone, industries compete strongly with other land uses such as agriculture and housing for an expanding urban population. Some industrial activities, especially the agro-food sector, the iron and steel and the paper industries, are also highly demanding of water. The industrial need for water in the Mediterranean countries is close to 14,000 m^3 a year. Although three quarters of this water is consumed by industries in the northern part of the Mediterranean, the effect is most serious in areas with low water resources. Industrial pollutants impact the air primarily through emissions of sulphur oxides, nitrogen oxides and carbon monoxide, some of which are responsible for acid rain phenomena in the Mediterranean. Carbon dioxide emissions are also largely due to industry. Industrial solid wastes consisting of slag from coal mining, coal processing and steel making, sludge from the processing of ores, dust and combustion ashes and mine tailings may end up on land, in the form of landfill, into rivers or into the Mediterranean sea directly. The mining of mercury is an especially important problem since Mediterranean countries, occupying about 0.5% of the Earth's surface, undertake more than half of the world's mercury mining (from 60% to 85% according to estimates for different years) and provide no less than half of the world supply. Industrial wastewater is an important carrier of pollutants, including oils, heavy metals, detergents, solvents and organic chemicals as well as heated cooling water to the Mediterranean aquatic environment.

Industrial wastewater is either discharged directly to the sea or through municipal sewerage systems, outfalls, uncontrolled disposal sites and rivers. A survey of pollutants from land based sources in the Mediterranean, which was carried out by WHO as part of the MED POL Programme, showed that the annual load of 66 million m^3 untreated industrial wastewater which entered the sea directly from several Mediterranean countries, was responsible for roughly 36% of BOD, 30% of COD, 3% of nutrients, 92% of phenols, 7% of mercury, 37% of lead, 40% of chromium, 24% of zinc and close to 100% of mineral oils, relative to the total pollution load entering the sea from those countries each year. Rivers are important conveyors of industrial pollutants to the Mediterranean. There is documented evidence of contamination of the Po, Ebro and Rhone, large rivers draining into the Mediterranean, with polychlorinated biphenyls (PCBs), polycyclic aromatic hydrocarbons (PAHs) and solvents.[2]

The State of Pollution

The open waters of the Mediterranean are considered as oligotrophic (nutrient depleted) and in some parts as ultra-oligotrophic, except in areas where the upwelling of nutrient-rich waters occurs. Although there is a reported increase in the last ten years of the concentrations of nitrates and phosphates in the intermediate and deep waters of certain parts of the Mediterranean,[3] it is mainly along certain coastal sites and the offshore areas nearby, where eutrophication occurs.

Almost all coastal Mediterranean countries are affected by eutrophication, although at varying levels and most incidents have been reported for the northern Mediterranean (i.e. the bays of the Ebro delta, the Albufera of Valencia, the bays of the Rhone delta, the gulf of Saronikos, the gulf of Thermaikos, the bay of Izmir)[4] . The most important areas of extensive eutrophication are the gulf of Lyons and the northern Adriatic coast, particularly along the semi-enclosed bays of the Po delta, the gulf of Venice and the gulf of Trieste on the Italian coast. The Slovenian coast and the bays of Pula, Rijeka, Kastela, Sibenik and Dubrovnik in Croatia also suffer. The key features of the Adriatic, which make it most vulnerable, are believed to be its shallowness, low turbulence during the summer and the high riverine nutrient input. Although not documented as extensively as for the northern Mediterranean, serious eutrophication problems also exist in the southern countries (as in the coastal waters and lagoons of the Nile delta in Egypt and the coastal lagoons of Tunisia and Algeria) and are likely to increase in the future, following increases in the population and further industrial development.

The main cause of microbiological contamination of the Mediterranean Sea is the discharge of untreated or partially treated sewage in coastal waters. Considerable

---

2 *M. Meybeck/A. Ragu*, River discharges to the oceans: An assessment of suspended solids, major ions and nutrients, in: *UNEP*, *Environmental Information and Assessment* (April 1997).

3 *E. Souvermezoglou/E. Krasakopoulou/A. Pavlidou*, Temporal variability in oxygen and nutrient concentrations in the South Aegean Sea and the Straits of the Cretan Arc, in: *PiO* 44 (1999), 573–600.

4 *UNEP/FAO/WHO*, Assessment of the state of eutrophication in the Mediterranean Sea, in: *MAP TRS* 106, 456 *et seq.* (UNEP Athens 1996).

amounts of untreated municipal wastewater enter the Mediterranean each year.[5] Upstream wastewater discharges carried by rivers to the sea also contribute to the problem, in addition to wind blown bacteria, viruses and parasites carried from the continents and rain-deposited into rivers and the sea. The large number of bathers may be the source of pathogenic microorganisms in crowded bathing waters that are not affected by sewage effluent.

The health risk from microbiological contamination is particularly significant in the Mediterranean, owing to the warm climate which allows an extended exposure to seawater and sand of a large number of bathers on crowded beaches in the summer, coupled with the consumption of large quantities of seafood in the coastal areas of the Mediterranean, while considerable amounts of untreated sewage are discharged into coastal waters, in many cases in the vicinity of recreational and shellfish-growing areas.

The presence of the heavy metals mercury, cadmium and lead and chlorinated hydrocarbons in the marine environment has been the focus of attention in recent years as these substances are persistent, toxic and easily bioaccumulated and have detrimental effects on marine life and human health.

Heavy metals enter the marine environment from natural and man-made sources. Land based inputs of heavy metals to the Mediterranean cause local pollution problems, usually near river-mouths and coastal industrial outfalls. At the coastal industrial zones with high mercury concentrations, identified in the early 1970's (in Tuscany, Kastella Bay near Split, St Gilla Lagoon in the Sardinia Channel, Haifa Bay and Alexandria) the highest concentrations of mercury were measured near the outfalls. Background concentrations may be reached at distances of up to 20 km from an outfall.

With the exception of mercury in sediments and biota, the concentrations of heavy metals in open waters, sediments and biota are generally low.[6] The higher mercury levels are possibly the result of the region being in the Mediterranean-Himalayan "mercuriferous" belt.[7] Pollution of the Mediterranean Sea by man-made inputs of mercury occurs through the atmosphere and through riverine runoff. A part of the riverine runoff of mercury, i.e. between 10–40 tonnes per year, and the bulk of the atmospheric deposition which is also between 10–40 tonnes per year come to the Mediterranean Sea as soluble mercury compounds which can be assimilated by the marine biota and can affect marine life.[8]

Most mercury values of total (organic and inorganic) mercury in marine organisms (extracted from the MED POL database, only values obtained after 1987) are below

---

5 *UNEP/WHO* (*supra* note 1).

6 *UNEP/WHO*, Identification of Priority Pollution Hot Spots and Sensitive Areas in the Mediterranean, in: *MAP TRS* 124, 102 *et seq.* (UNEP Athens 1999).

7 *G.W. Bryan*, Heavy metal contamination in the sea, in: *R. Johnston* (ed.), *Marine Pollution*, pp. 185–302 (London 1976); *M. Bernhard*, Mercury in the Mediterranean, in: *RSRS* 98 (UNEP 1988).

8 *UNEP/WMO*, Atmospheric Input of Mercury to the Mediterranean Sea, in: *MAP TRS* 122, 78 *et seq.* (UNEP Athens 1998).

the minimum legal limit for seafood intended for human consumption (500 ng/g). The concentrations in tuna are for small specimens and are much lower than the levels of mercury found in the larger specimens. Total mercury concentrations exceeded 1000 ng/g only in swordfish from the central Mediterranean and the gastropod *Gibbous nassa* from Israel.

High concentrations of cadmium (up to 50 mg/kg) have been measured in the sediments of coastal lagoons and other hot spots in the Mediterranean.[9] Elsewhere, the values obtained in the surface sediments are lower than the limits adopted for sediment quality criteria.[10] The mean cadmium values[11] do not exceed 200 ng/g FW. Cadmium concentrations exceeded 1000 ng/g in some other species (the gastropod *Nassarius gibbosulus* from Israel, the bivalve *Scapharca inequivalis* from Italy and the limpet *Patella caerulea* from Greece).

Increased concentrations of lead are found near highly industrialized coastal areas. In estuarine sediments lead concentrations drop off rapidly within a few kilometers from known anthropogenic point sources.[12] Elsewhere, the concentrations of lead in the surface sediments are lower than the limits adopted by different countries (55–500 mg/kg) for sediment quality criteria.[13] The concentrations of lead shown for demersal fish are very low, rarely exceeding 600 ng/g.

Tributyltin (TBT) is an organo-metallic compound, used mainly as a biocide in antifouling paints of ships and boats. It is an endocrine disrupting chemical whose toxic effect is well documented in mollusks, including sex reversal effects in dogwhelks. Now the effects on seabirds, marine mammals and fish are becoming evident all over the world. TBT is detected all over the Mediterranean basin. The levels in seawater are highest (up to 12.150 ng/l) in marinas, commercial shipping areas and shipyards.[14] Elsewhere, most of the seawater concentrations reported are comparable to a "No Observed Effect Level" (20ng TBT/l), although the provisional safe level recommended by the WHO to protect aquatic life and seafood consumers is 10ng TBT/l.[15]

Organochlorines are the most important group of POPs. They are released into the marine environment only from man-made sources. In the 1980s at least 560

---

9 *UNEP/FAO/WHO*, Assessment of the State of pollution of the Mediterranean Sea by cadmium and cadmium compounds, in: *MAP TRS* 34, 175 *et seq.* (UNEP Athens 1989).

10 *R. Baudo/H. Muntau*, Lesser Known In-Place Pollutants and Diffuse Source Problems, in: *R. Baudo/J. Gisey/H. Muntau* (eds.), *Sediments: Chemistry and Toxicity of In-Place Pollutants*, pp. 1–14 (1990).

11 *F. Voutsinou-Taliadouri*, Survey of metal pollution in Greek sediments, in: *VIIes Journées Etud. Pollutions*, pp. 251–259 (CIESM Lucerne 1984).

12 *Baudo/Muntau* (*supra* note 10); *J. Giesy/R. Hooke*, Freshwater Sediment Quality Criteria: Toxicity Bioassessment, in: *R. Baudo/J. Gisey/H. Muntau* (eds.), *Sediments: Chemistry and Toxicity of In-Place Pollutants*, pp. 256–348 (1990).

13 *UNEP*, The State of the Marine and Coastal Environment in the Mediterranean Region, in: *MAP TRS* 100, pp. 142 *et seq.* (UNEP Athens 1996).

14 *WHO*, Tributyltin Compounds, in: *Environmental Health Criteria* 116 (WHO Geneva 1990).

15 *UNEP*, State of the Mediterranean Marine Environment, in: *MAP TRS* 28, pp. 225 *et seq.* (UNEP Athens 1989).

tonnes of organochlorines were discharged into the Mediterranean each year, including 196 tonnes of DDTs and similar compounds.[16] The two main types of organochlorines monitored in the Mediterranean are chlorinated pesticides and polychlorinated biphenyls. The concentration of DDT in the sediments of the Rhone delta (675 ng/g dry weight) is typical of the concentrations found in heavily polluted areas. PCB concentrations in sediments are elevated (up to 228 ng/g dry weight) in the vicinity of coastal industrialized zones in the Mediterranean.

The distribution of concentrations of PCBs and DDTs in Mediterranean marine organisms, based on data from the MED POL database show a lower level than the pre-1987 values. The maximum concentrations of PCBs and DDTs in mussels are much lower than the permissible limits for seafood consumption (1–5 μg/g) adopted in some countries.[17] The concentrations of PCBs and DDTs in sardines from the northwestern Mediterranean and swordfish from the central Mediterranean exceeded the values shown. Marine mammals are the most susceptible to minute concentrations of PCBs and other organochlorines in the marine environment, as these contaminants are biomagnified and bioaccumulated in the food chain. Because the sea is the final destination of the bulk of the PCBs released into the environment, the fatty tissue of marine mammals contain concentrations far greater than those found in terrestrial top predators. Dolphins in the Mediterranean are among the marine mammals most highly contaminated by PCBs and DDTs and evidence exists for a link with reproductive disorders and immunosuppression.[18]

Although incidents at oil terminals account for just above one tenth of the accidents causing pollution of the sea by petroleum hydrocarbons in the Mediterranean, these incidents along with routine discharges from land-based installations contribute to elevated concentrations of petroleum hydrocarbons in the marine environment around the 40 or so oil related sites (pipelines, terminals and refineries) and at industrial outfalls scattered along the Mediterranean coast. The survey of pollutants from land-based sources in the Mediterranean, which was carried out by WHO as part of the MED POL Programme showed that the equivalent of 12.5 metric tons processed oil per million were discharged annually into the marine environment from 13 refineries in 6 countries (Albania, Algeria, Cyprus, Spain, Syria and Turkey) submitting information during the period of the land-based sources survey.

The Measures Taken

As early as the 1970s it became obvious to the countries surrounding the Mediterranean Sea that although human activities at sea led to marine pollution, its origin was mainly to be found in land-based activities. As a result, the countries

---

16 *WHO/UNEP*, Health Risks from Marine Pollution in the Mediterranean, Part II: Review of Hazards and Health Risks, Doc. EUR/ICP/EHAZ 94 01/MT01 (2), pp. 225 *et seq.* (World Health Organization Regional Office for Europe Copenhagen 1995).

17 *UNEP* (*supra* note 13).

18 *UNEP/WHO* (*supra* note 16).

devoted particular attention to the preparation of an appropriate legal instrument to cover this aspect of marine pollution. Shortly after adopting the Mediterranean Action Plan (MAP) and the Barcelona Convention for the Protection of the Mediterranean Sea Against Pollution, the Contracting Parties adopted and signed the Protocol for the Protection of the Mediterranean Sea against Land Based Sources (LBS Protocol).

The LBS Protocol entered into force in June 1983 and a calendar of activities for its implementation through the MED POL Programme of Monitoring and Research in the Mediterranean Sea was set by the countries in the period from 1985 to 1995, including assessments of priority pollutants listed in the Annexes I and II of the LBS Protocol, as well as the development of guidelines on various aspects of waste management covered by the protocol. On the basis of the assessments of the state of pollution of the Mediterranean Sea by individual substances listed in the LBS Protocol, the Contracting Parties progressively adopted, between 1985 and 1993, a number of Common Pollution Control Measures.

The 1992 Earth Summit in Rio signaled a change in the pace of events that eventually consolidated the shift in the direction of the MED POL Programme towards action for the prevention and control of pollution from land based activities. Shortly after the Rio summit the Mediterranean States, wanting to give effect at the Mediterranean level to the Agenda 21 resolutions, approved an Agenda MED 21 promoting the integration of environmental concerns in environmental policies in the Mediterranean. This was closely followed by the revision of the Barcelona Convention in 1995, to give legal status to the commitments made at Rio. In the same year, 108 countries and the European Commission adopted the Washington Declaration, a commitment to protect and preserve the marine environment from the impacts of land based activities through *inter alia* giving priority to the implementation of the Global Programme of Action for the Protection of the Marine Environment from Land-Based Activities (GPA). The subsequent events in the Mediterranean in the field of land based pollution control show that the Mediterranean countries are putting into practice the goals of the GPA on a regional level.

In 1996, the Contracting Parties to the Barcelona Convention signed a revision of the Protocol for the Protection of the Mediterranean Sea Against Pollution from Land-Based Sources (LBS Protocol).

Under the revised LBS Protocol, the Mediterranean States agreed to take measures to prevent and control the degradation of the Mediterranean Sea area caused by land based sources and activities originating in their territories, including discharges from rivers, outfalls and coastal establishments. Substances that are toxic, persistent and liable to bioaccumulate are placed first in the list of priority substances to be phased out.

The amended protocol, under the new title of "Protocol for the Protection of the Mediterranean Sea Against Pollution from Land-Based Sources and Activities" covers not only the Mediterranean Sea itself, but also the entire watershed area within the territories of the riparian states draining into the Mediterranean Sea, the waters on the landward side of territorial boundaries as well as communicating brackish waters, marshes, coastal lagoons and ground water.

The signature of the amended LBS Protocol is a milestone in the history of the Mediterranean Action Plan, as it sets the legal framework for a progression from land-based pollution assessment to taking strong action on pollution control.

One of the major breakthroughs in the Mediterranean countries' efforts to combat land-based pollution, which was prompted by the signature of the revised LBS Protocol, is the preparation and adoption by the Contracting Parties of a Strategic Action Programme (SAP) of regional and national activities to address land-based pollution.[19]

The SAP is an action-oriented MED POL initiative identifying priority target categories of substances and activities to be eliminated or controlled by the Mediterranean countries through a timetabled schedule for the implementation of specific control measures and interventions. The SAP is the basis for the implementation of the Land Based Sources Protocol by the Mediterranean countries in the next 25 years. In addition, the SAP represents the regional adaptation of the principles and aims of the Global Programme of Action (GPA) to address pollution from land-based activities, adopted in Washington in 1995.

The key land-based activities addressed in the SAP are linked to the urban environment (particularly municipal wastewater treatment and disposal, urban solid waste disposal and activities contributing to air pollution from mobile sources), and to industrial activities, targeting those responsible for the release of toxic persistent and bioaccumulative substances into the marine environment, giving special attention to persistent organic pollutants (POPs).

A FOCUS ON THE THIRD PHASE OF MED POL

Bringing the MED POL Programme closer to the spirit of the amended LBS Protocol

In the first and second phase of MED POL (1975–1995) the coastal states participated in a Mediterranean research and monitoring programme and eventually designed and implemented marine pollution national monitoring programmes. At the same time research provided continuous new information on the state of the Mediterranean Sea and contributed to the improved understanding of the effects of pollutants. In 1996 MED POL entered its third phase. Known as the Programme for the Assessment and Control of Pollution in the Mediterranean Region (1996–2005) or MED POL Phase III, the third phase of MED POL combines the experience gained from the two previous phases, with the new concepts for assessment, prevention and elimination of marine pollution set out in MAP Phase II which, in line with UNCED and Agenda 21, focuses on activities that contribute to sustainable development. Through placing greater emphasis than in the past on pollution control, the countries have brought the programme closer to the spirit

[19] *UNEP*, Strategic Action Programme to Address Pollution from Land-Based Activities (UNEP Athens 1999).

of the amended LBS Protocol. *This is presently being achieved in practice through giving priority to activities that are directly linked to the implementation of the SAP, in effect also contributing to the implementation by the Mediterranean countries of the goals of the GPA. The MED POL component has an essential coordinating role in this direction.*

Providing the scientific basis for the implementation of the LBS Protocol

Through the continuous assessment of pollution related problems, MED POL Phase III provides the Mediterranean countries with the scientific basis and the rationale for the implementation of the amended LBS Protocol. The assessment component of MED POL Phase III is designed to assist the countries to take measures to combat marine pollution, particularly from land-based sources, through providing them with appropriate information to identify the sources and loads of pollution, the levels and trends of contaminants and to assess potential threats to the Mediterranean environment. A new type of monitoring introduced in the third phase of MED POL aims at providing the countries with a tool for assessing the change over time in the environmental levels of chemical contaminants, with a given degree of confidence. This is known as *trend monitoring*. To achieve this, the trend monitoring programme must be designed in such a way that will minimize variations from other sources of change such as biological and environmental variables and variables in analytical methods. *When this type of monitoring takes place in areas under the direct influence of pollution sources, the countries can assess the efficiency of national pollution control measures.* Trend monitoring in MED POL Phase III involves coastal zone trend monitoring, trend monitoring in pollution hot spot areas, trend monitoring of loads and trend monitoring of biological effects.

Effective pollution control needs to be backed by a *compliance monitoring* programme to assist countries in determining whether their regulatory provisions for pollution control for any given activity are complied with. The data obtained are used for making decisions as to whether appropriate enforcement measures should be imposed. The Mediterranean countries carry out compliance monitoring of bathing waters, aquaculture waters, and seafood for health related pollution control, as well as on urban and industrial effluents, and at hot spots to determine if their environmental quality objectives are complied with.

Also addressed are the release of harmful concentrations of nutrients into the marine environment, the storage, transportation and disposal of radioactive and hazardous wastes and activities that contribute to the destruction of the coastline and coastal habitats.

The Contracting Parties adopted the SAP in 1997 and are expected to bring it up to date and review some aspects of its operation in 2001.

The SAP has a built-in scope for the review of detailed operational timetables at two to three year intervals and a detailed work-plan and time-schedule for 2000–2001 has been prepared by the Secretariat and approved by the countries. The activities earmarked for the biennium will create the infrastructure for the implementation of the SAP and are essential to equip all the countries with the necessary tools (regional guidelines, strategies, plans and programmes for sharing technical information and advice, priority capacity building and preparatory public participation activities) that will allow them to eventually fulfil their priority objectives under the SAP.

The adoption of the SAP and the initiation of activities for its implementation even before the entry into force of the amended LBS Protocol, is a clear indication of the determination of the countries to take concrete action to combat land-based pollution and at the same time contribute to maintaining and restoring marine biodiversity, safeguarding human health and promoting the sustainable use of marine living resources.

Shortly after its adoption, the SAP was recognised by the Council of the Global Environment Facility (GEF) as an important programme dealing directly with some of the major concerns relating to international waters. As a result of this recognition the GEF Council approved in 1998 a three-year Mediterranean GEF Project due to start in January 2001, entailing a contribution of six million US$ for the realization of a number of important groundwork activities of the Strategic Action Programme that are essential for the Programme's long-term success, such as the preparation of National Action Plans (NAPs).

NAPs are intended to follow on from the adoption in each country of all the targets and activities of the nationally relevant components identified in the SAP. Funds from the Mediterranean GEF Project will be used to support national inter-ministerial committees in the development and implementation of NAPs in 12 eligible countries. The implementation of country specific National Action Plans to combat pollution from land-based activities is the operational long-term output of the SAP.

One of the most important components of the SAP which is expected to lead directly to a reduction in polluting inputs to the Mediterranean Sea from land-based activities is the package of actions which accompany the evaluation of the impacts of pollution hot spots and the environmental audit of pollution-sensitive areas (i.e. those areas of natural or socio-economic value at risk of becoming future pollution hot spots) in the Mediterranean, taking into consideration their regional and trans-boundary significance.

Pre-investment studies will be conducted in the most important hot spots and detailed environmental assessment reports will be prepared in the most important pollution sensitive areas from a regional perspective. This will lead to investment by countries and donors in projects aiming at the elimination or reduction of trans-boundary pollution from the priority hot spots as well as in environmental protection projects and comprehensive integrated management plans in the selected pollution-sensitive areas. GEF funds will be used for the preparation of pre-investment studies in GEF eligible countries.

Recent experience from coastal management projects in Mediterranean countries shows that applying economic instruments greatly contributes to effective environmental protection and pollution control. When the costs for the SAP remedial actions are considered, it becomes evident that the success of the SAP will largely depend on the sustainable financing of its individual components on a national level. The goal of the Secretariat is to develop administrative, legal and fiscal mechanisms for the sustainable financing of the SAP and to assist the governments in implementing these mechanisms by adapting them to meet their national requirements.

This will involve setting priorities for financing and mobilizing the financial community and international donors. In a first stage pilot projects will be implemented in six Mediterranean GEF eligible countries.

Setting the administrative, legal and technical groundwork for the implementation of the SAP by the countries is steered through regional guidelines and plans, which should be integrated into the National Action Plans. Funds from the Mediterranean GEF project have been allocated for their preparation. The selected guidelines and plans address those processes and activities for which the MED POL Programme identified the need for further assistance, including sewage treatment and disposal, disposal of urban solid wastes, industrial wastewater treatment and disposal, riverine and estuarine pollution monitoring and environmental inspection systems. A number of guidelines and plans are intended to strengthen the technical capacity of the countries to take on board the principles introduced by the amended LBS Protocol such as the application of clean technology and best environmental practice.

In addition to adequate financial and technical resources, combating pollution from land-based activities also requires specific competencies in areas such as environmental policy formulation and enforcement, scientific capability in the assessment of pollution, for example river pollution monitoring, as well as technical and managerial capabilities for the implementation of clean production techniques and environmentally sound technologies, for example the proper operation and maintenance of wastewater treatment facilities. The SAP makes provision for a series of regional training for trainers that aims at enhancing the capacities of Mediterranean countries in the above fields as well as to assist countries in overcoming existing inadequacies. Funds from the Mediterranean GEF project will support a number of SAP training courses earmarked for 2001–2003. Modern training techniques are deployed and the training package delivered to the trainers at the end of regional courses includes transparencies and explanatory notes in hard copy and software form, prepared in a way that facilitates translation and desk top publishing in any of the Mediterranean languages.

MAP is actively involved in the distribution of information material on all its projects and carrying out public information campaigns and special activities involving the public in environmental protection. MAP has recently set up an ambitious international information and public awareness strategy, which will reach out to broader audiences such as consumers, the private sector and youth, using multilingual literature and modern dissemination methods such as the Internet. Funds from the Mediterranean GEF project will be used to organise a workshop in 2001–2002 on the role the public and non-governmental organisations (NGOs) in particular can play in the implementation of the SAP.

The SAP is an ambitious undertaking, spanning a lengthy period of 25 years and addressed to countries with different degrees of socio-economic development, technical, scientific and administrative competencies, different cultural values and environmental priorities. To increase the prospects for the success of the SAP it is appropriate to set up from its onset a mechanism which will take on board issues such as the nature of the body that will coordinate the SAP activities at the national level, the effective conveyance and assimilation of all the "support structures" of the SAP at the national administrative level, the successful dissemination and assimilation of the tasks by the local stakeholders in each country as well as the nature of the body which will monitor the progress of all the activities that are being carried out in each country and of the body which will evaluate the outputs. In addition, the operational plan will tackle important practical issues for achieving the financial sustainability of the SAP in the long-term. Equally importantly the operational plan will provide detailed instructions for the countries on how to address the technical concerns that are being raised in the deliberations leading to the updating of the SAP. As an example, detailed instructions will be provided to the countries on how to calculate the national budgets for individual targeted pollutants and the actual pollutant reductions required on a national basis, to reach the targets stated in the SAP. To achieve this, the operational plan will also provide directions for the identification of the baseline values against which the pollutant reductions should be estimated. These are just some of the crucial issues that will be tackled by a SAP implementation operational plan that is currently in the process of being developed by MED POL.

Most importantly, the Mediterranean countries moved one step further towards acting on combating land-based pollution, by preparing and adopting a Strategic Action Programme for the implementation of the revised Land Based Sources Protocol in the next 25 years. The MED POL Programme, known in its present phase (1996–2005) as the Programme for the Assessment and Control of Pollution in the Mediterranean Region, is playing an essential coordinating role in this direction, giving priority to activities that are directly linked to the implementation of the SAP. Through a timetabled schedule, the Mediterranean countries are implementing specific measures for the elimination or control of priority land-based target groups of substances and activities which are of global concern, paying special attention to toxic, persistent and bioaccumulative substances, particularly persistent organic pollutants. Through these actions, the Mediterranean countries are in effect also implementing the goals of the Global Programme of Action.

The adoption of the SAP and the initiation of activities for its implementation even before the entry into force of the amended LBS Protocol, reflects the determination of the Mediterranean countries to take tangible action to combat land based pollution, at the same time contributing to upholding and restoring marine biodiversity and safeguarding human health and marine living resources.

Vladimir V. Efimov and V.N. Eremeev***

THE DEVELOPMENT OF THE BLACK SEA AREA

The Black Sea has an extreme importance for the six riparian countries and for about 150 million people living in its catchment basin which is among the most contaminated basins of the World Ocean. The environmental crisis in the Black Sea resulting from anthropogenic forcing is manifested by dramatic changes in its ecosystem and resources.

The Black Sea is of global interest as a nature's warning for other regions of the world and as a suitable "laboratory" basin to study the anthropogenic forcing, geophysical and climatic problems.

Regional environmental/oceanographic programs of the last 5–7 years such as the Black Sea Environmental Program, Environmental Program for the Danube River Basin, Azov Sea Project, Tracer Applications, Cooperative Marine Science Program for the Black Sea, Black Sea Regional Program (IOC), NATO TU-Black Sea Project, NATO TU-WAVES Project and others, gave a new understanding and perception of some environmental characteristics of the Sea and, especially, the possibility to collect interdisciplinary data as a baseline for future activities.

The new program "The Black Sea Ecosystem Processes and Forecasting/ Operational Database Management System" combining the efforts of scientists and institutes from the six riparian countries is successfully carried out.

The Black Sea needs increased vigilance and effective environmental management due to the current environmental and climate changes.

Introduction

The Black Sea is an area of scientific, ecological and economic interests of the six riparian countries – Ukraine, Russia, Turkey, Bulgaria, Romania, Georgia. About 160 million people live in its catchment basin with about 40 million summer visitors. On the one hand, the Black Sea is a deep basin, with a maximum depth of more than 2000 meters. Below 150–200 meters there are only anoxic waters making it the

* Professor, Marine Hydrophysical Institute, Sevastopol, Crimea, Ukraine.
** Marine Hydrophysical Institute, Sevastopol, Crimea, Ukraine.

P. Ehlers, E. Mann-Borgese and R. Wolfrum (eds.), Marine Issues, 177–186

largest anoxic basin on our planet. 90% of its water is contaminated by hydrogen sulfate. Together with very small vertical mixing in the deep sea this means, on the other hand, that the Black Sea, in terms of ecology, can be considered a shallow water basin, where different human pollutants are distributed in the upper sea layer. In the main volume only anaerobic bacteria exist. As a result, the Black Sea is the most contaminated sea among 12 examined world basins according to the estimation of the IOC (Intergovernmental Oceanographic Commission).[1] This sea has experienced more severe environmental degradation. The Black Sea was rated as having the highest concerns in many categories of ecological degradation.

Environmental Degradation of the Black Sea

It is necessary to mention the next key contributing factors of the ecological degradation. The fishing yields and biodiversity have declined badly. Overfishing resulted in 80% reduction in the total catch in the last 20 years. Significant changes in phytoplankton species composition, eutrophication and algae blooms in the northwestern part of the Black Sea have taken place in the last years. The Euphotic zone, where the sunlight is sufficient for biological production, decreased from 50–60 to 30–40 meters. Intrusion of the jellyfish *Mnemiopsis leidyi* led to the explosive increase in organic matter falling to the sea floor from blooming and decaying organisms. Chemical and microbiological pollution, the enormous increase in the nutrient and pollutant load are accompanied by periodical epidemics of water-born cholera and hepatitis in the northern near-coastal regions. Tourism has severely decreased.

A notable danger is the oil pollution. At present, the average oil concentration in the open sea exceeds two times the water FSU Standard. Plans of using the Black Sea as a future transport corridor for oil and gas transportation represent a serious potential danger of further oil pollution particularly in the regions of inadequate port reception facilities and possible oil spills.

Among major sources of all pollution the largest contribution falls on the Danube river. Its average run-off amounts to about 200 km^3/yr which is almost three times more than the amount all other rivers discharge in the Black Sea. Namely, the Danube river discharges about half of total 110,000 t/yr of oil pollution into the Black Sea, as well as phosphorus, inorganic nitrogen, heavy metals and others. From all riparian countries approximately 2/3 of all pollution falls on the Ukraine, having the large Dnieper River discharge and the industrialized and populated northwestern coast.

It is interesting to compare the Black Sea and the Mediterranean. According to the data given by Ragaini[2] the pollutant loads into these seas for the main selected

1 *IOC*, A Strategic Plan for the Assessment and Prediction of the Health of the Ocean: A Module of the Global Ocean Observing System, IOC/INF – 1044 (Paris 1996).

2 *R.C. Ragaini*, Monitoring Black Sea environmental conditions: workshop summary 1999, in: *Monitoring Black Sea Environmental Conditions, Proceedings of the World Federation of the Scientific Working Group on Water and Pollution*, vol. 3 (Italy).

pollutants differ 1.5 ÷ 3 times. However, the volume of the Black Sea is 7 times smaller, and its area is 6 times smaller. So it is understandable that the pollutant load on the Black Sea is much more severe than on the Mediterranean, especially if the low vertical mixing rates in the Black Sea are taken into account.

The Black Sea as a Laboratory Basin

The importance of the Black Sea is related not only to the problems of ecological degradation. The Black Sea can be considered as a region of global scientific interest, as a natural laboratory basin. In fact, it is a relatively large basin where hydrophysical, chemical and biological models can be more easily adapted for hindcasting and forecasting.

The Black Sea is an interesting region in relation to local climate changes. For instance, in the scenarios of fixture climate change[3] the Black Sea region is located in the area of the large meridional near surface temperature gradients. So the issue of downscaling for this region is important and not a trivial problem. As it is known, before computations of scenarios of climate change, the coupled atmosphere-ocean numerical models are fitted to the observed data. In some of such fittings, the Black Sea region differs significantly from the observed temperature data. Thus, for January temperatures, for 1961–1990, the difference between the observed mean temperature and the ECHAM4 model amounts to 10–12°C.[4] It is interesting that contrary to air temperature in this region, which became warmer during last 40 years for about 0.3–0.5°C, the sea surface temperature of the Black Sea decreased about 0.8°C (see Figure 1). That means that this region needs a special thoughtful consideration.

Environmental Programs for the Black Sea

In addition to national scientific programs, many international environmental ones have been performed during the last decade in the Black Sea. Table 1 lists recent major international environmental programs, main sponsors and dates. We will consider in more detail only those of them, in which the Marine Hydrophysical Institute National Academy of Sciences of Ukraine was involved.

Cooperative Marine Science Program for the Black Sea (CoMSBlack)

The Program began in 1991 and aimed at establishing a scientific basis for the effective and integrated management of the entire Black Sea region. The IOC assembly established the program to be the first truly inter-institutional coordinated marine program. The major scientific objectives were:

---

3 *IPCC (Intergovernmental Panel on Climate Change)*, Climate Change 1995, The Science of climate change (*J.T. Houghton/L.C. Meira Filho/B.A. Callander/N. Harris/A. Katteribery/K. Maskell* eds.) (Cambridge, U.K. 1996).

4 *Ibid.*

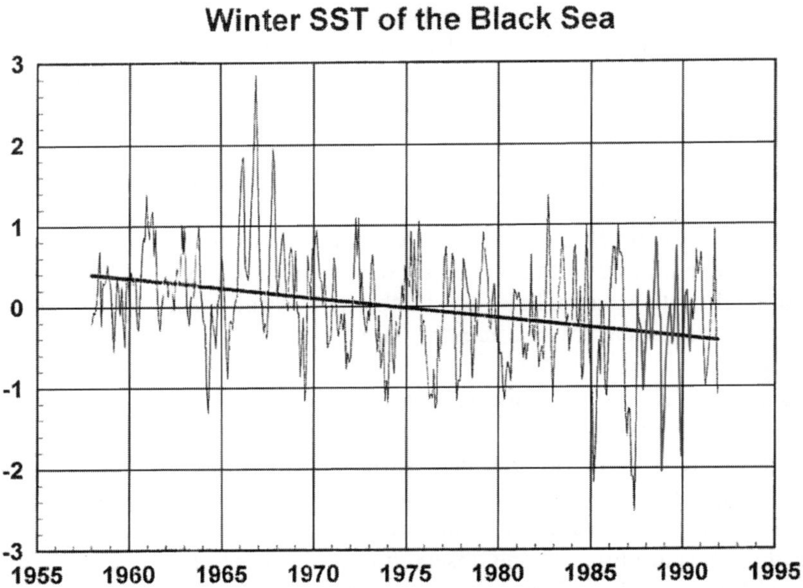

Figure 1. Winter sea surface temperature of the Black Sea for 1958–1992.

Table 1. Black Sea environmental programs.

Sponsor(s)	*Program*	*Dates*
IOC	CoMSBlack	1991 –
EU/GEF	Danube River	1992 – 1999
GEF	BSEP I & II	1993 – 1998
EU	EROS	1993 – 2001
NATO	TU BS	1993 – 1997
NATO	TU-Waves	1993 – 1998
Netherlands	Azov Sea	1993 – 1995
IAEA	Tracer Applications	1994 – 1996
GEF	Danube Delta	1994 – 1998
IOC	STOPS	1996 – 1998
IOC	Sediment Flux	1996 – 2002
IOC	BS GODS	1999 – 2002

– to assess the natural and anthropogenically induced changes using historical data;
– to determine the past and present fluxes of all pollutants, from rivers, atmosphere, straits, across shelves;
– to provide a quantitative description of the physical-biochemical processes governing the transport and cycling of carbon, nutrients, suspended sediments within the basin.

Numerous basin and sub-basin ship oceanographic surveys have been carried out in the period of 1991–1993 and new important and interesting scientific results were obtained relating to the interdisciplinary understanding and prediction of physical and biochemical processes in the Black Sea.

NATO TU-Black Sea Project

The Project was carried out in 1993–1998 in the framework of the NATO Science for Stability Program and aimed at establishing scientific collaboration with the central and eastern European countries. It was conducted through the Institute of Marine Sciences, Middle-East Technical University in Turkey. Major objectives were:

- development and application of interdisciplinary ecosystem models to analyse the physical processes, effects of anthropogenic forcing and natural variability on dynamics of the lower trophic levels of the biological community;
- capacity-building focused on providing cross-training, scientific equipment, joint observations including satellite monitoring, analysis data, joint publications, developing a communication network;
- a data base management system (DBMS).

More then 100 scientists from 12 oceanographic institutions took part to accomplish the objectives of the Project. DBMS was a major achievement of the TU-Black Sea Project. It included the last 30 years of environmental and oceanographic data, nearly 150 megabytes of data, including observation, from 13,000 stations quality-checked, processed and stored in the data base.

NATO TU-Waves

TU-WAVES was another NATO Science for Peace supported Project carried out in 1993–1998. The project was conducted also through the Middle-East Technical University in Turkey with participation of specialists from the coastal countries of Ukraine, Russia, Bulgaria, Romania. Main objectives were:

- direct measurements of wind and waves in several given sites of the Black Sea;
- processing of archive meteorological data;
- modeling using modern numerical wave models.

Within the project all available synoptic maps were digitized. As a result, the wind and wave atlas of the Black Sea was created, which is the most modern wind-wave handbook for the Black Sea, it is extremely useful for coastal and marine planning, management and operations. For the Marine Hydrophysical Institute, this project was also valuable because it created the possibility to conduct wind-wave measurements by means of new instruments installed on an oil rig in the northwestern part of the sea, which are continuously operating at present.

Ongoing Black Sea Programs

Black Sea Ecosystem Processes and Forecasting/Operational Data Base Management System (ODBMS)

The program is supported by the NATO Science for Peace Program. It commenced in January 1999 and involves the development and application of coupled interdisciplinary physical-biogeochemical models, field observations and analysis for the identification and interpretation of interactive physical and biogeochemical processes. Main objectives are:

- to explore, quantify and predict the ecosystem variability through process studies and development of coupled interdisciplinary models that allow the prediction of future states of the sea, description of the present and past states;
- to develop further the Data Base Management System for the Black Sea for the management-oriented operational marine forecasting and research, on the base of quality-controlled data received from various types of wave instruments and satellites in near-real time mode.

Eight prominent oceanographic institutes representing all coastal Black Sea countries are participants of the project:

The Marine Hydrophysical Institute (Sevastopol, Ukraine);
The Institute of Biology of Southern Seas (Sevastopol, Ukraine);
The Institute of Marine Sciences of the METU (Erdemly, Turkey);
The P.P. Shirshov Institute of Oceanology (Moscow, Russia);
The Southern Branch of the P.P. Shirshov Institute of Oceanology (Gelendgic, Russia);
The Romanian Marine Research Institute (Constanza, Romania);
The Institute of Oceanology (Varna, Bulgaria);
The Tbilisi State University (Tbilisi, Georgia).

The Project consists of several sub-projects: modeling, observations, data base management, dissemination. The goal of modeling is to predict the ecosystem variability through coupled interdisciplinary models with near-real data assimilation. The observational component focuses on the understanding of a set of poorly studied processes and of some key elements of the Black Sea ecosystem, and, especially, interaction between the physical, biological and chemical processes of the oxic, suboxic and anoxic layers, exchange between the coastal-shelf regions and the interior of the basin. The data management issues include the processing and analysis of data received from field operations of research vessels, satellites, buoys and coastal stations. The data base management system will be the further development of the DBMS created within the NATO TU-Black Sea Project.

In May 2000 the first Project evaluation meeting took place in Istanbul in order to:

- discuss the first year scientific activities of the project among its key scientific and external advisors;

- hold an assessment meeting with the Science for Peace Program representatives;
- have a scientific steering committee meeting for planning forthcoming field survey and other activities.

The high level of the Black Sea interdisciplinary studies (both observational and modeling) carried out currently within the framework of this project was ascertained. The existing efforts constitute a baseline of the future interdisciplinary predictive modeling efforts, which should specifically pay attention to obtaining compatible, interdisciplinary data for the predictive modeling studies with reasonably good time and spatial structures. This data should include measurements of some key biogeochemical parameters at several specific locations complemented also by selected regional and basin-wide multi-disciplinary surveys, which are necessary to initialize or update physical and biogeochemical properties of the water column computed by predictive models. The satellite data are another potentially important data source, especially if difficult economical situations in the Black Sea coastal countries are taken into account. Data management systems should be capable of handling the near-real time data transfer and storage issues among participating institutions.

Let us mention only one result of last year's studies having direct relation to the problem of ecological degradation of the Black Sea. Using data from 52 cruises from 1960 to 1995 Konovalov and Murray[5] examined decadal variability in basic chemical properties (oxygen, sulfide, nitrate, phosphate and silicate) throughout the water column. This analysis revealed some new features, which indicate an increase in the inventory of sulfide and nutrients in the anoxic zone, a decrease in the inventory of oxygen, and variations in the thickness of the sub-oxic zone due to anthropogenic changes reflected in the distribution of nitrate and oxygen. This trend, displayed in Figure 2 as a steady shoaling of oxygen isolines in the upper layer of the sea up to 1987–1989, has been interrupted after 1990. In recent years, this tendency was reversed and the lower boundary of the upper oxygen layer began to deepen.

Such positive changes, indicating the decrease of the flux of sinking particulate organic matter in the upper layer, which is some decrease of the entrophication, is confirmed by the latest measurements of the nutrient and organic loads in the north-western shelf of the Black Sea.[6]

A slight tendency of the increasing silica content parallel to a continuous decrease of nitrogen and phosphorus has been detected. These changes have been reflected in the reduction of the total phytoplankton biomass, reduction in the magnitude of

---

5 *S.K. Konovalov/J.W. Murray*, Variations in the basic chemical properties of the Black Sea on a scale of decades (1960–1995), in: *Black Sea Ecosystem Processes and Forecasting/Operational Database Management System, Report of the Workshop and Project Evaluation Meeting* (Istanbul 2000).

6 *A. Cociascu/L. Popa/L. Buda*, Long-term evolution of the nutrient concentrations in the north-western shelf of the Black Sea, in: *Black Sea Ecosystem Processes and Forecasting/Operational Database Management System, Report of the Workshop and Project Evaluation Meeting* (Istanbul 2000).

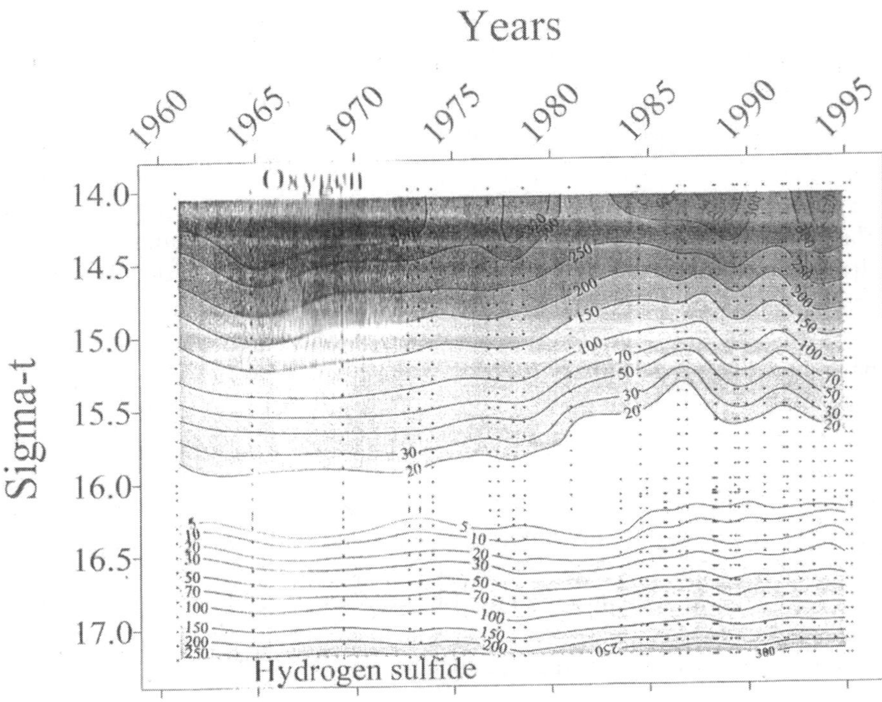

Figure 2. Isolines of oxygen and sulfide in the Black Sea for 1960–1995.

algae blooms. This can be considered as signs of further evolution of the normal status of the phytoplankton community.[7]

Even though, a decreasing tendency has been recorded in the last three years, the inorganic nitrogen species kept their content at high value, exceeding 3–5 times the level of the 1960s period, i.e. the period before eutrophication. Phosphorus and silica values display a similarity to the ones before eutrophication frequently reaching the exhaustion stages.

And thus, this positive trend in the recent period (1991–1997) is still fragile and should be treated rather tentatively. These years are *a priori* considered as a period of the decrease of anthropogenic pressure on the basin mainly as a result of the collapse of the economy in the former socialist Black Sea countries. The positive ecological tendency is a simple result of such economical stagnation, but not a special complex of anti-pollution actions. In any case, returning to the Black Sea as a natural laboratory basin, this last period can be considered as a case study of

7 *N. Bodeanu/S. Moncheva/G. Ruta/L. Popa*, Long-term evolution of the algae blooms in Romanian and Bulgarian Black Sea waters, in: *Black Sea Ecosystem Processes and Forecasting/Operational Database Management System, Report of the Workshop and Project Evaluation Meeting* (Istanbul 2000).

decreasing anthropogenic pollution forcing and a very favorable possibility to develop and test interdisciplinary physical, biogeochemical models for the Black Sea.

A system of regular standard hydrophysical, chemical and biological measurements over the Black Sea (hydrological sections by hydrometeorological research vessels, navy, monitoring on the coastal stations) existing in the former Soviet Union is now almost completely interrupted. Without its restoration any progress in understanding and forecasting future anthropogenically induced ecological changes seems to be impossible.

In this regard, international regional cooperation can be especially important because it creates a possibility to attract the attention of the governments and officials of riparian countries for the necessity of the assignment of financial resources. One of the most important endeavors is the formation of a regional sub-program of the Global Ocean Observing System – the Black Sea GOOS.

The "Science and Implementation Plan for the Black Sea GOOS" was adopted in May 1999 as a regional project of IOC.[8] The Program has to provide regions with information by the following ways:

- Monitoring, estimations and further prognosis of ecological and climatic changes on regional and sub-regional levels that influence decisively the quality of life and perspectives of economic development.
- Investigations aimed at better understanding, modeling and prognosis of the sea medium state as the most important climate, weather and resource forming factor, and its marine industrial complex of the country and the region.
- Propagation of data and results of data analysis urgently required for effective and rational use of sea resources and other practical purposes.
- Scientific and technical foundation and support of industrial pry of regional, sub-regional and local scales (construction of terminals, pipelines, undersea communication lines, development of gas and oil resources).

The structure of the Project in the Ukraine includes:

- System of observation of long-term variations of the marine environment induced by anthropogenic and natural causes;
- System of observations and assessment of the living resources of the sea;
- System of observations of the environment in the coastal zone and control of its changes;
- System of estimation, diagnosis and prognosis of the health of the sea;
- Generation of a national integrated system and technology of operative control of the state of marine environment and overlying atmosphere;
- Construction of measuring and metrological complexes and system providing marine investigations.

Seven scientific organizations in the Ukraine will take part in the Black Sea GOOS:

[8] *IOC*, IOCBSRI-II/3, Annex VIII.

Marine Hydrophysical Institute (Sevastopol);
Institute of Biology of Southern Seas (Sevastopol);
Southern Scientific-research Center of Fishing and Oceanography (Kerch);
Marine Science-information Department of the Ukrainian Hydrometeo Institute (Sevastopol);
Odessa Branch of Institute of Biology of Southern Seas (Odessa);
Ukrainian Research Center of Marine Ecology and Nuclear Safety (Odessa).

CONCLUSIONS

In spite of the successful development of the Black Sea Programs an achieved level of our knowledge and assigned resources does not correspond to the urgency of the problem of ecosystem degradation. The most important object is to restore and expand the interdisciplinary monitoring of the Black Sea environmental conditions (BS GOOS activity) to develop the operational database management system, accessible to the scientific and policy-making communities as a basis for the effective arid integrated management, including restoration of the ecosystem and its biodiversity.

*Gerd Hubold**

FISHERY AND SUSTAINABILITY

By the turn of the century, a world-wide over-capacity of high-technology fishing equipment is threatening the sustainable use of wild-living fish stocks in the sea. At the same time, anthropogenic impacts deteriorate the marine environment and imminent climatic change may alter the biological processes in marine ecosystems to an unknown extent. In the face of this challenge, the fishing industry, fishery science, and fishery management have to depart from the traditional single-species "maximum yield" approach in fisheries. An ecologically *and* socio-economically oriented "network for responsible fishing" with revised tasks for the stakeholders must be developed. New approaches to fisheries management have to consider models of resource privatisation by leasing or licensing schemes. Under such a scheme, the *fishing industry* should have more responsibility for the sustainable management of their exploited fish stocks *and* the maintenance of the ecosystems on which they depend, according to the standards set and supervised by society. Public responsibility could then be focused on the strategic research and monitoring necessary to define and control the ecologic and economic threshold criteria for the sustainable use of the marine ecosystems.

The Problem of Over-capacity

Since 1950 world fishery production has increased from 20 mill. t to more than 100 mill. t today. An estimated 20–27 mill. t of not utilized (discarded) catches have to be added to this figure. About 30 mill. persons make their living directly from fishing, an additional 150 mill. are indirectly linked to this activity. The world's fishing fleet has steadily increased by number and efficiency, and today an estimated 3.5 mill vessels from small artisanal boats to giant floating factories chase fish in the sea.

This significant increase in fishing power today has resulted in a dramatic over-capacity, which is threatening the sustainable use of wild-living fish stocks in the sea. According to an analysis by FAO,[1] 60–70% of the worlds 200 most important commercial fish stocks are fished at or beyond the maximum, and need urgent management action to safeguard their future productivity.

* Bundesforschungsanstalt für Fischerei, Hamburg.

1 *FAO*, The state of world fisheries and aquaculture 1996, pp. 1–125 (FAO Rome 1997).

P. Ehlers, E. Mann-Borgese and R. Wolfrum (eds.), Marine Issues, 187–193

While the fishing sector responds to an increasing demand for fish from a growing human population, aided by advances in ship-building and catching technology and sustained by ample public subsidies, its resources, the fish stocks, cannot be exploited beyond a maximum biologically determined limit. For many fish stocks this limit has now been reached. To balance present-day catching capacity with the natural biological productivity of the marine ecosystems, a massive reduction of fishing efforts (not just the number of vessels, but also their performance on the fish stocks) will be necessary.

The North Sea Cod Example

An example of the development of a well-documented fishery can be drawn from the North Sea cod fishery. For almost 40 years, consistent data have been collected and analysed by the European fishery institutes under the coordination of the International Council for the Exploration of the Sea (ICES). The data allow for a rather detailed reconstruction of how the cod stock developed since 1963.[2]

In the early 1960s, annual landings of about 120,000–130,000 t (Figure 1a) were based on a spawning stock biomass of 150,000–170,000 t of cod (Figure 1d). The fishing mortality (F) as a measure of the relative share taken from the stock by fishery (spawners plus young fish) was in the order of $F = 0.5$ (Figure 1c). An $F = 0.5$ indicates that, considering a natural mortality of $M = 0.1$, about 38% of the fish (ages 2–8) present at the beginning of each year are taken by the fishery. Incoming year classes of 200–400 mill. young fish (recruits; Figure 1b) balanced the stock. Due to probably favourable environmental conditions over a number of years, a continuous sequence of good to excellent year classes allowed increased catches until the early 1970s and a sufficient number of fish survived to add to the adult biomass, which rose to 277,000 t in 1971 (this phase was termed the "gadoid outburst", a period in which several of the North Sea cod-like fish species showed increased population sizes). Fishing mortality rose to 0.8 in 1972 (taking about 53% of the fish annually) and landings amounted to 350,000 t.

From 1972 on, a number of poorer year classes have been produced. Fishing, however, continued on a high level until the early 1980s, fuelled by only a few abundant recruit classes. This led to a steadily declining adult spawning stock (Figure 1d). With a fishing mortality of $F = 0.9$ since 1982, an annual share of 57% of the fish has been landed. In fact, many more fish were taken by the fishery, because actual catches regularly exceed the registered landings considerably, because many cod are caught and discarded (as undersized fish, as by-catches in other fisheries without quota, etc.). From the mid-eighties, the reduced spawning potential then aggravated the low recruitment problem (Figure 1b) and well below 200 mill. young fish appeared per year, which was not sufficient to re-build the stock even when the fishery was reduced.

[2] *ANON*, Report of the ICES Advisory Committee on Fishery Management, in: *ICES CRR* 237 (2000).

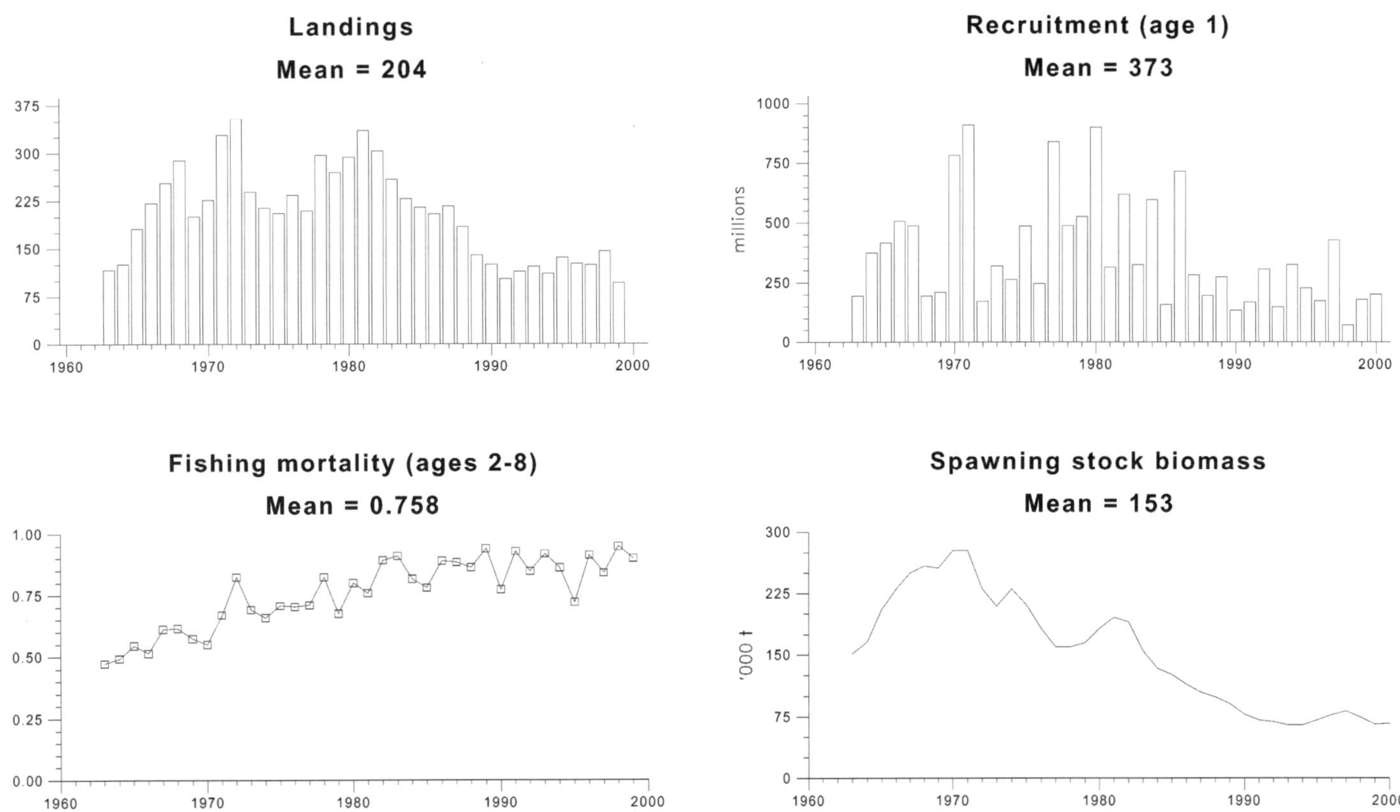

Figure 1a–d. North Sea cod 1963–2000. (a) Landings; (b) recruitment; (c) fishing mortality; (d) adult fish biomass.

As a consequence, in the 1990s the adult cod stock was at its lowest ever-observed size, and protection measures had to be taken by the management to rebuild it. A fishing intensity of $F_{pa} = 0.65$ and a biomass of B_{pa} of 150,000 t are the targeted reference points according to a precautionary approach (pa) in the management now. In no case, the fishing intensity should exceed the limit values $F_{lim} = 0.86$ and the biomass should not fall below a minimum limit of $B_{lim} = 60{,}000$ t.

In retrospective, the precautionary reference points have been transgressed since 1971 for fishing mortality and since 1984 for biomass, respectively. Since 1982, the stock has been fished beyond the threshold limit F_{lim} of 0.86, and in 1996 it arrived close to the B_{lim} value for a minimum acceptable spawning biomass.

The Management System

Yearly assessments such as for North Sea cod are provided by the national fisheries institutes for more than 130 stocks in the North Atlantic within the ICES structures. These assessments are the basis for the North Atlantic fisheries management. Regulatory commissions like the European Union (EU), International Baltic Sea Fisheries Commission (IBSFC), North East Atlantic Fisheries Commission (NEAFC), North Atlantic Salmon Commission (NASCO), North West Atlantic Fisheries Commission (NAFO) and member countries are clients for the advice given by ICES. This scientific infrastructure is one of the best and most efficient scientific bodies world-wide, although over the last years a decrease in national contributions to the scientific programme has hampered the performance of the ICES advice system.

Given this excellent scientific infrastructure, the question remains why fisheries management so often fails to maintain the stocks at a productive, sustainable biomass level.

The basis for traditional fisheries management is input control (i.e. control on fleet size, engine power, mesh regulations, restricted areas etc.) and output control (Total Allowable Catch (TAC), landed catches, minimum fish sizes, by-catch regulations etc.).

The control of input parameters in fisheries is difficult due to the rapid advances in high-tech equipment which increase fishing efficiency, illegal practices at sea, which are hardly controllable, and a high capitalisation of modern fisheries, which increases the pressure on fishermen to pay back their bank duties rather than to perform a reasonable and sustainable profession. Both fishermen and their governments hesitate to reduce fishing capacity to the necessary lower levels fearing to loose catch opportunities in a suddenly appearing fish boom.

The output control (catches, minimum sizes etc.) is equally complicated and involves expensive control at sea by fishery inspectors, and systematic statistics of fish landings in ports. Catches have to be documented by the fishermen themselves at sea in log-books, but the precision of these documents does not always meet the needs of exact statistics. Furthermore, listing of discarded catches is optional, and thus the figures often do not reflect the true amounts. Therefore, at the end of the year, the landings represent only a fraction of real catches, but only the official landings are counted against the internationally agreed total allowable catch (TAC), which is established to protect the stocks from over-fishing.

Scientific models for stock assessment have to rely both on scientific survey data and fisheries statistics. If one of these two sources of data fails, the entire system flaws. The gap between recorded landings and the actual catches, which could not be compensated fully by independent scientific data on the population development of these species may be one of the primary reasons, why the management of North Sea cod had to fail.

The Common Fishery Policy (CFP) of the European Union, which operates with an ever increasing number of regulations and restrictions, could not halt the decrease of many important fish stocks such as cod. In its complexity, the CFP does not produce common sense and correct behaviour by the fishermen, which would be needed to improve the data basis. Instead, it rather created resistance and confrontation between fishermen, public authorities, and scientists. In this climate of tension, neither party can work successfully. New approaches to fisheries management should therefore consider a different distribution of tasks and responsibilities, giving a stronger part to the private sector to contribute to the maintenance of the fish stocks.

Privatisation of the Fish Resources

Simple models of privatisation in the form of individually transferable quota (ITQ) have been successfully applied e.g. in New Zealand, and partly in Iceland. ITQs attribute a market value to the fish in the sea before it is caught, which might encourage the fishing industry to handle the stocks more carefully. An ownership of quota would probably also diminish "black" landings due to a stricter social control within the fishing communities. In the European multi-species fisheries, however, ITQs are not straightforward, because they would have to be attributed to a mix of species with different catch characteristics and different quota. In addition, they would probably involve increased discarding of lower value fish ("high-grading" of catches) to maximise the profit from the individual quota, and they could lead to an undesired concentration of ownership in the hands of few big investors. Also, within an ITQ model, the basic problem of control of illegal practices at sea remains.

Therefore, a privatisation of the resources may be one step into a right direction, but a more holistic approach to fisheries with a system of co-management involving governments, consumers, NGOs and the fishing sector should be envisaged.

A Holistic Approach to Fisheries

Under such a new scheme, all stakeholders, rather than the public sector alone, should be responsible for the sustainable management of the exploited fish stocks in a defined area (within given threshold parameters for the stocks) and be responsible for the preservation of the utilised ecosystem according to the ecosystem quality standards set by society. In this scenario, the *fishery* should be allowed to

- take free decisions on how, when, where, and how much to fish within the respective area
- decide by itself on (and pay for) all measures deemed necessary for input or output control of their fellow fishermen
- decide on (and pay for) scientific stock assessment, gear development, technical measures etc. necessary to obtain optimum economic results.

The fishing sector would be responsible for fish stock assessment, catch and environmental protection, including the necessary scientific analyses and management. A large part of the necessary operational science could be found within the ICES system which could be co-financed by the industry for this purpose.

Public responsibility could be focused on

- the definition of the socio-economic parameters for the fishery (e.g. a balanced relation between fleet sectors, limited ownership, consideration of regional development etc.),
- the setting of ecological quality targets and management objectives for the ecosystems (e.g. minimum stock sizes of commercial and other species to maintain ecosystem balance),
- the prevention of ecological risks by scientific monitoring and analysis of the respective ecosystems under the privatised fishery regime,
- immediate action on the fishery, when environmental targets are endangered;
- mediation between user groups of conflicting interest (e.g. Fishery and environment, but also other uses of the sea such as gravel extraction, construction of wind-parks, shipping, military use etc.).

The public sector would thus be responsible to conduct strategic (operational) research, to monitor and control the health of stocks and the ecosystem and to control the private management performance. The applied long-term research necessary for this has to be conducted by public agencies linked to the responsible ministries, and should continue to be part of the present ICES scientific advice system. In addition, targeted academic research must continue to provide the scientific basis for rational utilisation of the marine ecosystems on a larger scale, and should find adequate funding e.g. in the European Science Plans and scientific framework programmes.

All interested parties including NGOs, consumers, and other users of the seas should form a common "Network for responsible fishing". The Network would allocate and revise responsibilities of the stakeholders and define the standards for sustainable fishing and ecosystem protection. Within the fishing industry, efficient mechanisms of co-management, including the necessary research and management structures should be created. An operational monitoring and strategic research for the fisheries and ecosystems should be developed under the objective leadership of public authorities to verify the sustainability of the activities in the form of a "result control" for fisheries performance. In case of infractions a legal basis for draconic measures should be created including the possibility to withdraw fishing licences, or close areas for fishing on a precautionary basis.

In the longer term, the "Network" should develop a strategic plan not only for fisheries, but for the more general use of the seas to mediate present and future conflicts between fishery and other users, including public interests such as environmental protection and research. With these steps towards a "Holistic Fisheries Management system", it might be possible to improve the presently deficient management, which could not prevent an almost world-wide resource depletion in the seas.

*Alexander Yankov**

REFLAGGING OF FISHING VESSELS: CRITICAL ASSESSMENT OF ITS IMPACT ON THE ENFORCEMENT OF FISHING REGULATIONS AND THE RESPONSES THERETO

Introduction

The present situation of fisheries on the high seas has caused well-justified concern about the present fishing practices of non-compliance with conservation and sustainable management rules and regulations. Unregulated fishing has resulted in over-exploitation and depletion of fish stocks. As pointed out in the Agreement for the Implementation of the Provisions of the United Nations Convention of the Law of the Sea of 10 December 1982 Relating to the Conservation and Management of Straddling Fish Stocks and Highly Migratory Fish Stocks (*hereinafter* Straddling Fish Stocks Agreement), among the unregulated fishing should be singled out "vessel reflagging to escape controls."[1]

Reflagging of fishing vessels and the use of fishing vessels flying "flags of convenience" have become a significant part of the illegal fishing activities on the high seas. This relatively recent development has added new dimensions to the irregular fishing practices of unregulated fishing and overfishing.

The growing concern about reflagging of fishing vessels on the high seas was raised already at the International Conference on Responsible Fishing held under the auspices of FAO in 1992. The Conference adopted the Agreement to Promote Compliance with International Conservation and Management Measures by Fishing Vessels on the High Seas of 1993 (*hereinafter* FAO Compliance Agreement).[2] The Preamble of the Agreement states that the Agreement "will form an integral part of the Code of Conduct for Responsible Fishing"[3] (*hereinafter* FAO Code of Conduct).

Among the FAO multilateral treaties and other instruments relating to conservation and management of marine living resources, including reflagging of fishing vessels, fall the Rome Declaration on the Implementation of the Code of Conduct for Responsible Fisheries, adopted by the FAO Ministerial Meeting on Fisheries of

---

* Prof. Dr., Vice President, International Ocean Institute.

1 See UN General Assembly doc. A/CONF.164/37 of 8 September 1995.

2 *FAO*, International Fisheries Instruments with Index, p. 41.

3 See FAO Code of Conduct for Responsible Fisheries, article 1, para. 1.1, *FAO*, International Fisheries Instruments with Index, p. 56; and FAO Conference resolution 15/93.

P. Ehlers, E. Mann-Borgese and R. Wolfrum (eds.), Marine Issues, 195–202

1999, the Draft International Agreement on the Flagging of Vessels on the High Seas (*hereinafter* Flagging Agreement), and relevant resolutions of FAO governing bodies on this matter.[4]

The problem of reflagging of fishing vessels should also be considered within the broader framework of several relevant international instruments such as the United Nations Convention of the Law of the Sea (*hereinafter* UNCLOS), Article 92 on the status of ships on the high seas, and Articles 118, 119 and 120 on the conservation and management of living resources of the high seas; UNCED – Rio Declaration on Environment and Agenda 21: Programme of Action for Sustainable Development, section 2, chapter 17, C (Sustainable Use and Conservation of Marine Living Resources of the High Seas); and the Straddling Fish Stocks Agreement of 1995.

Reflagging of fishing vessels as an illicit activity constitutes a violation of international law and the provisions of UNCLOS relating to the legal regime of the high seas. It has harmful effects on enforcement and compliance measures for the conservation and sustainable management of the fish stocks therein.

Thus, reflagging has to be considered in close relation with compliance and enforcement for the protection, rational use and sustainable development of marine living resources at the regional and global level. The implementation of effective measures to deter reflagging and fishing activities carried out by fishing vessels flying "flags of convenience" entail the responsibility of all states parties involved in marine affairs, and in particular, the flag State and the port State.

It is suggested in this paper to examine reflagging in connection with the relevant provisions of the appropriate international instruments entailing specific duties to undertake preventive, enforcement measures and control against illegal, unregulated and unreported fishing activities, including reflagging, with the view to ensuring responsible fisheries.

It is also envisaged in the concluding part to consider some suggestions *de lege ferenda* at the international and national level, for enhancing the genuine link of fishing vessels, and in particular, emphasising the responsibility of the master of the ship not only towards the flag State but also the State of his nationality. These suggestions are contemplated to follow the objectives of the Draft FAO Flagging Agreement and the relevant provisions of the FAO Compliance Agreement.

1. Reflagging of Fishing Vessels – Violation of International Law on the Legal Status of Ships and Compliance with Conservation and Management Rules and Regulations on the High Seas

The legal status of ships counts among the well-established customary rules of the international law of the sea. They have been transformed into treaty law particularly

4 Report of the Twenty-seventh Session of FAO (Rome, 6–24 November 1993), paras. 254–265, containing reference to the Draft International Agreement on the Flagging of Vessels on the High Seas (*hereinafter* FAO Flagging Agreement) and resolution 15/93 for adoption of this Agreement. The provisions of the Draft Agreement were later incorporated in the FAO Compliance Agreement.

after the adoption of the Geneva Convention on the High Seas of 1958 (Article 5 on the nationality of ships), and UNCLOS.

Under Article 92 of UNCLOS ships shall sail under the flag of one State and shall be subject to its exclusive jurisdiction on the high seas. It is further stipulated that a ship may not change its flag during a voyage or while in a port of call, save in the case of a real transfer of ownership or change of registry.

Consequently, reflagging of a fishing vessel as a means of avoiding compliance with applicable conservation and management international rules and regulations for fishing activities on the high seas, in some instances, may lead to a violation of international law regarding the legal status of the fishing vessel and the flag State's responsibility in respect of that vessel.[5] In line with Article 92 of UNCLOS, Article 111 para. 4 of the FAO Compliance Agreement stipulates that:

> "Where a fishing vessel that has been authorized to be used for fishing on the high seas by a Party ceases to be entitled to fly the flag of that Party, the authorization to fish on the high seas shall be deemed to have been cancelled".

The reflagging or use of fishing vessels with "flags of convenience" on the high seas as a means of avoiding compliance with conservation and management rules and regulations are not only violations of international law concerning the legal status of ships on the high seas. They have also important legal implications as an encroachment of applicable international rules and regulations governing the conservation and sustainable management of the living resources of the high seas.

Therefore, modern international law has assigned particular duties to flag States, Port States and other States parties to fisheries agreements and regional fisheries arrangements. States are requested to pursue international cooperation for compliance with and enforcement of conservation and management rules and regulations for fishing activities on the high seas.

2. Duties and Responsibilities of the Flag State

Considering the major role of the flag State on the high seas in accordance with general international law of the sea, most of the international treaties and other instruments concerning fishing activities contain specific rules on the duties and responsibilities of the flag State. In this connection may be singled out the Straddling Fish Stocks Agreement (Articles 18 and 19), FAO Compliance Agreement (Article 111), FAO Flagging Agreement, and FAO Code of Conduct (Article 8.2).

The provisions on the duties and responsibilities of the flag State are numerous. For the purpose of this paper, they could be set out in two main problem areas:

---

[5] See FAO Compliance Agreement, in: *FAO, International Fisheries. Instruments with Index*, pp. 39, 41; also Cancun Declaration, adopted by the FAO International Conference on Responsible Fishing, held in 1992 in Cancun, Mexico.

compliance with conservation and management rules and regulations, and enhancement of the genuine link between the State and the vessel flying its flag. Enforcement measures undertaken by the flag State are instrumental in both instances.

(a) Enforcement and Compliance with Conservation and Management Rules and Regulations

Articles 18.1 and 19.1 of the Straddling Fish Stocks Agreement establish the duty and responsibility of the flag State to take appropriate measures necessary to ensure that vessels flying its flag comply with conservation and management rules and regulations. In addition, Article III.1(a) of the FAO Compliance Agreement stipulates that appropriate measures shall be taken in order to ensure that fishing vessels entitled to fly the flag of a State Party "do not engage in any activity that undermines the effectiveness of international conservation and management measures."

Monitoring, control and surveillance referred to in Articles 18.3 and 19.1 of the Straddling Fish Stocks Agreement contain a list of enforcement powers of the flag State including investigation, physical inspection, instituting judicial proceedings in case of alleged violations of conservation and management measures carried out by the flag State.

These enforcement measures may be applied *mutatis mutandis* also to deter reflagging of fishing vessels on the high seas.

(b) Enforcement Measures to Enhance the Genuine Link between the State and the Vessel Flying its Flag

The general requirement for a genuine link between the State and the vessel flying its flag has been substantiated and further elaborated in several provisions of the Straddling Fish Stocks Agreement, the FAO Compliance Agreement and the Flagging Agreement.

Under Article 18. 2 of the Straddling Fish Stocks Agreement the flag State "shall authorize the use of vessels flying its flag for fishing on the high seas *only where it is able to exercise effectively its responsibilities in respect of such vessels*" (emphasis added). This provision not only reiterates, in other words, the rule of genuine link, proclaimed in Article 91 of UNCLOS, but also may be interpreted as opposing the practices of reflagging or the use of fishing vessels of a "flag of convenience" on the high seas.

The genuine link is further confirmed through the control of fishing vessels by means of fishing licences, authorizations or permits. The establishment of national record of fishing vessels authorized to fish and the requirements for recording and timely reporting of relevant fishing data and information on the operation of the vessel, are new developments introducing appropriate enforcement measures for strengthening the control of the State over fishing vessels flying its flag. In the same direction are the technical requirements for marking fishing vessels and fishing gear for identification in accordance with uniform and internationally recognizable vessel and gear marking systems, established by FAO.

The enforcement measures referred to above are to be supported by monitoring, control and surveillance through national inspection schemes, national observer programmes and vessel monitoring systems.

All these measures taken together testify to the new policy for the establishment of a viable international regime of regulated fisheries on the high seas. International cooperation of all States is the main prerequisite for the implementation of this policy. The jurisdiction of the flag State – though not exclusive – should be further strengthened in the two indicated directions, namely in enforcement and compliance measures, and in enhancing the genuine link between the State and the fishing vessel flying its flag.

3. Port State Assistance for Compliance With Conservation and Management Measures, and Enhancement of the Genuine Link

The enforcement by the port State for violation of international rules and regulations of fishing activities, is an extension of the port State jurisdiction relating to the enforcement of the applicable rules and standards in respect of discharge from a vessel outside the port State's internal waters, territorial sea or continental shelf.[6]

The main requirements and constitutive elements of the port State jurisdiction under Article 218 of UNCLOS are the following:

(a) The vessel must be voluntarily within a port or at an offshore terminal of the port State;
(b) The port State is entitled to undertake enforcement measures for violations of applicable international rules and regulations committed outside its internal waters, territorial sea, exclusive economic zone or continental shelf;
(c) The Port State shall institute no proceedings in respect to the alleged violation unless requested by the coastal State damaged or threatened by the violation or the flag State;
(d) The records of the investigation carried out by the port State shall be transmitted to the flag State or the damaged coastal State; and
(e) The transmittal of evidence and records of the case, together with any bond or other financial security posted with the authorities of the port State shall preclude the continuation of the proceedings by the port State.

The powers of the port State consist of investigation through inspection, instituting proceedings when appropriate, and arrest of the vessel to carry out the proceedings. The relevant provisions of the fisheries agreements, in general, follow these requirements, since they have been modeled upon the substantive elements of Article 218 of UNCLOS. Article III.2 of the FAO Compliance Agreement on international

---

6 For more details about the novel concept of port State jurisdiction and its legislative history see: *Myron H. Nordquist* (ed.): United Nations Convention on the Law of the Sea 1982 a Commentary, vol. IV (*Shabtai Rosenne/Alexander Yankov*, vol. eds., *Niel Grandy*, ass. ed.), pp. 260–272 (Dordrecht/Boston/London 1991).

cooperation, indeed, reflects closely the text of Article 218, para. 1 of UNCLOS which is the core of the concept of port State jurisdiction.

In the operation of the port State jurisdiction in respect to fisheries, special emphasis is made to assistance rendered by the port State. Article 8.3.1 of the FAO Code of Conduct specifies that port States should take, through their national legislation and in accordance with international law, such measures as are necessary to assist other States in achieving the objectives of responsible fishing and fisheries activities, conservation of fisheries resources and fishing management It further sets out, in Article 8.3.2, that the port State should provide such assistance to flag States as is appropriate, when a fishing vessel of the flag State is voluntarily in a port or at an offshore terminal of the port State.

This assistance should be rendered on the request by the flag State for assistance in respect of non-compliance with conservation and management measures or with internationally agreed minimum standards for the prevention of pollution and for safety, health and conditions of work on board fishing vessels. On its part Article 23 of the Straddling Fish Stocks Agreement provides for the rights of the port State to inspect documents, fishing gear and catch on board fishing vessels of the flag State. In accordance with para. 3 of the same article, the port State may adopt regulations empowering its authorities to prohibit landings and transshipments where it has been established that the catch has been taken contrary to the conservation and management rules and regulations on the high seas.

It may be inferred from the provisions relating to the assistance by the port State that they could apply also to reflagging as a violation of applicable international rules and regulations committed by a fishing vessel voluntarily within a port or offshore terminal of the port State. This kind of port State jurisdiction is residual in its scope and complementary to the flag State jurisdiction on the high seas. Nevertheless, it will acquire an important part in the cooperative efforts of all States to promote the effectiveness of a well-regulated regime of fisheries.

4. Some Suggestions Relating to Compliance and Enforcement Measures, and Determent of Reflagging of Fishing Vessels on the High Seas

The existing international instruments provide a viable legal framework in the field of fisheries in general, and in particular, in respect to illegal fisheries activities, including reflagging of fishing vessels or use of fishing vessels flying "flags of convenience" on the high seas. The compliance with and the enforcement of these instruments have acquired high priority. The mechanism of effective implementation needs coordination and harmonization of applicable rules, regulations and recommended practices and procedures at the global, regional and national level.

The international fisheries instruments comprise special provisions on cooperation of States directly or through sub-regional or regional fisheries management organizations or arrangements, to ensure compliance with and enforcement of conservation and management measures (*inter alia* Article 20 of the Straddling Fish Stocks

Agreement). They refer to mutual assistance between States, listing specific measures, such as assistance to be rendered to the flag State when conducting an investigation of alleged violation of conservation and management measures, or in case of investigation undertaken by the flag State in cooperation with other interested States; assistance in identifying vessels reported to have engaged in activities undermining the effectiveness of conservation and management measures, consultations and exchange of information, including evidentiary material relating to fishing activities.

It is important to point out the special attention attributed to the cooperation between the flag State and the coastal State in appliance and enforcement. This is the situation where there are reasonable grounds to believe that a foreign vessel on the high seas has been engaged in unauthorized fishing within an area under the jurisdiction of a coastal State. Fishing activities carried out in the exclusive economic zone of a coastal State adjacent to the high seas have become growing fishing practice. In that case the flag State of the intruding vessel, at the request of the coastal State concerned, shall immediately investigate the alleged offence and is under the obligation to cooperate with the coastal State in taking appropriate enforcement action, including authorization of the authorities of the coastal State to board and inspect the vessel on the high seas.

In conformity with Article 20.7 of the Straddling Fish Stocks Agreement, States members of a sub-regional or regional fisheries management organization or arrangement may take action in accordance with international law, to deter vessels engaged in activities that undermine the effectiveness or otherwise violate the conservation and management measures established by that organization or arrangement from fishing in the high seas in the region or sub-region until such time as appropriate action is taken by the flag State. This new type of a sanction is imposed in order to discourage violations of international fisheries rules and regulations and compel flag States to comply with the conservation and management measures.

The implementation of the fisheries agreements and related international instruments depends upon, to a great extent, the adoption of adequate legislative and administrative measures within the internal legal system of States. Violations of international rules on fishing should be qualified as offences under municipal law, including penal law. This approach is substantiated in Article 8.2.7 of the FAO Code of Conduct which stipulates that flag States should make the contravention of applicable conservation and management measures an offence under national legislation.

Reflagging, which is recognized as a breach of international law of the sea, must also be qualified as an illicit act under domestic penal law of States parties to the respective international agreements and other international instruments. There are already treaty provisions in this direction. It is appropriate in this connection to refer to the FAO Compliance Agreement which "calls upon States to take effective action, consistent with international law, to deter reflagging of vessels by their nationals as a means of avoiding compliance with applicable conservation and management rules for fishing activities on the high seas." It is evident that such a provision would apply to the master of the fishing vessel committing infraction of the law of the sea in respect of the status of ships and their nationality, operating on the high seas.

The incorporation in municipal law of the incrimination of violations of rules of the law of the sea concerning illegal fishing activities, including undermining applicable conservation and management measures, reflagging and other offences committed by fishing vessels on the high seas, has to be made in accordance with the general principles and rules of international law and the law of the sea. This novel concept should not, in any way, detract from the established principle of the jurisdiction of the flag State on the high seas: It has to be introduced with great caution and after thorough evaluation of the legal implications that may derive therefrom. The consensus of States on such a reform is of paramount importance for the effective implementation of this new concept.

*Nele Matz**

THE INTERACTION BETWEEN THE CONVENTION ON BIOLOGICAL DIVERSITY AND THE UN CONVENTION ON THE LAW OF THE SEA**

1. Introduction

In the face of virtually thousands of international treaties and a continuously growing number of multilateral and so called "global" conventions it is not at all surprising that many of these instruments, due to their thematic and geographical scopes, overlap or collide with one another. Two facts, however, are truly surprising; first, the fact that the resulting situation has rarely been discussed other than in the context of collisions between Multilateral Environmental Agreements and the General Agreement on Tariffs and Trade (GATT)[1] and, second, that approaches to solve these difficulties and preventative mechanisms during the negotiation processes of new agreements are still underdeveloped. In fact, particularly the second aspect leads to a continuing tendency towards so-called treaty congestion.[2]

Conflicts of different treaties on the one hand and the doubling of efforts by two or more agreements regulating the same subject matter on the other hand can significantly decrease the effectiveness of international law. The phenomenon of treaty congestion becomes particularly apparent in the field of international environmental law, because environmental issues are closely interrelated and the number of agreements has significantly increased over the last three decades.

In the scenario concerning the interrelation of the United Nations Convention on the Law of the Sea 1982 (UNCLOS)[3] and the Convention on Biological Diversity

* Ph.D. Candidate, University of Heidelberg.

** This paper is based upon an article by *Rüdiger Wolfrum/Nele Matz*, The Interplay of the United Nations Convention on the Law of the Sea and the United Nations Convention on Biological Diversity, *MPY UNL* 4 (2000), pp. 445–480.

1 See for example *D. Brack*, Reconciling the GATT and Multilateral Environmental Agreements with Trade Provisions: the Latest Debate, in: *RECIEL* 6 (1997), 112–120; *S. Charnovitz*, Multilateral Environmental Agreements and Trade Rules, in: *EPL* 26 (1996), 163–169; *J. Cameron/J. Robinson*, The Use of Trade Provisions in International Environmental Agreements and their Compatibility with the GATT, in: *YIEL* 3 (1992), 3–30.

2 On the phenomenon of treaty congestion see *B. Lukitsch Hicks*, Treaty Congestion in International Environmental Law: The Need for Greater International Coordination, in: *UoRLR* 32 (1999), 1643 *et seq.*

3 21 *ILM* 1261 *et seq.* (1982).

P. Ehlers, E. Mann-Borgese and R. Wolfrum (eds.), Marine Issues, 203–220

1992 (CBD)[4] potential overlaps and collisions can lead to ineffectiveness concerning the protection and sustainable management of marine biological, i.e. living and genetic, resources. The following discussion analyses the underlying philosophies, concepts and approaches to the protection of marine living and genetic resources as envisaged by the two instruments. The aim is to provide the reader with a brief yet comprehensive summary on whether and to what extent marine biological resources are adequately protected under international law and which regulations prevail in this respect.

2. The Management and Protection of Marine Living Resources

The management and protection of marine living resources has gained growing international attention since the worldwide serious depletion of fish stocks and the economic breakdown of many fishing industries and fishing communities as a result of overfishing. In this respect an economic, utilitarian position and a more protectionist, environmental standpoint on how to address the problem of management and protection of marine life and, particularly overfishing, differ considerably. The following discussion will show to what extent opposing opinions are reflected by the approaches taken by the UN Convention on the Law of the Sea and the Convention on Biological Diversity concerning marine living resources.

2.1. Scope of the UNCLOS and the CBD in Respect to Marine Living Resources

Under the law of the sea regime as codified in the UN Convention on the Law of the Sea the regulations on the management and protection of marine living resources to a large extent depend upon the respective maritime zone. The rules on responsibility for a sustainable management and the protection of marine life as related to fisheries differ for the territorial sea, the exclusive economic zone and the high seas. The situation is further complicated by the fact that the regime on fisheries is supplemented by the provisions on environmental protection of marine life in Part XII of the UN Convention on the Law of the Sea[5] and by the 1995 Agreement on Fish Stocks.[6]

In territorial and archipelagic waters the UN Convention on the Law of the Sea's fisheries regime grants exclusive sovereignty to the coastal state without indicating a conservation or management policy to be pursued. While the provisions applicable

4 31 *ILM* 818 *et seq.* (1992).

5 In the order of 27 August 1999, Southern Bluefin Tuna Cases (New Zealand v. Japan; Australia v. Japan), Requests for Provisional Measures, 38 *ILM* 1624 *et seq.* (1999), in para. 70 the International Tribunal for the Law of the Sea states that "... the conservation of the living resources of the sea is an element in the protection and preservation of the marine environment."

6 Agreement for the Implementation of the Provisions of the UNCLOS of 10 December 1982 relating to the Conservation and Management of Straddling Fish Stocks and Highly Migratory Fish Stocks, 1995, 34 *ILM* 1547 *et seq.* (1995).

to the natural resources in the exclusive economic zone also grant sovereign rights to the coastal states concerning the exploration, exploitation, conservation and management of natural resources, the states' rights concerning straddling and highly migratory fish stocks and the conservation and management policy adopted by the coastal states are subject to restrictions. In contrast to the freedom enjoyed with regard to the policies applicable in territorial waters, the coastal state is, according to arts 61 and 62 UNCLOS, obliged to establish an appropriate management and conservation regime. Under these provisions the coastal state must, subject to further specifications, protect living resources against over-exploitation and maintain and restore levels that can produce the maximum sustainable yield of harvested species. The same – rather minimalist – protection standards also apply to high seas fisheries, article 119 UNCLOS. An important aspect of the conservation regime of marine living resources in the high seas, that is necessary to counterbalance the freedom of the high seas, is the duty to co-operate with other states concerning the exploitation of living resources.

By the application of Part XII to fishery policies other environmental considerations are taken into account when dealing with marine living resources under the UN Convention on the Law of the Sea. Article 193 UNCLOS emphasises that the sovereign right to exploit marine living resources does not release states from the obligation to protect and preserve the marine environment. With regard to the further protection of marine living resources according to the UN Convention on the Law of the Sea, the general rules of Part XII of the Convention dealing with the protection and preservation of the marine environment are applicable to the formulation of the national fishery policy in the territorial waters, the archipelagic waters and the exclusive economic zone. The respective obligations accordingly represent a limit to the exercise of sovereign rights. In contrast to the first impression the preservation and protection of the marine environment, including the management and protection of marine living resources, is thus not fully left to the discretion of states.

The regimes on fishing in the exclusive economic zone and on the high seas are further supplemented by the 1995 Agreement on Fish Stocks. This agreement provides for more detailed regulations on species management that were found necessary in the face of a serious decline of several fish stocks, the lack of co-ordination between national fisheries and conservation policies and the lack of compliance control and enforcement. Measures to address these issues are a central focus of the agreement.

Concerning the seabed, again, the rules applicable to marine living resources differ with regard to the respective zones. In this respect the continental shelf and the deep seabed, the so-called Area, have to be distinguished. The rules concerning the continental shelf, although mentioning sedentary species, do not provide for policy guidance concerning a regime on the protection and management of the continental shelf's living resources. However, the general principles on marine environmental protection are applicable.

The status of marine living resources of the deep-seabed is problematic. The UN Convention on the Law of the Sea regime on the Area is restricted to mineral resources. Even the provisions that give institutional competence for a potential broadening of the regime, article 162 para. 2 lit (o) (ii) UNCLOS, can be understood to exclude the establishment of rules that directly address biological resources. However, in the face of the potential need to establish rules and regulations for activities concerning biological resources, particularly genetic resources, the competence of the Seabed Authority in this respect will gain growing attention in the near future.

One main reason for the failure of UNCLOS to address the biological resources of the deep seabed must be seen in the only rather recent discovery of living organisms in the deep seabed and their potential significance. Mankind, or rather the industrialised world, has only a short while ago developed the technical and technological capabilities to explore the deep seabed. However, the issue of biological resources in the Area gains more significance in regard to the exploration of and access to genetic resources, since, due to the adverse living conditions on the deep seabed, the organisms concerned are mainly bacteria and other microorganisms found in connection with hydrothermal vents. Commercial fishing and the threat of overfishing of species are not directly relevant for the regime of the deep seabed.

If compared with the different zones and regimes concerning living resources under the UN Convention on the Law of the Sea, the application of the Convention on Biological Diversity's rules to the living resources of the marine environment seem, on first sight, rather simple. The Convention on Biological Diversity is, in principle, applicable to terrestrial and marine biodiversity.

The negotiations preceding the conclusion of the Convention on Biological Diversity had almost exclusively focused on terrestrial biological diversity, the issues of marine and coastal biodiversity have been introduced later in the negotiating process. Nevertheless, they have never been intensively discussed,[7] before the issue was finally addressed by the second Conference of the Parties (COP) to the Convention on Biological Diversity in 1995. On that occasion COP 2 expressed its deep concern "... at the serious threats to marine and coastal biodiversity caused by factors, including physical alteration, destruction and degradation of habitats, pollution, invasion of alien species, and over-exploitation of living and marine coastal resources." As a result the Subsidiary Body on Scientific, Technical and Technological Advice (SBSTTA) established a work programme – the Jakarta Mandate – which focused on five thematic issue areas: integrated marine and coastal area management; marine and coastal protected areas; sustainable use of marine and coastal living resources; mariculture; and alien species.[8]

Yet, while it follows from the general inclusion of marine biodiversity and the specific programmes that the Convention on Biological Diversity is applicable to marine species, ecosystems and genetic resources, the Convention on Biological

---

7 *G. Verhoosel*, Prospecting for Marine and Coastal Biodiversity: International Law in Deep Water, in: *IJMCL* 13 (1998), 91.

8 See Report COP2, Annex II, Decision II/10, Doc.UNEP/CBD/2/19.

Diversity's juridical scope of application is subject to a restriction that is most important for its application to the marine environment. Art. 4 CBD on the juridical scope of the convention holds every state responsible for the application of the convention in regard to components of biological diversity located within areas of national sovereignty and to activities and processes under its control within and without areas of national jurisdiction regardless of where the effect of that activity occurs. When establishing which marine areas are areas of national sovereignty, the distinction of different marine zones of sovereignty and competence under the UN Convention on the Law of the Sea have a crucial effect on the Convention on Biological Diversity's scope.

It follows from the distinction of maritime zones in the UN Convention on the Law of the Sea and art. 4 CBD that in the archipelagic waters, the territorial sea, the exclusive economic zone and on the continental shelf the Convention on Biological Diversity applies to components of biological diversity, whereas beyond these zones of sovereignty states parties have to co-operate either directly or through competent international organisations to promote the conservation of components of biological diversity. In the case of the marine environment several international organisations already exist which may serve as an appropriate forum, such as the IMO, the International Whaling Commission as well as regional or species-oriented organisations. Outside the limits of national sovereignty the Convention on Biological Diversity is only applicable in regard to activities and processes under the states' control and not to "components of biological diversity". The distinction between components of biological diversity on the one hand and processes and activities potentially harmful to biodiversity on the other hand has been considered arbitrary.[9]

2.2. The Ecosystem Approach v. the Maximum Sustainable Yield

Concerning the approach how and, particularly, to what extent living resources should be protected the UN Convention on the Law of the Sea and the Convention on Biological Diversity differ considerably. The 1995 Agreement on Fish Stocks to some – yet limited – extent bridges the gap between their underlying approaches. The main difference is to be found in relation to the ecosystem approach as envisaged by the Convention on Biological Diversity on the one hand and the restoring or maintaining of levels that can produce the maximum sustainable yield as provided by the UN Convention on the Law of the Sea for the regimes on high seas and exclusive economic zone fisheries on the other hand. The rules on the restoration and maintenance of the maximum sustainable yield are significantly less comprehensive than an ecosystem approach to the protection and management of marine life.

The ecosystem approach to the management and protection of marine life does

---

[9] *L. Glowka/F. Burhenne-Guilmin/H. Synge* in collaboration with *J.A. McNeely/L. Gündling*, A Guide to the Convention on Biological Diversity, p. 27 (1994).

not only focus on particular, harvested or other, species but includes the protection of all living organisms and non-living features and their interdependence in the marine environment.[10] These interdependencies take into account biological and ecological interactions between all marine species in the same as well as in neighbouring jurisdictional zones, and the ecological conditions of the physical surroundings. The Convention on Biological Diversity very clearly reflects the ecosystem approach and constantly stresses the significance of the protection of ecosystems rather than species. It not only incorporates the variability of ecosystems into the definition of biological diversity in art. 2[11] hence including the protection of ecosystems within all measures envisaged to save biological diversity but also more specifically refers to the protection of ecosystems in art. 8 lit. (d). In this article the Convention on Biological Diversity states that contracting parties must pursue the conservation of biological diversity by establishing a system of protection areas or areas where special measures need to be taken to conserve biological diversity and promote the protection of ecosystems, natural habitats and the maintenance of viable populations of species in natural surroundings. Contracting parties are also required to rehabilitate and restore degraded ecosystems and to promote the recovery of threatened species, article 8 lit. (f).

In defining the maximum sustainable yield according to the UN Convention on the Law of the Sea environmental and economic factors may be taken into account. The environmental factors referred to by the respective provisions are the interdependence of stocks (i.e. the effect exploitation has on species associated with or dependent upon harvested species) and generally recommended international minimum standards. While the interaction between species is part of this approach, dependent and associated species to those protected for human exploitation represent only a small percentage of all living organisms that build the marine community in an ecosystem. The majority of interdependencies and other factors characterising a marine ecosystem are not addressed by the approach taken to conserve marine living resources under the UN Convention on the Law of the Sea, despite the fact that fishing alters the relative abundance of species in marine communities and, additionally, fishing gear can physically destroy or alter habitats and disrupt bottom-dwelling communities.[12] As a result marine ecosystems can be significantly changed,[13] even if

---

[10] See also *S. Iudicello/M. Lytle*, Marine biodiversity and international law: instruments and institutions that can be used to conserve marine biological diversity internationally, in: *TELJ* 8 (1994), 124 *et seq.*

[11] Art. 2 CBD "Use of Terms": "*Biological Diversity*" means the variability among living organisms from all sources including, *inter alia*, terrestrial, marine and other aquatic ecosystems and the ecological complexes of which they are part; this includes diversity within species, between species and of ecosystems.(…).

[12] *A. Rieser*, International Fisheries Law, Overfishing and Marine Biodiversity, in: *GIELR* 9 (1997), 251 *et seq.*, 254; *G. Rose*, Marine Biodiversity Protection through Fisheries Management – International Legal Developments, in: *RECIEL* 8 (1999), 284.

[13] The effect fisheries have on species and marine ecosystems due to ecological inter-dependency is considerable; stock depletion affects *inter alia* coral reefs, mangroves, estuaries as well as mammal species and turtles; *A. Rengifo*, Protection of Marine Biodiversity: A New Generation of Fisheries Agreements, in: *RECIEL* 6 (1997), 313 *et seq.*

policies comply with the provisions of the UN Convention on the Law of the Sea on the interdependence of species.

Part XII contains one concrete provision on the protection and preservation of marine living resources, namely article 194 para.5. According to it, measures are to be taken to protect and preserve rare or fragile ecosystems as well as depleted, threatened or endangered species and other forms of marine life. This provision may not be understood as requiring reactive measures only, but calling additionally for preventive action.[14] While the provision clearly mentions ecosystems and the need for their protection, one cannot conclude that hence the more specifically outlined UNCLOS fisheries regime was also reflecting an ecosystem approach. As a consequence of this unclear relation of rules within UNCLOS, the ecosystem approach must at the very least be regarded as underdeveloped.

The UN Convention on the Law of the Sea has largely been negotiated before the general acknowledgement of the ecosystem's significance for effective environmental protection and its provisions quite clearly focus on single species management and protection. In fact, since the convention's fisheries regime focuses on harvested species, it reflects not only a single species but furthermore a clearly utilitarian point of view. The Convention on Biological Diversity, although also promoting the sustainable use of biodiversity and consequently also taking a utilitarian point of view, at least acknowledges the intrinsic value of biological diversity in its preamble. The focus on an ecosystem approach tends to be more ecocentric, since those features not primarily useful for human purposes are included in the concept. In the end the reasons why a specific approach has been taken, for ecocentric or utilaristic reasons, is not important, provided that the approach in itself is far-reaching and comprehensive.

To some extent the Fish Stocks Agreement of 1995 modifies the reliance on species protection. The Agreement has improved some shortcomings of the UN Convention on the Law of the Sea regarding the protection of ecosystems. However, as opposed to the Convention on Biological Diversity, it does so mainly in respect to additional stocks and not to marine life in general.[15] States must take into account the biological unity and other biological characteristics of the stocks and the relationship between the distribution of the stocks, the fisheries and the geographical particularities of the respective region. The reference to the notion of "biological unity" emphasises that the Agreement is at least more clearly based upon an ecosystem approach than the UN Convention on the Law of the Sea. The Agreement provides for conservation and management measures for species belonging to the same ecosystem as the protected straddling and highly-migratory fish stocks.[16] Furthermore, the protection

---

[14] *R. Wolfrum* The Protection of the Marine Environment after the Rio Conference: Progress or Stalemate?, in: *U. Beyerlin et al.* (eds.), *Recht zwischen Umbruch und Bewahrung – Festschrift für Rudolf Bernhardt*, pp. 1003 *et seq.*, 1009 (1995).

[15] Out of the number of fish stocks that have reached their yield limit, however, many species are classified as straddling and highly migratory stocks, see *Rengifo* (*supra* note 13), p. 314.

[16] Article 5(e) 1995 Agreement on Fish Stocks.

of biodiversity in the marine environment is one of its objectives. The diversity of ecosystems can be regarded as one component of biodiversity; the 1995 Agreement on Fish Stocks, however, does not give any definition of the term. Although the 1995 Fish Stocks Agreement has retained the concept of maximum sustainable yield as a valid reference point, it does not face the same critique as the respective provisions of the UN Convention on the Law of the Sea. This reference point is to be considered a limit reference point, which constrains utilisation within safe biological limits.[17]

3. Genetic Resources and Marine Scientific Research

Many marine genetic resources have been recognised or are supposed to bear a significant potential for applied research and biotechnology. Genetic resources cannot only be important for medical developments and applications, but, particularly those from the bacteria and other microorganisms living in the realm of deep-seabed hydrothermal vents, can also be significant for industrial use e.g. because of heat resistant capacities. The organisms found in connection with deep-seabed vents survive in a sulphur atmosphere without oxygen and at very high temperatures, which makes their characteristics especially valuable for further exploration.

The present forms of bioprospecting i.e. the taking of samples of genetic material for further research cannot be compared with the exploitation and depletion of marine living resources as occur in fishing activities. Since the collection of samples for the sake of their genetic resources is not concerned with the mass of material but rather with the further research on its content, the activity, although highly commercial, resembles scientific research.

3.1. Applicability of Regulations to Marine Genetic Resources

When the UN Convention on the Law of the Sea was negotiated and finally concluded, the issue of marine genetic resources and their potential significance for developments in the biotechnological, medical and industrial field was not yet recognised. Consequently, neither the management and protection of nor access to genetic resources are directly addressed by the UN Convention on the Law of the Sea. In contrast thereto, genetic diversity as one explicit aspect of biological diversity is part of the Convention on Biological Diversity's regime on the conservation and sustainable use of biodiversity. In fact, the Convention on Biological Diversity makes genetic resources, their sustainable use and access thereto one of its central issues.

Under the UN Convention on the Law of the Sea the protection of living resources from over-exploitation, as weak as that regime might be, indirectly also protects the

---

[17] See *D. Nelson*, The Development of the Legal Regime of High Seas Fisheries, in: *A. Boyle/D. Freestone* (eds.), *International Law and Sustainable Development: Past Achievements and Future Challenges*, pp. 126/127 (1999), with further references.

respective genetic resources. As unsustainable fisheries can reduce genetic diversity by changing population characteristics, the protection of sustainable yields indirectly promotes the genetic variability of the targeted species. Yet, as the Convention refers to living resources with the implicit meaning of fisheries, microbial genetic diversity in the deep seabed like those organisms found in hydrothermal vents might be outside the Convention's ambit. Consequently, an unknown variety of marine genetic resources, and particularly those considered valuable for commercial use, would not even indirectly be addressed by the Convention.

Because of the resemblance of the exploitation of genetic resources with scientific research, in respect to the UN Convention on the Law of the Sea the provisions on marine scientific research could be applicable. In general terms the expression "marine scientific research" is most often used to describe activities to expand scientific knowledge of the marine environment and its processes and includes *inter alia* oceanography, marine biology, marine chemistry, scientific ocean drilling and coring, geological and geophysical surveying.[18] The expansion of knowledge on marine genetic resources and activities as to their exploration, consequently, are to be considered marine scientific research. According to article 238 UNCLOS all states have the right to conduct marine scientific research subject to the rights and duties of other states. These rights and duties depend upon the maritime zone in which the research is to be conducted and the nature of the research activity. Article 239 formulates a general rule on promotion and facilitation of the development and conduct of marine scientific research.

3.2. Access to Genetic Resources

Under the UN Convention on the Law of the Sea access to genetic resources in the cause of marine scientific research depends on the maritime zone. In its territorial waters a state enjoys exclusive sovereignty to regulate, authorise and conduct marine scientific research and is – under the UN Convention on the Law of the Sea – not obliged in any way to provide for access to genetic resources for their scientific exploration. Any marine scientific research by other states or international organisations or nationals of other states may be conducted only with the express consent and subject to the conditions of the coastal state.[19] Further, the UN Convention on the Law of the Sea expressly states that passage through territorial waters for the purpose of carrying out research activities does not qualify as innocent passage.[20]

As to the exclusive economic zone and the continental shelf, the coastal states have jurisdiction with respect to marine scientific research; however, their authority is subject to limitations, if compared with the regime in the territorial sea and archipelagic waters. Marine scientific research may only be conducted with the

[18] *J.A. Roach*, Marine Scientific Research and the New Law of the Sea, in: *ODILA* 27 (1996), 59 *et seq.*, 60.
[19] Art. 245 UNCLOS.
[20] Art. 19(2)(j) UNCLOS.

express consent of the coastal state but, as opposed to the provisions concerning territorial waters, states can be obliged to grant this consent. The obligation to establish regulations and procedures to ensure that consent is granted without unreasonable delay or denial[21] is in conformity with the obligation to facilitate access to genetic resources under the Convention on Biological Diversity.

Article 246 paras 3–5 UNCLOS distinguishes between scientific research to increase the knowledge on the marine environment (purely scientific research) and scientific research, which is of direct significance for the exploration and exploitation of the natural resources of the given exclusive economic zone or the continental shelf. In the latter case the coastal state may withhold its consent subject to state discretion, whereas in the former the state has under normal circumstances the obligation to grant permission. The objective of this provision is to make the regime for marine scientific research compatible with the regime concerning the use of the exclusive economic zone and the continental shelf. Since bioprospecting is not meant to exclusively increase the general scientific knowledge on the environment of a given zone but is rather commercial-use-oriented it should come under article 246 para. 5 UNCLOS. Consequently, the coastal state may withhold its consent and is according to the UN Convention on the Law of the Sea, under no obligation to facilitate access to genetic resources in its exclusive economic zone.[22] The same is valid for access to genetic resources located on the continental shelf as far as this area does not extend 200 nautical miles from the baselines. For projects to be conducted on the continental shelf beyond the 200 miles limit, states can only perform their discretion to withhold consent for research projects, if they have publicly designated the area in question as an area "in which exploitation or detailed exploratory operations focused on those areas" are occurring or about to occur in a reasonable period of time.[23]

As far as the high seas are concerned, the conduct of marine scientific research is free.[24] Equally free is marine scientific research concerning the Area.[25] Research on marine biological resources of the deep seabed does not come under the jurisdiction of the International Seabed Authority since its jurisdictional power does not extend to marine living resources of the Area.[26]

The provisions of the UN Convention on the Law of the Sea on marine scientific research are predominantly aiming at a distribution of jurisdictional powers rather than at the protection of the research object and at the distribution of benefits resulting from such research. The only general duty states parties to the Convention have is to promote and facilitate marine scientific research as such according to

---

21 Art. 246(3) UNCLOS.

22 *G. Henne*, Genetische Vielfalt als Ressource, p. 328 (1998); different *Verhoosel* (*supra* note 7), pp. 100 *et seq.*, who seems to qualify bioprospecting as purely scientific research.

23 Art. 246(6) UNCLOS.

24 Art. 238 in connection with art. 87 UNCLOS.

25 Art. 256 in connection with art. 143 UNCLOS.

26 See above at I.1.

article 239. This obligation does not even allow the conclusion that research by foreign scientists must be facilitated. Regulations for the promotion of marine scientific research can be focused on conditions for national scientists and still comply with article 239 UNCLOS. There is no customary law of the sea that deals with genetic resources or access thereto. Therefore, they do not cover the scope covered by the Convention on Biological Diversity.

The Convention on Biological Diversity's regime on access to genetic resources is very elaborated and relies heavily on benefits for the sustainable use of genetic resources as an incentive to protect and maintain genetic resources on a long-term basis. The CBC provides for a network of trade-offs. States hosting genetic resources may bargain access to genetic resources against the sharing of benefits[27] derived from their use. The possibility of benefiting from the utilisation of genetic resources in itself is meant to constitute an incentive for the conservation of biological diversity and to ensure that biological resources under the jurisdiction of the host state are used in a sustainable manner. To stabilise a system of access and benefit-sharing several provisions of the Convention on Biological Diversity restate that states have sovereign rights over or the sovereign right to exploit their biological resources.[28] This principle is, however, to a certain extent balanced by the statement in the Preamble of the Convention that biological diversity has an intrinsic value and that the conservation of biological diversity is the common concern of humankind. Under article 15 para. 2 CBD each contracting party shall endeavour to create conditions to facilitate access to genetic resources. This provision balances the sovereign rights some more and might be seen as the rudimentary expression to regard biological diversity not only as a common concern but a common heritage of humankind. The introduction of a concept of common heritage into the Convention on Biological Diversity has been heavily opposed by the biodiversity-rich developing countries. While many environmentalists regretted the omission of the common heritage and the emphasis on sovereign rights, these rights and a system of benefit-sharing might just be the only viable incentive to make a system of protection of genetic resources work.

4. Questions of Divergence and Prevalence

4.1. Divergences: A Comparison of the Two Regimes on Marine Living and Genetic Resources

The regimes as described so far differ in several respects. Fundamental differences relate to the underlying philosophies of the Conventions and their respective focus and structure. This has consequences for the approach to the protection of marine

[27] See arts. 15, 16 and 19.

[28] The fourth preambular paragraph and art. 15(1) reaffirm that states have sovereign rights over their own biological resources, whereas article 3 CBD refers to the sovereign right to exploit such resources.

living and genetic resources as well as to marine scientific research and access to genetic resources for scientific reasons.

The regime on marine living resources under the UN Convention on the Law of the Sea is predominantly exploitation-oriented and focuses on marine living resources harvested for human consumption or other human uses. In contrast to this feature the protection of other stocks or species, in particular those that compete with human activities in the utilisation of harvested stocks, is weak. While both Conventions, the UN Convention on the Law of the Sea as well as the Convention on Biological Diversity, are based upon an anthropocentric approach, they differ with regard to the underlying objectives and targets in time.

The UN Convention on the Law of the Sea aims at short-term efforts to secure stocks valuable for human consumption, whereas the Convention on Biological Diversity includes in its concept the potential needs of future generation as well as – in the preamble – the recognition of an intrinsic value of biodiversity. As a result the instrument rather aims at comprehensive long-term efforts that include all components of biological diversity and not only those that are momentarily considered valuable. The 1995 Agreement on Fish Stocks links both described approaches. The objective to ensure the long-term conservation and sustainable use, based upon *inter alia* a – cautious – ecosystem approach is generally compatible with those of the Convention on Biological Diversity.[29]

Another area of discrepancy derives from the conservation obligations under the Convention on Biological Diversity. The implementation of the obligation to provide for protected areas, to promote the protection of ecosystem and natural habitats and to rehabilitate and to restore degraded ecosystems may come into conflict with the coastal states' obligation to allow innocent passage in the territorial sea or in archipelagic waters, to respect the right of archipelagic sea lanes passage, of transit passage and the freedom of navigation in the exclusive economic zones.

Specific areas of environmental protection are not explicitly envisioned by the UN Convention on the Law of the Sea. States can take measures "... necessary to protect and preserve rare or fragile ecosystems as well as the habitat of depleted, threatened or endangered species and other forms of marine life,"[30] yet such measures must not be an "unjustifiable interference with activities carried out by other states in the exercise of their rights and in pursuance of their duties in conformity with this Convention."[31] Given the importance that the right of innocent passage and freedom of navigation claims throughout the Convention, it is unlikely that areas that exclude ships from making use of these rights can be established. Although the coastal states may adopt laws and regulations in respect of the preservation of the environment,[32] this right is balanced by article 24 para. 1 lit. (a) UNCLOS according to which

[29] *Rengifo* (*supra* note 13), p. 318.
[30] Art. 194(5) UNCLOS.
[31] Art. 194(4) UNCLOS.
[32] Art. 21(1)(f) UNCLOS.

regulations on foreign ships which have the practical effect of denying or impairing innocent passage cannot be imposed. As a consequence, areas in the territorial waters, archipelagic waters, archipelagic sea lanes and in the exclusive economic zones from which shipping would be totally excluded would be contrary to the objective of the UN Convention on the Law of the Sea concerning innocent passage and freedom of navigation for these zones and would, as a result, be considered unjustifiable.

However, many activities that are capable of depleting marine living resources in protected areas such as fishing or the catch of living resources for scientific research can be prohibited because they are not covered by the activities considered to come under "innocent passage."[33] The Convention on Biological Diversity does not define the term "protected areas." Although certain measures must be undertaken to fulfil the commitment to establish and manage protected areas, the Convention does not oblige states parties to establish areas that are free from any human use. As a consequence there is not necessarily a conflict of obligations between the Conventions but rather a conflict of objectives or targets. From the perspective of environmental protection, however, conflicts of objectives often have the same negative effect as conflicts that arise from incompatible obligations and result in insufficient protection regimes.

Both instruments also differ considerably concerning the protection of and access to genetic resources and respectively concerning marine genetic research. As already discussed, there is no obligation to facilitate access to genetic resources in the territorial waters or exclusive economic zones under the law of the sea, whereas article 15 para.2 CBD – one of the essential structural elements of the framework for biodiversity protection – calls for the facilitation of access.

Although article 15 CBD does not oblige states parties to grant access to genetic resources, its provisions go further than the UN Convention on the Law of the Sea. The discretion states have to grant or not to grant access to genetic resources for bioprospecting in the exclusive economic zone and on the continental shelf collides with the obligation to facilitate access to marine genetic resources under national sovereignty according to the Convention on Biological Diversity. The obligation not to impose restrictions that run counter to the objectives of the Convention is of special significance. One of the objectives is to protect biodiversity via the incentive to make use of genetic resources and to share benefits with and transfer technology to developing countries of origin. A rigorous restriction of access to genetic resources of the territorial and archipelagic waters runs counter the objectives to establish a comprehensive system of access, benefit sharing and co-operation. As a result an incentive-based framework of protection would not be promoted and, hence, the protection of biological diversity could be diminished. Furthermore, the regime on marine scientific research – although bioprospecting resembles sampling for scientific

33 Art. 19(2)(i) and (j) UNCLOS.

research – lacks the protective component, which is essential under the Convention on Biological Diversity.

For the high seas and the Area the legal situation for marine genetic resources is even more unsatisfactory. For marine genetic resources outside national jurisdiction access to genetic resources to undertake scientific research is free under the UN Convention on the Law of the Sea. Neither is access to genetic resources outside national jurisdiction part of the complex system of access and benefit-sharing under article 15 in connection with article 4 CBD. According to article 4 lit (b) the Convention on Biological Diversity applies to processes and activities under the control of states parties outside the limits of national jurisdiction, hence, also concerning the activities on the high seas and the deep seabed. However, the provisions on access are based upon national sovereignty and cannot be transferred to access to genetic resources in the high seas. As long as scientific research does not collide with other objectives of the Convention on Biological Diversity it can be performed by contracting states' nationals beyond areas of national jurisdiction without further conditions.

This circumstance – again – is capable of severely diminishing the significance of access to genetic resources as an incentive for their protection.[34] If states can conduct bioprospecting on the high seas without having to agree on benefit-sharing and technology transfer as they would have concerning resources under national jurisdiction, they undermine the objectives of the Convention on Biological Diversity as there is less incentive for developing states to protect genetic resources under their sovereignty. This reasoning is to some extent theoretical as many areas of genetic richness are located near coasts i.e. under the sovereignty of the coastal state. Furthermore, scientific research on the high seas is more difficult and expensive to undertake. As a result developed states might in fact be more interested in gaining access to genetic resources in areas under national jurisdiction accepting agreements on benefit-sharing and transfer of technologies, and consequently strengthen an incentive based system of protection of genetic resources. Yet, this discussion shows that the underlying rationale of the UN Convention on the Law of the Sea can to some extent undermine the objectives and efforts of the Convention on Biological Diversity.

4.2. Conflict Clauses and Rules of Preference

In this context the Vienna Convention on the Law of Treaties is particularly valuable with regard to its rules on the interpretation of treaties, since its rules on the solution of conflicts refer only to treaties dealing with the same subject matter (article 30 VCLT). These provisions must be considered inapplicable when dealing with overlapping treaties on different aspects of environmental protection. The UN Convention on the Law of the Sea and the Convention on Biological Diversity cannot be

---

34 See *Verhoosel* (*supra* note 7), p. 102.

regarded to be successive treaties on the same subject matter, even if their focus on the protection of the marine environment overlaps to some extent; too different are the scopes and primary aims of both agreements.

The feasibility of interpretation to perform a conciliatory function, however, must not be underestimated. Still, interpretation can only be employed to address conflicts, if the respective colliding provisions are unclear or vague. If the states parties to an agreement wilfully establish provisions that collide with other agreements and express their intention in clear unambiguous wording, interpretation cannot be used to conciliate the conflict. The basic rule of interpretation according to article 31 para.1 Vienna Convention on the Law of Treaties states that treaties have to be interpreted "in good faith in accordance with the ordinary meaning to be given to the terms of the treaty in their context and in the light of its object and purpose". Especially the teleological element to this rule is important when dealing with the interpretation of colliding treaty provisions and related matters.

Although there is, with the potential exception of Article 103 Charter of the United Nations, no hierarchy of treaties in international law, treaties themselves can establish conflict clauses that recognise the superiority of other agreements. In the case of treaty clauses that regulate the relation to other agreements, interpretation is an essential element of conciliation. Generally, the provisions of the referring instrument must be interpreted so as to conform to the superior treaty. This proceeding reflects the will of the parties with regard to the object and scope of the agreement laid down in the clause of precedence. Hence, the precedence of the one agreement is recognised, while the widest possible scope of application of the inferior instrument is maintained.

The most common provision is to prevent conflicts of obligations by establishing precedence of those instruments adopted prior to the respective treaty. Like many other international agreements the Convention on Biological Diversity contains such a clause of precedence of those rights and duties that bind the contracting parties at the time of the ratification of the Convention, article 22. Yet, the agreement adds that this preference shall not be valid if "the exercise of those rights and obligations would cause a serious damage or threat to biological diversity". This exemption to the rule is unusual and can lead to a *de facto* precedence of the Convention on Biological Diversity in respect to other instruments. This conclusion is emphasised when considering that the phrase to "cause a serious damage or threat to biological diversity" is subject to a wide margin of interpretation by the contracting parties. Article 22 para. 2 CBD deals specifically with the relation to the law of the sea. The implementation of the Convention on Biological Diversity must be in consistence with the rights and obligations of states under the law of the sea.

The expression "rights and obligations of states under the law of the sea" can either be interpreted to limit the prevailing power of the law of the sea to rights and duties only, or to include in fact the law of the sea in general. The limitation to rights and obligations in a strict sense of meaning excludes general principles and institutional or administrative matters. This question has not yet been discussed in the respective literature. Authors seem to understand "rights and obligations" as being equivalent to the law of the sea in general.[35]

It is doubtful whether the contracting parties intended the exclusion of general principles. A conflict of treaties most often arises, if rights and obligations collide, but general principles can be used to interpret certain rights and obligations and, as a result, play an indirect role in the said collisions. Furthermore, general principles can as well lead to conflicts of different conventions' objectives and the interpretation of agreements.

Two thoughts speak in favour of adopting a narrow interpretation of article 22 para. 2 of the Convention on Biological Diversity. The drafters could have easily chosen a different wording, if they had wanted to give the UN Convention on the Law of the Sea precedence over the Convention on Biological Diversity. Regarding the fact that otherwise the states parties wanted to give the Convention on Biological Diversity the widest possible scope e.g. in article 22 para. 1, it is more likely that instead the Convention on Biological Diversity means that the two regimes exist in parallel and supplement and reinforce each other. Although article 22 para. 2 CBD clearly is *lex specialis* to article 22 para. 1, the general approach to the widest possible application should remain valid. Only if the application of the Convention on Biological Diversity does infringe upon the rights or obligations of states, the law of the sea rules prevail.

The UN Convention on the Law of the Sea also contains a provision on the relation with other international treaties: article 311. Only article 311 paras 2–4 deal with the relation to other treaties in general. In relation to all international agreements the UN Convention on the Law of the Sea claims priority.[36] According to article 311 para. 2 the UN Convention on the Law of the Sea does not alter the rights of other treaties as long as they are compatible and do not affect the application of basic principles or the enjoyment by other states parties of their right or the performance of their obligations under the UN Convention on the Law of the Sea. Consequently, these provisions lead to the result that the UN Convention on the Law of the Sea claims the right to alter all those obligations arising from other treaties that are not compatible. Hence, all incompatible agreements must be as far as possible interpreted to comply with the UN Convention on the Law of the Sea or the respective provisions cannot be applied at all. It follows that global treaties like the modern environmental agreements and respectively the Convention on Biological Diversity are affected by article 311 as far as the obligations they impose on contracting states that are also states parties to the UN Convention on the Law

---

35 See e.g. *Glowka/Burhenne-Guilmin/Synge*, (*supra* note 9), p. 109, who simply state "the law of the sea prevails in instances where the Convention's implementation conflicts with it"; *Henne*, (*supra* note 22), speaks of colliding norms of the law of the sea and the CBD; no distinction is made to the expression of rights and obligations she uses in the same context.

36 See *Vukas*, The Law of the Sea Convention and the Law of Treaties, in: *V. Götz/P. Selmer/R. Wolfrum* (eds), *Liber amicorum Günther Jaenicke – Zum 85. Geburtstag*, pp. 631, 649 (1998), who states that the UNCLOS "pretends to play the role similar to the one of article 103 of the United Nations Charter".

of the Sea collide with the latter. Concerning the relation to the Convention on Biological Diversity this conclusion is not fully coherent with article 22 para. 2 CBD.

5. Conclusions

Both conventions establish regimes of management and protection of marine biological resources, and can, on the one hand, collide, but can, on the other hand, supplement and reinforce one another. In any case, the different approaches of the UN Convention on the Law of the Sea and the Convention on Biological Diversity cannot completely be brought into coherence; too different are their underlying philosophies and objectives.

In territorial and in archipelagic waters the Convention on Biological Diversity does not directly modify the obligations of coastal states to protect marine life. The underlying principle of the Convention on Biological Diversity that biological diversity has an intrinsic value and that the international community is interested in its protection is not necessarily implemented with respect to marine living resources. However, as long as fundamental rights and obligations of states with regard to the UN Convention on the Law of the Sea are respected, states are free to give the Convention on Biological Diversity its widest possible application and implementation.

Although under the Convention on Biological Diversity coastal states are not obliged to change or amend the policies concerning the conservation of marine life, they may use the Convention on Biological Diversity to do so. Further, the coastal states may use the Convention on Biological Diversity to strengthen the protection of marine life in the exclusive economic zone, but again they are according to the UN Convention on the Law of the Sea not under an obligation to do so. As far as the establishment of protected areas is concerned, they face the same limitation as under the territorial waters regime. Yet, a positive approach to the conservation of marine living and genetic resources can to a larger extent than so far envisaged incorporate the policy guidance of the Convention on Biological Diversity into the law of the sea regime on these resources.

Further co-operation and the joint negotiation on binding and soft law agreements concerning the biological resources of the high seas seem necessary to achieve a sustainable system of use and preservation.[37] The effectiveness of measures depends upon the degree of co-ordination and co-operation between both Conventions to promote a more coherent system of protection of marine living resources in the high seas. Further co-operation between the institutions of both agreements is also especially necessary to address issues like integrated marine and coastal area management, the establishment of protected areas in territorial waters and in the exclusive economic zone and bioprospecting.

---

[37] *D.K. Anton*, Law for the Sea's Biological Diversity, in: *CJTNL* 36 (1997/98), 341, 370 *et seq.* theoretically favours a protocol to the CBD but at the same time considers it to be politically infeasible.

Generally speaking, the UN Convention on the Law of the Sea provides for a framework that can be environmentally strengthened by the objectives of the Convention on Biological Diversity. Especially the provisions on the sustainable use of resources outside national jurisdiction are open for further development even by agreements that are wider in scope as is clearly shown by the 1995 Agreement on Fish Stocks. If linked by respective conciliatory agreements and strengthened by continuous co-operation, a viable framework for the protection of marine biological resources can be established under the UN Convention on the Law of the Sea and the Convention on Biological Diversity. This – as always in international law – depends upon the will of the state community to not only negotiate agreements concerning the conservation and sustainable management but to also comply with the respective obligations.

*Michael Bothe**

THE PROTECTION OF THE MARINE ENVIRONMENT AGAINST THE IMPACTS OF SEABED MINING: AN ASSESSMENT OF THE NEW MINING CODE OF THE INTERNATIONAL SEABED AUTHORITY

1. Introduction

On 13 July 2000, the Assembly of the International Seabed Authority approved "Regulations on Prospecting and Exploration for Polymetallic Nodules in the Area". The environmental impact of exploration activities may be considerable, but the relevant Part XI of UNCLOS is completely silent on the matter. However, Part XII of the Convention, dealing with the protection and preservation of the marine environment, also applies to activities in the Area. But the obligations expressly formulated in this Part are very general. Standing alone, they do not achieve much. They are designed so as to be supplemented and implemented through additional norms. As far as the Area is concerned, this is recognised by Art. 209 which refers to the rule-making powers which the Authority possesses according to Part XI, i.e. in relation to "prospecting, exploration and exploitation in the Area" (Art. 162 para. 2 (o)(ii), 160 para. 2 (f)(ii). This is the legal basis for the Regulations just mentioned. This paper tries to evaluate whether and to what extent these Regulations are appropriate to restrain negative environmental consequences of deep seabed exploration activities.

What are the criteria for such an evaluation? Certain requirements of good environmental policy and administration, of good environmental governance can be pointed out which are well established in relation to environmental decision-making by States. In part, these principles have been codified in regional treaty regimes,[1] they are recognised by resolutions of international organisations and conferences, in particular the Rio Declaration,[2] and in part at least, they have acquired the status of rules of customary international law.[3] It is submitted that these principles have

* Professor of Public Law, Frankfurt am Main, Germany.

1 See in particular the relevant UNECE ("Espoo" and "Aarhus") conventions: Convention on Environmental Impact Assessment in a Transboundary Context, 25 February 1991, 30 *ILM* 800 (1991); Convention on Access to Information, Public Participation in Decision-Making and Access to Justice in Environmental Matters, 25 June 1998, 38 *ILM* 517 (1999).

2 31 *ILM* 876 (1992).

3 This is not to say that the Rio Declaration *in toto* constitutes customary law (rightly sceptical in this respect: *U. Beyerlin*, Umweltvölkerrecht, p. 53 (2000)), but certain substantive and procedural duties belong to that category, *inter alia* the precautionary principle, a general duty to protect the global

P. Ehlers, E. Mann-Borgese and R. Wolfrum (eds.), Marine Issues, 221–232

to apply, *mutatis mutandis*, to the activities of international institutions. This transfer of rules governing the activities of States is, by the way, a procedure which has been applied in many instances to develop the administrative law of international and supranational institutions.[4]

A first requirement is to ensure, as early as possible in the decision-making procedure, that information concerning the environmental consequences is collected and continuously updated. This is a precondition for the various actors to be able to take into account environmental considerations in the respective decision-making processes. For that purpose, the information has to be relevant and meaningful. The procedure which has been developed to achieve this is the Environmental Impact Assessment.

The second prerequisite, related to the first one, is to make sure that there is an informed decision-making in the sense that the decision can and does take into account all interests at stake. This requires, first, transparency, i.e. an appropriate information flow between all those concerned, in particular access to environmental information for all stakeholders. The information must be complete, relevant and meaningful. Second, there must be a possibility for all stakeholders to participate in the decision-making process, to make their views known and to defend the interests they are representing.

These first two principles are procedural in nature, but there purpose is a substantive one, namely a decision which takes due account of environmental concerns. To achieve this goal, substantive norms are also needed, in other words environmental standards for exploration activities as well as sufficient powers of the competent authority to impose concrete conditions in this respect.

Fourthly, standards are not enough, they must be implemented. Certain legal tools are necessary to make sure that this is the case. Violations of the applicable rules concerning the protection of the environment must be sanctioned in one way or the other, in particular by liability rules.

Finally, emergencies may occur, and rules dealing with this contingency are necessary, too.

These requirements have to be applied to the subject matter of the regulation, which is exploration. This is only a part of the activities relating to the Area. The regulatory powers of the Authority also relate to prospecting and exploitation, but rules concerning those two aspects of mining activities remain to be elaborated. It is, of course, appropriate to start the regulatory effort with the first phase of mining activities, which is exploration. The first key decision to be taken by the Authority in relation to exploration is the "approval" of a "work plan", meaning a permission to start the activity. The principles just explained are relevant in four different phases

commons against degradation, an obligation not to cause transboundary harm and certain procedural duties (information, consultation) to be derived from the latter principle (*Beyerlin ibid*, pp. 64 *et seq.*).

4 *G. Ress*, Die Bedeutung der Rechtsvergleichung für die Praxis internationaler Organisationen, in: *ZaöRV* 36 (1976), 227; *M. Bothe*, Die Bedeutung der Rechtsvergleichung für die Praxis internationaler Gerichte, *ibid* p. 280.

of the operation: The first one is the preparation of an application for approval, the second one the processing of this application by the Authority, in particular by the Legal and Technical Commission and by the Council, which is the final decision-maker, the third one the implementation of those decisions by way of a contract concluded between the Authority and the "explorer", the last one the operation of the exploration activities, subject to the supervision by the Authority.

The paper will now examine the fulfilment of the criteria just developed in relation to these different phases.

2. Collecting Environmental Information, Ascertaining Environmental Problems

The first question to be addressed is whether there are rules making sure that meaningful and complete information relating to the environmental consequences of the operation is collected early enough in order to avoid any *fait accompli* before the environmental problems have been ascertained. The application for the approval of a work plan must indeed, in order to be admissible, deal with the environmental consequences of the activities in a number of ways. First, the application must contain a written undertaking that the prospector will[5]

> "comply with the Convention and the relevant rules, regulations and procedures of the Authority concerning:
>
> ...
>
> protection and preservation of the marine environment;"

In addition, the application must show that the applicant is

> "financially and technically capable of carrying out the proposed plan of work."[6]

For that purpose, it must contain

> "a general description of the applicant's financial and technical capability to respond to any incident or activity which causes serious harm to the marine environment."[7]

These requirements mean that the applicant must make a critical self-evaluation of the environmental implications of its project and of its capacity to cope with them.

In addition, the application must contain specific information relating to the environment, namely the following:[8]

> "(a) a general description and the schedule of the proposed exploration programme, ... such as studies to be undertaken in respect of the environmental,

[5] Reg. 2(6)(a).
[6] Reg. 12(1).
[7] Reg. 12(7)(c).
[8] Reg. 18.

technical, economic and other appropriate factors that must be taken into account in exploration;

(b) a description of the programme for oceanographic and environmental baseline studies in accordance with these Regulations and any environmental rules, regulations and procedures established by the Authority that would enable an assessment of the potential environmental impact of the proposed exploration activities taking into account any recommendations issued by the Legal and Technical Commission;

(c) a preliminary assessment of the possible impact of the proposed exploration activities on the marine environment;

(d) a description of proposed measures for the prevention, reduction and control of pollution and other hazards, as well as possible impacts, to the marine environment; ..."

This means, in a nutshell, a kind of environmental impact assessment which the applicant has to include in its application. The list of information to be provided contains most of the elements which are usually required for that purpose,[9] except the consideration of alternative solutions and an indication of possible deficits in relevant knowledge.

The next phase of the procedure is the evaluation of the application by the Legal and Technical Commission. This body must make certain determinations in order to base its recommendation to the Council, which is the final decision-maker. Among these determinations, the Commission has to state that the plan of work will[10]

"provide for effective protection and preservation of the marine environment ..."

This means that the information to be provided by the applicant has to be meaningful enough as to enable the commission to make that determination. The Regulations are silent, however, concerning the question whether the Commission has any powers of inquiry of its own in this respect. This is somewhat problematic, as it is not a matter of course that the information basis furnished by the applicant is really adequate. No provision is made for the Legal and Technical Commission to have access to any additional information which might challenge the correctness of the data furnished by the applicant.

In the following phases of the project, the actual exploration, the collection of relevant information has to continue. This has to be an element of the clauses of the contract concluded between the Authority and the contractor. The relevant provisions of the Regulation which govern the contract contain the following:

"Each contract shall require the contractor to gather environmental baseline

9 See e.g. Annex III of the EC Directive on Environmental Impact Assessment (Dir. 85/337/EEC of 27 June 1985); Appendix II to the Espoo Convention (*supra* note 1).

10 Reg. 21(4)(b).

data and to establish environmental baselines... against which to assess the likely effects of its programme of activities under the plan of work for exploration on the marine environment and a programme to monitor and report on such effects ..."[11]

"Contractors, sponsoring States and other interested States or entities shall co-operate with the Authority in the establishment and implementation of programmes for monitoring and evaluating the impacts of deep seabed mining on the marine environment."[12]

"If the contractor applies for exploitation rights, it shall propose areas to be set aside and used exclusively as impact reference zones and preservation reference zones ..."[13]

These zones, to be monitored specifically, may serve as a basis for an exact determination of the environmental impact of the activities. These provisions are an important prerequisite of a meaningful assessment of the environmental consequences of exploration.

In conclusion, it appears that there are satisfactory provisions in order to make sure that environmental consequences of the proposed seabed mining activities are known early enough and can be evaluated, thus forming a basis for decisions to be taken by the Authority.

3. Transparency and Participation

Good environmental governance requires an open decision-making process. Information relating to the environmental consequences of a project must be accessible for the public. The decision-making must be open for an input from civil society. It is not appropriate to leave the elaboration of relevant decisions to a process which takes place exclusively between the interested economic actor and the public authority. This is formulated in Principle 10 of the Rio Declaration:

"Environmental issues are best handled with the participation of all concerned citizens, at the relevant level. At the national level, each individual shall have appropriate access to information concerning the environment that is held by public authorities, including information on hazardous materials and activities in their communities, and the opportunity to participate in decision-making processes. States shall facilitate and encourage public awareness and participation by making information widely available. Effective access to judicial and administrative proceedings, including redress and remedy, shall be provided."

These principles, it is submitted, should also apply to decisions by the Authority.

---

11 Reg. 31(4).

12 Reg. 31(6).

13 Reg. 31(7).

The first sentence clearly refers to all levels, including the international one. But also the remainder of the principle, although technically speaking addressed to States, simply contains modern rules of good environmental governance which the Authority should apply. It cannot be objected that the situation at sea, in the global commons, is not comparable, there being no "neighbours" who might be affected. First, there are competing interests in the vicinity of mining activities, in particular fishing. In addition, rules on access to information and public participation do not only serve the egoistic purposes of competing "neighbouring" interests, but also the common good of achieving a better informed balance of the interests at stake. This consideration applies with equal force also in the global commons.

It is a major flaw of the Regulation that it does not provide for this open type of decision-making process. The process, quite to the contrary, is a closed one. It is the task of the applicant to provide the information described above. This is then to be the basis for the decision of the Council to approve a plan of work. The Legal and Technical Commission, which evaluates the application, shall, as already indicated, "determine" whether the proposed plan of work would indeed provide for effective protection and preservation of the marine environment. What the regulations do not say is whether the Commission could or should use any additional information source.

Later, it becomes the task of the contractor, to be supervised by the Authority, to further monitor the impact of his activities on the environment. The problem remains the same.

This closed character of the process is aggravated by the fact that there are strict rules on the confidentiality of information transferred to the Authority in all phases of the procedures.[14] This makes any third party input in the information gathering process unlikely. There is no denying the fact that the protection of industrial secrets and of intellectual property rights relating to the proposed activity are important. But relevant national law and also the respective EC directive have developed rules which allow for this protection without forgoing the openness of all environmental information.[15]

Concerning the further exploration process, however, there is one provision which might allow a more open process, although this is far from being clear. As already indicated, contractors, sponsoring States and other interested States or entities "shall co-operate with the Authority in the establishment and implementation of programmes for monitoring and evaluating the impacts of the seabed mining on the marine environment."[16] States which may be affected by negative consequences (e.g. fishing states) or even interested associations ("entities") could thus be involved in this process of monitoring and evaluating environmental impacts. Whether and to

---

14 Regs. 6, 20(1)(b), 35, Annex 4 sec. 12.

15 Art. 3(2) of the EC Directive on Access to Environmental Information (Dir. 90/313/EEC of 7 June 1990), Art. 4(4) of the Aarhus Convention (*supra* note 1).

16 Reg. 31(6).

what extent the co-operation would also allow a disclosure of information which comes within the scope of confidentiality provisions is, however, quite doubtful.

It is fair to say that the transparency of the decision-making process, also as far as it relates to the protection of the environment, leaves to be desired. There is no possibility for participation by relevant non-governmental or even governmental organisations like UNEP in the licensing process, and the openness of the monitoring procedures concerning the actual operation is also not clear enough. This, it is submitted, contravenes principles of international environmental law relating to basic procedural requirements for decisions likely to have an adverse effect on the environment as they are reflected, as already stated, in Principle 10 of the Rio Declaration, in the Aarhus Convention and also under EC law.[17] Unfortunately, international institutions seem to be more restrictive than States as to the accessibility of the information they possess. Nevertheless, it is inconceivable that the standard of behaviour of international organisations does not respect basic standards to which States are subject under international law and which States respect in there national sphere. This is a simple principle which has sometimes had some difficulty to be recognised, but which has prevailed in matters as different as, for instance, the procedural rights of employees of international organisations[18] or the application of international humanitarian law by armed forces of the United Nations.[19] The protection of the environment cannot make an exception to this rule.

4. Substantive Obligations

There should be appropriate substantive yardsticks to make sure that the proposed activities are subject to the necessary environmental restraints. For that purpose, it is a condition for approving a plan of work that the plan

> "provides for effective protection and preservation of the marine environment."[20]

The question, then, is what this would mean in practice. This is for the Legal and Technical Commission and then, when taking the decision, for the Council to evaluate. Standards still have to be elaborated for that purpose. It is the task of the Authority to

> "establish and keep under periodical review environmental rules, regulations

---

17 See *D.A. Farber/F.L. Morisson*, Access to Environmental Information, in: *F.L. Morisson/R. Wolfrum* (eds.), *International, Regional and National Environmental Law*, pp. 845 *et seq.*

18 This is, in particular, the reason for the creation of administrative tribunals in the framework of international organisations, see *G. Vandersanden*, Administrative Tribunals, Boards and Commissions in International Organizations, in: *R. Bernhardt*, *EPIL* vol. I (1992), 227.

19 Observance by United Nations Forces of International Humanitarian Law, Bulletin issued by the Secretary-General, UN Doc. ST/SBG/1999/13, reprinted in: *M. Bothe/T. Dörschel* (eds.), *UN Peacekeeping*, p. 117 (1999).

20 Reg. 21(4)(b).

> and procedures to ensure effective protection for the marine environment from harmful effects which may arise from activities in the Area".[21]

Thus, there remains a need of concretisation, but the Authority has the power to achieve this. As a further guideline, the provision continues:

> "In order to ensure effective protection for the marine environment from harmful effects which may arise from activities in the Area, the Authority and sponsoring States shall apply a precautionary approach as reflected in Principle 15 of the Rio Declaration to such activities. The Legal and Technical Commission shall make recommendations to the Council on the implementation of this paragraph".[22]

This provision confirms and strengthens the precautionary principle as part of current international environmental law.[23] It is, thus, in line with recent treaty law on the protection of the environment which tends to include the precautionary principle in one way or the other.

It is a very important factor to ensure that negative environmental impacts of the seabed mining activities are excluded. The precautionary principle requires measures for the protection of the environment to be taken even in the absence of scientific certainty that a damage to the environment may occur if such measures are not taken. This is particularly important in relation to deep sea activities as this is an area where there still are important gaps in the knowledge of natural processes.

The major procedural device for implementing the precautionary principle is the environmental impact assessment, which, as already stated, plays indeed an important role in the Regulation. Another tool of the precautionary approach is the requirement of best available technology. The Authority must indeed require the contractor to restrain pollution and other hazards by using "the best technology available to it." This requirement to use "BAT" is a usual way of implementing the precautionary principle.[24] This requirement is mitigated, however, by adding the words "as far as it is reasonably possible,"[25] a formulation of the precautionary approach which leaves some doubt as to how strict it is. It is true that a certain limitation is implied in the application of the precautionary principle, namely the principle of proportionality. This means that the economic burden which an environmental requirement entails must not be excessive in relation to the environmental gain anticipated. This implies a somewhat problematic balancing of environmental and economic concerns.

---

[21] Reg. 31(1).

[22] Reg. 31(2).

[23] *Beyerlin* (*supra* note 3), p. 60; *A. Epiney/M. Scheyli*, Strukturprinzipien des Umweltvölkerrechts, pp. 103 *et seq.* (1998); for a more detailed analysis, see *J. Cameron/J. Abouchar*, The Status of the Precautionary Principle in International Law, in: *D. Freestone/E. Hey* (eds.), *The Precautionary Principle and International Law*, pp. 29 *et seq.* (1996).

[24] *Epiney/Scheyli*, (*supra* note 23) pp. 141 *et seq.*

[25] Reg. 31(3).

The problem involved in the formulation used really is whether it invites an interpretation which gives too much weight to economic concerns.

5. Implementation and Sanctions

Appropriate incentives have to make sure that the rules are really complied with. These incentives can be of a positive or of a negative nature, may constitute "sticks" or "carrots."[26] In the latter case, we usually speak of "sanctions." There are three types of sanctions regulated in the standard contract clauses which may be used to enforce the environmental obligations of the prospector, two general, the third one specifically designed for the purpose of strengthening the environmental obligations.

The first general sanction is the termination or at least suspension of the contract. This may be pronounced by the Council if

> "... the Contractor has conducted its activities in such a way as to result in serious persistent and wilful violations of the fundamental terms of this contract, Part IX of the Convention, the Agreement and the rules, regulations and procedures of the Authority ..."[27]

As the rules on the protection of the environment, in the light of the provisions already discussed in this paper, are indeed to be considered as "fundamental" in this sense, their violation may be sanctioned by a decision to suspend or to terminate the contract.

The Council may, this is the second instrument, impose monetary penalties upon the contractor, both in lieu of suspension or termination and in cases of violations which do not reach the same degree of seriousness.

The standard clauses for the exploration contract[28] also provide, thirdly, for a regime of responsibility and liability, which applies to all kinds of damages caused by the contractor and its agents. The liability is a no fault liability, only *force majeure* being excluded.[29] For these purposes, the contractor has to maintain appropriate insurance policies.

This liability regime has special provisions on environmental damages. The clause covers

> "any damage, including damage to the marine environment."

The latter includes

> "the costs of reasonable measures to prevent or limit damage to the marine environment, account being taken of any contributory acts or omissions by the Authority."

---

26 *P.H. Sand*, Transnational Environmental Law, pp. 313 *et seq.* (1999).

27 Annex 4 sec. 21.1(a).

28 Annex 4 sec. 16 and 17.

29 Annex 4 sec. 17.1.

This is a usual element of the reparation of environmental damages. It is important to note that the damage to be compensated by the contractor not only relates to life, health, property or similar individual rights, but to the environment as such. There are, however, two additional problems involved. The first one is the question who takes, and who decides on, the necessary measures. Is this the task of the Authority, acting in the global interest for the protection of the global commons? The second one is a somewhat problematic *a contrario* argument which might be made on the basis of the text, that a damage which cannot be prevented or limited would not have to be compensated. It is submitted that this exclusion is not necessarily involved in this formulation. But the yardstick for quantifying an environmental damage where no mitigation operations are made remains a difficult question.[30]

It can be concluded that if there is enough political will on the part of the Authority to enforce environmental obligations, the system is one "with teeth". What is then essential is the political will of the Authority to use this instrument.

It is regrettable, on the other hand, that the liability scheme shares the major flaw of the entire Regulation, namely that it constitutes a kind of closed circuit between the Authority and the contractor. The rules on liability are not contained in any legal document which would apply *erga omnes*, they are contained in contract clauses and therefor only valid between the parties. There is no indication that this contract is meant to be a *pactum in favorem tertii*. Thus, it would appear somewhat difficult that the Authority may claim also the compensation of damages suffered by private third parties, e.g. shipowners or fishermen. It would have been useful and desirable to provide for some third party role in this context. This concern both the compensation of damages suffered by those parties and their possible position as claimants or plaintiffs. In this respect as well, there is a need for further development in international environmental law.

6. Emergencies

Emergencies may happen during exploration activities and which cause or are likely to cause serious harm to the marine environment. The fundamental requirements of an effective response are swift information of all those concerned and preparedness for a swift reaction. These questions are dealt with in a rather strict manner by the Regulations. Contingency plans are obligatory.[31] There is a duty to report and a power of the Authority to take the necessary measures.[32] The Secretary General is

[30] *P. Sands*, Liability for Environmental Damage and the Report of the UNEP Working Group of Experts, Introductory Article by the Rapporteur, in: *UNEP*, *Liability and Compensation for Environmental Damage*, pp. 1, 9 *et seq*. (1998), and in particular *R. Stewart*, Outline of Linkage between Valuation, Methodologies and the Categories of Environmental Damage in Paragraph 35 of Decision 7 of the Governing Council of the United Nations Compensation Commission, *ibid* pp. 77 *et seq*.

[31] Annex 4 sec. 6.

[32] Reg. 32.

entitled to take immediate measures before the Council, on the basis of recommendations of the Legal and Technical Commission may issue final emergency orders. If the contractor does not comply with them, the Authority shall itself, or through arrangements with others, take these measures. This is, on the one hand, very important. It poses, on the other, the question of the resources of the Authority to do this.

An additional problem consists, in this respect as well, in the relative closeness of the information flow. Information to a broader range of persons or entities concerned is reduced to a minimum.

> "(T)he warning of ships which might be about to enter the immediate vicinity"[33]

is provided for, also "cooperation with other contractors."[34] But an essential element of emergency responses is that all those who are likely to be affected or in a position to help should know as soon as possible. The Authority is probably entitled to spread the necessary information accordingly, but an express provision to that effect might have been desirable. The lack of such a provision points to a structural problem which has already been indicated.

7. Conclusion

The Regulations can be characterised as a systematic and serious attempt to include appropriate legal safeguards for the marine environment. On the whole, this attempt has been quite successful. The obligations to collect and provide relevant environmental information before exploration can start and afterwards are sufficiently complete and strict. The environmental standards which may be imposed are high. In particular, it has to be stressed that a precautionary approach is obligatory. There is provision for contingency planning and swift information flow in case of emergencies. Enforcement tools are strict.

Although the Regulation and the Annexes are an significant step in concretising general obligations of international environmental law, there is a need for further development in this respect. Standards giving more precision to the precautionary principle are a particular case in point.

The major flaw is the closed character of the decision-making process which, it appears, is not open to an appropriate third party input, for instance by environmental associations. This will diminish the information basis for the Authority. A more transparent decision-making process, access to environmental information for third parties, including environmental NGOs and a possibility for these parties to have a hearing in the decision-making processes remain an important *desideratum.*

---

[33] Annex 4 sec. 6.1(c).

[34] Annex 4 sec. 6.1(g).

*Karin Lochte**

THE DEEP SEA FLOOR – NEW DISCOVERIES AND VISIONS

In this contribution I want to take you to an excursion into the largely unknown parts of our earth, the deep abyss. I will highlight in this short talk just a few aspects of this interesting and very large component of our earth.

Three arguments why the deep sea deserves our attention:

- The deep sea floor is less known than any other ecosystem on earth
- Major new discoveries are made – even today
- The deep sea floor is one of our last unexploited resources

The Deep Sea Floor is Less Known than any Other Ecosystem on Earth

The deep sea floor and the continental slopes deeper than 200 m are a vast expanse covering 65% of the surface of the globe, but it seems to be hardly recognized in its size and importance for this world. It is the largest ecosystem and it is also the least known one. If all benthic investigations in the North Atlantic are put together, the size of the well investigated area covers less than a few football fields. So we draw our knowledge from a very small and not very representative set of samples and we base far reaching economic and political decisions on scant data. It is also rarely recognized how close the links between land, surface water and the deep sea are and that there are a number of direct links. Therefore, the processes occurring in the deep sea are not cut off from the life at the surface.

While the latest new discoveries of unknown lands were made at the beginning of the 20th century with the exploration of Antarctica, major new discoveries in the deep sea are made even today. Most of the interesting recent findings are made along the continental slopes, like the gas hydrate deposits and cold water corals. The reasons for this are the physical gradients at the continental slopes which provide in various ways the basis for life.

---

* Insitut für Meereskunde an der Universität Kiel. The author gratefully acknowledges the help of Olaf Pfannkuche, Peter Linke (GEOMAR Kiel) and André Freiwald (Universität Tübingen) who supplied ideas and the wonderful pictures.

P. Ehlers, E. Mann-Borgese and R. Wolfrum (eds.), Marine Issues, 233–240

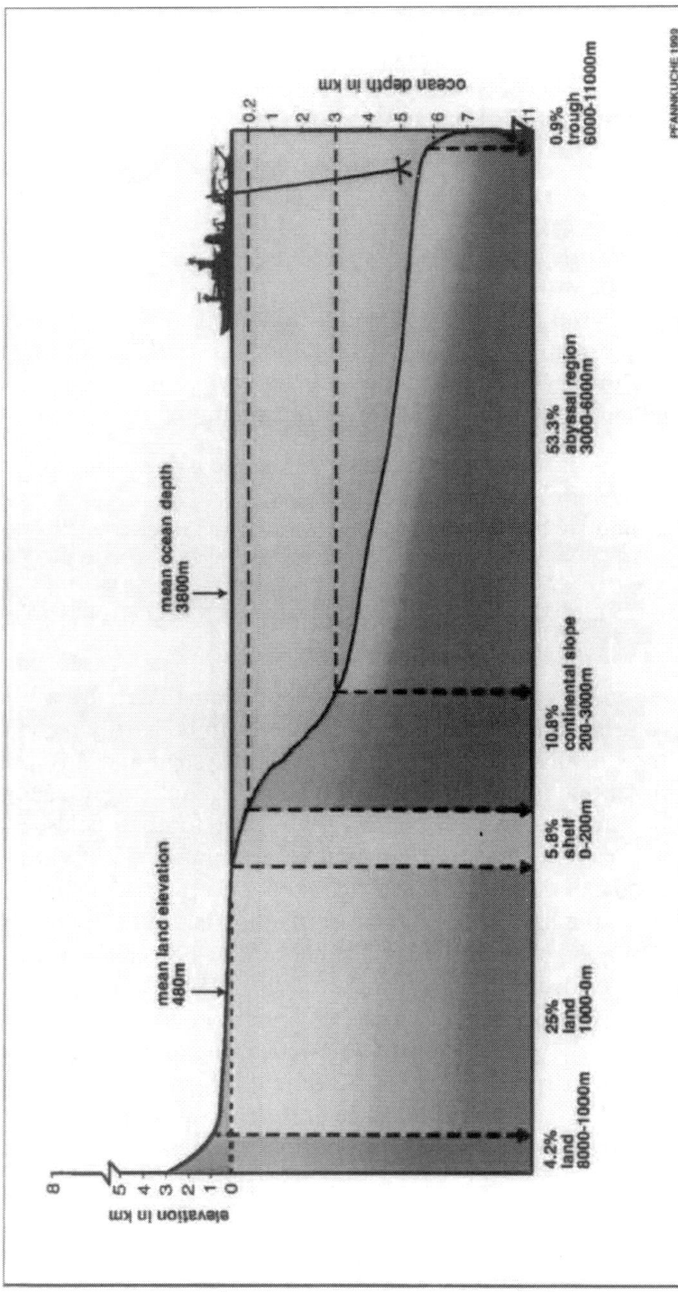

Figure 1. Hypsographic curve.

In many ways the deep sea is similar to the desert. Life in the desert is limited by the supply of water, life in the deep sea is limited by the supply of food.

However, the desert can bloom when it rains and an abundant plant life develops for a short time. This is also true for the deep sea; under certain circumstances, when sufficient food is available, abundant life with very special life forms can develop.

Most people have the idea that the deep sea is remote, cold, dark and sparsely populated (which is true). Figure 2 is a photograph of the normal deep sea floor. Most of the deep sea looks like this and you have to scan many pictures before one larger animal can be seen. Most organisms are very small (bacteria and meiofauna), they are living within the sediment and are mainly responsible for processing the organic material in the deep sea.

The main food source for all organisms living at the deep sea floor are sedimenting organic particles which are mainly made up of decaying microscopic algae. It takes on average between 3–5 weeks for these particles to sink about 4000 m from the surface to the bottom of the ocean. Most of this organic rain from the surface waters

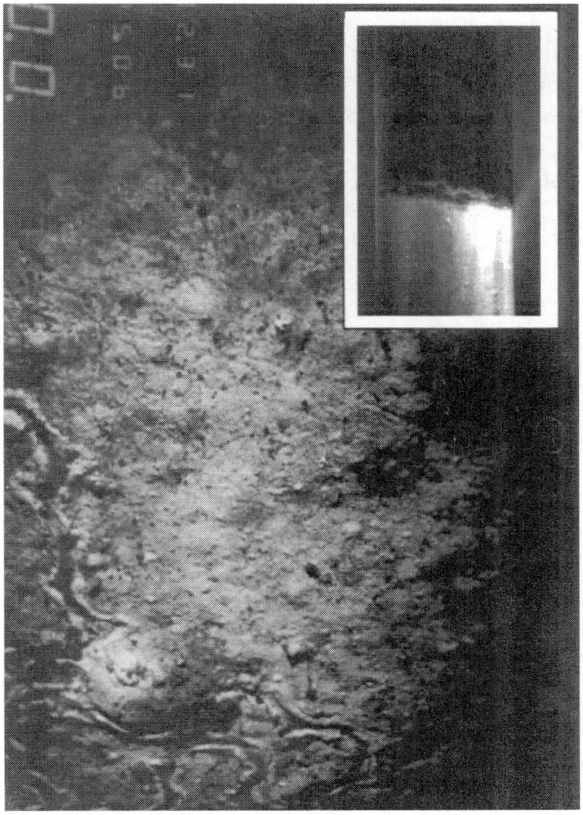

Figure 2. (a) and (b) Normal deep sea.

is processed by deep sea bacteria and small animals which react to such events within less than a week.

Major New Discoveries are Made Even Today

However, life in the deep sea can also look quite different. We can also find rich fauna at a deposit of gas hydrates. Such surprising observations have been made in the last years and they are evidence of alternative supplies of food (= organically bound energy) in the deep sea.

Methane trapped in gas hydrates is not only a potential energy source for humans but also an energy source for life in the deep sea. Certain types of bacteria can oxidize methane and gain energy to produce biomass from this process. Mats of such bacteria (*Beggiatoa*) can be seen covering the sediment. Some bacteria are living as symbionts within larger animals, with the white mussel *Calyptogena*, and are supplying them with the necessary food. Furthermore, large numbers of egg clutches of the snail *Buccinum* have been seen. They are probably feeding as predators on other organisms. Thus methane deposits provide the basis for an abundant life in an otherwise barren environment. The investigation of these communities from bacteria to large animals promises many more new discoveries; part of these are of potential interest for biotechnology.

We trapped Methane under high pressure and low temperature in a cage of water molecules forming an ice-like substance called gas hydrate. 1 dm^3 of gas hydrate contains 36 litres of methane gas. When the hydrate is retrieved from the sea floor, pressure decreases and temperature rises which destabilizes the gas hydrate and methane is released. We have made these experiments on board of the research vessel SONNE which investigated the gas hydrate deposits off the coast of Oregon in about 700–800 m depth. The existence of gas hydrates has been known for a while, but new is the discovery of how much methane is bound in marine sediments in form of gas hydrates and what a rich life is supported by these hydrates.

In total in marine sediments and in permafrost soils, it is estimated that 10.000 billion tons of methane are locked in gas hydrates worldwide. This is more than all known resources of oil and coal estimated at 5.000 billion tons. Gas hydrates are a potential energy source, but they are difficult to mine and, hence, exploitation is not a near target. Secondly, gas hydrates are very instable and may under changed environmetal conditions release very suddenly large amounts of methane into the atmosphere. Methane is a much more effective green house gas and, hence, such release may have climatic impacts. There are indications that this may have happened in the geological past.

The instability of gas hydrates has been demonstrated by an experiment with a piece of hydrate sampled from 700 m depth. The gas hydrated piece was held in the manipulator arm of a remotely operated vehicle (ROV). Firstly, it remained stable and of similar size in the deep part of the water column. When the ROV ascended and the critical depth was exceeded, the piece of hydrate turns into gas bubbles and disappeared.

In some locations the gas hydrates are deposited in the sediment so closely to their stability limit that even the tides (i.e. slightly changing water pressure) can release methane. Gas bubbles can be detected by sonar rising through the water column and can be seen bubbling up at the sea surface.

Along most continental slopes, cold water corals of the species *Lophelia* are found. These corals live from a few hundred to 6000 m water depth in the dark and cold. Unlike tropical corals they do not contain algal symbionts for their nutrition, but they filter small organic particles from the water column. They give shelter for many other animals (here a red fish) and are an oasis of life in the otherwise rather poor surrounding. They are mainly found on the continental slopes where internal waves break providing the high currents which transport particles towards the corals.

As seen from the map, these corals have been found in many locations around Europe. In other parts of the world they have also been discovered, but we simply did not have enough surveys to investigate the continental slopes around third world countries to know how far-spread they really are.

Trawling for deep water fish is now extending to 1000 m and these corals are sustaining extensive damage. This has reached such a level that protective measures in the deep sea are now beeing discussed.

One of the most exciting discoveries was the observation that living bacteria exist in sediments up to 750 meters below the sea floor. They have been isolated from the rest of the living world for a few million years. We still do not know how deep this deep biosphere extends into the depth. One estimates that 10% of the world's biomass is contained in this totally unexplored ecosystem. Since these bacteria have been able to develop without link to the rest of the living world, it is expected that many new discoveries in respect to new organisms and biochemical processes can be made which may be of use for biotechnology.

The Deep Sea Floor is One of Our Last Unexploited Resources

The deep sea floor is one of our last unexploited ecosystems. It is a vast area and it harbours living and non-living resources. There are numerous potential uses, but their feasibility, both in respect to economic gain and to environmental impact, are generally poorly known.

The deep sea is by no means free of human impact! Anywhere in the world's ocean rubbish is found in the trawls. There was found trash in 4100 m in a remote area of the Arabian Sea. The coke tin had a clearly visible date stamp on the bottom. It was from 1974 and well preserved.

One of the major industrial uses of the deep ocean is drilling for oil. As the shallow resources are already exploited to a large extent, the attention turns to the oil fields in greater depths. Drilling has progressed down the continental slopes. At present the deepest commercially exploited fields are the Roncador and Marlin oil fields off Brazil in ca. 1500–1800 m water depth. This is not the limit and oil fields in 2000 m are being explored. This advance has been made possible by new technologies, like tension leg platforms.

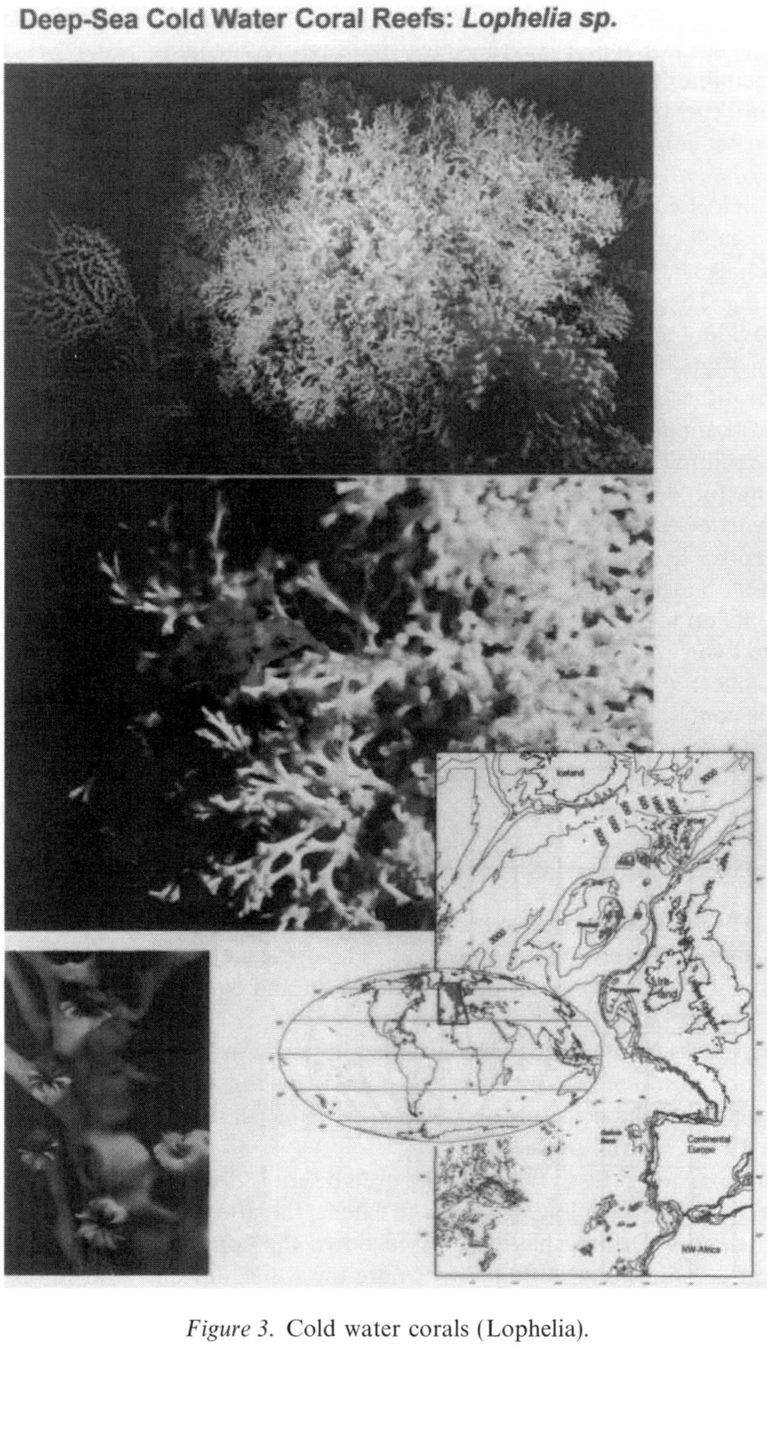

Figure 3. Cold water corals (Lophelia).

At the sea floor a host of remotely operated instruments are docked and linked to the central drill unit covering several hundred meters of sea floor. Such hi-tech instrumentation in the deep sea relies critically on high precision forecasts of currents, in particular of sudden deep sea storms with high current speed. Another danger is slope instability, i.e. when sections of the continental slope become instable and slide into the deep sea. Slides of more than several thousand km^3 of sediment are known from the past, but smaller events have been occurring in the recent past and there is no safeguard against slope instabilities.

We Need New Tools to Access and to Understand this Largest Ecosystem on Earth

The major problem is that the deep sea is very inaccessible for observation. Most instruments do not function under the high pressure in the deep sea. Automatic registration of a few variables is now possible, but suffers from the limitation of power supply. While in the last decade major progress has been made in global observations via satellites, a similar progress was not possible in the deep sea. Hence, all our observations are still based on "snap shots". It is fair to say that the key to the deep sea lies with technological advances.

Lander Systems

At present, measurement in the deep sea can be made by lander systems. Such a measuring system is lowered from the ship on a glass fibre cable and drifts across the sea floor while observing the bottom with a camera. The pictures are transmitted to the ship. Once the right position is found, the lander is released from the launching unit. When settled on the sea bed it carries out the measurements autonomously for a time. It returns to the surface with the stored data when it receives an acoustic command to drop its balast weights. These systems can only operate for a limited period of time.

Other systems are moored at the sea floor for long periods of time and transmit their data via a surface buoy and satellite to the home laboratory. Their problem is mainly a limited power supply.

Remotely Operated Vehicles (ROV)

Remotely operated vehicles (called ROV) are a more sophisticated and also a much more costly way to gain access to the sea floor. These ROV are lowered to the sea floor and are connected by an umbilical cable to the ship. They can then be steered from the ship; there are a number of cameras to observe the sea floor and mechanical arms are available to collect specific samples or to carry out simple experiments. *Kaiko* as the deepest diving ROV can go to even the deep trenches in 10 km depth, whereas *Ropos* can dive to 6000 m.

There are more technical possiblities to access the deep sea. One of the most promising ones is to use deep sea cables to which monitoring units are connected. This way power supply and data transmission are provided by the cable and a long term monitoring would be possible.

Conclusion

In the following I would like to present a few glimpses of the possibilities and problems of observing the deep sea. It has some resemblance to space exploration, both in respect to the inaccessiblitiy of its object of study and in respect to the high costs. However, development of such technologies is the key to gain access to the deep sea and its secrets. It is my conviction that we need to make greater efforts to understand the deep sea much better than up to now. This is not because of curiosity, but because the deep sea harbours many promises and challenges for our future. Human pressure on the deep sea will inevitably increase and we need to make sure that we manage and protect this largest ecosystem on earth wisely.

Summary Statements

The deep sea is an integral part of the earth system and it harbours a number of resources which we just begin to recognize.

Our understanding of the processes in the deep sea and of its lifeforms is still rudimentary.

We need new technologies and visions to access and monitor this highly inaccessible ecosystem.

Human pressure on the deep sea will inevitably increase and we need to make sure that we manage and protect this largest ecosystem on earth wisely.

*Markus Böckenförde**

THE INTRODUCTION OF ALIEN OR NEW SPECIES INTO THE MARINE ENVIRONMENT: A CHALLENGE FOR STANDARD SETTING AND ENFORCEMENT

INTRODUCTION

The introduction of alien species is second only to land use/land cover change in driving global losses of biological diversity.[1] But since alien species are self-perpetuating, they can have a permanence unmatched by other threats to biodiversity. Probably the most illustrative case of the negative effects caused by an alien species that has been introduced in an area where it had not habitated before is the establishment of the European rabbit in Australia which was introduced in 1859 for hunting purposes. Due to the absence of natural enemies, such as weasels and foxes, the rabbit population increased dramatically, soon colonizing most of the Australian continent. Native plants became endangered and were close to extinction.[2]

The introduction of alien species into the marine environment, by purpose or by accident, may be less well-known. However, their negative impacts for health, wealth and environment are severe, as the examples given further below will demonstrate (Part 1). Within the last twenty years, almost every part of the world had been afflicted with this problem that has already been anticipated in the mid-seventies by the negotiators of the United Nations Convention on the Law of the Sea (UNCLOS).[3] Hence, pertinent parts of the final UNCLOS provision[4] that deals with alien species are central to the paper and its starting point. Therefore, some

---

* Dr. jur. Candidate, University of Heidelberg.

1 *Wissenschaftlicher Beirat der Bundesregierung Globale Umweltveränderung*, Welt im Wandel: Erhaltung und Nachhaltige Nutzung der Biosphäre, pp. 99–106 (Berlin 2000).

2 Initiatives to reduce the number of rabbits started soon after and have continued until today without solving the problem entirely.

3 Most of the cases in which the introduction of alien species caused significant harm occurred during the eighties. However, the issue was already discussed during the UNCLOS negotiations in 1974. See A/CONF.62/C.3/L.18 (1974), III Off. Rec. 266.

4 Art. 196 (1) UNCLOS (Use of technologies or introduction of alien or new species), reprinted at 20 *ILM* 1245 (1982), states: (1) States shall take all measures necessary to prevent, reduce and control pollution of the marine environment resulting from the use of technologies under their jurisdiction or control, or the intentional or accidental introduction of species, alien or new, to a particular part of the marine environment, which may cause significant and harmful changes thereto.

P. Ehlers, E. Mann-Borgese and R. Wolfrum (eds.), Marine Issues, 241–263

preliminary thoughts are made with regard to the wording of Art. 196 (1) and the underlying assumptions behind the interpretation: the introduction of alien species as a form of pollution (Part 2). The two following parts focus on the provision's purpose, the control of the introduction of species, alien or new, whereby new species cover those that have been bred traditionally or through modern biotechnology. As indicated by Art. 196 (1), alien or new species may be introduced in two different ways: intentional or accidental. Each of those two ways of introduction needs distinct legal and institutional mechanisms and is addressed separately (Parts 3 and 4). Part 5, finally, focuses on the standard setting and enforcement policy with respect to ballast water management.

1. Alien Species and Their Negative Impact on Health, Wealth and the Environment

1.1. Health Impacts

A cholera epidemic (disease agent: *Vibrio cholerae*) commenced in Indonesia in the early 1960s and finally completed its encirclement of the globe in South America at the beginning of the 1990s. There, the epidemic wave started on the coasts of Peru and was documented later from several ports of Latin America. It is believed that the cholera had been introduced by maritime traffic. In November 1991 and June 1992, the USA documented the detection of active cholera bacteria in ballast water of vessels coming from South America.[5] The introduction in coastal waters of Latin America caused a serious threat to thousands of people's health after consumption of seafood, such as oysters and finfish caught in affected areas.[6]

1.2. Economic Impacts

(a) The comb jelly *Mnemiopsis leidyi*, originating from the American east coast is believed to have been introduced into the Black Sea through ballast water in the 1970s and caused one of the most devastating biological explosions ever recorded by science in the early 1980s. Having no known predators to control it, the comb jelly spread suddenly and incontinently through the Black Sea. It fed voraciously on zooplankton, the food of young fish, and on fish larvae, depriving them of this source of food. It has been largely responsible for the collapse of the local anchovy fishing industries in the Black Sea which decreased to 10% compared with fisheries of the times before the comb jelly invaded the Black Sea.[7]

---

5 *S.A. Mc Carthy/F.M. Khambaty*, International Dissemination of Epidemic *Vibrio Cholerae* by Cargo Ship Ballast and other Nonpotable Waters, in: *AEM* 60(7) (1994), 2597–2601.

6 *Stefan Gollasch*, Removal of Barriers to the Effective Implementation of Ballast Water Control and Management Measures in Developing Countries (GEF/IMO/UNDP project), p. 73, Internet: http://www.imo.org/imo/focus/gollasch.pdf.

7 *E.A. Shushkina/E.I. Musayeva*, Structure of Planktic Community of the Black Sea Epipelagic Zone and Its Variation Caused by Invasion of a New Ctenophore species, in: *Oceanology* 30(2) (1990), 225–228.

(b) Another example is the North Pacific seastar, *Asterias amurensis*, native to Japanese and Alaskan waters and known from Tasmanian waters since the late 1980s. The introduction is believed to have occurred with the discharge of water containing the larvae of the species. The pacific starfish threatens the shellfish industry causing damages of around US dollars 350 million by eating mussels.[8]

(c) The ruffe, *Gymnocephalus Cernuus*, a small but aggressive fish native to Eurasia, was introduced into the Great Lakes via ballast water in the 1980s. Because it grows very fast, has a high reproductive capacity and adapts to a wide variety of environments, it is considered a serious threat to commercial and sport fishing.[9]

2. Environmental Impacts

(a) The European Shore Crab, *Carcinus maenas*, has been introduced at several places around the world presumably with the discharge of ballast water. In northern California, it has already displaced common red rock crab species.[10]

(b) The tropical green alga *Caulerpa taxifolia* was probably introduced into the Mediterranean Sea in the 1980s. It replaces native and endemic sea grasses (such as the flowering *Posidonia oceanica*) and limits the natural habitat for larval fish and invertebrates.[11] In 1984, it was first recorded covering an area of just one square meter off Monaco. Today it covers thousands of hectares along the coasts of France, Spain, Italy and Croatia.[12]

(c) But the invasion of alien species may also alter the structure and/or function of an ecosystem even if all native species survive. In other words, they do not just add players to the game, they change its rules. The zebra mussel, that had been introduced to the Great Lakes in the 1980s, is generally known for its economic impact. One may remember that water supplies of power plants have been densely clogged by this species causing billions of dollars of damage in the Great Lakes area. Often the impact to the ecosystem is thereby forgotten. Zebra mussels are filter feeders. Each adult is capable of filtering a liter of water per day removing almost every microscopic aquatic plant (phytoplankton or algae) and animal (zooplankton). Due to their astounding density, experts estimate that Lake Erie's zebra mussel population filters the entire volume of the lake's western basin once a week. The water clarity thereby has increased up to 600% which has allowed light to penetrate deeper into the water column, allowing rooted aquatic vegetation to greatly increase in density changing the whole ecosystem.[13]

---

8 *Gollasch* (*supra* note 6), p. 69.

9 Alien Invaders – Putting a Stop to the Ballast Water Hitchhikers, IMO Graphic Document, Internet: *http://www.imo.org/imo/focus/graphic.pdf.*

10 *Gollasch* (*supra* note 6), p. 70.

11 *A. Meinesz et al.*, Suivi de l'invasion de l'algue tropicale Caulerpa taxifolia en Méditerranée. Situation au 31 Décembre 1996, *Laboratoire Environnement Marin Littoral – CNRS UMR "DIMAR"* (1997), 191.

12 *Gollasch*, (*supra* note 6), p. 64.

13 Zebra Mussels and Other Nonindigenous Species, p. 2, Sea Grant, Internet (visited: 11/07/00): *http://seagrant. wisc.edu/greatlakes/glnetwork/exotics.htm.*

2. Alien Species as a Form of Pollution

2.1. The Interpretation of Art. 196 (1) UNCLOS

Art. 196 (1) UNCLOS is an amalgam of two different concepts: the duty of states to control negative effects to the marine environment either resulting from the use of technologies under their jurisdiction or resulting from alien or new species. From a textual point of view, the regulation of two different topics in one paragraph offers different ways to allocate the "introduction of alien species" to the remaining text, as illustrated below:

First Version
Article 196
Use of technologies or introduction of alien or new species

(1) **States shall take all measures necessary to prevent, reduce and control pollution of the marine environment resulting from** [the use of technologies under their jurisdiction or control, or] **the intentional or accidental introduction of species, alien or new, to a particular part of the marine environment, which may cause significant and harmful changes thereto**.

Second Version
Article 196
Use of technologies or introduction of alien or new species

(1) **States shall take all measures necessary to prevent, reduce and control** [pollution of the marine environment resulting from the use of technologies under their jurisdiction or control, or] **the intentional or accidental introduction of species, alien or new, to a particular part of the marine environment, which may cause significant and harmful changes thereto**.

In contrast to the second version, the first one considers the introduction of alien species as a form of pollution. In this author's view the pure wording itself does not indicate which of both alternatives should prevail. A clarification of this question is not purely academic, since the legal consequences differ considerably with regard to Art. 211 UNCLOS.[14] In situations where the text can be interpreted in different ways, the general rules of treaty interpretation in international law, as codified in the Vienna Convention on the Law of Treaties, provide further assistance: pursuant to Art. 31 (1) of the Vienna Convention, the text of Art. 196 (1) UNCLOS has to be interpreted in context and in the light of the treaty's purpose and object. Furthermore, Art. 31 (4) suggests that a "special meaning shall be given to a term if it is established that the parties so intended". The parties' intention might be deduced from the systematic context within Art. 196 (1) and in comparison with other relevant

---

[14] See *infra*, 5.4.(a).

provisions of UNCLOS. The structure of Art. 196 (1) seems to support the interpretation that alien species are not regarded as a form of pollution: undoubtedly, alien species refer to the last part of the provision addressing the cause of significant and harmful changes to the marine environment. An additional reference to the pollution, defined in Art. 1 (4) UNCLOS[15] as something which results in deleterious effects such as harm or hazards, would therefore be redundant. Moreover, to meet the requirements of pollution as defined in Art. 1 (4), alien species, in other words living organisms, have to be considered as "substances" or "energy".[16]

On the other hand, the International Maritime Organization's (IMO) initial idea to elaborate an instrument to reduce specific ways of the introduction of alien species as an Annex to MARPOL is premised on the implicit notion that regulations preventing marine pollution from ships are to be adopted.[17] Although not explicitly mentioned as a tool of treaty interpretation in Art. 31 of the Vienna Convention, it nevertheless demonstrates how the alien species issue may be interpreted in other fora.[18]

As a supplementary means of interpretation, reference may also be made to the preparatory work of UNCLOS. The legislative history indicates that the two topics are to be read not as different facets of the concept of marine environment pollution but rather as two distinct duties.[19]

However, most scholars have read Art. 196 (1) in a way that alien species may be regarded as pollution of the maritime environment.[20] According to them, species as a natural part of the ocean may become a "pollution" to it as soon as they do not live in the region in which they are expected to be. Beside the legal impact,[21] such a statement is more than a semantic concern. Indeed, this interpretation as the basis

---

15 Art. 1(4) UNCLOS reads: For the purpose of this Convention: [...] (4) "pollution of the marine environment" means the introduction by man, directly or indirectly, of substances or energy into the marine environment, including estuaries, which results or is likely to result in such deleterious effects as harm to living resources and marine life, hazards to human health, hindrance to marine activities, including fishing and other legitimate uses of the sea, impairment of quality for use of sea water and reduction of amenities.

16 In contrast, the definition of "pollutant" provided in the Clean Water Act of the USA (*CWA* § 502(6), 33 *U.S.C.* § 1362(6)) includes "biological materials". Other international conventions with the purpose of protecting the maritime environment also do not define "marine pollution" in a way that clearly includes alien species. See *M. Tomczak*, Defining Marine Pollution, in: *MarPol* 8 (1984), 311.

17 *David J. Bedermann*, International Control of Marine "Pollution" By Exotic Species, in: *EcoLQ* (1991), 715.

18 Meanwhile, the MEPC decided at its 45th Session, that an independent convention on that issue is to be adopted. See *infra*, 5.a).

19 *Shabtai Rosenne/Alexander Yankov*, in: *Myron H. Nordquist*, *The United Nations Convention on the Law of the Sea 1982, A Commentary*, vol. IV, p. 74 (Dordrecht 1990).

20 *Bedermann*, (*supra* note 17), p. 689; *Stephen M. Schwebel*, Third Report on the Law of the Non-Navigational Uses of International Watercourses, U.N. International Law Commission, 34th Sess., 312, U.N. Doc. A/CN.4/248. However, some authors regard the effects caused by the introduction of alien species as "Alteration of the Physical [Marine] Environment". See *Suzanne Iudicello/Margaret Lytle*, Marine Biodiversity and International Law: Instruments and Institutions That Can Be Used To Conserve Marine Biological Diversity Internationally, in: *TELJ* (1994), 144.

21 See *infra*, 5.a).

for a standard setting concept fundamentally determines the role of humans within the environment.

2.2. The Meaning of Alien Species in the Context of Art. 196 (1)

Species, in order to be covered by Art. 196 (1), have to be "alien".[22] A definition of alien species is not provided by UNCLOS itself. Scholars have described this term as "a species occurring outside its normal distribution";[23] "any species that enters an ecosystem beyond its historic range;"[24] or a species that "has spread beyond its natural range".[25]

Of course, the question follows: where does the natural range of a species end? In the human context – since an alien is defined as someone who is not a naturalized citizen of the country – the natural range is zoned by the frontiers of his or her country. Those clear borders do not exist within the plant or animal world at least not in the maritime world that knows only a few physical barriers, such as temperature and salt content. Range expansion as natural extensions of a species range can occur as a result of changing environmental conditions or chance events such as the attachment of fouling organisms to drifting objects. Are those invading species "aliens" because they are outside their natural range, their historical region? Relying on a historic perspective, how much time is needed for an established non-native to be treated as indigenous? A definition which includes changes to the oceanic environment from a primordial so-called "natural" state has to explain what the true natural state of a particular ecosystem is supposed to be over the time.[26] It therefore may be asked in how far the notion of "alien species" is already interlinked with human influence?[27] Hence, should the term alien species be defined as an organism that has been transported by human activity into regions where there is no natural precedent

---

[22] In the scientific and legal literature, the term "alien" is used more or less interchangeably with broadly equivalent terms such as "non-indigenous", "non-native" or "exotic". See *Bedermann*, (*supra* note 17), note 1; *David M. Whalin*, The Control of Aquatic Nuisance Nonindigenous Species, in: *EL* 1998, 70 with further references at note 25; *Claire Shine*, Legal and Institutional Dimensions of Invasive Alien Species Introduction and Control, Paper prepared for the Workshop held at IUCN Law Centre, Bonn, 10–11 December, p. 2 (on file with author).

[23] *Shine*, (*supra* note 22), p. 2.

[24] *Whalin*, (*supra* note 22), p. 71.

[25] *Bedermann*, (*supra* note 17), p. 681.

[26] See *Bedermann*, (*supra* note 17).

[27] A similar definition can be found in *Ulrike Doyle*, Alien Organisms in Germany – Results of a Conference at the Federal Environmental Agency in March, 1998, in: *Ulrike Doyle* (ed.), *Alien Organisms in Germany*, (Berlin 1999): "The term alien organism includes neozoans, neophytes and neomycetes. Neozoans are animals which have been introduced directly or indirectly by human activities in modern times (since 1492) into faunal regions to which they had not had access previously and which have established new populations there. Alien plants and fungi are defined correspondingly.".

for such invasion.[28] The inclusion of human influence seems also to be presupposed by Art. 196 (1): the distinction between an intentional and accidental introduction presumes that the introduction takes place by someone who is able to act intentionally or accidentally.

This view opposes human action that influences the environment from the course of nature in time. Humanity is not integrated into nature but put apart from it. However, what does nature mean in a world dominated by human impacts?[29] It should not be forgotten that almost all parts of the landscape on the European continent are in one way or the other cultivated. Without human influence, meadows and grassland could only thrive and prosper in a few places in Central Europe such as the edges and shores of lakes, fens and the sea.[30]

Nature protection, understood as leaving nature to its evolutionary process without human influence, would cover Central Europe almost entirely with wood. One-third of the species living in this region at present would disappear within a couple of generations.[31] The Lüneburg's heather is known as Germany's eldest legally protected nature sanctuary.[32] However, it is a manmade landscape, meager with regard to its biodiversity.

Coming back to Art. 196 (1) UNCLOS, according to the last two lines of this provision, those alien species are to be controlled that may cause significant and harmful changes to a particular part of the marine environment. But who determines, whether a change of the marine environment caused by an alien species is harmful? What timescale must be used as a basis to pass judgement on the value of the new ecosystem that may come into being through the introduction of an alien species over the time? The IUCN Guidelines[33] are clearer in this respect, not relying on value-loaded terms such as "harmful": an alien species is upgraded to an "alien invasive species" if it "becomes established in natural or semi-natural ecosystems or habitat, is an agent of change, and threatens native biological diversity." But do we really protect nature if we want to conserve our existing inventory as much as possible? It should be kept in mind that an estimated 99% of all species that have ever lived are extinct and that more kinds of creatures may be alive today than at any other single time in the planet's 4.6-billion-year history. Of course, there are

---

28 In this way: Art. 3 IUCN Guidelines for the Prevention of Biodiversity Loss Caused by Alien Invasive Species (approved by the 51st Meeting of the IUCN Council (Feb. 2000)): "Alien Species" [...] means a species [...] occurring outside of its natural range (past or present) and dispersal potential (i.e. outside the range it occupies naturally or could not occupy without direct or indirect introduction or care by humans) [...]. Available at: *www.iucn.org/themes/ssc/pubs/policy/invasivesEng.htm*; and *Iudicello/Lytle*, (*supra* note 28), p. 146.

29 *Holly Doremus*, The Rhetoric and Reality of Nature Protection: Toward a New Discourse, in: *WLLR* 57 (2000), 15.

30 WBGU (*supra* note 1), pp. 103–107.

31 WBGU (*supra* note 1), pp. 103–107.

32 WBGU (*supra* note 1), pp. 103–107.

33 Art. 3 (*supra* note 28).

legitimate reasons to control the introduction of "alien species": economic, socio-economic and the idea of preserving one special ecosystems for coming generations. But then we act for human's and not for nature's sake.

2.3. The Meaning of "Pollution to the Marine Environment" in the Context of Art. 196 (1) UNCLOS

Fragmentary reference to the definition of the term "pollution of the marine environment" as used in Art. 1 (4) UNCLOS has been made above. The entire definition reads as follows:

> Article 1
> 1. For the purpose of this Convention:
>
> [...]
>
> (4) "pollution of the marine environment" means the introduction by man, directly or indirectly, of substances or energy into the marine environment, including estuaries, which results or is likely to result in such deleterious effects as harm to living resources and marine life, hazards to human health, hindrance to marine activities, including fishing and other legitimate uses of the sea, impairment of quality for use of sea water and reduction of amenities.

Thus, in order to qualify for a pollution, invading species, regarded as substances, have to be introduced, directly or indirectly, by man and result in deleterious effects. The enumeration of those effects covers a vast variety of situations (such as the reduction of amenities) so that they do not seem to imply an additional straitening criteria. However, the crucial point is what kind of introduction of alien species can or should be traced back to a human activity.

Four examples may highlight this problem:

- Manmade canals, like the Suez Canal or the Panama Canal, that create the opportunity for species to enter new areas they were unable to reach before.
- Global warming caused by humans that also affects the oceans and may force species to move to other areas in order to keep the thermal level required for their survival.
- Human caused decimation of species which dominated a habitat allows other formerly repressed species to move in and establish a viable population.
- What – with special regard to the definition of Art. 1 (4) – if human controlled reintroduction of an extinct species represses the population that has established itself in the meantime and generated economic benefits for humans?

3. The Intentional Introduction of Alien Species in Marine Waters

Intentional introductions are generally planned and purposeful for management and economic reasons (exception: the disposal of unwanted pets or ornamental plants and research organisms).[34] In maritime waters intentional introductions occur primarily for mariculture production of *e.g.* salmon, shrimp, oysters, mussels, and algae. An additional significant pathway is by release of hatchery-spawned organisms into the wild for the purpose of augmenting wild populations, generally for future capture in fisheries or in an attempt to enhance a population that is under threat.[35] Intentional introductions are usually associated with the release of a single species.

Some alien species introduced for beneficial purpose unexpectedly produce harmful consequences.[36] For instance, the non-native Japanese oyster species has out-competed and displaced native oysters in the pacific Northwest of America. Nevertheless, devastating effects from the intentional introduction of alien species in maritime waters, like the destruction of whole ecosystems and the extinction of endemic species that have been reported from aquacultural projects in freshwater areas (Nile perch in Lake Victoria[37]), are hardly known. However, this scenario may change in the future: according to new research, genetically modified (GM) fish released into the wild could wipe out local populations.[38] The researchers studied transgenic Japanese *maedaka* carrying the human growth hormone gene, which increases growth rate and final size. The transgenic fish became sexually mature faster than the normal fish, produced more eggs and attracted – because of its size – four times as many mates as its smaller rivals. But beside the reproductive advantages, only two-thirds of the transgenic *maedaka* survived to reproductive age. Thus, the spread of the growth hormone gene through the population could cause reduction in population size and eventual extinction.[39]

As the above paragraphs have already indicated, standard setting mechanisms with regard to the intentional introduction of alien species have to strike the right balance between the benefits of introduced species and the costs involved, including the long-term impacts, and take into consideration the inherent uncertainty as to future consequences of intentional introductions.

---

34 For instance, New Zealand's economy depends heavily on about 50 introduced species. See *Shine*, (*supra* note 22), p. 2.

35 UNEP/CBD/SBSTTA/1/8, Annex.

36 Harmful consequences that are a general side effect of marine large-scale production such as the destruction of mangrove forests through shrimp farming are not included, since they are not specifically related to the alien species issue.

37 The invasion of Lake Victoria by the Nile perch has led to the loss of about 70% of the lake's cichlid species, a unique evolutionary suite of small fish; on the other hand however, the Nile perch is highly valued by local communities for food value and as an important economic asset. See *Shine*, (*supra* note 22), p. 2.

38 *W.M. Muir/R.D. Howard*, One GM Fish Could Destroy Wild Populations, in: *BINASNews* 5 (1999), Issues 3 & 4, p. 12.

39 *Ibid*, p. 12.

One approach emerged during the *travaux préparatoires* of the present Art. 196 (1) UNCLOS, introduced by Norway during the fourth session of the Third Committee in 1976. The draft article[40] required an assessment on the potential effects of any planned introduction to a particular part of the marine environment and prohibited an introduction where the outcome of such an assessment may indicate significant and extensive harmful changes to the marine environment. Furthermore, advanced consultation on planned releases of new organisms with "interested states and appropriate international organizations" was required. But the language of this draft article was considered too far-reaching and was not adopted.

Similar, the IUCN Position Statement on Translocation of Living Organisms, approved in 1987, lays out steps to follow when considering future releases. This paper did not directly focus on maritime species, but it was nevertheless of guiding value and applicable.[41] In the initial draft for the Convention on Biological Diversity (CBD) prepared by IUCN, the alien species provision included parts of the ideas of the 1987 paper and even suggested creating a new international expert body on alien species within the CBD.[42] Again, the draft was weakened considerably, ending in the hortatory statement of Art. 8 (h) CBD,[43] a vague and probably unenforceable provision. After all, the introduction of alien species has become a bigger issue within the CBD.[44]

The – so far unsuccessful – attempts to regulate the issue of intentional introduction of alien species comprehensively relied on a preventive framework, considering the unpredictability of the impacts.

New instruments that are about to be elaborated may be guided[45] by the mechan-

---

40 The proposal read (introduced as Art. 5 bis (1)): States shall to the fullest extent possible assess the possible effect of any planned introduction of species alien or new to a particular part of the marine environment, and shall not undertake or permit any such introduction where they may cause significant and extensive harmful changes to the marine environment. Whenever the effects of any planned activity could give rise to uncertainty in respect of significant and extensive harmful changes to the marine environment, the State concerned shall duly consult with competent international organizations and other States that may be affected by such changes (reprinted in *Nordquist*, (*supra* note 19), p. 74).

41 In summary it provides that: release of an alien species should be considered only if clear and well defined benefits to humans or natural communities can be foreseen; releases should be considered only if no indigenous species is suitable; no alien species should be deliberately released into any natural area; releases into seminatural areas should not occur without exceptional reasons; planned releases, including those for biological control, entail three critical phases: rigorous assessment of desirability; controlled experimental release; and extensive release accompanied by careful monitoring and pre-arrangement for control or eradication measures, if necessary.

42 *U.S. Congress, Office of Technology Assessment*, Harmful Non-Indigenous Species in the United States, in: *OTA-F-565*, p. 296 (Washington D.C. September 1993).

43 Convention on Biological Diversity, 31 *ILM* 818 (1992).

44 Decision V/4. UNEP/CBD/COP/5/3.

45 Of further guiding value may be the guidelines of the International Council for the Exploration of the Sea (ICES) adopted in 1973, the first version of the "Code of Practice" on the introduction of alien species for mariculture that had been revised several times, lastly in 1994. The code sets forth recommended procedures and practices to diminish the risks of detrimental effects from the intentional introduction and transfer of marine organisms. The Code is divided into five sections of recommendations relating to: (1) the steps to take prior to introducing new species, (2) the steps to take after

isms applied in the Biosafety Protocol,[46] adopted at the beginning of 2000. With regard to the deliberate introduction of "new species"[47] in the form of genetically modified organisms, the Protocol requires that an advanced informed agreement procedure[48] take place and that decisions be based on a risk assessment[49] and may apply the precautionary approach.[50]

However, new standards may have to be balanced with the Agreement on the Application of Sanitary and Phytosanitary Measures (SPS),[51] requiring the recognition of several trade principles while applying protective measures.[52] Another question is whether Art. 196 (1) UNCLOS allows the application of precautionary measures. On the one hand, it requires the causation of harmful or significant changes to the marine environment. However, on the other hand, those effects do not have to be proven, it is rather sufficient that they *may* happen through the introduction of alien species. Hence, precautionary measures may be taken under Art. 196 (1).

4. The Accidental Introduction of Alien Species

Whereas control and management systems for intentional introduction involve identified actors and attempt to anticipate the species' behavior in the new host environment, the systems for accidental introductions focus on the unknown. Operational measures have to be targeted at those human activities (pathways or vectors) that present the highest risk of unwanted alien invasion. The best known vectors for introductions that directly effect the maritime environment are: unintentional introductions via mariculture, ship fouling, and ballast water.

4.1. Unintentional Introductions via Mariculture

In the past, the introduction of species for mariculture has often also resulted in the unintentional introduction of diverse associated flora and fauna, including encrusting, epifaunal and infaunal species.[53] However, modern mariculture practices, particularly

---

deciding to proceed with an introduction, (3) the prevention of unauthorized introductions by member countries, (4) policies for ongoing introductions or transfers which have been an established part of commercial practice, and (5) the steps to take prior to releasing genetically modified organisms.

46 Cartagena Protocol on Biosafety to the Convention on Biological Diversity (CPB), 39 *ILM* 1027 (2000).

47 Art. 196 (1) UNCLOS not only refers to the introduction of "alien" but also to "new" species, whereby new species cover those that have been bred traditionally or through modern biotechnology.

48 Art. 7–10 CPB (*supra* note 46).

49 Art. 10(1); Art 15; Annex III CPB (*supra* note 46).

50 Art. 10(6) CPB (*supra* note 46).

51 See Annex 1 of the Marrakesh Agreement Establishing the World Trade Organisation, 33 *ILM* 1125 (1994).

52 For a detailed discussion see *Steve Charnovitz*, The Supervision of Health and Biosafety Regulation by World Trade Rule, in: *TELJ* (2000), p. 271.

53 *CRIMP (Center for Research on Introduced Marine Pests)*, Introduction Mechanisms for Exotic Marine Species, Internet (visited: 10/25/00).

the movement of culture species in the larval stage, have greatly diminished the incidence of accidental introduction. Furthermore, species that are imported lawfully for contained use often manage to escape into the natural environment without the deliberate intention of effecting an introduction. For instance, the Atlantic salmon has continuously escaped through holes in net pens. There is concern that they may compete for food or nesting sites with native Pacific salmon.[54] In order to prevent such an effect, one strict approach is general exclusion if it is shown that the cultivated species may survive in the wild, whether or not it has been proven that such a species displaces native ones.[55] Other imports could be controlled on the basis of reliable data.

4.2. Ship Fouling

Another long known vector is the introduction of alien species as fouling organisms on the hull of ships. Therefore, antifouling paints are used to coat the bottoms of ships to prevent sea-life such as algae and molluscs from attaching themselves to the hull. In the early days of sailing ships, lime and later arsenic were used to coat ships' hulls, until the modern chemical industry developed tributylin (TBT) paints. This biocidal antifoulant widely available to the shipping industry since the beginning of the 1970s has significantly reduced the potential for dispersal of fouling organisms.[56] But studies have shown that TBT slowly "leaches" into the sea water, killing sealife, harming the environment and possibly entering the food chain. As a result, in 1990, MEPC adopted a resolution recommending that governments adopt measures to eliminate antifouling paints containing TBT.[57] In November 1999, the IMO Assembly adopted Resolution A.895(21) on Antifouling Systems Used on Ships stating that the MEPC should develop a global, legally-binding instrument to address the harmful effects of antifouling systems used on ships, ensuring a ban on the application of TBT by 2003 and a complete ban on ship hulls by 2008. Meanwhile, MEPC approved the draft convention in principle at its 45th session in October 2000. The individualistic approach of the MEPC working group has been criticized as blindly ignoring the benefits TBT has had in stopping species from inoculating on ships' hulls and opponents forecast a growing contamination of ecosystems with exotic organisms as a consequence.

---

54 *Massachusetts Bay Information Server Marine Bioinvaders*, Aquacutlure, Internet (visited: 10/23/00): *http://massbay.mit.edu/ExoticSpecies/aqua/index.htm.* For further detail see: Impacts of Farmed Salmon Escaping from Net Pens, Internet (visited: 10/23/00): *http://www.eao.gov.bc.ca/project/aquacult/salmon/escape.htm.*

55 Western Australia has established a hierarchy of controls to regulate activities generating escape risks. See *Shine* (*supra* note 22), p. 11.

56 CQD Journal for the Maritime Environment Industry, vol. 5, #2 (June 1999), p. 3, Internet (visited: 10/28/00): *http://cqdjournal.com/html/env_5.2.htm.*

57 Resolution MEPC 46(30).

5. The Accidental Introduction of Alien Species through Ballast Water

Probably the primary method of alien species introduction has been through the ballast water of shipping vessels. Global shipping moves 80% of the world's commodities and is fundamental to world trade.[58] All the different cases of alien species introduction into maritime waters described at the beginning of this article are caused through ballast water.[59] Scientists estimate that as many as 3,000 alien species per day are transported in ballast water around the world.[60]

5.1. Ballast Water and Alien Species

Ballast water is fresh or saltwater held in the ballast tanks and cargo holds of ships. It is used to provide stability and maneuverability during a voyage when ships are not carrying cargo, not carrying cargo heavy enough, or when more stability is required due to rough seas. Ballast water may also be used to add weight so that a ship sinks low enough in the water to pass under bridges and other structures.

Usually ballast water is pumped into ballast tanks when a ship has delivered cargo to a port and is departing with less cargo or no cargo. Ballast water is then transported and released at the next port-of-call where the ship picks up more cargo. If a ship is receiving or delivering cargo to a number of ports, it may release or take on a portion of ballast water at each port. In such cases, the ship's ballast water contains a mix of waters from multiple ports.[61]

Taken from coastal port areas, this water (and associated sediments) is home to multiple marine organisms. The ships, in loading ballast, also load the living organisms, ranging in size and phyla, from tiny microorganisms to larger species, including even whole schools of fish! At the next port of call, the water may be discharged or exchanged. Parts of the sediment and organisms, which have survived the voyage also will be discharged. Some unpumpable ballast water and sediment may always remain on board and form a virtually permanent layer, with the concomitant capability of supporting a living community on the tank bottom composed of polycheate

---

58 *Committee on Ships' Ballast Operations, National Research Council*, Stemming the Tide: Controlling Introductions of Nonindigenous Species by Ships' Ballast Water, p. 1 (1996).

59 See *supra*, part I.

60 *J.T. Carlton/J.B. Geller*, Ecological Roulette: The Global Transport of Non-Indigenous Marine Organisms, in: *Science* 261(6) (1993), 78–82. *S. Gollasch*, Untersuchung des Arteneintrages durch den Internationalen Schiffsverkehr unter Besonderer Berücksichtigung Nichtheimischer Arten, p. 314 (Hamburg 1996).

61 One illustrative example is provided in: Stemming the Tide (*supra* note 58), p. 17: A vessel off-loads its cargo in a discharge port, having arrived with some ballast on board from a prior harbor (site 1). After completing cargo discharge, the vessel ballasts (site 2) in preparation for its transoceanic crossing to pick up cargo for another port. During passage additional water is loaded into storm ballast and cargo/ballast holds because of rough sea conditions (site 3). Some days later, due to fuel and freshwater consumption, more ballast is added mid-ocean for additional stability (site 4). Finally, additional ballast is taken aboard for clearance under a harbor bridge in the arrival port (site 5).

worms, amphipods, shrimp, hydroids etc.[62] While the resident adult community would remain on the bottom of the tank, they would release continuously planktonic larvae into the overlying incoming and outgoing ballast water.

5.2. Ballast Water Treatment and Control Strategies

The primary objective of developing strategies for managing ballast water is to reduce the likelihood of the introduction of alien species to an acceptable level. In other words, preventive instead of reactive programs should be preferred wherever possible. Beside, appropriate strategies need to also be safe for a ship and its crew, environmentally acceptable, practicable in application, compatible with normal ship operations and cost effective.

Successful standard setting has to consider three different levels of action: first, a precautionary practice should apply; second, appropriate treatment of ballast water is required; and third, a monitoring system should be established.

(a) Precautionary Measures

Minimizing the uptake of potentially harmful aquatic organisms should be the first step. Therefore, particularities of the location should be considered: at ports with high sediment loads or with areas of sewage discharge or global hot spots, where targeted organisms are known to be present in the water column, the intake of ballast water should be kept to an absolute minimum at the cargo discharge berth and be finished upon departure but while still in calm waters. Furthermore, the intake of ballast water should be avoided at night, when some planktonic organisms migrate higher up the water column.

(b) Treatment options for ballast water

The wide spectrum of suggested treatment options may be categorized following the three different stages in a ship's voyage: during ballasting at the cargo discharge port; en route, between the ports; and during deballasting at the cargo loading port. Each of these scenarios has significantly different constraints with respect to treatment options. In the first and third scenarios, large quantities of water must be treated in a short period of time, while water is taken on board or discharged and flow rates through the treatment system are high. In the second scenario, between the ports, more time is available for treatment.

On or before departure, control is based on preventing or minimizing the intake of organisms during loading of ballast water at the port of origin. This can be done through filtering ballast water as it is loaded.

En route, control is based on the removal of viable organisms prior to discharge of ballast water at the destination port either by chemical, physical, mechanical, or biological treatments or by open ocean ballast water change. Changing ballast water

---

[62] Stemming the Tide, (*supra* note), p. 31.

Table 1. Ballast water treatment methods

Ballast water treatment	*Advantages/disadvantages*
Ballast water exchange in deep sea – i.e. depths of 2,000 meters or more	Seen as most effective practical method of minimizing risk of transfer of unwanted species. Deep ocean water contains few organisms and these are unlikely to survive transfer to coastal or fresh water environment. Ship safety aspects may inhibit operations – deep sea exchange may not be considered safe under certain weather/sea conditions. Flow-through exchange is preferred option as emptying and filling ballast tanks is unlikely to be a safe option for structural/stability reasons.
Taking on clean ballast	May be achieved through precautionary measures such as avoidance of shallow water, dredging operations and areas of known outbreak of disease or plankton bloom. But there may be little choice over where ballasting can take place.
Relying on differences of temperature/salinity	Significant changes in ambient conditions between area of take-up/receiving area can affect ability of aquatic organism to survive. But more research is needed and it depends on locations.
Keeping water in ballast for long periods	Water maintained in ballast tanks for more than 100 days represent minimum risk, as most organisms do not survive the absence of light and higher iron content of ballast water. But tankers and bulk carriers may not have option of maintaining ballast water for three months.
Sediment disposal	Many aquatic organism are present in sediment and all sources of sediment retention such as anchor cables should be routinely cleaned. Ships should be designed to 'minimise' sediment retention.
Reception facilities	Discharge of ships' ballast into reception facilities may provide adequate means of control. Dependent on these facilities being provided.
Filtration	Filtering ballast water as it is taken on board would remove large particles such as small seaweeds, but would not rule out the uptake of microscopic organisms. Residues would be released in the area of ballasting, but capital costs to provide infrastructure to do this could be high.
Ultra violet radiation	Effect varies with type of organism, with some highly resistant to UV radiation. But could be effective in combination with filtration. No toxic side effects, and no adverse effects on pipework, pumps or coatings.
Ballast water heating	Potentially attractive solution. Heating to temperatures of 36–38°C for 2–6 hours has been shown to kill zebra mussels. Temperatures above 40°C for eight minutes can be lethal to all organisms. Dependent on availability of heat to treat ballast water during voyage; thermal stresses also need to be addressed.
Use of chlorine as disinfectant	Effectiveness influenced by temperature, contact time and pH level. But there are environmental concerns about discharge of chlorinated ballast water. The reaction of chlorine with some organic compounds produces carcinogens.
Electrolytically generated copper and silver ions	Effectiveness seen as superior to chlorination, but some organism can enhance their tolerance to high copper and silver concentrations. Environmental implications of concentrations required need further study.

Source: IMO at: *www.imo.org/imo/focus/1998/ballast.pdf.*

at sea is currently the favored technique. Ballast water loaded in port is exchanged for ocean water during passage between port of call. This method is usually effective because most freshwater, or inshore coastal organisms cannot survive when discharged into the ocean environment. Similarly, freshwater, or inshore coastal waters are inhospitable to oceanic organisms. However, altering the ballast condition while under way may jeopardize vessel safety. In order to reduce that risk another option has been developed in which the original ballast water is flushed out by pumping in ocean water at the bottom of the tank and continuously overflowing the tank from the top until sufficient water has been changed to minimize the number of original organisms remaining in the tank.[63] A physical inactivation of organisms in ballast water may be undertaken through thermal treatment, using excess engine heat and/or the exhaust from the engine cooling unit so that the ballast water becomes part of the main engine cooling water system.[64] Yet another option is the use of ultraviolet radiation, which operates by causing photochemical reactions of biological components such as DNA or RNA.[65]

Chemical removal of species in ballast water through chlorination, the use of ozone and hydrogene peroxide or salinity and pH adjustments, is a further alternative. However, those applications are also not free from negative side-effects.[66]

On arrival, control strategies are aimed at preventing the discharge of unwanted organisms that could survive in the target environment. Beside the possibility to apply the aforementioned methods while at berth, ballast could also be transferred ashore to land-based facilities and either be treated there before discharge or be directly repumped in ballast water tanks of other vessels so that ballast water is used in an isolated circle.

(c) Monitoring system

Finally, a monitoring system should be established for two purposes: First, monitoring is needed to audit ballast water control methods and check for compliance with regulations or guidelines; therefore it is an integral part of the ballast water management process. Second, monitoring is a research and development tool that permits assessment of the effectiveness of ballast water treatments, allows increased understanding of the non-indigenous species problem and may assist in developing plans to manage ballast water.[67]

5.3. Status of National Regulations on Ballast Water

Some of the above-mentioned options are already unilateral mandatory requirements in several countries to inhibit the introduction of alien species in the future.

63 *Ibid*, p. 37.
64 *AQIS*, Ballast Water Treatment for the Removal of Marine Organisms, in: *BWRS* 1, 1–99 (Canberra 1993).
65 *Gollasch*, (*supra* note 6), p. 91.
66 *Ibid*, pp. 95–106.
67 Stemming the Tide, (*supra* note 58), p. 74.

In the United States, exchange of ballast water is mandatory for vessels entering the Great Lakes; vessels arriving at the British Columbia port of Vancouver, Canada, must exchange ballast water at sea; those ships destined for Israel must change ballast water outside the Red Sea if visiting Eilat and in the Atlantic if visiting the Mediterranean ports; in Chile, any ship coming from zones affected by cholera or similar contagious epidemic should renew ballast water a minimum of 12 nautical miles from the coast. Where no proof of ballast water exchange is available, chemicals must be added to ballast water prior to deballasting in port. China also requires a chemical ballast water treatment on board if its area of origin is listed as an infected point by the WHO. Vessels calling for the port of Odessa have to change their ballast water immediately upon entry into the Black Sea area. In Panama the discharge of any kind is prohibited while passing through the Canal. Buenos Aires Port Authorities requires chlorination for ships calling at port.

5.4. Status of International Regulations on Ballast Water

So far, only voluntary guidelines are available on an international level. Many of the above-listed unilateral responses are generally consistent with those IMO Guidelines while others impose new and different requirements on shipping.[68] Different mandatory ballast water control measures at the port, regional or national level, in the absence of a governing international framework would lead to a complicated patchwork of differing requirements. Uniformity in operating procedures and training standards militates strongly in favor of a coordinated, international approach to the development of a regulatory framework for managing ballast water. Hence, in the following paragraphs, the existing legal structure within which a binding framework could be established has to be analyzed. The starting point of this analysis is again the legal basis for the protection of the maritime environment, part XII of UNCLOS.

(a) The Standard Setting Process within UNCLOS and IMO.

Art. 196 (1) itself has no "norm setting" function but is rather a hortatory call for member states to take "all measures necessary" to control accidental introductions that may cause significant and harmful changes to the marine environment.[69]

Partly designed to operate as an umbrella convention, UNCLOS delegates in Part 7 the elaboration of global and regional rules *for the protection and preservation*

---

68 The IMO International Guidelines based on Resolution A.868(20) are discussed in detail below.

69 Although the text of Art. 196 (1) requires the causation of "significant or harmful changes" to the marine environment for both the intentional and the accidental introduction of alien species, this qualified requirement seems to focus on the intentional introduction only. Since the actors are not identified in the case of accidental introduction, and hence no risk assessment can be undertaken to evaluate harmful effects in advance, no preventive measure could be taken. *Bedermann*, (*supra* note 17), p. 702.

of the marine environment to other international fora, but requires that those international rules and standards be established in consistency with it (see Art. 197).

In contrast, Art. 211, obliging states to establish international rules and standards to prevent, reduce and control *pollution of the marine environment from vessels* through the competent international organization, which means through IMO, does not have a saving clause like Art. 197 but is subject to the regulation set out in Art. 237. It states that the provisions of Part 7 are without prejudice to agreements which may be concluded in furtherance of the general principles set forth in UNCLOS. In other words, as long as the international rules and standards fall within IMO's authority in the context of Art. 211, they do not have to be consistent with UNCLOS, but only follow its general principles.

Furthermore, according to Art. 211 (2), once the standards set in the IMO are "generally accepted", they have to be implemented and enforced by the parties to UNCLOS even if the pertinent state is not a member of IMO or is a member of IMO but has not consented within IMO to be bound by the particular standard. According to some scholars, UNCLOS incorporates, by reference, international standards with an obliging *erga omnes* effect, even if the standard itself is only a legally non-binding guideline under IMO.[70]

The crucial question in this context is at which level the requirement of "general acceptance" is met. Some authors suggested that this will be the case if the pertinent rule enters into force,[71] others postulated a higher degree of acceptance[72] and few even required the status of customary international law.[73] Guidelines, adopted at IMO's General Assembly through resolutions, are not binding and hence cannot enter into force. Is, in this case, the mere adoption of the resolution sufficient to be regarded as generally accepted?

The above-discussed issue of how to read Art. 196 (1)[74] is of some importance in the present context. If the introduction of alien species is considered as a form of pollution, Art. 211 is applicable and the legal frame set by Art. 196 could be filled by the IMO in any way as long as the general principles of UNCLOS are respected. Additionally, regulations with regard to ballast water elaborated under IMO's authority may become a legally binding minimum level for UNCLOS members.

If they are not regarded as a form of pollution, the legal frame of Art. 196 (1) has to be filled through Art. 197. However, in that case agreements elaborated under

---

70 *R. Wolfrum/V. Röben/F.L. Morrison*, Preservation of the Marine Environment, in *Fred L. Morrison/R. Wolfrum* (eds.), *International, Regional and National Environmental Law*, pp. 259–260 (The Hague 2000).

71 See Discussions of the Evensen-Group of 1976, reprinted in: *Platzöder*, *Documents of the New York Session 1976*, p. 219.

72 See *Doris König*, Durchsetzung internationaler Bestands- und Umweltschutzvorschriften auf Hoher See im Interesse der Staatengemeinschaft, p. 147 (Berlin 1990).

73 *W. van Reenen*, Rules of Reference in the New Convention on the Law of the Sea, in: *NYIL* 12 (1981), 15.

74 See *supra* part 2.1.

IMO as well as those established under any other competent international organization (e.g. CBD), have to be consistent with UNCLOS and do not evolve in a minimum standard for UNCLOS members.

With regard to the special relation between UNCLOS and IMO, the evolution of pertinent IMO activities are analyzed in greater detail.

aa) Standard Setting Process within IMO

In 1973, IMO convened a conference to adopt a new international convention which would address all aspects of marine pollution by ships – The International Convention for the Prevention of Pollution from Ships.[75] At this conference, the ballast water problem was raised specifically in the context of the transport of pathogens harmful to humans. The conference adopted a resolution, which noted that "ballast water taken in waters which may contain bacteria from epidemic diseases, may, when discharged, cause a danger of spreading of the epidemic diseases to other countries." The resolution requested IMO and the World Health Organisation to "initiate studies on that problem on the basis of any evidence and proposals which may be submitted by governments".[76]

In the late 1980s, Canada and Australia were among countries experiencing particular problems with unwanted species, and they brought their concerns to the attention of IMO's Marine Environment Protection Committee (MEPC). In 1990, during its 31st session the MEPC set up a working group on ballast water, which developed guidelines on addressing the problem of alien species.[77] A MEPC Resolution[78] – the Guidelines for Preventing the Introduction of Unwanted Organisms and Pathogens from Ships' Ballast Waters and Sediment Discharges – was adopted in 1991. The guidelines were aimed at providing administrations and port state authorities with information on procedures to minimize the risk from the introduction of unwanted aquatic organisms from ships' ballast water and sediment. The guidelines recommended care in loading ballast water to ensure only clean water and clean sediments were taken on board. Where the discharge of ballast water was unavoidable, ballast water exchange in the open sea provided a means of limiting the introduction of unwanted species, but also other ballast water management practices were mentioned as acceptable.

In 1993, those guidelines were adopted as an Assembly Resolution giving them more weight than a MEPC Resolution. The resolution additionally requested MEPC and the Maritime Safety Committee (MSC) to keep the guidelines under review

---

75 The Convention and its Protocol adopted in 1978 is known as MARPOL 73/78. It initially consisted of five annexes dealing with oil, chemicals, goods in packaged form, sewage and garbage. In 1997 an annex on air pollution was added.

76 *IMO*, Alien Invaders – Putting a Stop to the Ballast Water Hitch-Hikers, p. 2, available through internet: *www.imo.org.imo/focus/1998/ballast.pdf*.

77 *Gollasch*, (*supra* note 6), p.84.

78 MEPC 50(31).

"with a view to further developing the guidelines as a basis for a new, then legally binding, Annex to MARPOL 73/78."

An updated version of the guidelines was adopted by the 20th Assembly of IMO in November 1997.[79] The revised guidelines incorporate further recommendations on tackling the problem, including how to lessen the chances of taking harmful organisms on board along with ballast water. The guidelines contain 13 paragraphs and two appendices. Defining themselves as a tool to minimize the risks associated with ballast water the guidelines are structured like an agreement while using a soft language. Paragraphs 2–4 contain general provisions, defining pertinent terms, the guidelines' application and their objectives. Training and education is recommended for ships' masters and crews and information, such as the availability of reception and treatment facilities at ports should be provided through IMO. Paragraphs 7–9 describe several procedural measures: every ship carrying ballast water should have a specific ballast water management plan, should record the treatment procedures on board and the ballast water's amount, temperature and salinity and report it to the port state authorities. Paragraph 9 recommends ships apply precautionary practices. The recommendations include informing local agents and/or ships of areas and situations where uptake of ballast water should be minimized, such as areas with known populations of harmful pathogens or areas near sewage outlets. Ballast water exchange has been considered as the appropriate operate measure at least in the short term. However, if reception facilities are provided by a port state, they should be utilized.

The resolution also asks the MEPC to work towards completion of legally binding provisions on ballast water management in the form of a new annex to MARPOL 73/78, together with guidelines for their uniform and effective implementation with a view to their consideration and adoption in the year 2000. However, at its 45th Session in October 2000, MEPC postponed the possible date of adoption to 2002–2003 and proposed the instrument to be a new international convention "for the control and management of ships' ballast water and sediments."[80]

The instrument is being developed on the basis of a two-tier approach. Tier 1 includes requirements that would apply to all ships, including mandatory requirements for a ballast water and sediments management plan, a ballast water record book and a requirement that new ships shall carry out ballast water and sediment management procedures to a given standard or range of standards. Existing ships would be required to carry out ballast water management procedures after a phase-in period, but these procedures could differ from those to be applied to new ships. Tier 2 includes special requirements which could apply in certain areas and would include procedures and criteria for the designation of such areas in which additional controls

[79] A.868(20) Guidelines for the control and management of ships' ballast water to minimize the transfer of the harmful aquatic organisms and pathogens.

[80] See IMO's template of the 45th Session of the MEPC, pp. 3–4, available at *www.imo.org/imo/meetings/mepc/45/mepc45.htm.*

may be applied to the discharge and/or uptake of ballast water. The text for Tier 2 remains to be developed.[81]

bb) Enforcement of UNCLOS/IMO Standards

IMO itself does not have jurisdiction to enforce these regulations. It is primarily the responsibility of the flag states to ensure compliance of the ships flying their flags. By exercising their flag state jurisdiction, flag states implement their commitments under UNCLOS. Since flag state jurisdiction proves to be ineffective in situations like the one in our case, the flag state jurisdiction has to be supplemented to ensure effective implementation of IMO regulations. Therefore, when enforcing the rules against marine pollution, coastal states (Art. 220) or port states (Art. 218) have the right to investigate into violations of applicable international rules and standards for the prevention, reduction and control of pollution from vessels (Art. 220 (3)), or "the violation of applicable international rules and standards through the competent international authority" (Art. 218 (1)). The power to invoke rules and standards does not depend upon whether the flag state of that particular ship is party to the relevant convention, or, according to one scholar, whether the standard invoked is enshrined only in guidelines issued by IMO.[82]

(b) The Standard Setting Process within the Convention on Biological Diversity (CBD)[83]

The issue of alien species in the maritime environment has been approached from two different aspects within the CBD: first, through the implementation of Art. 8 (h) CBD addressing the introduction of alien species and second as part of the conservation and sustainable use of marine and coastal biodiversity. With regard to the first aspect, the Conference of the Parties (COP) took its first steps to comprehensively address the alien invasive species issue at its third meeting in November 1996.[84] It decided that alien species' introduction should become a thematic issue and hence has to be addressed comprehensively as a stand-alone matter. At its fourth meeting in May 1998, the COP built on this initiative directing the Subsidiary Body for Scientific, Technical and Technological Advice (SBSTTA) to develop "guiding principles" on the prevention, introduction and eradication of alien species for the fifth COP meeting in May 2000.[85] However, at that meeting the adoption of elaborated draft guidelines was not suggested, since further comments were needed on several issues. Instead, the draft version was included in Annex I[86] of Decision V/8 as

---

[81] *Ibid*, p. 4.

[82] *R. Wolfrum*, IMO interface with the law of the sea convention, in: *Myron H. Nordquist/John Norton Moore* (eds.), *Current Maritime Issues and the International Maritime Organization*, pp. 222–236, 232 (The Hague 1999).

[83] See *supra* note 43.

[84] Decision III/9, para 9 (c).

[85] Decision IV/1 C.

[86] See UNEP/CBD/COP/5/3.

"Interim Guiding Principles for the Prevention, Introduction and Mitigation of Impacts of Alien Species". In this document, the discharge of ballast water is explicitly addressed as one of the common pathways leading to introductions of alien species. The main part of Decision V/8 was the parties' conclusion to decide on the appropriate instrument to address the alien species issue (either in form of an international instrument or by further developing the guiding principles).

"The Jakarta Mandate on the Conservation and Sustainable use of Marine and Coastal Biological Diversity" adopted through COP decision II/10 in 1995 is the second approach in which the ballast water issue may be addressed in further detail. Within the Jakarta Mandate, five thematic issues have been identified, one of them focusing on the introduction of alien species. In the annex of Decision IV/5, three operational objectives were identified for the alien species issue, but ballast water management was not explicitly mentioned.

(c) Other Fora, in Which the Ballast Water Management Issue Has Been Addressed

(aa) Model Ballast Water Management Plan[87]

The International Chamber of Shipping (ICS) and the International Association of Independent Tanker Owners (INTERTANKO) have published a Model Ballast Management Plan giving practical guidance for the implementation of the IMO guidelines.

(bb) Global Ballast Water Management Program[88]

IMO, alongside with UNDP and GEF began a project in 1997 on "Removal of Barriers to the effective Implementation of Ballast Water Control and Management Measures in Developing Countries". The initial stage of the project has been completed involving a report on ballast water management in a number of countries. Beginning in May 2000, and continuing for another 3 years, the program will this time assist less industrialized countries to implement effective measures to control the introduction of marine species through ballast water. Six demonstration sites have been chosen with the intent to represent the six main developing regions of the world.

(cc) Invasive Species Specialist Group (ISSG)[89]

The New Zealand based ISSG is a specialist group of the Species Survival Commission of the International Union for the Conservation of Nature: The ISSG is a global group of more than 100 scientific and policy experts and has recently finished developing invasive species policy guidelines which have been accepted by IUCN. They were also used as orientation for the guidelines elaborated under the CBD. Ballast Water management is not addressed in detail.

87 Available for Members at: *www.intertanko.com.*

88 Further information available at: *http://globallast.imo.org.*

89 Further information available at: *www.issg.org.*

(dd) Global Invasive Species Programme (GISP)[90]
GISP is a component of DIVERSITAS (international program on the science of biodiversity) and is coordinated by SCOPE (Scientific Committee on Problems of the Environment), in conjunction with IUCN, UNEP and CABI with initial financial support from GEF, UNEP, ICSU and NASA.

The program will *e.g.* lay the groundwork for new tools in science, information management, education, and policy. Again, the ballast water issue has not been addressed so far.

SUMMARY

Art. 196 (1) UNCLOS, which addresses the introduction of alien or new species into the marine environment, may be interpreted in a way that alien species are regarded as a form of pollution. Such a classification raises the question of the role assigned to humans with respect to the (marine) environment. It highlights the bizarre position of humans, who are living in a world dominated by their impacts, and who attempt to oppose themselves to the course of nature within their standard setting mechanisms.

The introduction of alien species has caused devastating effects to health, wealth and environment around the globe. While the consequences of the intentional introduction of alien species seem to be somehow measurable, the accidental introduction as a by-product of international trade is yet extremely difficult to manage. Effective and safe control mechanisms are still to be elaborated; at present, no legally binding instrument on an international level has been adopted, although some voluntary guidelines in place may have evolved a binding character for UNCLOS-members. At the moment, an independent international convention "for the control and management of ships' ballast water and sediments" is under negotiation. The planned date of adoption is between 2002 and 2003.

90 Further information available at: *http://jasper.Stanford.EDU/gisp.*

*Christian Stienen**

GERMAN MARINE SCIENCE – A CASE STUDY

This contribution is divided in five parts, which will allow for a short overview of the past and present marine research in Germany. It starts with the history of German marine science and its development from the first beginnings in the 70s of the 19th century, followed by the establishment of the German marine research infrastructure from the end of World War II to German reunification. I will then go on to describe the present situation of marine research in Germany. In the final part some details are given about the current plans for German marine research in the next few years.

1872–1945

One of the first German institutions which did scientific work on the subject of oceans was founded in 1872 by Anton Dorn – not in Germany but in Italy, more precisely in Naples. The year 1892 saw the foundation of the Biological Research Institute on the island of Heligoland, followed in 1900 by the first institute of oceanography in Germany, which was established in Berlin. This institute continued to exist until shortly after the Second World War and can be regarded as the predecessor of the institutes established in Kiel in 1937 and in Warnemünde in 1958.

Between 1874 and 1925, into the Weimar Republic, five large research expeditions have been launched, all of which gained international recognition. I would like to mention in particular the voyage of the research vessel "National" in 1889 under the direction of Victor Hensen, who coined the term plankton to describe all organic material, whether dead or living, drifting in sea currents. The results of this expedition gave rise to a major controversy because many scientists – among them the well-known and scientifically highly-acknowledged Ernst Haeckel – were unable at the time to imagine that the subarctic North Atlantic harboured substantially more living organisms than tropical and subtropical seas, i.e. that the situation in the oceans was the exact opposite of that on land.

After several decades during which research voyages had been aimed at making geographical discoveries and investigations, the METEOR research cruise to the South Atlantic in 1925 was the first expedition involving all oceanographic disciplines

* Dr., Federal Ministry for Education and Research.

P. Ehlers, E. Mann-Borgese and R. Wolfrum (eds.), Marine Issues, 265–269

and focusing on one main issue: high-resolution measurements of the surface and deep-sea currents in the South Atlantic, including testing of new ocean current calculation methods which had been introduced into marine research following World War I. The METEOR voyage can be regarded as the starting point of and frequently cited argument for the construction of several German research vessels after World War II as well as for the continuation and consolidation of German marine research during the last few decades.

1946–1989

As a result of Germany's division after the Second World War, the community of marine scientists, too, was divided. During the following decades, things developed separately, but often in parallel. Contacts were confined to rare, at best regular, meetings at scientific conferences. Especially the research work in the Baltic Sea carried out by the Marine Research Institute in Kiel and by the Marine Research Institute in Warnemünde brought together oceanographers of the two countries for occasional meetings.

During the International Geophysical Year at the end of the fifties, the Federal Republic of Germany was reaccepted into the international community of marine scientists. When the second research vessel named METEOR was commissioned, Germany was able to operate an efficient and modern research tool. During the following decades, METEOR 2 set off on cruises to the Atlantic Ocean, the Mediterranean and the Indian Ocean. The research vessel "Alexander von Humboldt", built for the Warnemünde Marine Research Institute of the GDR in the early 60s, operated on all world oceans.

In the mid-70s, the Federal Republic of Germany saw a great upswing of marine research, which brought an increase of the funds available and a considerable expansion of the research fleet.

By the mid-80s, three major research vessels were available to German marine science: the SONNE, a converted trawler, was used mainly for prospecting and geosciences research in the Pacific Ocean; the third research vessel named METEOR went on cruises to the Atlantic and the Indian Ocean and to the Mediterranean from 1986 onwards and served to celebrate the centennial of the formerly mentioned Plankton-Expedition during the first JGOFS-Expedition in 1989. And finally there was the ice-breaking research ship POLARSTERN, which had been built to demonstrate Germany's new commitment to research on the ice-covered seas. It is operated by the Institute for Polar and Marine Research set up in Bremerhaven in the early 80s. The Federal Republic's commitment to Antarctic research has to be seen as a response to the commitment by the German Democratic Republic, which, together with the Soviet Union, as signatories of the Antarctic Treaty, maintained a permanently manned station on Antarctica. The Federal Republic of Germany followed suit, building the Georg von Neumayer Station.

The upswing also led to an expansion of institutions. The Kiel Institute of Marine

Research was enlarged; the Alfred Wegener Institute for Polar and Marine Research was newly established; the university institutes in Bremen and Hamburg increased their oceanographic research, and new institutes were established at Oldenburg University to deal with the chemistry and biology of the sea and at Kiel to deal with marine geosciences.

1990–2000

The period of expanding resources for marine and polar research ended in 1989. Today fewer research vessels are available, the staff at research institutions is being cut at an annual rate of approximately 1.5%, and the funds available for marine research have been increased only slightly if at all.

On the other hand, the participation of German scientists in the large-scale international research programmes such as JGOFS, WOCE, ACSYS and TOGA has been considerably increased over the last few years. While project work was initially aimed chiefly at quantitative studies, during recent years scientists have increasingly succeeded in obtaining qualitative results on the current condition of the oceans. Success came not only as a result of improved model calculations, but also owing to markedly improved international cooperation.

Today

Today, both marine and polar research in Germany can rely on a still decent infrastructure. A map of the institutions and research establishments engaged in marine research shows that such work is done everywhere in this country (figure 1). We have a fleet of three large-scale research vessels operating worldwide and four medium-sized vessels as well as a number of smaller research vessels operating within our coastal zones. In order to replace an old research vessel which is to be decommissioned within the next few years, the construction of a new vessel is being planned which will be able to address new scientific tasks, i.e. the role of the Arctic Ocean in the climate system. Hence it shall operate in the North Atlantic Ocean up to the ice edge. However, Germany is less well-equipped at present as regards large-scale facilities such as submersibles and autonomous or remotely operated underwater vehicles.

German marine and polar research institutions together employ more than 2,000 scientists and technicians at present. The Federal Ministry for Education and Research alone will spend more than 160 million Euro on marine and polar research this year. The ongoing German marine research programme has marked the transition from descriptive and quantitative marine research conducted during the second half of the last century to research activities that will study the oceans as an overall system including the ocean margins, the sea floor, coasts and the atmosphere.

The New Millenium

In the years to come, marine research in Germany, together with polar research and the geosciences, will have to make contributions to earth system science. The Federal Ministry for Education and Research will present a new integrated research programme by the middle of 2002 with scientific issues closely related to the focuses identified by the Deutsche Forschungsgemeinschaft. These include:

- The role of oceans in climate variability, mostly mechanisms of decadal variations and rapid climate change;
- Biogeochemical substance cycles and biodiversity, mostly distribution and reactivity of trace substances, regulating mechanisms and sensitivity of substance flows, functional biology at the level of cells, individual organisms and populations; habitats under extreme living conditions at the sea floor;
- Variability and predictability of shelf systems, mostly effects of climate variability and human activities, exchange processes between shelf seas and oceans;
- Geological constraints influencing the energy and substance balances within oceans, mostly tectonic processes influencing oceanic circulation and sea level, cycling of matter at continental shelves and plate boundaries; and
- general conditions for marine research, i.e. cooperation with other disciplines, infrastructures, international research planning.

It is envisaged to spend about 1.8 billion Euro over the next ten years for carrying out these research tasks.

Apart from these scientific topics, the new programme will be dedicated to three aspects not directly related with the above research topics. These aspects are:

1. Improving support for young scientists through more intensive cooperation with universities and by setting up international research groups of young scientists;
2. Improving the research infrastructure and its use. This will be achieved by improved coordination of investments into vessels and large-scale facilities at the European level. The new German research vessel which will be able to operate up to the ice edge, will be made available to other European countries by means of multilaterally agreed barter schemes for vessels and major equipment, just as new vessels built in other EU partner countries can be useful for German marine research. Together with these countries it is our aim within the next 10 years to replace old vessels by new and differently designed and equipped ships so as to have a complete European research fleet to address all necessary scientific topics while avoiding any duplication of infrastructure; and
3. The new marine and polar research programme will give more support to small and medium-sized enterprises, either through outsourcing or through consolidating support.

Apart from improving cooperation in the use of the marine infrastructure, Germany is seeking increased participation in EU research programmes, which means that we will call for and encourage more research proposals by German scientists to be sent to Brussels. As written elsewhere, there exists already a number of scientific links between our national programme and the programme of the European Science Foundation. In addition, Germany will continue to participate in internationally agreed, large-scale research programmes.

Co-operation between marine scientists from many countries already is more common and much closer than many of us may be aware of. Oceanographers from all countries have always regarded the sea as an element linking rather than separating nations.

However, marine research must remain independent and autonomous if it is to be able to obtain results which, in the last analysis, will help to achieve more sustainable use of marine resources and better protection of the oceans as stipulated in part XIII of the UN Convention of the Law of the Seas.

International marine science has reached a point where many issues can only be tackled through joint international efforts. The collection of data, which by far exceeds the financial possibilities of any individual country, will in future be operationalized using special observing systems in the case of some programmes and experiments.

Since funds will be only slightly increased in the next few years, it is absolutely necessary to intensify cooperation by making better use of and selectively developing the European marine research infrastructure.

In addition to its participation in European and international research programmes, Germany will, in the next decade, expand cooperation with numerous countries in Asia and South America. We will conduct joint research projects in the coastal zones of the respective countries, and we will do more: Under the new German marine research programme we will invite and train young scientists from these countries in Germany as part of international cooperation in marine science.

What do We Need Internationally?

1. *Improving research infrastructure.* Inefficient use hampers good science which results in a sub-optimal use of money.
2. *Enhancing communication and co-operation between major international programmes.* Considering joint meetings of the scientific steering committees on a regular basis, e.g. under the auspices of the Marine Board of the ESF.
3. *Securing long-time financial support for operational measurements and long time-series investigations.* Since we are now facing an increasing number of operational oceanographic measurements we need an internationally agreed commitment to share the financial burden between all participating countries.

*Klaus-Günther Barthel**

IS MARINE RESEARCH AN ECONOMIC FACTOR IN EUROPE?

The General Economic Background

In looking at the link between research, industry and economic development in the marine sector, it is useful to first have a look at these issues in a more general context.

A recent OECD publication on the perspectives of science, technology and industry in the year 2000 points out that a good deal of the economic growth in the last decade has only been made possible through significant innovation in the relevant sectors. This innovation has been made possible through a new partnership between scientific research and industry. Research and Technological Development (RTD) are therefore highlighted in the report as very important for the national economies, an experience shared by many industrialists and researchers.

Thus, it is not amazing to note that the RTD expenditure has increased in many countries during the last decade. This includes 13 of the 15 EU member countries; only in Italy and the UK RTD expenditure has on average decreased between 1990 and 1998. In the European Union as a whole, average annual growth in real values has been 1.2% in the same period;[1] in the USA and Japan, however, it has been much higher than in Europe namely 3.3% and 1.9% respectively. As the Gross Domestic Product (GDP) in these countries has grown as well, we can note that the total expenditure on RTD, expressed as percentage of the GDP, has decreased from 2.0 to 1.8% in the EU, has been maintained at 2.7% for the USA and has risen from 2.9 to 3.1% for Japan. A comparison of RTD expenditure per capita confirms that the European Union, although it is increasing its effort, is investing much less into research than the USA and Japan and that the gap has been rapidly getting bigger during the last years.

Research is funded by a multitude of institutions: directly by research performers including industry, indirectly through research grants and contracts awarded by public and private bodies. The major part of all research expenditures in Europe, namely 65%, is made by industry; only 35% of RTD funds are spent by government

---

* Dr., European Commission, Research Directorate-General, D.1.3 Sustainable Marine Ecosystems, Infrastructure, Rue de la Loi 200, B-1049 Brussels, Belgium. This contribution represents the author's opinion and does not commit the European Commission.

1 Figures from: Towards a European Research Area: Science, Technology and Innovation, Key Figures 2000, EUR 19396.

P. Ehlers, E. Mann-Borgese and R. Wolfrum (eds.), Marine Issues, 271–278

research or higher education institutions. Of the industrial research expenditure, 82% come from the industry's own resources and 18% from public grants. Thus, industrial research activity based on its own resources makes up more than 50% of total RTD efforts and is therefore clearly the most important factor in innovation.

The Need for Marine Research

While the afore-mentioned figures are valid for research across all topics, it is much more difficult to obtain comprehensive figures on marine research specifically. Looking at *all* marine-based activities and services, in other words most of them not research, it shows that they represent 3–5% of the GDP of maritime countries in the EU. Although this figure looks low at the first glance, it is by no means insignificant. Furthermore, marine activities are very important in certain sectors, such as:

Maritime Transport

Ninety per cent of external trade of the EU is conducted through shipping; more than 300,000 persons are employed in the maritime and river transport chain in Europe, consisting of: ship builders and repairers, ship owners and operators, maritime and river ports, providers of services, ship outfitters, and the corresponding human resources directly or indirectly attached to these categories.

European shipyards account for 25% of international shipbuilding, often in specialised and high-quality sectors. Thus, shipbuilding remains of strategic importance, depending on high-technology added-value sectors, in which Europe has or could have a leading position and must maintain it (use of modern materials and designs, information and communication technologies, integrated management systems, operational forecasting technologies etc.).

Maritime transport carries also with it the risk of catastrophic accidents; here RTD can contribute greatly to developing integrated prevention and intervention approaches. And prevention and intervention are not only public tasks; they offer commercial opportunities as well.

Living Resources

Fishing, sea farming and the associated processing industries employ more than 600,000 people and have a turnover of 12 billion € per year. Seas and oceans are a major source of food, but it is well established that stocks of many fish species are depleted (in March 1997, FAO pointed out that 60% of the world fish stocks were fully or over-exploited). The increasing competition for fish resources could lead to serious conflicts, if drastic limitations on the availability of the resources is experienced. Obviously this would affect the economic basis of many coastal communities. Better understanding of the boundary conditions to fish stock exploitation, and a development of integrated socio-economic approaches to fishery activities, which takes into account ecosystem limitations and variability, is therefore an essential contribution to maintaining economic viability of this sector.

Sea farming, another important area of activity, is also facing difficulties that require a holistic view encompassing veterinary, environmental, socio-economic and ethical aspects. The contribution of this sector to European competitiveness and welfare is considerable. Therefore, RTD must provide solutions to existing difficulties.

There is furthermore an economic potential in the exploitation of marine biota in biotechnology, pharmacology etc. The USA, Australia and Japan are strong in this field while Europe does still not properly exploit the possibilities offered by this sector. Exploitation of marine biota requires also a serious effort in the area of marine biodiversity research.

Examples of EU-funded activities: The biotechnology industry is supported to explore the future potential for anti-cancer/anti-virus drugs from bioactive substances in marine organisms, e.g., sponges, and to determine the potential for biotechnological applications of microbial communities from extreme hypersaline anoxic basins. Another project develops a novel technology for the environmentally sound creation of underwater structures for mariculture purposes or environmental restoration. This offers prospects for commercial exploitation in both biotechnology and environmental management.

Non-Living Resources

Half of Europe's gas and oil needs are met by the exploitation of offshore hydrocarbon resources in the North Sea. On average, the North Sea produces 350 million tons of petroleum and about 220 million tons of equivalent petroleum gas per year. Even though these resources are limited, they will remain very important for much more than another decade. Annual investment in the area varies between 15 and 20 billion € and the equipment and service industries, which have developed to meet these needs, account for more than 200,000 jobs, the majority of which are highly technical.

In addition, as a consequence of the rapid development of deep-sea hydrocarbon exploitation and extraction, these enterprises are capable of exporting their know-how to the new and extremely competitive South Atlantic and Asian markets.

Examples of EU-funded activities: The EUROMARGIN cluster. Commercial operations move into ever-deeper waters, and the challenge of sustainable use, previously focused on the coastal zone and the continental shelf, now extends over the shelf break and into the deep sea. Thus, the EUROMARGIN cluster of projects for multidisciplinary margin research has been formed to improve our understanding on gas-hydrates, submarine slope stability, quaternary evolution of the European margin, cold-water coral reefs, and seafloor and sub-seafloor biosphere activity. The cluster will help to inventory the deep-water mineral and biological resources of the European margins and will thus be of great interest to the industry. The projects will contribute to the safe and environmentally friendly exploration and exploitation of European deep-water resources. To ensure a timely and effective transfer of results to relevant end-users, the cluster interacts with the industry by establishing links with 4 ongoing Joint Industry Projects in Norway (SEABED), the Faeroes (the GEML Network), the UK (WAF) and Ireland (PIP). And therefore it does not only provide the industry with the necessary knowledge on resources, including environmental aspects, but allows also a better transfer of personnel between academic and applied sectors.

Implementation Tools

These operations, particularly in the hostile deep-sea environment, require the best possible co-ordination of existing knowledge and skills as well as development of new management approaches, instrumentation and technologies, which are based on multidisciplinarity and are developed with strong participation of the industry (e.g., automatic underwater vehicles, underwater industrial robots, remote driven vehicles, acoustic and seismic technologies, drilling technologies, floating platforms and storage and transport installations).

Safety and security aspects, including environmental safety, related to these activities are also crucial issues that have to be considered very seriously for the whole chain of operations, from the exploration for resources (e.g. the risk associated to drilling) to decommissioning of offshore platforms. The full range of operations needs reliable integrated risk assessment methods and strategies for risk containment.

These activities require also a capacity in operational forecasting, which needs to be developed in both the scientific and the technological aspects. Operational forecasting is a field, which cannot be built up by public funds alone, but where industrial involvement will be very beneficial.

Examples of EU-funded activities: Operational forecasting of the sea state becomes more and more important in the context of marine transport, environmental protection, tourism and coastal ocean management. Thus, the EU supports projects to develop forecasting criteria for 'rogue waves', pre-operational forecasting systems and satellite-supported monitoring schemes.

Higher storm frequencies and potentially rising sea levels require new efforts in coastal protection, i.e., protection of the population, the installations and the landscape against extreme events. Coastal engineering is an area where industry will not only profit as a user of research results but where they are deeply involved in generating these results themselves.

Industry Participation in Marine EU Programmes

In the European Commission Framework Programmes Marine Science and Technology funding since 1989 has seen an increase from €13 million to about €60 million per year, which is an increase in proportion to the entire Framework Programme growth. It is difficult to quantify how much has been contributed to marine research funding by national bodies and the industry itself. It is, however, safe to say that EU funding of marine research and technology has become an important factor in research at public institutions in Europe and that international collaboration facilitated through EU grants has become a general feature in marine research. A large research is also being funded by the industry directly, notably in hydrocarbon exploration and marine transport.

What is the participation of industry in the EU Marine Science and Technology Programmes? Ever since the start of specific marine research programmes in 1989, industry participation has ranged from 10–12% of total EU contributions awarded, with a roughly even balance between big companies on the one side and small and medium enterprises (SMEs) on the other. However, in the last two years a clear shift from bigger companies to small and medium enterprises has taken place; now 9% of total EU contributions go to SMEs and only 2% to larger companies. This is a sign that the special efforts of the European Commission to support SME better than in the past are coming to fruition.

But does it also show a declining interest of bigger companies to get involved in EU projects? I don't think so. The re-orientation of the Framework Programme two years ago meant that some large and heavy technologies in the marine field, such as AUVs and ROVs, are no longer funded in the Key Action Sustainable Marine Ecosystems. It is these technologies, which the big industry was traditionally interested in, so that their decline is most likely influenced by this shift in funded topics. On the other hand more emphasis has been given to monitoring and operational forecasting, a topic, for which in particular small and medium enterprises can offer services and technologies.

The EU Research Philosophy in the Second Half of FP5

By supporting specifically the cross-frontier collaboration of European researchers, the European Commission aims at increasing the competitiveness of the European industry, to solve societal problems of a European nature and to create a coherent, mobile and highly skilled community of European researchers. For marine RTD this means that EU support focuses on pollution-related studies, preserving ecosystem integrity, designing coastal management strategies and developing technologies for sustainable exploitation of the seas. Marine Science and Technology is needed to maintain a high capacity in exploiting the sea commercially but in an environmentally acceptable, sustainable manner. Most of the benefits will go to the coastal population and it is important to note that about half of the EU population lives within 50 km from the sea and that European maritime regions account for 41% of the EU gross national product.

In the second half of FP5, there are a number of new grand challenges opening up for marine research.

Commercial operations are increasingly carried out in the deep-sea. In conjunction with a better use of existing technology, new technological developments are needed to survey, characterise and monitor the marine environment. Operational oceanography figures high on the political agenda. GOOS, the Global Ocean Observing System, and its regional partners such as EuroGOOS and MedGOOS, could well become a motor for RTD in the next decades.

Given the diversity, importance and international use of European seas, an applied knowledge base is needed to understand the impacts of various activities on marine ecosystems, to contribute to the protection of these ecosystems from pollution and to develop long-term, viable management strategies. Monitoring the coastal zone and managing coastal processes is therefore one area that is emphasised.

Thus, the European Commission has recently revised the work programme for the Sustainable Marine Ecosystems Key Action in the 5th FP with a view to addressing these challenges.

Outlook to ERA and FP6

But it is not only necessary to identify the correct research topics to address the current problems in our society; it is also important to choose the right approach and provide the necessary basis and infrastructure that research can flourish and bring about the necessary solutions. The European Commission is therefore developing a strategy for creating a European Research Area (ERA) in the next years, which will allow for strengthening the link between research activities, policy-making and the needs of society. This will reflect positively on the development of industry-relevant marine research topics in the upcoming Sixth Framework Programme, and will also allow generating the necessary background knowledge for the application of the precautionary principle and the sustainable development approach in environmental research.

More specifically the European Commission plans to address the following issues:

- The environment for private investment in research needs to be improved. The sufficient provision of capital, and in particular risk capital, to R&D partnerships and high technology projects is essential for effective industrial research. Better co-operation between the industry and the research community is a further issue to be advanced.
- Public resources and facilities devoted to research must be used in a more coherent way: this includes the networking of national and European research programmes and closer relations between existing organisations for scientific co-operation. Research organisations should link to each other and exploit potential synergies through the more efficient use of modern telecommunication technologies. The mapping of excellence across all member states will allow focusing on particularly promising areas for European co-operation.
- The establishment of a common system of scientific and technical reference needs to be achieved through the alignment of methods and harmonisation of procedures. This will give both policy-makers and industry a more reliable basis for decision-making and definition of performance indicators. This would

include a set of guidelines at Union level, the comparison of best practices, a process of regular monitoring and the adoption of measures, which take account of national and regional differences.

- The European patent should be made available so that industry can obtain comprehensive Community-wide protection of research results simply and inexpensively. Only if the protection of intellectual property can be easily obtained, will we have a stronger impact of industrial research on European economies.
- Human resources are a key factor and, at the same time, the prime asset of European research. Obstacles to mobility of researchers should be removed, to retain high-quality research talent in Europe and to attract other researchers to come to Europe. This includes the under-used potential of women in research, which must be activated. Furthermore, the young people's interest in science must be stimulated in order to achieve a higher recruitment into scientific subjects.
- Regions are playing a more and more important role in research by linking universities, companies and research centres locally. Mechanisms must be put in place to adapt research policies to the geographical socio-economic context and thus facilitate a closer co-operation of research providers and users.

Thus, the European Research Area is a wide-ranging approach to formulate an integrated European Research Policy, which goes beyond the pure implementation of Framework Programmes as you know them from the past. The next Framework Programme will therefore not be the only means of making ERA a reality, but it will be an important building block.

The Sixth Framework Programme (FP6)

What does the creation of a European Research Area mean for marine science and technology? On 4 October 2000 the European Commission published a second Communication on ERA, which gives political guidelines for the implementation of EU research activities. For marine research this translates into two main points:

- The need to improve competitiveness of European marine activities;
- The need to put RTD at the service of the sustainable exploitation of marine ecosystems and resources for the welfare of European citizens.

Although the preparation of FP6 has only just begun, one can already identify on the basis of these two main points some likely corner-stones for FP6:

- The concept of problem-oriented research as in the current Key Actions will most likely be retained;
- Projects will probably become larger and a number of very large projects will be set up;
- A higher risk element may be allowed in certain projects;
- Contracts might be concluded for longer periods where the size or nature of the work requires it;

- The regional dimension will be given more importance;
- The international co-operation with non-EU partners will receive more attention;
- The link between science and the citizen will remain a central feature.

CONCLUSIONS

- Marine-based activities and services are a factor in European economy and play a significant role in coastal regions.
- Marine research is essential in supporting competitiveness of the industry and much of the research has to be carried out by the industry itself.
- The task of the public bodies is to provide appropriate framework conditions to allow the industry to carry out or commission the research necessary for innovation.
- The establishment of a common market in Europe was an important prerequisite to allow development of competitive technological products for a sufficiently large market.
- The participation in European research projects helps establishing a Europe-wide marketing strategy.
- The next EU Framework Programme will contribute to improved competitiveness of the European industry and put RTD at the service of the European citizen.

Dik Tromp and Nicholas C. Flemming***

A EUROPEAN APPROACH TO OCEAN OBSERVATION

Europe needs ocean data, obtained in real-time or near real-time, with interpretations and forecasts based on ocean data, to meet important practical socio-economic objectives. The Global Ocean Observing System (GOOS) has been under development sponsored by a consortium of UN Agencies since the Second World Climate Conference in 1990, and is now in the early stages of implementation. The Third Report of the Intergovernmental Panel on Climate Change (IPCC)[1] indicates more strongly than ever the importance of understanding and monitoring the coupled ocean-atmosphere system.

Within GOOS 30 European national Agencies from 16 countries have established EuroGOOS in order to gather ocean data in operational mode, supplementing those existing programmes of data-gathering in the scientific research mode, where data are gathered through discontinuous cruises and experiments. Europe needs operational ocean data so as to run numerical computer models, and provide forecasts and management information.

The operational information products provide socio-economic benefits on all time scales from hours to decades, and can be applied to numerous sectors of activities such as coastal protection, fisheries, pollution control, flood prevention, navigational safety, and offshore oil and gas production. Physical and bio-ecological models also provide the basis for environmental management, and help to forecast the mechanisms and effects of climate change and global warming.

EuroGOOS Member Agencies collaborate to use *in situ* instrumentation, subsurface profiling floats, ship-borne instruments, and observations from space, in a long-term programme of sustained observation and modelling. All data can be exchanged between Member Agencies in real time within the terms of the EuroGOOS Data Policy.

EuroGOOS focuses its effort by having specialist Task Teams working in each of the regional and shelf sea areas, with additional zones of activity dedicated to Atlantic and Arctic observations. Other technical project teams and working groups provide

* Chairman EuroGOOS, Senior Advisor, UNEP, P.O. Box 16227, 2500 BE The Hague, The Netherlands.

** Director EuroGOOS, Room 014/12, SOC, European Way, Southampton, SO14 3ZH, UK.

1 *IPCC*, Third Report of the Intergovernmental Panel on Climate Change (2001 Forthcoming).

P. Ehlers, E. Mann-Borgese and R. Wolfrum (eds.), Marine Issues, 279–298

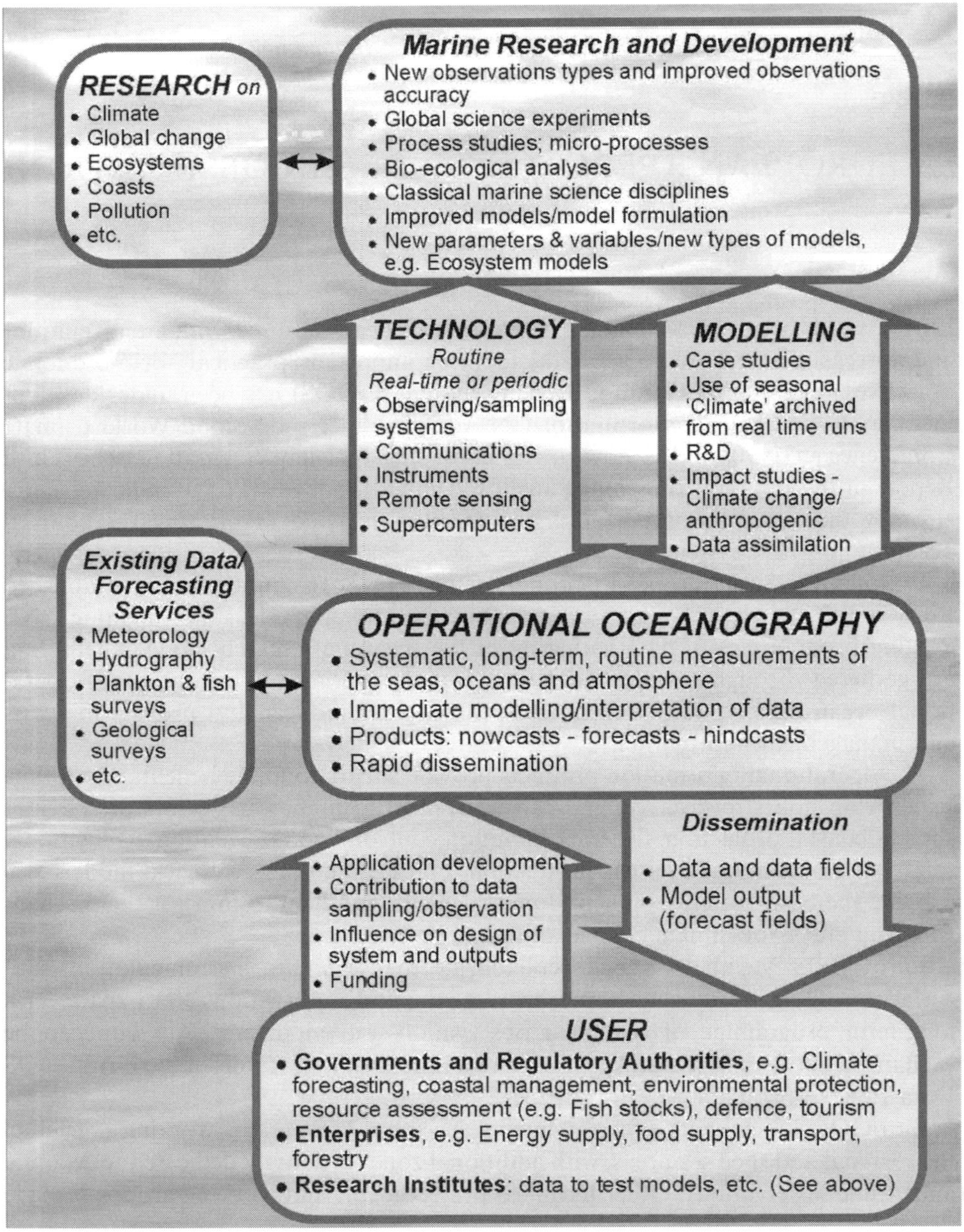

Figure 1. Operational oceanography builds on the experience of a century of marine scientific research. Where the underlying processes are sufficiently well understood, they can be measured in a routine way and the data transferred to analysis centres and modelling groups, where information products are processed for delivery to end users. Operational oceanography depends upon many branches of science and technology to achieve these objectives.

support for technological instrument development, planning of remote-sensed observing systems, and scientific underpinning.

Introduction

Operational oceanography is the provision of scientifically based information and forecasts about the state of the sea (including its chemical and biological components) on a routine basis, and with sufficient speed, such that users can act on the information and make decisions before the relevant conditions have changed significantly, or become unpredictable (see Figure 1). National meteorological offices have been providing such a service for the atmospheric weather for many years, and military and fisheries agencies have been providing some operational information on marine sub-surface conditions since the 1960s. Since the late 1980s it has been possible to envisage a global system, similar to the World Weather Watch, and linked to national and regional observation and modelling services, which could provide an analogous service for many parameters of the marine water column and coastal zone. Figure 2 illustrates how observations are combined through models to provide calculated values on a fine spatial grid. Users searching for information or forecasts are thus more likely to find what they need close to the site where they need it.

Operational oceanography has been defined at some length in the publication devoted to setting out the long term plans for GOOS[2] and in the EuroGOOS Strategy.[3] Although the emphasis is on obtaining and processing data in real time, or near real time, the products required by customers may be nowcasts, hindcasts, or forecasts, all based on the most recently obtained data. The EuroGOOS Data Requirements Survey[4] shows that these products are required in approximately equal proportions. Table 1 shows the aggregate ranking of all sectors' requirements for all variables.

Table 1. A survey of 200 users of operational marine data were asked to list the data variables they needed ranked by priority of importance. This table, taken from Fischer and Flemming,[5] shows the aggregated ranking of all variables requested in operational mode by all users.

Rank	*Variable*	*Variable group*	*No.*
1	Current velocity	Surface fields	94
2	Current direction	Surface fields	93
3	Waves Hs	Surface fields	85
4	Wave period	Surface fields	81
5	Sea surface temperature	Surface fields	79

2 *IOC*, GOOS 1998 Prospectus, pp. 7–10.

3 *J.D. Woods/H. Dahlin/L. Droppert/M. Glass/S. Vallerga/N.C. Flemming*, The Strategy for EuroGOOS, EuroGOOS Publications No. 1, p. 10 (Southampton 1996).

4 *J. Fischer/N.C. Flemming*, Operational Oceanography: Data Requirements Survey, EuroGOOS Publication No. 12, p. 22 (Southampton 1999).

5 *Fischer/Flemming* (*supra* note).

Rank	*Variable*	*Variable group*	*No.*
6	Wave direction spectrum	Surface fields	75
7	Sea surface wind stress	Surface fields	71
8	Wave spectrum	Surface fields	68
9	Wave swell	Surface fields	67
10	Coastal bathymetry	Coastal and shelf	60
11	Sea surface salinity	Surface fields	60
12	Coastline map	Coastal and shelf	58
13	Bathymetry	Sea bed	56
14	Surface currents	Upper layer fields	55
15	Hourly mean sea level	Sea surface topogr.	48
16	Sediment transport	Coastal and shelf	44
17	Shelf bathymetry	Coastal and shelf	41
18	Surface sediments	Sea bed	39
19	Oceanic tides	Sea surface topogr.	38
20	Geostrophic currents	Sea surface topogr.	35
21	Tidal constants	Coastal and shelf	35
22	Upper ocean salinity	Upper layer fields	35
23	Precipitation	Surface fields	35
24	Meteorological forcing	Sea surface topogr.	34
25	Monthly mean sea level	Sea surface topogr.	34
26	River runoff	Coastal and shelf	34
27	Phytoplankton	Biogeochemical	34
28	Suspended sediments	Biogeochemical	34
29	Sea level anomaly	Sea surface topogr.	33
30	Chlorophyll	Biogeochemical	33
31	Gridded bathymetry	Sea bed	32
32	Nitrate	Biogeochemical	31
33	Oxygen	Biogeochemical	31
34	CTD sections	Deep ocean	30
35	Stratification	Coastal and shelf	30
36	Eddies, jets, fronts	Upper layer fields	30
37	Sound velocity profiles	Acoustics	29
38	Upper ocean veloc. fields	Upper layer fields	29
39	Phosphate	Biogeochemical	29
40	Surface outcrops	Sea bed	26
41	Heat flux	Surface fields	26
42	Deep ocean salinity	Deep ocean	25
43	Extent, boundary, leads, %	Sea ice	25
44	Upwelling velocities	Upper layer fields	25
45	Zooplankton	Biogeochemical	24
46	XCTD sections	Upper layer fields	23
47	Concentration	Sea ice	22
48	Marine geoid	Sea surface topogr.	22
49	Hinterland topography	Coastal and shelf	22
50	Land non-river runoff	Coastal and shelf	22
51	Tidal ellipses	Coastal and shelf	22
52	XBT sections	Upper layer fields	22
53	Moisture flux	Surface fields	22
54	Downwelling velocities	Upper layer fields	21

Rank	*Variable*	*Variable group*	*No.*
55	Silicate	Biogeochemical	21
56	Wetlands characteristics	Coastal and shelf	20
57	Trace metals	Biogeochemical	20
58	Biological pigments	Biogeochemical	19
59	Air, sea, ice, temperatures	Sea ice	18
60	Fresh water transport	Upper layer fields	18
61	Petroleum hydrocarbons	Biogeochemical	18
62	Acoustic scattering	Acoustics	17
63	Aquatic toxins	Biogeochemical	17
64	Inter-basin straits currents	Deep ocean	16
65	Ocean boundary currents	Deep ocean	16
66	Ice motion	Sea ice	16
67	Thickness	Sea ice	16
68	Upper ocean fresh water	Upper layer fields	16
69	Artificial radionuclides	Biogeochemical	16
70	PAHs	Biogeochemical	16
71	Pesticides and herbicides	Biogeochemical	16
72	Transmissivity	Optics	15
73	Albedo	Sea ice	15
74	Ambient noise spectrum	Acoustics	15
75	Seabed acoustic prop's	Acoustics	15
76	Magnetics	Sea Bed	15
77	Salt transport	Upper layer fields	15
78	Carbon dioxide	Biogeochemical	15
79	Sea surface CO_2	Surface fields	15
80	Acoustic tomography	Acoustics	14
81	Gravity	Sea bed	14
82	Fresh water flux	Upper layer fields	14
83	Upper ocean heat content	Upper layer fields	14
84	Iron	Biogeochemical	14
85	Distribution	Icebergs	13
86	Numbers	Icebergs	13
87	Trajectories	Icebergs	13
88	Depth of photic zone	Optics	13
89	Ocean tracers	Deep ocean	13
90	Acoustic models (shelf)	Acoustics	13
91	Sound ray paths	Acoustics	13
92	Surface ice state	Sea ice	13
93	Reverberation charact.	Acoustics	12
94	Surface ice roughness	Sea ice	12
95	Momentum fields	Upper layer fields	12
96	Salt flux	Upper layer fields	12
97	Human health risks	Biogeochemical	12
98	Pathogens	Biogeochemical	12
99	Synthetic organics	Biogeochemical	12
100	Anthropogenic noise	Acoustics	11
101	Temperature	Sea ice	11
102	Carbon transport	Upper layer fields	11
103	Sea surface GHGs	Surface fields	11

Rank	*Variable*	*Variable group*	*No.*
104	Area, volume	Icebergs	10
105	Secchi disk depth	Optics	10
106	Extent, boundary	Ice shelves	10
107	Buoyancy flux	Upper layer fields	10
108	Upper ocean heat flux	Upper layer fields	10
109	Upper ocean heat transport	Upper layer fields	10
110	Deep ocean ht storage	Deep ocean	9
111	Acoustic models (oceanic)	Acoustics	9
112	Snow on ice	Sea ice	9
113	Water on ice	Sea ice	9
114	Heat flow	Sea bed	9
115	Tritium	Biogeochemical	9
116	Bioluminescence	Optics	8
117	Surface ice velocity	Ice shelves	8
118	Deep ocean carbon storage	Deep ocean	8
119	Deep ocean water storage	Deep ocean	8
120	Carbon budgets	Upper layer fields	8
121	Carbon inventory	Upper layer fields	8
122	Tropic. upper ocean, struct.	Upper layer fields	8
123	Bottom topography	Ice shelves	7
124	Sub-shelf ocean circulation	Ice shelves	7
125	Surface temperature	Ice shelves	7
126	Acoustic thermometry	Acoustics	7
127	Mass balance	Ice shelves	6
128	Snow line	Ice shelves	6
129	Surface state	Ice shelves	6
130	Topography	Ice shelves	6
131	Pharmaceutical wastes	Biogeochemical	6
132	Phosphorescence	Optics	5
133	Roughness	Ice shelves	5
134	Albedo	Ice shelves	5
135	Incident light spectrum	Optics	4
136	RS reflected light spectrum	Optics	4

Variables ranked in the order of number of requests by all respondents. No. = number of respondents requesting variable.

This paper summarises the arguments for investing in a global system of continuous ocean observations supplementing the traditional pattern of scientific cruises, and addresses the European priorities within the global scale, and within the European marginal seas. It examines the structure which has evolved in Europe to promote and implement operational oceanography, and presents some brief conclusions. The Members of EuroGOOS are listed in Table 2.

The Need for Ocean Observations in the 21st Century

The justification for spending money on routine long-term ocean observations can be based either on the short-term economic benefits, or the long-term forecasting of

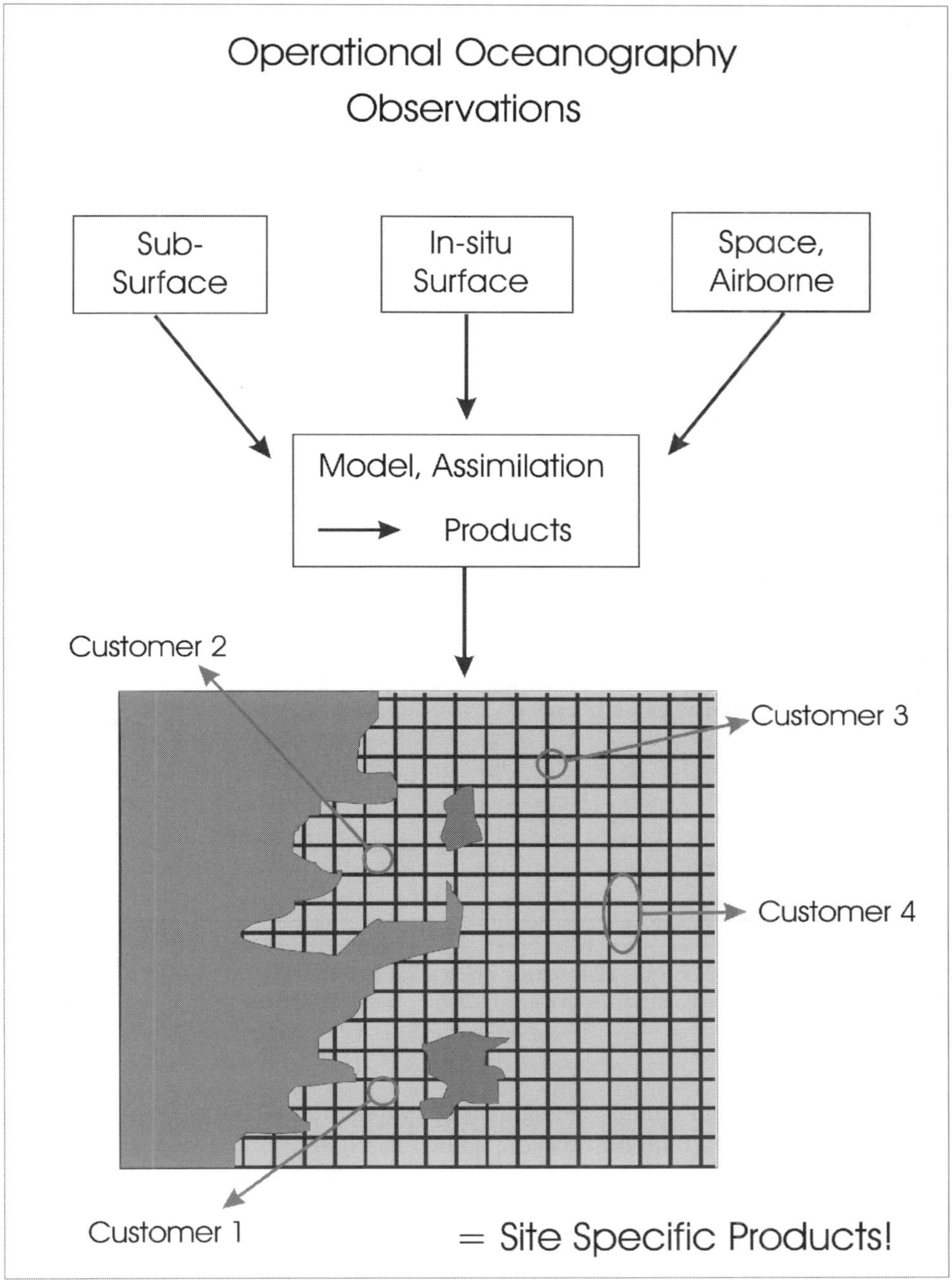

Figure 2. This diagram shows in a very simplified form that measurements of marine variables such as temperature, salinity, or chlorophyll can be observed in many different ways, and the data transmitted automatically to computer centres where models re-construct the best achievable representation of the state of the sea, and present the output as maps or grids. This approach to ocean observation means that a wide range of different customers or users can be given accurate products based on the same original data.

Table 2. List of Members of EuroGOOS

Bundesamt für Seeschiffahrt und Hydrographie (BSH), Germany	Natural Environment Research Council (NERC), UK
CERFACS, France	Norwegian Meteorological Institute (DNMI), Norway
Consiglio Nazionale Delle Ricerche (CNR), Italy	NWO Earth and Life Sciences Council, Netherlands
Danish Meteorological Institute, Denmark	Puertos del Estado, Clima Marítimo, Spain
ENEA, Italy	Royal Danish Administration of Navigation and Hydrography, Denmark
Environment Agency (EA), UK	Russian Federal Service for Hydrometeorology and Environmental Monitoring (Roshydromet), Russia
Finnish Institute of Marine Research, Finland	Swedish Meteorological and Hydrological Institute (SMHI), Sweden
IFREMER, France	**30 members in 16 countries:**
Institute of Marine Research, Bergen, Norway	Belgium
Institute of Marine Sciences, Turkey	Denmark
Institute of Meteorology and Water Management (IMWM), Maritime Branch, Poland	Finland
Institute of Oceanology, Polish Academy of Sciences, Poland	France
Institution of Marine Biology of Crete, Greece	Germany
Instituto Español de Oceanografia (IEO), Spain	Greece
Koninklijk Nederlands Meteorolologisch Instituut (KNMI), Netherlands	Ireland
Marine Institute, Ireland	Italy
Maritime Institute, Gdansk, Poland	Netherlands
Météo France	Norway
Meteorological Office, UK	Poland
Management Unit of the North Sea Mathematical Models (MUMM), Prime Minister's Services, Belgium	Russia
Nansen Environmental and Remote Sensing Center, Norway	Spain
National Centre for Marine Research of Greece	Sweden
National Institute for Coastal and Marine Management (RIKZ), Rijkswaterstaat, Netherlands	Turkey
	UK

EuroGOOS Members are government departments and research institutes of national standing. Agencies can join EuroGOOS from all countries which are members of the EU or the Council of Europe. This Table shows the Members in January 2001.

climate variability and climate change, or a combination of both. The broad links between timescales and applications are shown in Figure 3.

Throughout the 1990s the importance of understanding the risks of climate change has been growing steadily, but the timescales are so long, 50–100 years, and the economic and social changes so difficult to quantify, that governments find it difficult to justify expenditure now, combined with a commitment for continuous observations, in response to a calculated probable threat in the distant future. Thus it is important to establish that the same expenditure on an integrated ocean observing system can provide benefits now and in the immediate future, and will, over the

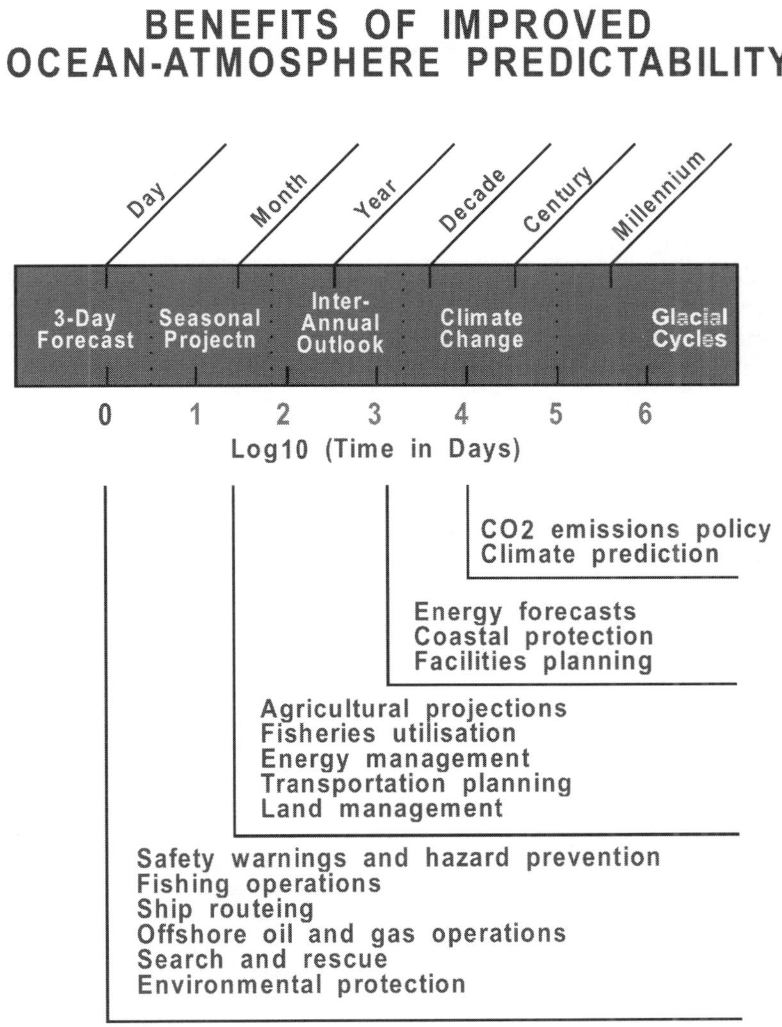

Figure 3. Some information products from ocean observation are used within hours to provide emergency warnings or forecasts. Other products have benefits or pay-off times which extend to months or decades. Different user communities tend to benefit from different types of information or forecast. This diagram was first prepared by Dana Kester for GOOS meeting in 1993.

years, provide the information needed to understand and anticipate the effects of climate change. When it became clear that the shorter term economic benefits provided the main justification for early investment in GOOS, particularly in Europe, it was then necessary to find a way of evaluating and summing the benefits which would accrue year-by-year to a wide range of maritime and coastal industries, support services, and regulatory organisations.

In the USA, central Americas, and much of the tropical Pacific and South-East Asia, the El Niño–Southern Oscillation phenomenon provides a well-publicised target for monitoring and understanding the ocean-atmosphere system, with predictable benefits on time-scales 1–5 years. The effect of ENSO is minimal in Europe, so that there are no peak periodicities of predictable economic or social gain between the operational maritime services with forecasts and benefits in days or weeks, and the North Atlantic variability on the order of 10–14 years. There are real benefits to be obtained at all scales from predicting monthly ocean and climate variability, inter-seasonal forecasts, and so on, but in Europe there is no single phenomenon with a short periodicity where understanding will produce a uniquely high benefit. We have to concentrate on the whole spectrum of ocean and coastal processes and the benefits from forecasting them, and build the system up pragmatically stage by stage.

Since 1990 there has been an increasing effort to evaluate the economic and social value of the marine and coastal industries and services, and the implicit value of the marine environment.[6] Recent work by EuroGOOS[7] shows that, from a list of 115 categories of activity, representatives of almost every industrial, commercial, and environmental and conservation service in the marine environment can specify marine operational data which would improve the efficiency of their activity. The only activities which did not respond to the survey were deep sea mining and extraction of minerals from sea water.

---

6 *United Nations*, Agenda 21: United Nations Conference on Environment and Development, Rio de Janeiro 3–14 June 1992, Doc. A/CONF.151/4, ch. 17 (1992); *OECD*, Megascience: The OECD Forum, Oceanography (OECD Paris 1994); *M.H. Glantz* (ed.), Climate variability, Climate Change and Fisheries (Cambridge 1992); *National Research Council, Committee on Opportunities to Improve Marine Observations and Forecasting*, Opportunities to Improve Marine Forecasting (Washington, DC. 1989); *Woods Hole Oceanographic Institution*, Preliminary analysis of benefits and costs of a proposed Coastal Forecast System, Report on workshop held at Woods Hole Oceanographic Institution, 7–8 June 1993 (Woods Hole, MA. 1993); *P.G. Sassone/R.F. Weiher*, Cost benefit analysis of TOGA and the ENSO Observing System, Proceedings of First International Conference on EuroGOOS, The Hague, The Netherlands, October 1996, pp. 36–50 (1997); *R.M. Adams/B.A. McCarl/K. Bryant/A. Solow/D. Legler/J. O'Brien/R. Weiher*, Value of improved long-range weather information, in: *CEP* 13 (1995), 10–19; *Woods/Dahlin/Droppert/Glass/Vallerga/Flemming* (*supra* note 3); *R. Costanza/R. D'Arge/R. de Groot/S. Farber/M. Grasso/B. Hannon/K. Limburg/S. Naeem/R.V. O'Neill/J. Paruelo/R.G. Raskin/P. Sutton/M. van den Belt*, The value of the world's ecosystem services and natural capital, in: *Nature* 387 (1997), 253–260; *D.P. Pugh/L. Skinner*, An analysis of marine-related activities in the UK economy and supporting science and technology, in: *IACMST Information Document No. 5* (Southampton 1996); *IFREMER*, Données économiques maritimes françaises (*R. Kalaydijan* ed.), in: *Service d'économie maritime* (IFREMER France 1999); *R.F. Weiher* (ed.), Improving El Niño Forecasting: The potential economic benefits, U.S. Department of Commerce, NOAA Office of Policy and Strategic Planning (1999); *RASCL*, Canada's Ocean Industries: Contribution to the Economy 1988–1996, Prepared for Economic and Policy Analysis Division, Department of Fisheries and Oceans (1998).

7 *Fischer/Flemming* (*supra* note 4).

If we add to this range of environmental and commercial activities the objectives of managing, predicting, and possibly controlling climate variability and climate change, it is clear that the base now exists for justifying operational oceanography in the same way that meteorology was justified 20–30 years ago.

In September 1993 the Organisation for Economic Co-operation and Development (OECD) convened an Experts Meeting of the Megascience Forum in Tokyo to discuss the economics of GOOS, and from this a book was published in August 1994.[8] The Megascience Forum established for the first time the approximate scale of the aggregate of all maritime industries and services, and their contribution to national and global GNP. Since 1993–4 several countries have set up national committees to develop policies and projects in support of GOOS, and analysis of the benefits and economics of GOOS has been a high priority. In 1999 27 countries signed the GOOS commitments agreement in Paris, confirming their intention to make nationally funded observations available to GOOS. All the European countries represented signed the commitments agreement. See also, for example, a catalogue of national contributions to GOOS.[9]

In October 2000 EuroGOOS organised a meeting to develop the case for European investment in operational ocean observing satellite missions. The meeting was hosted by EUMETSAT, and the proceedings will be published by EuroGOOS during 2001.[10] Papers were presented outlining the economic benefits of ocean forecasting for a wide range of economic and commercial activities, together with a general estimate of the commercial market for ocean forecasting data products. The global commercial market for marine environmental data products and forecasts (excluding marine geophysics for the oil and gas industry) is substantial, of the order of 100 million euros annually, but the majority of information and data products relate to services and activities in the public domain, and have the economic characteristics of a public good. *Woods et al.*[11] estimate that the nominal price of information which governments and industry together should be prepared to pay annually for marine environmental data is of the order of 100–200 million Euro for Europe alone.

The importance of the public domain investment is not surprising. There are measurable financial markets for providing offshore oil and gas companies with data which makes platforms safer, or cheaper; and there are markets for enabling ships to operate more efficiently, or engineers to build a breakwater without damage to their equipment.[12] But in many cases the best method for delivering information is through governmental services broadcast to everyone, and in a large number of

---

8 *OECD* (*supra* note 6).

9 *BSH*, German programme contribution to the Global Ocean Observing System (GOOS) (Hamburg and Rostock 1999).

10 *J. Font/P. Gaspar/T.H. Guymer/J. Johannessen/G.H. van der Kolff/C. le Provost/A. Ratier/D. Williams/N.C. Flemming,* EuroGoos Conference on Operational Ocean Observations from Space, EuroGOOS Publication No. 16 (Southampton 2001).

11 *Woods/Dahlin/Droppert/Glass/Vallerga/Flemming* (*supra* note 3), p. 21.

12 *OECD* (*supra* note 6), p. 143.

cases both the information service and the user agency are in the public domain, although the agency may employ commercial contractors. Many aspects of coastal defences, safety and rescue at sea, public health, fisheries regulation, management of rivers, freshwater, and pollution, have huge economic impact, and are in the public domain. The economic value of public domain provision of environmental data far exceeds the commercially marketable data. This means that most of the cost of the infrastructure for the observing system should be publicly funded. This conclusion is endorsed by *Adams et al.*[13] for the USA.

In January 2001 the Intergovernmental Panel on Climate Change (IPCC) meeting in Shanghai announced the forthcoming publication of its third report, stating that global warming is almost certainly of anthropogenic origin, and that warming is expected now to be faster than previously predicted in 1995. This announcement increases the urgency for developing a permanent ocean observing and forecasting system, but does not alter the fact that the observing system is much more affordable if we obtain useful data from it on a continuous basis for socio-economic applications.

Adams et al.[14] present the most sophisticated analysis so far of short- and medium-term socio-economic benefits, presented in general terms, for the seasonal to inter-annual benefits arising from better marine observations and their effect upon weather and inter-annual climate forecasting across the USA, as well as for marine exploitation and conservation. A combination of forecast techniques incorporating ENSO analysis, the Pacific Decadal Oscillation, and the North Atlantic Oscillation, would provide benefits measured in hundreds of millions of dollars per year in the USA for each of several management sectors related to fresh water reservoirs, agriculture, oil and gas storage, and agriculture. Medium term to multi-year forecasting in the European region does not have the advantage of a clearly dominant signal like the ENSO cycle, but analysis of Atlantic and Arctic processes is beginning to yield several potential mechanisms and cycles in addition to the NAO, which may permit valuable forecasts. If this is the case, the improved boundary conditions for shelf seas models, and the climate forecasts for the whole continent, could have user values of the same order of magnitude as those derived for the USA.

The largest potential benefits from long-term integrated ocean observations are those which accrue 5–10 years into the future, or beyond, and the largest figures are also those shrouded in the greatest uncertainty given present knowledge. It is therefore prudent to use the observing system as intensively as possible in the short term to generate truly operational products with economic and social benefits. By this tactic the total cumulative discounted cash flow, including expenditure and computed

---

13 *R. Adams/M. Brown/C. Colgan/N.C. Flemming/Kite-Powell/B. McCarl/J. Mjelde/A. Solow/T. Teisberg/R.F. Weiher*, The economics of sustained ocean observations: Benefits and rationale for public funding, Joint publication of the National Oceanic and Atmospheric Administration and the Office of Naval Research (2000).

14 *Ibid.*

value of benefits, is prevented from dipping too far into deficit,[15] and will show a total net benefit to society as quickly as possible. The EuroGOOS Economics Working Group has held two meetings in order to develop further methodology[16] and EuroGOOS plans to employ a professional consultant during 2001 to synthesise all available documentation on the economics and socio-economic valuation of operational oceanography.

Operational oceanography is following rapidly along the course taken decades ago by meteorology, but we still require a great deal of strategic planning on timescales of 5 to 10 years, with a steadfast consistency of purpose, to reap the full potential benefits. The justification for European investment depends upon understanding the regional European benefits, as well as the global objectives.

European Priorities in Ocean Observations

Different global regions identify different timescales of the whole spectrum of forecastable marine processes as potentially important. In the USA and central and southern Americas the impact of the El Niño Southern Oscillation (ENSO) with a period of 3–5 years dominates economic and social value assessment. In China, South East Asia, and southern Asia it is the Monsoon cycle. In Europe it is the impact of short term ocean and coastal processes on marine industries and services, followed by potential climate forecasts of the impact of fluctuations in the North Atlantic Oscillation and the Gulf Stream, and the frequency and intensity of cold deep water formation. The European/Atlantic climatic variability has a periodicity in the range of 10–15 years, making it less tractable than the ENSO cycle, resulting on a higher relative importance of the shorter term economic analysis of benefits.

Between 3% and 5% of input to the European GNP (EU) is generated directly by marine-based industries and services.[17] The value added directly by these activities is of the order of $140–230 bn/yr. The industries and services are subject to uncertainty, loss of efficiency, and direct costs and damage caused by the unpredictable forces of the marine environment such as storms, sea level surges, waves, erosion, transport and resuspension of pollutants, shifts in fish stock migration, and toxic algal blooms. The temperature and salinity of the North Atlantic determines the weather and climate of Europe, Russia, and the Mediterranean. Europe has a great need to understand, monitor and predict the state of its coastal seas, the Mediterranean, and the adjacent oceans, Atlantic and Arctic. The monitoring and forecasting of the North Atlantic Oscillation, the fluctuations of the Gulf Stream,

---

15 *N.C. Flemming*, Dividends from investing in ocean operations: a European Perspective, Paper Presented at the OceanObs Conference, CNES, St. Raphael, October 1999 (To be published also as a book).

16 *EuroGOOS*, Report of the second meeting of the EuroGOOS Economics WG, Genova, Italy, 21–22 September 1998, *EuroGOOS report EG98.44* (1998), see website: *http://www.EuroGoos.org*.

17 *Woods/Dahlin/Droppert/Glass/Vallerga/Flemming* (*supra* note 3), p. 2.

convection and deep water formation, and Arctic sea ice formation, are particularly important at the oceanic scale.[18]

Improvement of the short- to medium-term prediction services for maritime conditions would improve the value of maritime industries and services by a few percent. If we accept 1% as a most conservative estimate, the value added to the GNP of the EU by a prediction system is of the order of \$1.4–2.3 bn/yr.[19] This is a minimum which should be exceeded by a factor of 2–3. In addition there are the longer term benefits of climate prediction, and its impact on agriculture, energy generation, water supply management, land use and other social activities, which would be of the same order. More recent economic studies under way now are suggesting the methods for quantifying in comparable ways the benefits from short-term commercial activities, through specific short and medium-term public good benefits, to long-term public good, environmental, and climate scale risks and benefits.

Europe is dependent upon and influenced by marine conditions more than any other developed continental region. Changes in the mean sea level, changes in storm conditions and coastal erosion have a greater impact on economic and industrial activities in shelf-seas and on oceanic fisheries, tourism, land use, shipping and ports and offshore oil than in other continents. From a European perspective these factors require regional attention, and are of comparable significance to the inundation of coastal floodplains and oceanic islands which threaten Bangladesh or the islands of the Pacific. Concern about possible global sea level rise and its combination with regional vertical earth movements is of high priority, as evidenced by the activity of the European component of the Global Sea Level Observing System (GLOSS). A recent COST project (COST Action 40)[20] has been completed on the design of a European Sea Level Observing System, and at the Annual Meeting of EuroGOOS in December 2000 the implementation of this system (ESEAS) was linked by technical procedures to EuroGOOS.

---

18 *W.S. Broecker*, The great ocean conveyor, in: *Oceanography* 4(2) (1991), 79–89; *G. Parilla/A. Lavin/H. Bryden/M. Garcia/R. Millard*, Rising temperatures in the subtropical North Atlantic Ocean over the past 35 years, in: *Nature* 396(6475) (1994), 48–51; *F. Schott/M. Visbeck/U. Send*, Open ocean deep convection, Mediterranean and Greenland Seas, in: *P. Malanotte/A.R. Robinson* (eds.), *Ocean Processes in Climate Dynamics: Global and Mediterranean Examples*, pp. 203–226 (1994); *DYNAMO Group*, DYNAMO: Dynamics of North Atlantic Models: Simulation and assimilation with high resolution models (Kiel 1997); *R.T. Sutton/M.R. Allen*, Decadal predictability of north Atlantic sea surface temperature and climate, in: *Nature* 388 (1997), 563–567; *C. Le Provost/N.C. Flemming* (eds.), The EuroGOOS Atlantic Workshop Report, *EuroGOOS Publication* No. 9 (Southampton 1998); *EuroCLIVAR*, Climate Variability and Predictability Research in Europe, 1999–2004: EuroCLIVAR Recommendations (*D. Anderson et al.* eds.) (The Netherlands 1998); *R.A. Wood/A.P. Keen/J.F.B. Mitchell/J.M. Gregory*, Changing spatial structure of the thermohaline circulation in response to atmospheric CO_2 forcing in a climate model, in: *Nature* 399 (1999), 581–575; *D.T. Shindell/R.L. Miller/G.A. Schmidt/L. Pandolfo*, Simulation of recent northern winter climate trends by greenhouse-gas forcing, in: *Nature* 399 (1999), 452–454.

19 *Woods/Dahlin/Droppert/Glass/Vallerga/Flemming* (*supra* note 3).

20 *H-P. Plag*, European sea-level observing systems (EOSS): Status and future developments, COST Action 40, European Commission, Directorate General for Research (2000).

The regional seas and adjacent ocean basins each require analysis to identify their distinct oceanographic processes, and the economic needs of their bordering populations. The Mediterranean is an almost closed basin with unique circulation which requires a relatively high resolution observation and modelling scheme.[21] The Mediterranean Forecasting System proposed by EuroGOOS in collaboration with the Mediterranean GOOS organisation (MedGOOS) emphasises regional nested modelling and forecasting.[22] This modelling is important both for the Mediterranean coastal states, and to provide accurate assessment of the Mediterranean outflow of dense water into the Atlantic. The Baltic region has a highly developed set of collaborational structures, with a sophisticated programme of linked hydrodynamic models, interfacing with biological productivity models.[23] Operational data products and models will be developed in support of HELCOM.

The ability to monitor and predict North Atlantic changes on the multi-year timescale would provide the boundary conditions for models of the shelf seas, and hence permit prediction of conditions in the coastal areas. In addition to the Atlantic variability it is important to understand the variability of Arctic sea ice, and the variability of the ocean waters under the ice. European countries will benefit greatly from a programme of remote sensing of the Atlantic and Arctic Oceans, combined with *in situ* instrumentation. The ocean scale models should be run so as to provide seasonal, inter-annual and multi-year predictions. Most EuroGOOS activities to date, and the forecasts and models run by member agencies, are intended to provide short- to medium-term forecasts of coastal and marine processes. The full value of incorporating seasonal and inter-annual ocean models into climate variability forecasting has not yet been tested. This is likely to occur soon, as basin scale models such as FOAM and MERCATOR are implemented at higher resolution, and integrated with climate models. Forecasts on this scale will influence the planning of fresh water utilisation, management of dams and reservoirs, river management, agriculture, and energy planning. In 1997 EuroGOOS held a joint workshop with participants from the USA to analyse requirements for operational modelling of the Atlantic.[24] EuroGOOS Member Agencies are prominent in the planning of the Atlantic ARGO Pilot Experiment, jointly with the USA.

The North Sea is one of the most densely used sea areas of the world, with an enormous coastal urban population, and major European rivers draining into it. Because of the high level of economic and scientific activity in the North Sea, and

---

21 *M. Golnaraghi/C.J. Lozano/A.R. Robinson*, Dynamical adjustment of quasi-synoptic data sets in the eastern Mediterranean: testing a full basin coastal methodology, in: *JMS* 7(1) (1996), 9–42; *L. Jeftic/J.D. Milliman/G. Sestini* (eds.), Climatic Change and the Mediterranean (London 1993); *L. Jeftic/S. Keckes/J.C. Pernetta* (eds.), Climatic Change and the Mediterranean, vol. 2 (London 1996).

22 *N. Pinardi/N.C. Flemming*, The Mediterranean Forecasting System Science Plan, in: *EuroGOOS Publication* No. 11 (Southampton 1998).

23 *E. Buch/H. Dahlin* (eds.), The BOOS Plan: Baltic Operational Oceanographic System, 1999–2003, in: *EuroGOOS Publication* No. 14 (Southampton 2000).

24 *Le Provost/Flemming* (*supra* note 18).

the adjacent North West Shelf Seas, EuroGOOS has developed its plans here very carefully and slowly. There is no point in duplicating work already being carried out by well-established, technically sophisticated bodies such as ICES or OSPAR. After consultation and several joint workshops, EuroGOOS is developing its North West Shelf Ocean Observing (NOOS) Plan. This is designed to bring the advantages of real time data transmission and modelling in support of the existing agencies with statutory responsibilities in the area.

Although the most technically feasible components of GOOS are the physical observations and predictions, the biological requirements are both scientifically important and politically essential. Biological processes, particularly phytoplankton growth, strongly influence the carbon cycle and the penetration of light and heat into the upper layers of the ocean. Biological productivity, water quality, and public health issues are of vital public interest in the coastal zone. International global science programmes such as JGOFS and GLOBEC provide some of the basic understanding needed in ecosystem modelling. In April 2000 EuroGOOS and ICES jointly sponsored a workshop on bio-ecological modelling, which was held at RIKZ, the Netherlands.[25] This workshop identified the stages by which the recent research on ecosystem models can be developed and tested so as to produce genuinely operational real-time information services. In September 2000 ICES held a joint meeting with GOOS to plan the further development of operational bio-ecological monitoring in support of fisheries management and conservation. This will be followed up by a joint ICES-GOOS-EuroGOOS workshop in Bergen during 2001 to produce recommendations for the North Sea Secretariat.

European Organisation and Logistics for Operational Oceanography

EuroGOOS was established in 1994 and has for the first two years devoted its activities to strategic analysis of the needs of Europe for operational ocean services, and defining objectives. This period culminated in the publication of the Strategy for EuroGOOS[26] and the First EuroGOOS Conference held at the Hague in 1996, with a Conference Proceedings volume published in 1997.[27]

Two key elements were created during that phase, which have stood the test of time. The first of these was the network of regional sea Task Teams, each responsible for identifying needs and developing strategies for implementation in the sea areas of the Baltic, North West Shelf Seas, Arctic, Atlantic, and Mediterranean. These areas are so radically different in terms of oceanographic conditions and economic exploitation of the sea and coastal zones that they have to be treated as separate

25 *J. Fischer/J. Baretta/F. Colijn/N.C. Flemming*, Bio-ecological observations in operational oceanography, *EuroGOOS Publication* No. 15 (Southampton 2000).

26 *Woods/Dahlin/Droppert/Glass/Vallerga/Flemming* (*supra* note 3).

27 *J.H. Stel* (ed.), Proceedings of the First EuroGOOS Conference, 7–11 October 1996, The Hague, The Netherlands (1997).

and distinct units. The scale of such subdivisions would naturally vary in different regions of the globe, but it is equally clear that the Mediterranean itself would benefit from detailed analysis at the sub-regional level, and then implementation of observations at an integrated level.

The second key principle established early on was the so-called Virtuous Circle (Figure 4), whereby sectors of activity are continuously reviewed and progressed through a changing suite of projects. The sectors of activity are Customer and User analysis; Economic assessment; Scientific research to remove obstacles; Technology development; Trials and case studies; Operational Observing Systems; Numerical assimilation of data, models and forecasting; Product design and services; and thence back to the Customers and Users.

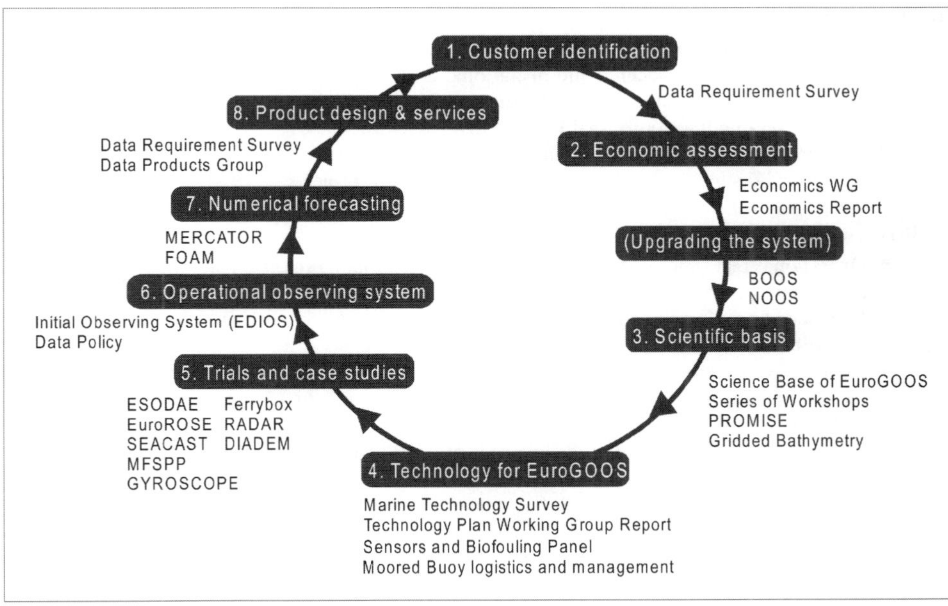

Figure 4. EuroGOOS identified in 1996 a number of sectors of activity which always need attention and effort. These are shown in the dark boxes. The actual work required in each sector will vary from year to year, and the activities and projects carried out to achieve the objectives of the sector are shown below each box.

From 1997 to 1999 EuroGOOS developed a range of projects on different scales related to various problems, technological requirements, and regional studies, designed to test pre-operational systems. Some of these projects have been funded by the European Commission under the MAST programmes MAST-2 and MAST-3, and more recently under Framework 5. At the same time, existing operational services provided by national agencies were analysed to see how they could fit together or reinforce each other on a European scale. In March 1999, EuroGOOS held its Second Conference in Rome, and the development of operational and pre-operational observing systems and products was manifest. The speed of development has been greatly assisted by the increased speed and range of services on the Internet. At the end of 1999 EuroGOOS published a short document entitled "The EuroGOOS Forward Look".[28] This sets out in a brief way the targets which EuroGOOS hopes to achieve by the year 2008. The next few years will be dedicated to implementing operational and pre-operational systems to achieve those targets. See Table 3 for a list of the benchmarks of achievement set out in the EuroGOOS Forward Look.

Table 3. At the beginning of 2000 EuroGOOS published its Forward Look. Planned achievements are summarised above. A) Benchmarks to be attained in the period up to 2002; B) Benchmarks to be attained before 2008

(a) Benchmarks from Forward Look: Near Field, 1999–2002

- Develop regional and Atlantic operational systems and services
- Support ecosystem modelling and operational development
- Agree EuroGOOS real time data-sharing policy
- Develop self-funding status for EuroGOOS
- Members expand and develop national operational projects
- Apply for F5 support for pre-operational development projects

(b) Benchmarks from Forward Look, Far Field, 2003–2008

- Operational real time services with substantially less than 1km grid resolution in coastal seas, and 1–5km in the Mediterranean
- Expanded list of forecast variables, including nutrients, water quality, and ecosystem parameters
- Ocean basin and shelf edge models fully operational
- Strong regional seas operational systems, such as BOOS, MSF, NWSTT, etc.
- Expanded network of deployed ocean profiling floats and time-series fixed stations (ARGO, GODAE, etc.)
- Greatly increased computer modelling capacity and high data rate real time network
- Operational ocean satellite missions scheduled on an agreed programme at European level
- Fully functional real time data sharing agreement (EuroGOOS Data Policy)
- Agreements to deliver products to non-research directorates and European agencies

CONCLUSIONS

Operational oceanography in the civilian sector has now been developing for about a decade, and the results are encouraging. The technically developed countries of the world now have experience of delivering local and regional services for a range of physical oceanographic parameters, and the simplest ecosystem and biogeochemical parameters are becoming manageable. EuroGOOS is in the vanguard, working with a number of other European agencies (CEC, EUMETSAT, EEA, ESA, ICES, ECMWF), to ensure that governments and commercial organisations in Europe

[28] *EuroGOOS*, EuroGOOS Forward Look; *EuroGOOS doc.* EG98.22 v5 (1999), see website address: *http://www.EuroGOOS.org.*

obtain the best operational data products, using the most efficient technology, and the most advanced scientific methods of analysis. At the global scale a number of collaborative projects such as GODAE and ARGO are being developed within the framework of GOOS to provide operational data services, and to provide the long term system which will support global coupled ocean-atmosphere models for climate study. The participants in the GOOS Intergovernmental Committee include many developing countries, and EuroGOOS Members work through this to provide technical aid and assistance, and additionally work in collaboration with the developing countries in the Mediterranean and Black Sea regions. EuroGOOS is ensuring that the national member agencies of European countries are fully involved at this global scale.

Annex: Acronyms

ARGO	Array for Real-time Geostrophic Oceanography
BOOS	Baltic Operational Oceanographic System
BSH	Bundesamt für Seeschiffahrt und Hydrographie (Germany)
CEC	Commission of the European Communities
DYNAMO	Dynamics of North Atlantic Models
ECMWF	European Centre for Medium-Term Weather Forecasting
EEA	European Environment Agency
ENSO	El Niño Southern Oscillation
ESA	European Space Agency
ESEAS	European Sea Level Observing System
EU	European Union
EUMETSAT	European Meteorological Satellite Organization
EUREKA	European Research and Co-ordination Agency
EuroCLIVAR	European Climate Variability and Predictability
EuroGOOS	European (component) Global Ocean Observing System
FOAM	Forecasting Ocean Atmosphere Model
GLOBEC	Global Ocean Ecosystems Dynamics
GLOSS	Global Sea Level Observing System
GNP	Gross National Product
GODAE	Global Ocean Data Assimilation Experiment
GOOS	Global Ocean Observing System
HELCOM	Helsinki Commission (Baltic Marine Environment Protection Commission)
IACMST	Inter-Agency Committee on Marine Science and Technology (UK)
ICES	International Council for the Exploration of the Seas
IFREMER	French Institute for Research and Exploitation of the Sea
IOC	Intergovernmental Oceanographic Commission (UNESCO)
IPCC	Intergovernmental Panel on Climate Change
JGOFS	Joint Global Ocean Flux Study
MedGOOS	Mediterranean Global Ocean Observing System

MERCATOR	French Operational High-Resolution Global Ocean Prediction Project
NAO	North Atlantic Oscillation
NOOS	North West Shelf Ocean Observing System
OECD	Organisation for Economic Co-operation and Development
OSPAR	Oslo-Paris Convention
RASCL	Roger A Stacey Consultants Ltd.
RIKZ	Netherlands Institute for Coastal and Marine Management
TOGA	Tropical Oceans and the Global Atmosphere

*Arne Nielsen**

TOWARDS A EUROPEAN MARINE INFORMATION HIGHWAY

Over the past ten years it has become common knowledge that the wealth of information contained within the nautical charts is of value not only to the mariners but also for many other users within the marine industry including coastal zone management, offshore industry and manufactures of equipment. Government agencies dealing with physical planning and environmental issues are also users of hydrographic information. The growing demand for high-resolution hydrographic data sets from the new user groups is a challenge for the hydrographic offices and calls for broader co-operation between the European hydrographic offices and co-operation with commercial distributors.

The national hydrographic services – hydrographic offices – are a vital part not only of the national and international transport infrastructure[1] but also of the national and international spatial data infrastructure.

The main objectives of a hydrographic office are to:

(a) Ensure the production, distribution and updating of charts.
(b) Ensure the timely dissemination of maritime safety information.
(c) Collect georeferenced data related to
  – depths of the sea,
  • coastal configuration,
  • hazards to navigation and other marine activities,
  • sea bottom composition,
  • tides, currents and physical properties of the water column.
(d) Process the collected information in order to create databases capable of feeding the productions of chart and thematic maps for the following most common uses
  – maritime navigation and traffic control,
  • naval operations,
  • laying of submarine cables and pipelines,
  • maritime boundaries definition.

---

* Royal Danish Administration of Navigation and Hydrography.
1 More than 80% of international trade in the world is carried by sea.

P. Ehlers, E. Mann-Borgese and R. Wolfrum (eds.), Marine Issues, 299–303

Although intended primarily to support safety of navigation, the extensive volume of data held by hydrographic offices are of considerable value not only to the mariners and fishermen, but also for many other users. Coastal zone management including construction of new harbours or development of existing ones; control of coastal erosion; establishment of dumping grounds for industrial waste; extraction of mineral deposits; aquacultural activities; exploration and exploitation of marine resources; environmental protection management; marine science; tourism and design and production of navigational equipment are examples of other user groups. For these user groups the chart provides the spatial framework for the collection, processing and management of marine data sets.

The hydrographic offices have learned that there is an established demand for the type of data held in their databases. This awareness has grown in line with the development of the electronic navigational chart – including the development of the electronic chart and information system, the so-called ECDIS.

ECDIS is an integrated navigation tool. In order to carry the name ECDIS the system must comply with the specification issued by the International Maritime Organisation (IMO). The first ECDIS, which complies with the IMO requirements, was issued in spring this year.

Originally ECDIS had been defined as an equivalent to paper charts, but the mariners have learned that an ECDIS is more than just that. The mariners are starting to realise that an electronic chart system such as ECDIS represents an entirely new approach to maritime navigation. The mariners (or any other user) can choose what type and level of information is most appropriate for the conduct of safe navigation (or any other operations) in the current situation. The system has the ability to show – on the same display – chart related hazards on the seafloor together with the ship traffic on the water's surface, thereby helping the mariners to conduct safe navigation. – No wonder that the greatest benefit of ECDIS is in confined waters – in rivers, harbours and harbour approaches.

In parallel with the development of ECDIS, a data exchange format – the so called S57 – has been developed. This means that hydrographic and oceanographic data sets may be absorbed smoothly and effectively into the ECDIS. The exchange format S57 has been developed by the International Hydrographic Organisation (IHO). The S57 format focuses on electronic chart databases. In order to meet the requirement from the market, work has been initiated to include also time varying objects (currents, waves, ice cover etc.), which in this context are named Marine Information Objects (MIOS).

ECDIS and S57 is a success. It is used or recommended for use by many user groups outside the hydrographic community. The era of ECDIS has just started.

In addition to ECDIS, we see many more systems with functionalities similar to the ones included in ECDIS. These systems, which do not comply with the specifications issued by the IMO, are called electronic chart systems or integrated bridge systems. These latter systems are in common use on board fishing vessels, buoy tenders and the like.

As a spin-off to the development of the electronic chart, all information in the paper chart must be transformed into an electronic version. It is this transformation – the digitisation of the source data that makes the production of the electronic chart possible – that gives new added value to the information in the chart even though this information may have been collected more than a hundred years ago.

The development of shallow water multibeam echo sounders during the past decade is another important factor for the growing interest in hydrographic data sets. The ability to map the seafloor has changed fundamentally. Today it is possible to obtain complete coverage of large areas of the sea-floor with details never seen before. It is also possible to simultaneously collect backscatter data resulting in sidescan sonar like imagery.

Many potential users have already heard about these possibilities, but do not know who to contact to get access to the hydrographic data sets. Other users – working mainly in the field of hydrography, geophysics or related disciplines – know that they should contact the World Data Centre System. However, having done so, they quickly learn that the data sets they need are not included in the databases at World Data Centres. Instead they are advised to address the hydrographic offices in the countries in question. Doing so many of the users get frustrated because the data sets they are looking for are not available – or only partly so.

One disappointing factor is the generally poor data density of the hydrographic data sets and/or the age of the available data sets. It is true that modern technology of today offers incredible opportunities. However, most of the data sets held by the hydrographic offices are more than a hundred years old. These old data sets do have the same data density as is expected from a modern survey. Furthermore, the hydrographic surveys were and still are focused on shallow water surveys in harbour approaches and waters otherwise difficult to navigate.

It must be remembered in this context that the main objectives of the hydrographic offices are collection, validation and quality control of data for the design and production of paper charts or electronic chart databases. Even though it is anticipated that the hydrographic offices have a total overview of all hydrographic data sets of relevance for the production of charts, this does not mean that the hydrographic offices also are the data owners of all the relevant data sets. Other organisations or private companies collect many of the data sets held within the hydrographic databases. This fact raises questions such as ownership, copyright etc.

Since the International Hydrographic Organisation (IHO) was established in 1921 the hydrographic offices have co-operated on standardisation of charts, development of exchange formats and free exchange of nautical data. – But much has happened since 1921. New international copyright conventions have come into force and forced the IHO to disband the free exchange principle. Cost recovery is an issue, which is often raised in relation to present and future funding of the hydrographic offices. In this respect copyright issues and national cost recovery efforts counteract a wider use of hydrographic data sets.

The growing demand for high-resolution hydrographic data sets from the new user groups is a challenge for the hydrographic offices.

Initiatives have been taken to investigate how best to facilitate wider access to hydrographic data by user groups such as coastal managers and fishermen. One such investigation is the AVID Project. AVID stands for Added Value Information Dissemination from hydrographic data sets. The project was carried out in the framework of the INFO2000 programme of the EC/DG XIII (contract number PUB 1123 AVID 24854). The full report of the work is to be found at *http://hydrostore.org*. The report concludes among other things:

- Internet technology is mature enough to develop a viable solution for the delivery of publicly funded hydrographic data sets to different user groups.
- Political issues such as copyrights, pricing, liability are far greater barriers for wider access to hydrographic data sets than the technological ones.

These statements stress the need for further initiatives and a broader co-operation between the European hydrographic offices and co-operation with commercial distributors. The MISD – Marine Information Service Database – project is a step in this direction. MISD in its original form is a joint Norwegian, Icelandic, Danish and UK enterprise initiated by the Norwegian Hydrographic Service. All hydrographic offices in the countries around the North Sea have been invited to participate in the project – and all addressees have responded positively to the invitation.

The main objective of the MISD project is to serve the professional mariners and the fishermen as well as other user groups not familiar with the use of an electronic chart system (SCS). MISD must provide access to the hydrographic data sets so that these data sets may be integrated into geographical information systems (GIS) other than ECS or ECDIS.

Mandatory layers in MISD should be:

- Bathymetry.
- Up-dated oil & gas related information, i.e. pipelines, platforms, oil rigs, abandoned well heads.
- Submarine cables.
- Geographical names.
- Information on wrecks.
- Fishing prohibited areas.

Optional layers could include amongst others:

- Fishermen fasteners.
- Nature of seabed.
- Limits of fishery zones/fishery protection zones and EEZs.
- National administrative fishery boundaries.
- Sediment type.
- Information on fishery resources and the environment, including weather, sea temperature and current information.
- Information on algae.

The final outcome of MISD will, of course, depend on further talks with potential partners and available funding for the project.

Challenge

- Broader co-operation between the European hydrographic offices and co-operation with commercial distributors.
- Resolve the problems related to copyrights and pricing.

Literature

National Maritime Policies and Hydrographic Services, International Hydrographic Bureau, Monaco, 1999.

Useful web sites

European Commission, Directorate General XII "Science, Research and Development", Marine Science and Technology (EC DG XII)
http://europa.eu.int/comm/research/marine1.html

European Environmental Agency (EEA)
http://www.eea.eu.int

European Global Ocean Observing System (EuroGOOS)
http://www.eurogoos.org

Global Ocean Observing System (GOOS)
http://www.unesco.org

Intergovernmental Oceanographic Commission (IOC)
http://ioc.unesco.org/iocweb/default.htm

International Council for the Exploration of the Sea (ICES)
http://www.ices.org

International Hydrographic Organisation (IHO)
http://www.iho.shom.fr/

International Hydrographic Organisation Data Center for Digital Bathymetry (IHO DCDB)
http://www.ngdc.noaa.gov/mgg/bathymetry/iho.html

International Oceanographic Data and Information Exchange (IODE)
http://ioc.unesco.org/iode/

World Data Center System
http://www.ngdc.noaa.gov/wdc/wdcmain.html

Adalberto Vallega and Stefano Belfiore***

OCEAN AND COASTAL ZONES IN GLOBAL PROGRAMMES AND THE OCEAN 21 PROJECT

PREMISE

In 1996, in the framework of the 28th International Geographical Congress "Land, Sea, and Human Effort" (The Hague, 4–10 August), the extended paper Agenda 21 for Ocean Geography was presented by *A. Vallega* discussing the role of geography facing the need for inter-disciplinary and multi-spatial scale research. On the basis of this approach, the ocean subject was included in the 1996–2000 programme, adopted by the 19th General Assembly of the International Geographical Union (10 August), and *A. Vallega*, as newly-elected Vice-president of IGU, was appointed to take care of this field. To deal with this task, the *Oceans* programme was drafted and discussed in a joint workshop of the International Geographical Union (IGU) and of the Intergovernmental Oceanographic Commission (IOC). The programme was finalised and, on this basis, in 1998 the IGU-IOC Seminar *The role of ocean science and geography in facing ocean management for the third millennium* was held in Sagres, Portugal, 3–5 September. As a conclusion of that event, the *Oceans 21* programme was adopted.

Meanwhile, the conceptual and methodological discussion about ocean geography led the participants in the IGU Regional Conference The Atlantic: Past, Present, and Future (Lisbon, 31 August – 2 September) to adopt the International Charter of Ocean Geography, which was called The Lisbon Charter. This solemn document, designing ocean geography in front of the development of ocean sciences in the framework of post-modern society, has been translated into 26 languages. The relevant book was published by the Italian Geographical Society.[1]

This paper provides a concise presentation of the conceptual background approach designed by *A. Vallega*, of the goals, content and main aspects of the *Oceans 21* programme, focusing on its role facing the research programme convened by IOC

* Vice-President, International Geographical Union (IGU), c/o Department Polis, University of Genoa, 37 Stradone di S. Agostino, 16123 Genoa – Italy, Phone: +39 (010) 209–5858 Fax: +1 (010) 209–5907, Email: *a.vallega@polis.unige.it*.

** Center for the Study of Marine Policy, Graduate College of Marine Studies, University of Delaware, 301 Robinson Hall, Newark, Delaware 19716 – USA, Phone: +1 (302) 831–8086, Fax: +1 (302) 831–3668, Email: *sbelf@udel.edu*.

[1] 1999.

P. Ehlers, E. Mann-Borgese and R. Wolfrum (eds.), Marine Issues, 305–320

and by the International Council for Science (ICSU) on ocean subjects. Finally, a call for collaboration will be addressed to geographers.

The Background Approach

The background approach is presented in Appendix 1 – *Geography for Holistic Ocean Science*. Here it is sufficient to recall some key statements which are closely concerned with the setting of the *Oceans 21* programme.

Ocean Geography in the Scientific Context

The conventional setting of ocean research is based on a multitude of disciplines – physical, biological, social, and juridical – which are not integrated by the adoption of a mutual epistemological design. This setting results from the positivist and structuralist approach and has led to the construction of *ocean sciences*. On the other hand, the constructivist approach is based on the adoption of mutual epistemological design by all the sciences involved in ocean research in order to build up *ocean science*. In this framework disciplines are clustered into disciplines of matter, disciplines of movement, and disciplines of engineering. Based on its historical ability to bridge natural and social perspectives, geography should play a leading role in building up the ocean science.

Geography as an Engineering Discipline

Within the constructivist scientific setting, ocean geography should be regarded as an engineering discipline. The physical and the human geography of the ocean should not be regarded as separate fields, but as the integrated components of a unique disciplinary area, which is concerned with research and education. To fulfil this demand, which has essentially arisen from the pursuit of ocean sustainable development, the organisation of ocean geography can be imagined as a four-co-ordinate epistemological matrix, incorporated in the set of engineering sciences. The co-ordinates relate to:

(i) the subject areas, selected and identified in accordance with the goal of knowledge;
(ii) the geographical parts of the ocean to which the subject areas are referred;
(iii) the geographical scales on which research is conducted;
(iv) the timing scale to which the processes are referred.

Key Geographical Subject Areas

As a result of the above mentioned approach, the key areas of geographical investigations, where the physical and the social perspectives are melted together by a mutual epistemological basis, include:

(i) coastal geography;
(ii) deep-ocean geography;
(iii) regional geography; and
(iv) ocean geographical information systems.

A Triple Reference Framework

The adoption of Agenda 21 by the United Nations Conference on Environment and Development,[2] enunciating principles and providing guidelines for deep ocean, coastal, and small island management, has led to an increased demand for the ecosystem-human community interaction assessment, as well as to the need of creating new collaborations between natural (physical and biological) and social sciences.

In the meantime, the design and implementation of global change programmes, convened in the framework of the International Council for Science (ICSU, formerly International Council for Scientific Unions) are deeply concerned with the ocean. Research is focused on two subject areas:

(i) the role of the ocean as a whole facing global change and biogeochemical cycles;
(ii) the physical processes involving the ocean and, to some extent, the interaction with the social processes which mainly involve the increasing human pressure on coastal areas.

As a result, the role of geography in contributing to the implementation of Agenda 21, Chapter 17, and that of the discipline potentially involved in the ICSU programme framework are worth of consideration.

Since the *Oceans 21* programme was meant as a co-operation tool between IGU and IOC, also its role facing the existing IOC programmes should be taken into account. This consideration is essential since IOC has moved from a merely physical approach to oceans and coasts to an increasingly sensible approach as far as the prospect of integrating physical and social perspectives to efficiently answer to the need of management patterns and tools is concerned.

Geography Facing Agenda 21

In order to holistically deal with ocean management and to harmonise the protection of the ecosystem with its use as a resource, Chapter 17 includes seven programme areas:

A. *coastal area management*, where the concept of integrated coastal management is adopted and where prescriptions on how environmental and development issues should be jointly dealt with are provided;

---

[2] UNCED 1992.

B. *environmental protection*, where prescriptions to prevent and mitigate land- and sea-based pollution are provided;
C. *management of living resources in the high seas*, where the need to develop fisheries by granting protection to biodiversity is addressed;
D. *management of living resources in national waters*, where prescriptions tailored to the complexity of this environment are defined, complementing those related to the high seas;
E. *addressing critical uncertainties*, where the impacts of atmospheric warming and climate change on the ocean are considered through a wide spectrum of *ad hoc* guidelines and prescriptions primarily concerned with the need for research implementation;
F. *international and regional co-operation and co-ordination*, where the principles by which the decision-making centres should be integrated on all the geographical scales are enunciated;
G. *small islands*, where the specific issues of small islands and small island states, marked by diffuse fragile ecosystems and important cultural heritage, are dealt with by *ad hoc* prescriptions.

With regard to this breakdown, the present literature[3] asserts that the scientific community should intensify its efforts in coastal and deep ocean areas, as well as in small islands, in order to design:

(i) *integrated approaches* among those sciences concerned with the various aspects of the ocean in order to provide holistic methods and more effective interdisciplinary views;
(ii) *strategies and programmes* able to grant protection of the ecosystem, of economic efficiency, and of social equity including the rights of future generations;
(iii) *co-operation patterns between decision-making systems* operating in different sectors and on different scales with the aim of optimising integrated management;
(iv) *data management* patterns tailored to the sustainable development concept applied to coastal areas, the deep ocean and small islands;
(v) *strategies and programmes* for the optimisation of social participation in sustainable development-aimed programmes;
(vi) *capacity-building* patterns focused on developing countries.

Connections are found among the above-mentioned six points, on which literature has concentrated, and the programme areas around which UNCED Agenda 21 has designed its mid- and long-term ocean strategies. The web of links presented in Table 1 not only shows the extent of the connections but also how strong and effective the interaction between science and policy could become.

---

[3] Cicin-Sain 1995; Mann Borgese 1995.

Table 1. Relevance of the issues discussed by the literature to the programme areas of UNCED Agenda 21, Chapter 17

Programme areas of Chapter 17		*Subject areas focused by the literature*					
		I	*II*	*III*	*IV*	*V*	*IV*
A	Coastal area management	■	■	■	■	■	■
B	Environmental protection	□	■	■	□	■	□
C	Management of living resources of the high seas	□	□	□	□	□	□
D	Management of living resources of the national waters	□	□	■	□	□	
E	Addressing critical uncertainties	■	□	■	■	□	
F	International and regional co-operation and co-ordination	□	■	■			□
G	Management of small islands	■	■	■	■	■	■

Degree of relevance: ■ high relevance; □ low relevance.

Geography Facing the ICSU Programme Framework

The second leading force between a heightened study of the oceans has been the network of international programmes on global change sponsored by the ICSU. In fact, the concerns of these programmes relating on the ocean overlap with those of UNCED Agenda 21, whose Paragraph 17.100, Area E, is entitled "Addressing critical uncertainties for the management of the marine environment and climate change".

Within the ICSU framework, the ocean has been – to various extents and from various points of view – included in core projects covered by six research programmes.[4] As it can be seen from Table 2, the time sequence these programmes have been convened by is meaningful. Most efforts have focused on climate change and subsequent impacts on physical and chemical contexts of the oceans. The ecosystem has been analysed only since the 1980s, socio-economic aspects have been included, with self-evident hesitation and reluctance, in the agenda of research. In this regard, it is expected that interaction will be established and will rapidly be implemented by International Geosphere-Biosphere Programme (IGBP) and by the International Human Dimensions of Global Environmental Change Programme (IHDP). At the present time, social aspects are incorporated into two core projects: Land-Ocean Interaction in the Coastal Zone (LOICZ), which is expected to also deal with the management of the coastal areas; Land-Use and Land Cover Change (LUCC), convened jointly by IGBP and IHDP, which is potentially concerned with the use of coastal resources. It is hoped that interaction will be implemented in a way to widen the correspondence of the ICSU programmes as a whole with the demand for research from UNCED Agenda 21, Chapter 17.

These two needs for interaction may be regarded as profoundly connected since the more effective the co-operation is among disciplines, the more successful the co-operation is between science and policy, and the social justification for research

4 ICSU 1996.

Table 2. The ICSU[(*)] research programmes and their relevance to the ocean[(a)]

Bodies/Programs	*Year of adoption*	*Projects relevant to the ocean*	*The role of programmes vis-à-vis UNCED Agenda 21, Chapter 17*
Programmes of the Scientific Committee on Problems of the Environment (SCOPE)	1969	Solving Environmental Problems of the Ocean	In 1996 the programme *Towards sustainability* was adopted to focus on the issues considered by Agenda 21.
World Climate Research Programme (WCRP)	1979	World Ocean Circulation Experiment (WOCE).	"The observational phase of WOCE (1990–1997) is the largest oceanographic programme ever undertaken"[(b)]. Main uses of the ocean are concerned: living resource exploitation.
	1985	Tropical Ocean-Global Atmosphere (TOGA)	Investigations on the predictability of flooding and extreme droughts due to the El Niño is a main component of the programme.
		Arctic Climate System Study (ACSYS)	Pilot research useful to develop models of interactive ocean-atmosphere-cryosphere processes.
International Geosphere-Biosphere Programme (IGBP)	1986	Land-Use and Land Cover Change (LUCC)[(c)]	The project has potential relevance to the investigation of coastal uses.
		Land-Ocean Interaction in the Coastal Zone (LOICZ)	Core subject areas: (i) the effects of changes in external forcing or boundary conditions on coastal fluxes; (ii) coastal biogeomorphology and global change; (iii) carbon fluxes and trace gas emissions; (iv) economic and social impacts on global change in coastal systems.
		Joint Global Flux Study (JGFS)	The project aims at investigating the dynamic exchanges of carbon within the ocean and across its atmosphere.
		Global Ocean Ecosystem Dynamics (GLOBEC)	Core subject areas: (i) multi-scale physical processes forcing large-scale changes in marine ecosystems; (ii) structure and dynamics in a variety of ocean ecosystems; (iii) impacts of global change on zooplankton and fish populations.

Bodies/Programs	*Year of adoption*	*Projects relevant to the ocean*	*The role of programmes vis-à-vis UNCED Agenda 21, Chapter 17*
Environmental Panel on Climate Change (IPCC)	1988	The IPCC Reports have strong relevance to sea-level rise, associated biogeochemical processes and socio-economic implications.	The role of IPCC in driving coastal management programmes has become essential.
Human Dimensions of Global Environmental Change (HDGEC)[(d)]	1990	Land-Use and Land Cover Change (LUCC)[(e)]	See above (IGBP).
Diversitas	1991	Marine Biodiversity.	The project has strict relevance to sustainable development-aimed approaches to deep ocean and coastal areas.
Global Observation Systems	1992	Global Ocean Observing System (GOOS).	The project is closely concerned with ocean living resource exploitation and ocean health.

(*) The International Council for Scientific Unions was recalled "International Council for Science" in April 1998 by its General Assembly. The acronym "ICSU" was maintained.

(a) Data is mostly from the International Council for Scientific Unions 1996.

(b) *Ibid*, p. 13.

(c) In co-operation with the International Human Dimensions on Global Environmental Change (IHDGEC) Programme.

(d) This programme is usually called the International Human Dimensions Programme (IHDP).

(e) In co-operation with the International Geosphere-Biosphere Programme (IGBP).

increases. It follows that the integration effectiveness among disciplines is the core issue to be faced by the scientific community in order to meet the demand for research and assessment arising from the Rio Conference. This deduction, which is generally valid, is particularly relevant to ocean science because of the extensive research fields to be harnessed so to support the programmes and actions designed by Chapter 17. Ocean research is an arena where the general need for inter-disciplinarity is very well demonstrated.

The framework of ocean sciences applies the concept of inter-disciplinarity in three fundamental ways. First, a conventional approach, which begins with natural sciences, is inspired by positivism and aims at providing determinist views of ocean reality. In this context, natural sciences simply absorb the assessment of the role of human communities as required by social sciences. For example, the physical disciplines involved in coastal area management use social concepts, such as those of economic system and resource use structure, in absence of effective theoretical and methodological integration. More recently in the physical scientific milieus, efforts have been made to tackle this issue more in depth and intense discussion about inter-disciplinarity has developed. Nevertheless, as far as the ocean sciences are concerned, these exercises are still far from being successful. The present state of research is marked by an assessment of components each one of which is supported by its own conceptual and methodological approach and connected to the epistemological statute of the discipline from which it derives. This seems more a Tower of Babel than a rational building of systems of knowledge, and causes embarrassment to the scientific community. It could be asserted that effective results might be achieved by moving from the admission that discussion about the methodological concerns should be integrated with that of the logical backgrounds supporting methods and the epistemological approach to the ocean, from which logic and method draw their legitimacy. It derives that only where discussion goes in-depth to the most profound level, i.e. epistemology, successful results may achieved. In this regard, two pathways are possible. On the one hand, the conventional pathway where positivism (nature's disciplines) and structuralism (social disciplines) start from the epistemological level, on which the disjunctive Cartesian logic and the analytical-deductive methods are based. As it has been said, in this context, inter-disciplinarity is intended as a mere assembling of disciplines. On the other hand, the innovative pathway, where the epistemology of complexity supports conjunctive (general system-referred) logical backgrounds, and inductive-axiomatic methods. In this context, inter-disciplinarity is intended as the construction of knowledge systems transcending the individual disciplinary theoretical statutes.

As an example, coastal area management may be taken into account. According to Agenda 21, Chapter 17 and the materials from the Preparatory Committee of UNCED, integrated coastal management is claimed as the tool to pursue the sustainable development of the coastal area. Integration has been diffusely considered[5] as contextually involving:

- *Teleological integration*, since integration must be tailored to the contextual pursuit of (a) ecosystem integrity, (b) economy efficiency, and (c) social equity including the rights of future generations.
- *Spatial integration*, since management should holistically involve the coastal land, the brackish belt, the marine areas, and the adjacent atmosphere.
- *Time integration*, since short-term actions and strategies need to be framed into long-term prospects and programmes.
- *Legal integration*, because national and international legal frameworks should provide integrated regulations to develop and diffuse effective management.
- *Jurisdictional integration*, because the administrative areas, extending landwards from the baselines, and the maritime jurisdictional zones, extending seawards, should be included in a unique management programme.
- *Decision-making integration*, because the actions of all the decision-making centres involved in coastal management should be co-ordinated in order to optimise the adoption and implementation of ICM programmes.

---

5 Cicin-Sain and Knecht 1998, ch. 2.

- *Social integration,* since top-down and bottom-up processes have to be harmonised and the local community participation in coastal management, including the design, adoption and evaluation of the management programme, needs to be improved.

There is no doubt that, where these concepts are regarded as basis for the scientific approach, efforts should be made to holistically describe and represent the coastal system, i.e. omitting the individual sectors of assessment and building systems of knowledge. It is not important to describe in detail how the coastal system is made, but rather to focus on how it is organised and on how it evolves and what target its changing organisation is heading to. Moreover, new subject areas should be regarded as worth of being included in the agenda:

(i) interactions between resource uses and the ecosystem in the framework of climate change and subsequent physical, chemical and biological processes;
(ii) the role of decision-making systems and their implementation prospects, as recommended by UNCED Agenda 21;
(iii) the role of legal and jurisdictional systems *vis-à-vis* the need to provide integrated coastal management and to optimise the management of ocean waters under an international regime;
(iv) the conceptual and methodological frameworks of ocean management concerned with global change and sustainable development.

Geography Facing the IOC Programmes

The IOC has played a leading role in the implementation of oceanography. It is useless to say that, if this organisation had not carried out such assertive action in the 1960s and 1970s, at the present time the whole ocean sciences would have been unprepared to meet the demand for knowledge and assessment from UNCED Agenda 21 and the subsequent approaches from the inter-governmental organisations concerned with ocean management. As it is well-known, the preparation of UNCED was assigned to the Preparatory Committee (PrepCom), who convened four sessions between 1991 and 1992. A core part of the extended amount of materials provided by the UN organisations was due to the IOC to the point that in most parts Chapter 17 is to be regarded as the result of the IOC approach to ocean management. From that circumstance a feedback arose since the guidelines and technical prescriptions from Chapter 17 were mostly addressed to the IOC calling for research implementation. The breakdown presented in Table 3 shows how much the role of the IOC has been implemented and how deeply it has evolved.

This breakdown highlights that a core objective of the IOC strategy is to set up close interaction between the satellite-based and land and marine monitoring systems with the aim of providing such a wide spectrum of real time data as to meet the demand for assessment from the inter-governmental organisations, multi-national and national bodies. This ambitious target is pursued through the Global Ocean

Table 3. The research programmes of the International Oceanographic Commission(*)

Partnership	*Objective*
IOC, WMO, UNEP	*Global Ocean Observing System*, GOOS(1) To ensure systematic observations adequate for: (i) forecasting climate variability and changes; (ii) assessing the state and health of the marine environment and its resources; (iii) supporting an improved decision-making and management process concerned with the ocean.
IOC, WMO	*Integrated Global Ocean Services System* (IGOOS) To exchange, in real-time, the oceanographic data acquired from ships of opportunity, volunteer observing ships and buoys.
IOC	*Global Sea Level Observing System* (GSLOS) To provide a co-ordinated basis for measuring sea-level changes throughout the oceans of the world.
IOC	*International Oceanographic Data and Information Exchange* (IODIE) To exchange non-operational (delayed-mode) oceanographic data through a system of national, regional (multi-national) and world data centres.
IOC, UNEP, IMO, IAEA	*Global Investigation of Pollution in the Marine Environment* (GIPME) To generate and evaluate data on contamination and pollution of the marine environment, and to provide a basis for the design of regulatory actions for preventing pollution.
IOC, UNEP	*Marine Pollution Monitoring* (MARPOLMON) To provide systematic observations of contaminants, mainly on the regional scale.
IOC	*Ocean Science and Living Resources* (OSLR) To investigate the relationships between living resources and ocean environmental variability with the aim of providing the scientific basis for rational fishery and environmentally-sound development and management.
IOC, UN	*Ocean Science and Non-Living Resources* (OSNLR) To investigate the interaction between the conditions and processes in oceans and coastal areas and the distribution of non-living resources.
IOC, UNEP, IUCN	*Global Coral Reef Monitoring Network* (GCRMN) To promote research, monitoring and assessment of coral reefs and related ecosystems and to provide information for more efficient and effective management for their long-term conservation.(2)
IOC, IHO	*General Bathymetric Chart of the Oceans* (GEBCO) To provide a digital atlas on ocean bathymetry.
IOC, IHO	*International Geological-Geophysical Atlases of the Atlantic and Pacific Oceans* (GAPA) To provide a digital atlas on the physical features of these two oceans.
IOC	*Training, Education, Mutual Assistance and Capacity Building* (TEMA) To fill the gaps in marine science knowledge and operational techniques in the fields.

(*) The breakdown presented in this table is deduced by *S. Keckes*, Review of international programmes relevant to the work of the independent World Commission on the Oceans, manuscript (1997).

(1) GOOS was adopted by the IOC General Assembly in 1989. It includes five modules: (i) Climate monitoring, Assessment and Prediction of Marine Living Resources; (ii) Monitoring of the Coastal Zone Environment and its Change; (iii) Assessment and Prediction of the Health of the Ocean; (v) Marine Meteorological and Oceanographic Operational services.

(2) This programme was convened in the framework of the International Coral Reef Initiative (ICRI) as a contribution to the Coastal Zone module of the GOOS.

Observing System (GOOS). In this view a main concern refers to the scale of data and approaches. Strong efforts have been made to "regionalise" information provided by GOOS and through other programmes with the aim of giving impulses to the management approaches on the multi-national and national scales. This task implies dealing with hard methodological problems.

In accordance with its nature of inter-governmental organisation dealing with oceanography, research is addressed to mapping, the implementation of which is achieved through the development of remote sensing-concerned and digital techniques. This task is far from being exhausted and the resulting products are expected to play an essential role in building up improved ocean management patterns.

Recently IOC has also dealt with issues which are only indirectly concerned with oceanography. This widening of scientific interest has been due to at least four factors:

(i) investigations on living and non-living resources have been undertaken with the aim of providing useful assessments for the rational use of natural ocean resources and, by doing so, attention has shifted to management patterns;
(ii) coastal area management has been included in the agenda of research;
(iii) education and training have been dealt with in an *ad hoc* programme (TEMA);
(iv) to a wide extent, the IOC programmes are topically linked to the ICSU programmes to the point that strong and effective co-operation has been established between the two arenas, the latter being concerned with a multi-disciplinary field much more extended than oceanography.

This widening of the role of research does not mean that all the subject areas UNCED Agenda 21 is concerned with are covered by the IOC programmes. In this respect the above comments on the ICSU programmes may be extended to the IOC framework. If this is agreed, it follows that a real challenge ought to be faced, namely that of widening the research areas tackled by IOC paying wider attention to the interaction between social and natural processes, to the role of decision-making systems, and to management. In this regard, on one hand the recently-born IOC proclivity to include social elements in some programmes, initially conceived to deal with natural processes should be regarded as an attractive evolution. Nevertheless, as far as the rationality and effectiveness of research are concerned, this does not seem sufficient since it would lead to considering the knowledge of social processes as merely instrumental to the knowledge of the natural ones. By doing so, the final result of research would be far from designing holistic views and effective integrated management patterns of coastal and deep-ocean areas. On the other hand, the proclivity to convene research projects only based on social sciences would be as fallacious as for those only based on the natural ones. The correct pathway would consist of building up effective inter-disciplinarity, supported by the adoption of a unique epistemological basis by both natural and social sciences.

The Oceans 21: An Overview

Oceans 21 aims at filling the gap between the physical and biological sciences on one hand, and the social sciences on the other in designing and implementing management approaches. Hence, this programme has self-evident complementary roles with both the programme frameworks of intergovernmental organisations, particularly IOC, and the research programmes convened in the context of ICSU and ISSC. *Oceans 21* is essentially addressed to decision-makers, managers and planners. As a result, most expected outcomes consist in guidelines and technical tools. Nevertheless, Project I is intended to bridge practice with theoretical and logical backgrounds with the final goal of contributing to effective inter-disciplinarity.

Basically *Oceans 21* deals with coastal area management. The deep-ocean is only considered by Project IV concerning ocean monitoring systems as a whole. In this framework:

- the *coastal area* is considered as the space extending seawards from the land up to the outer edge of the continental margin (physical criterion) or to the outer limit of the national maritime jurisdictional zones (legal criterion);
- the *deep-ocean*, is intended as the space extending seawards from the outer edge of the continental margin (physical criterion) or embracing the high seas and the deep seabeds (legal criterion).

According to its key scope, *Oceans 21* will essentially deal with the local scale, in which coastal managers and planners are involved, and with the national scale, on which master plans and state regulations are based. The regional (multinational) scale will only occasionally be taken into account.

Oceans 21 will be keen to implement a complexity-based inter-disciplinary approach, thought as the integration of disciplines on mutual conceptual and logical basis. It will be concerned with research, education, and training.

The main outcomes of *Oceans 21* will consist in:

- systems of knowledge for decision makers, managers and planners;
- conceptual, methodological and technical backgrounds on integrated coastal management;
- professional skills for decision-makers, managers and planners.

These kinds of products are expected:

- scientific events;
- educational and training courses;
- books (manuals and proceedings);
- journals;
- web-sites;
- distance learning systems;
- CD-ROMs;
- diskettes.

Oceans 21: The Programme Setting

Oceans 21, whose organisation is presented in *Appendix 2*, includes five projects and a special subject area.

Project I – Achieving Inter-disciplinary in ICM Research

This project has the role of providing conceptual and logical backgrounds the other projects may benefit from. In this sense it may be regarded as the basis for the development of *Oceans 21* as a whole. It will contribute to the discussion about the building up of ocean science, considered as an effective inter-disciplinary approach to the ocean. In particular, it will aim at: (i) designing and experimenting models for assessing, representing and simulating the interaction between the local ecosystem and the local communities; (ii) designing logical background and methodological inputs for collecting and processing data on the coastal systems, focusing on the interaction between ecosystems and human communities; (iii) designing logical background and methodological inputs to provide useful data for decision-making systems; (iv) exploring the literature on the above-mentioned subjects and reporting on the state of the relevant key results; (v) considering case studies concerned with the above-mentioned subjects and focusing on their use to improve concepts and methods; and (vi) convening discussions on the above subjects involving scientists, practitioners and decision-makers.

Project II – Marine Scientific and Technological Information Systems for ICM

This project will be concerned with the information systems on marine and coastal contexts. Linkage between Projects I and II will be due to the fact that Project I will be concerned with the conceptual and methodological issues relevant to the integration between data from various fields, while Project II will be concerned with the organisation of data in order to sustain coastal management.

As a key objective, this project will aim at: (i) serving as a clearing-house of marine scientific and technological information and data related to ICM; and (ii) developing management-oriented data banks.

Project III – Methodology Development in Support of ICM

Following the inputs from Agenda 21, Chapter 17, and from subsequent materials addressed by inter-governmental organisations to governments, local authorities and coastal managers, the need to design guidelines and other technical tools tailored to the concept of integrated management has arisen and spread. The preparation of these materials supposes that a well-defined spectrum of concepts and logical background has to be adopted. Hence, the close links between Project I dealing with theory and logical frameworks and Project III, dealing with decision-making processes are clear to see.

To fulfil to these needs, Project III will aim at providing methods and techniques consistent with integrated management principles and at dealing with issues considered pivotal by literature in order to optimise coastal management, and felt crucial by coastal managers for their daily work. In this prospect, a set of methodological and technical contributions will be provided aiming at: (i) assessing the coastal use structure and, *lato sensu*, the coastal system according to holistic criteria; (ii) representing and simulating the coastal use structure according to matrix- and GIS-based methods; (iii) mapping the coastal area involved in management programmes; and (iv) zoning the coastal area according to management purposes.

Project IV – Coastal and Deep-ocean Monitoring Systems

The evolving coastal and deep-ocean systems have been involved in accelerated changes due to the combined effects of climate change, increasing human pressure and globalisation. Hence, the need to monitor them to optimise management has acquired increasing importance. This need is concerned with both coastal areas and deep-ocean spaces but, for self-evident reasons, at the present time it is much more important in the former space. This justifies the efforts of scientists and practitioners to implement, design and apply monitoring and evaluation methods and techniques, and the wide room that technical literature has given to these subjects.

To meet this need Project IV of *Oceans 21* will aim at: (i) providing useful methods and techniques for monitoring key deep-ocean uses and simulating the consequences from new kinds of use; (ii) providing methods and techniques for evaluating the impacts of coastal development on the ecosystem, economic organisation and social context; and (iii) providing methods and techniques for monitoring and evaluating the efficiency of coastal management programmes.

Project V – Training, Education and Mutual Assistance in Marine Science for ICM

In 1998, in the context of the International Year of the Ocean, the Conference *Education and Training in Integrated Coastal Area Management* (Genoa, Italy, 25–29 May), designed and convened with the key co-operation of the IOC, was the ground for intense discussion. It was agreed that, at the present time, education has to deal with two basic issues: (i) to adopt conceptual and logical backgrounds effectively consistent with the need to holistically manage the coastal area – which implies referring to the epistemology of complexity; and (ii) to design, experiment and spread new techniques, such as GIS, distance learning and permanent education, to optimise productivity in courses and professional skills.

The specific background of IOC is based on the Training, Education and Mutual Assistance (TEMA) programme, which had a leading role in the design of the above mentioned Conference. TEMA aims at building marine scientific and technological capacity in ICM for the developing IOC Member States, by organising global, regional and national symposia, workshops, seminars, and training courses for different types and levels, as well as by provision of study grants, and, if possible, fellowships for marine scientists to have training in integrated coastal area management. This project is a part of the IOC/TEMA overall effort.

Moving from this wide background, as a main goal Project V will aim at:

(i) designing and spreading manuals on fundamentals, key sectors and issues of integrated coastal management; (ii) optimising efforts to use GIS in the field; (iii) designing and convening courses with the aim of optimising educational profiles and professional skills on a national basis; (iv) encouraging the design and experimentation of distance learning courses; and (v) experimenting permanent education techniques.

Special Subject Area: Coastal Urbanisation

The International Workshop *Challenges on Growing Urbanisation of the World's Coastal Areas* (Hangzhou, China, 27–30 September 1999), convened by the Intergovernmental Oceanographic Commission with the collaboration of the International Geographical Union, led participants to adopt a Final Declaration[6] including these subject areas: (i) Integrated Planning of Coastal Areas; (ii) Education, Training and Public Awareness; (iii) Establishing a network of large coastal cities. Due to their close linkage with the *Oceans 21* topics and approaches, the above-mentioned subject areas were considered by IOC and IGU as components of the *Oceans 21* programme.

The Role of Oceans 21 Dossiers

In order to mobilise scientific efforts from all over the world, *Oceans 21* is going to convene a series of *Dossiers* dealing with general and special issues which will be designed and worked out to implement educational tools on integrated coastal management (ICM). The potential Dossier users include: (i) education and training academical and extra-academical institutions and organisations; (ii) managers and planners; and (iii) governmental agencies and local authorities.

Dossiers will be published by IOC and will be presented as a joint IOC-IGU initiative in the framework of the *Oceans 21* programme. They will be available in: (i) hard copy; (ii) electronic format (CD-ROM); and (iii) *http://www.nos.noaa-gov/icm.* Promotion will be made through the linked web-sites.

The series is to be co-ordinated by *Julian Barbière* and *Adalberto Vallega* as editors-in-chief. Editor(s) of individual Dossiers, assisting the author(s), will be welcome. The Editorial Board includes the series co-ordinators, and: (i) the series secretary; (ii) the editing reviewer (language cleaning); (iii) the drawing assistant; and (iv) the web processing (transfer of materials to web pages).

Dossiers will be worked out in English. Translations into other languages will be made where needed and possible.

They will be worked out following this procedure:

(i) The Guest editor(s)/author(s) send the tentative project to the *Oceans 21* Secretariat (Paris);

---

[6] Available at *www.polis.unige.it/igu-vallega.*

(ii) The tentative project is evaluated by the *Oceans 21* Advisory Committee;
(iii) The final decision on whether operating the project is adopted by the co-ordinators and editors-in-chief of the series (*J. Barbière* and *A. Vallega*);
(iv) The author(s) work(s) out the issues;
(v) The Dossier is published in the series, and is circulated by IOC in hard copy, electronic format and Internet;
(vi) The author(s) get(s) 50 hard copies and 10 CD-Rom copies.

Each Dossier consists of 128 pages and, tentatively, includes these chapters:

Chapter 1. The issue (presentation of the subject)
Chapter 2. Exploring literature (consideration of the key conceptual and methodological references, and of contributions on technical aspects, such as GIS)
Chapter 3. Looking at experience (consideration of selected case studies)
Chapter 4. Optimising approaches (presentation of guidelines)
Chapter 5. Technical Appendices.

As a preliminary approach, these subjects may be considered as worthy of consideration: (i) the structure of the ICM programme; (ii) conflicts on coastal management; (iii) coastal biodiversity; (iv) coastal cultural heritage; (v) urban waterfronts; (vi) planning in coastal management; (vii) coastal fisheries; (viii) coastal tourism; (ix) coastal merchant seaports; (x) coastal recreational harbours; and (xi) coastal GIS.

Conclusive Considerations

Oceans 21 has three interests.

First, it aims at promoting geography in the context of a subject area, namely ocean management, which is acquiring such a strong importance that it has been included as a key subject in the 1990–1992 agenda of the United Nations Commission on Sustainable Development. In this framework, it designs possible pathways, where physical and human geography could effectively be integrated, an therefore overcoming a long, frustrating history of separate approaches. Moreover, the separation between coastal and marine geography, which has no epistemological justification, benefits from the prospect of being transcended.

Secondly, it aims at presenting geography as a science able to bridge perspectives from natural and social science in view of operating strategies and actions designed by Agenda 21 and subsequent materials from inter-governmental organisations. In this framework, the programme opens the way to the implementation of the programme setting convened by ICSU on ocean and coastal subjects.

Third, *Oceans 21* has the pilot role of experimenting how IGU, and the geographers' community as a whole, could establish co-operation with inter-governmental organisations – in this case, with IOC and UNESCO – therefore implementing their visibility in the international arena.

*Yang Jinsen**

ECO-ECONOMIC MANAGEMENT OF COASTAL ZONES

The ocean boasts immense economic, military, scientific and ecological values. However, an eco-economic crisis has occurred in the ocean, the ecological environment of a large area of the marine region has degenerated and the marine industries have receded, thus affecting the development of coastal areas. Strengthening the work of protecting the eco-environment and ensuring the sustainable development of the ocean has become the common mission facing man. The concepts of eco-economics and eco-economic management should be introduced into the work of marine eco-environmental management or the work of marine eco-environmental protection. The ocean is in itself a large ecosystem and at the same time divided into many secondary ecosystems; in the marine areas where there are human activities, the economic activities of man are combined with the natural marine ecosystems; from this then evolves the eco-economic system. Therefore, the marine eco-environmental management must be based on the basic theories of eco-economics, apply the method of eco-economic management and develop a model of regionalization in the scope of management, systematization in the contents of management and networking in the management system.

Regionalization in the scope of management (based on the natural sea areas, large marine ecosystems, special marine ecosystems and the key areas of marine eco-economy) should be a basic strategic measure for the work of marine eco-environmental protection. And China's work on marine eco-environmental protection should also be based on the marine eco-economic zones, carry out management by zonation, design integrated management plans in the light of the objectively different eco-economic zones and bring about the management activities with concerted behaviors of the government, market and public in the related administrative regions.

Systematization in the contents of management is the integration of the current marine environmental protection and marine resources management, which aims at bringing about a marine eco-economic management system and establishing new management models. This includes changing the environmental protection mode of purely controlling marine pollution into the management model of large eco-environmental systems so as to thoroughly prevent the marine eco-environment from degeneration; transforming the pattern of putting emphasis on the conservation of

* China State Oceanic Administration Institute for Marine Affairs, 100860 Beijing.

P. Ehlers, E. Mann-Borgese and R. Wolfrum (eds.), Marine Issues, 321–335

economic biological resources into the management model guided by the theory of large ecosystems, which attaches importance to the protection of the natural environment where economic organisms live, adjusts the economic and social relations and develops the fishery eco-economy; transforming the management model of stressing the short-term objectives into the one of stressing the long-term objectives so as to ensure the sustainable use of marine resources.

The interconnected management system is a new system suited to marine eco-economic management. The organisational framework related to coastal and marine eco-economic management includes the departments of oceanic administration, environmental protection, fishery administration and municipal construction. The objects of management include activities of tidal-flat development, coastal use, marine fishing, mariculture, marine tourism and marine minerals and resources development. In addition, the participation of the public in the coastal area is called for. The management system with a vertical-type structure under the charge of a single department is not fit for such a management, but it is essential to explore into establishing a net-structured system.

1. Structure of the Marine Eco-Economic System

The structure of the marine eco-economic system includes a number of levels such as the global marine ecosystem, regional marine ecosystems, large marine ecosystems, special marine ecosystem, key areas of marine ecosystem and marine ecosystem-protected areas, etc.

The global marine ecosystem is one that includes the global oceans covering an area of 360 million km^2 and is composed of about 0.2 million species of marine life, which is different from that on land.

The regional marine ecosystem refers to the marine ecosystem of sea areas with relatively independent geographical and ecological features, such as the Bohai Sea, Yellow Sea, East China Sea and South China Sea in China.

The large marine ecosystem refers to the sea areas with an area of 200,000 km^2 and unique ecological characteristics, such as the Yellow Sea large marine ecosystem, the East China Sea large marine ecosystem, the northern South China Sea large marine ecosystem and the Nansha large marine ecosystem.

The special marine ecosystem includes the coral reef, mangrove, estuarine, coastal wetland, upwelling and sea grass bed ecosystems, etc.

In carrying out marine ecosystem protection, it is necessary to choose key areas in different stages of economic development and transform them into protected areas, which cannot be achieved by general terms. It is neither necessary nor possible to carry out overall protection and management of all the oceans. There are many types of key areas, such as the key areas in the special marine ecosystem, and the key areas for biological species conservation, etc. The marine ecosystem-protected areas are generally chosen within the key areas, such as the protected areas of coral reef, mangrove, estuary, wetland, larval fish and rare species.

2. Marine Eco-Economic Crisis

2.1. Marine Environmental Pollution

In China, the major problems existing in the work of marine environmental protection are that the quality of marine water is tending to decline and that more than half of the nearshore seawater has been seriously polluted. The scope of offshore pollution is constantly expanding and, in the Bohai Sea, Yellow Sea, East China Sea and South China Sea, oil pollution is tending to rise in varying degrees. The heavily polluted sea areas have extended from the Pearl River mouth in the 1980s to West Guangdong, the sea area east of Vietnam, Beibu Gulf and even to part of the sea area of Hainan Island. Other heavily polluted sea areas include the north of Liaodong Bay, west of the Bohai Bay and the Haikou Bay, etc. Owing to the aggravation of seawater eutrophication in the sea areas, red tides occur frequently. According to incomplete statistics, during 1980–1992 nearly 300 red tides occurred in Chinas sea area while during 1972–1979 only 20 have been detected. Especially since the late 1980s, the number of red tide occurrences has been increasing year by year and its area is larger and larger, thus doing great harm to the marine living resources and the fishery production. Besides, offshore oil spill accidents occur frequently. Between 1980 and 1995, a total of 115 oil spill incidents of a certain scale have been detected.

2.2. Marine Habitat Degeneration

The seawater quality and the bottom habitat are deteriorating. For example, off Zhejiang Province there is virtually no Class-1 seawater available and about 30,000 km^2 of sea area have been polluted. The natural landscape of the tidal-flat wetland has been severely damaged. The living and breeding ground for important economic fish, shrimp, crab and shellfish has vanished. Many rare and endangered wild animals and plants have become extinct. This has also reduced the capacity of the tidal-flat wetland in regulating the climate, storing water and diverting floods, resisting the storm surge and protecting the bank and the farm land. The coastline of the bay has been reduced, the volume of the bay has shrunk, the proportion of artificial coast has increased, the shoal lost, the natural level of the coast dropped and the fish, shrimp, crab, shellfish and algae naturally living in the tidal zone and waters of the bay have generally declined.

2.3. Danger of Marine Desertification

Part of the bays and the sea area near cities have been subjected to desertification and become heavily polluted sea area, where marine life has decreased or become extinct, and the edible marine life cannot be eaten.

2.4. Special Ecosystems being Seriously Damaged

About 58% of the world's coral reef is in danger of degeneration, 80% of the coral reef in Southeast Asia is in danger. Besides, the mangrove, wetland and sea-grass beds have also suffered various kinds of destruction. The mangrove is decreasing. In the 1950s, China had about 50,000 km^2 of mangrove, of which only about 20,000 km^2 is left, and, as a result, 80% of the fringing reef in Hainan Island has been destroyed in varying degrees.

2.5. *Decline of Marine Fishery Resources*

Among the 200 species of marine fish in the world, 60% has been overfished or their resource biomass has been reduced. The catch in 13 of the 15 major fishing zones in the world has dropped. Fishing seasons cannot be set for the cod, small and large yellow croakers, Spanish mackerel, and flatfish in the Yellow Sea and Bohai Sea. The red porgy and hairtail have basically vanished from the Bohai Sea. And in the East China Sea, fishing seasons cannot be set for the large and small yellow croakers, and flatfish except the hairtail, and the large and small yellow croakers are on the verge of extinction. In the South China Sea, there are no fishing seasons for important offshore fish such as *Paragyrops edita* Tanaka.

2.6. *Decrease of Marine Biological Species*

A total of 20,278 species of aquatic life have been recorded in China's sea areas. The populations of the currently rare marine species are faced with the grave threat of disappearance and extinction. At the same time, some other species, which used to have large numbers and be widely distributed are gradually becoming new rare species.

2.7. *Coastal Erosion*

Coastal erosion is most severe along the coasts of Jiangsu, Hebei and Shandong Provinces. Erosion is comparatively less serious to the south of the Changjiang River, mainly occurring in the Hangzhou Bay, central Fujian, Guangxi and Hainan.

2.8. *Siltation of Important Estuaries*

Such as those of the Changjiang, Zhujiang, Haihe, Liaohe, Minjiang and Qiantangjiang Rivers.

2.9. *Decline of the Marine Fishing Industry*

The experts with FAO/UN suggest that 53% of the fishing vessels in the world are superfluous. The European Community decided in 1996 to cut down the number of fishing vessels by 40% within 6 years and Russia also wanted to reduce the number of fishing vessels considerably. Now 100,000 fishermen are out of work throughout the world.

2.10. Excessive Use of Cultivable Sea Areas

The offshore cultivation density in many bays and coastal areas which are suitable for developing mariculture is too high, the cultivated sea area is itself heavily polluted and the economic results are getting poorer and poorer.

2.11. The Development of Marine Tourism is Affected

Quite a number of sea areas used for swimming are polluted and sea beaches are destroyed, thus affecting the development of coastal bathing.

2.12. The Expenses for Controlling Coastal Pollution Must be Increased

In order to control the land-based pollution of the coastal area, it is essential to reduce the production of pollutants and their discharge into the sea, and confine the discharge of pollutants into the sea to the limits of the environmental capacity of the sea area. Therefore, some countries have begun to practice the system of pollutants total amount control. The total amount of pollutants is closely related to the extent of the economic development scale of the coastal area; so if the total amount is too large, the extent of economic development should be limited, or the expenses for controlling pollution should be increased so as to reduce the output of pollutants.

2.13. Scale of Population Carrying Capacity is Associated with the Marine Eco-economic Capacity

Too large a population, insufficient dwelling space and deterioration of the environment for production and life has become an important problem. Therefore, many countries are studying the population carrying capacity of the coastal area, to predict the trend of population growth there and to consider corresponding countermeasures. The coastal states of the United States have made predictions on the population in 2020 and the land used for construction, and considered all kinds of countermeasures.

2.14. Human Health is Affected

Owing to marine environmental pollution, marine products contain too much toxic matter, which causes adverse effects on the human health in coastal areas. The *mizu mata byo* in Japan is an early typical example, and similar problems also occur in many other parts of the world. A recent issue of the Japanese *Shukan Yomiuri* suggested that it is necessary to refrain from eating offshore fish, and it stated: small fish and microorganisms take in chemical substances in the sea and then are eaten by big fish. Owing to such a food chain, many chemical substances are concentrated in the bodies of large fish such as tuna. Sixty percent of the total amount of dioxins taken in by the Japanese through the food chain comes from fish. In 1988, many people (410,000 in Shanghai alone) in Shanghai and Jiangsu fell ill because of having eaten the blood clams in the Qidong sea area which had been infected by the hepatitis A virus. This incident has seriously damaged people's health and has created a very bad impression.

3. Impact and Challenge Encountered by Coastal Areas

3.1. Pressure of the Population Moving to the Coastal Area

Most coastal areas in the world boast favorable natural conditions and are fit for economic development and human dwelling. At present, 60% of the world's population is living in the coastal zone within 100 km of the coast. Thirteen of the 16 metropolises each with a population of over 10 million are coastal cities. The migration of the population to the coastal zone has become a global problem, and every day, 3600 people throughout the world are moving to the coastal areas. In America and other regions, most of the new plans for the development of residential quarters are carried out in the coastal zone. China's coastal provinces and autonomous regions have a total population of about 500 million as well as a large floating population. According to predictions by demographic experts, before 2020, there will not be much change in the trend of the population moving to the coastal zone. Each year there will be a population of 80–100 million from the central and western regions of China moving to the coastal zone. The fact that the coastal zone is filled with a large population would inevitably result in insufficient living space and aggravation of pollution as well as other eco-environmental and socio-economic problems.

3.2. Impact of the Large Amounts of Land-based Pollutants Discharged into the Sea

Densely populated and economically developed, the coastal zone generates a large amount of wastes. As the ocean is located in a lower position on earth, most of the polluting matter is dumped or lost into the sea, including sewage from the industry and domestic sewage, petroleum, toxic and harmful chemicals, radioactive matter. The sewage directly discharged into the sea by coastal factories and cities each year in China amounts to 10 billion tons, of which 1.46 million tons is the major harmful matter.

3.3. Destruction Resulting from Irrational Development

The irrational development of the ocean by man has brought severe damage to the marine resources, which generally may be attributable to the following three aspects:

- Concept of gaining gratis. It is believed that the marine resources are rich and therefore can be used gratis or without any limit;
- Behavior of seeking gains. Though knowing perfectly well that a certain marine

resource such as whales and sea turtles needs protection, some people may find all sorts of excuses to evade the law and management for the purpose of gaining profits;
- Development for subsistence, *i.e.*, excessive development of marine resources for one's own subsistence or for the subsistence of the current generation; for instance, the excessive use of cultivable bays in regions with large populations, overfishing of economic fish, and damage to such important ecosystems as mangrove and coral reef.

3.4. Conflict Between the Ecological and Economic Objectives

To realize sustainable development, it is essential to establish the goal of integrating ecological benefits with economic benefits in the course of marine development. However, in the regions with a low level of economic and social development, developing economy is usually taken as the priority objective while the ecological objective is easily neglected. In addition, due to lack of funds and backward technical means as well as for other economic and social reasons, the policy-makers are often in a dilemma as to whether to develop the economy or to protect the ecological environment, as a result of which it is often hard to realize the marine eco-environmental objective.

3.5. Effect of Natural Environmental Change

This may include the atmospheric environment, water cycle, cycle of sedimentation and the evolution of living things, all of which have significant effect upon the marine ecological environment.

4. Guiding Ideology of Marine Eco-Economic Management

4.1. Cultural Concept of Man-and-Sea Harmony

To improve the public's knowledge of the ocean's value, gradually foster the concept of manharmony and the sense of protecting the ocean and guide the population in the rational and scientific development and protection of the ocean.

4.2. Idea of Integrated Management for Sea and Land

To study the environmental capacity of each sea area and identify the total discharge of pollutants. On land, the emphasis is put on solving the problem of controlling the amount of pollutants discharged into the sea, while at sea on solving the problems of controlling the pollutants at sea and excessive development and use of marine resources.

4.3. *Creation of Development Patterns in Keeping with the Principle of Sustainable Development*

To harvest marine living resources in a rational way and moderately develop mariculture, develop the technologies and industries for utilization of marine biological wastes as well as wastewater reuse industries in the coastal areas.

4.4. *Umbrella-Structured Regional Cooperation Pattern*

To establish a regionally cooperative management system (international), taking the sea areas closely related with the natural environment, resources and development activities as geographical units; an interprovincial cooperative management system within a country and an inter-county coordinative system within a province, thus forming an umbrella-structured system which would gradually enfold at the regional, national, provincial and county levels.

4.5. *Principle of Sustainable Development*

Development and use rate of marine living resources in the sea area must be less than or equal to the regeneration rate of the resources; wastes discharged into the sea must be less than or equal to the environmental capacity of the sea area; the amount of the population in the coastal area must be less than or equal to the carrying capacity of the coastal area and the ocean.

5. Theories and Systems of Marine Eco-Economic Management

5.1. *Establishing the Property Right System of Marine Ecological Resources by Applying the Capital Theory of Ecological Resources*

Based on the capital theory of ecological resources, the government may establish the property right system of marine ecological resources, and through various policies, carry out resource management in a scientific way. As regards the exhaustible resources, such as submarine coal, submarine oil, beach places etc., the government may raise the land tax if their exploitation rate is too high. The higher the land tax is, the quicker the increase in the exploitation rate is. The government may also levy a tax on exploitation, which increases the unit exploitation cost for the owners of resources and reduces the rate of resource exploitation. The higher the exploitation tax is, the more the exploitation rate would be reduced. The government may establish allowances for exploitation, which is a negative exploitation tax and aims at increasing the rate of exploitation. If the property right of the biological resource is not partitioned, it may be managed very well. Otherwise, its management would be difficult. For instance, the management of the publicly owned marine fishery resources is very difficult. The biological resources are generally managed by controlling the rate of harvest. Some biological resources may be controlled by levying taxes on exploitation and pollution discharge.

5.2. Studying the Problem of Sustainable Use of Marine Ecological Resources by Applying the Supply-and-Demand Theory of Eco-economic Management

The supply-and-demand theory includes the supply of ecological resources and the economic demand for ecological resources. The supply of ecological resources refers to the potential of the ecological resources for meeting the demand in the course of man's production, including the quantity of matter and energy in stock and for renewal. The economic demand for ecological resources refers to the potential and practical demand for ecological resources to satisfy the population growth and the improvement of the quality of life. For such demand, it is up to the macro-management department to propose the planned quantity and the production sector to carry out the exploitation, among which the planned quantity is the potential demand, and the actual exploitation quantity the practical demand. The supply trend of ecological resources is composed of three basic quantitative relations: the current stock, new increment and reduction of matter and energy. The economic system also involves three key elements: economic growth, ecological resource input and social demand. The economic growth and the ecological resource input are in a positive feedback circle: The economic growth needs more ecological resources while the constant input of ecological resources promotes the economic growth. The economic growth and the social demand is also in a positive feedback circle: Along with the constant growth of consumer demand, the economic growth rate is continuously rising, as a result of which the socio-economic demand is further satisfied. In the marine eco-economic management, it is necessary to formulate the policies and measures which help increase the quantity of ecological resources, such as those encouraging release of biological resources for enhancement, expanding the exploration and exploitation of mineral resources, and encouraging the development of resource-saving industries.

5.3. Improving Environmental Management by Applying the Externality Theory of Ecological Resources

Externality is an overflowing phenomenon, i.e. the producer or consumer of a certain commodity himself does not bear the responsibility for the side-effects of the harmful or beneficial influence. For example, the China Ocean News reported on 20 November 1998: The sewage discharged into the sea without being treated by seven newly constructed fish meal plants around the Jimiya harbour area of Weiling Town, Jiaonan City caused the death of all the perch and blackheaded fish cultivated in 50 net cages, thus resulting in a direct economic loss of nearly one million yuan (RMB). One of the important tasks of eco-economic management is to intervene in externality by taking various measures so that the eco-environment would become a part of the capital and the loss of the eco-environment is incorporated into the cost. By means of tax, subsidy, market, laws and regulations and property rights, education and planning, etc., such externality could be internalized so as to attain the goal of protecting the ecological environment.

5.4. Establishing the Integrated Management System

This would include the formulation of integrated management laws and regulations, establishment of the high-level planning coordination and decision-making mechanism, creation of marine administrative organs at all levels and formation of the marine protection system with wide participation of the public and the scientific and a technological support system for the integrated management.

5.5. Strengthening Governments' Management of Marine Eco-economy

As the main body of macro eco-economic management, the government has the functions of formulating the key eco-economic management plans and strategies; coordinating the work of ecological environmental protection among various regions, industrial sectors and enterprises; developing the policies, laws and regulations, and criteria, etc. for eco-economic management, organizing and fostering the ecological resource market; promoting the infrastructure construction in the eco-environmental field; pushing forward the development of eco-environmental science and technology, and taking charge of the work of eco-environmental supervision and management.

6. Marine Eco-Economic Management Model

6.1. Regionalization in the Management Scope

The marine eco-economic system is regional and different regions have different characteristics. The management work must be based on the eco-economic regions. The regions include the natural sea area, special ecological areas, and administrative regions. Each sea area in China may be divided into several sub-areas and a sub-area management system may be established by applying the pattern of 1 + x. Unified planning may be made for the natural sea areas or special eco-economic zones and implemented according to administrative zones. The goal of regional eco-economic management is the sustainable development of the regional economy. The principles of regional eco-economic management include: rate of development and use < renewal rate of resources; wastes discharge < environmental capacity; population development scale < population carrying capacity; development scale of cultivation < carrying capacity of tidal flood and waters.

The several major natural seas of China may be divided into 10 zones:

1 + 4 pattern of the Bohai Sea:

Taken as an eco-economic area, the Bohai Sea is planned in a unified way and the sea areas are managed as falling within the jurisdiction of Liaoning Province, Shandong Province, Hebei Province and Tianjin Municipality respectively.

1 + 2 + 1 pattern of the northern Yellow Sea:

Taken as an eco-economic area, the Yellow Sea is planned in a unified way and the sea areas are managed as falling within the jurisdiction of Liaoning and Shandong respectively. In addition, cooperation must be carried out with Korea.

1 + 2 + 1 pattern of the southern Yellow Sea:
Taken as an eco-economic area, the southern Yellow Sea is planned in a unified way with the coastal sections of Liaoning and Jiangsu managed separately. In addition, cooperation must be carried out with the Republic of Korea

1 + 4 + 2 pattern of the East China Sea:
Taken as an eco-economic area, the East China Sea is planned in a unified way and managed by the four areas of Zhejing, Shanghai, Fujian and Taiwan. Besides, cooperation must be carried out with Japan and the Republic of Korea.

1 + 1 pattern of the Taiwan Straits:
The work of marine eco-economic management of the Taiwan Straits is planned in a unified way and management is carried out by the areas falling within the jurisdiction of Taiwan and Fujian respectively.

1 + 3 pattern of the northern South China Sea:
The northern South China Sea, which is taken as an eco-economic area, is planned in a unified way and managed by the sea areas falling within the jurisdiction of the Guangdong, Hainan and Taiwan administrative regions.

1 + 1 + 1 pattern of the Beibu Gulf:
The marine eco-economic management work of the Beibu Gulf is planned in a unified way and the areas falling under the jurisdiction of Guangxi and Hainan respectively carry out management. In addition, cooperation must be conducted with Vietnam.

1 + 1 pattern of the eastern and southern Taiwan:
The work of marine eco-economic management for the sea areas of eastern and southern Taiwan is planned in a unified way and management is carried out jointly by Taiwan and the Philippines.

1 + 1 pattern of the sea areas around the Xisha Islands:
Falling under the jurisdiction of Hainan Province, the sea areas around the Xisha Islands should be planned and managed in a unified way by Hainan Province.

Multi-national cooperative management of the Nansha Islands.

6.2. Systematization in the Contents of Management

To form a systematized management model with the marine eco-economic system as the point of departure should be the basic guiding ideology for marine eco-economic management. Systematization means to combine marine environmental protection with the management pattern of marine resources, form the marine eco-economic management system and establish a new mode of management; transform the environmental protection pattern of purely controlling marine pollution into the management model of large eco-environmental systems, and prevent the marine eco-environmental degradation once and forever; transform the model of stressing the conservation of economic living resources into the management model guided by the theory of large ecosystems which attaches importance to the protection of the natural environment where economic organisms live, adjusts the economic and social interactions and develops the fishery eco-economy; transform the management model of stressing the short-term objectives into the one stressing the long-term objectives so as to ensure the sustainable use of marine resources.

Controlling marine pollution: control the land source of pollution, marine source of pollution and atmospheric source of pollution.

Improving ecological management: protect the ecological environment of marine life, laying special emphasis on the protection and management of the ecosystems with special ecological value, such as the coastal wetland, sea beach, estuaries, mangrove, coral reef, sea-grass beds, upperwelling sea area, etc.

Rationally using the marine resources and developing clean production: develop the sustainable mode of production for the marine development industries, rationally utilize the marine living resources, marine mineral resources, seawater resources and marine spatial resources and evolve the mode of clean production, which is an important task of the department responsible for marine industries and a key measure to maintain a sound marine eco-economic system.

Building coastal eco-economic cities: The 21st century is an ecological one, in which all cities should develop toward the goal of becoming an ecological city. With respect to the marine eco-environmental protection, the main way of solving the problem of point source in the land sources of pollution is to build coastal ecological cities by summing up the experiences of Xiamen and Dalian, etc. in building clean cities.

Developing ecological agriculture in the coastal areas: The pesticides, chemical fertilizer and sewage from the non-point sources discharged into the sea come mainly from the coastal agricultural areas; the way of solving this problem is to develop ecological agriculture. In some coastal areas, the chemical fertilizer is rationally applied, the use of pesticides is strictly controlled, crabs and fish are cultivated in the paddy fields and the tidal flat and shallow sea are not polluted, all of which are very good experiences.

7. Industrialization Policies for Marine Eco-Economic Construction

Industrialization of ecological construction includes the environmental protection industry, environmental engineering service industry, and environmental software service industry; resource industry, mineral resource prospecting, and marine survey and exploration, aquatic products breeding and ranching, and waste water reuse as well as the resource conservation industry.

Ecologically sound development of industries, including developing clean production, reducing the generation of wastes, adjusting the industrial distribution, so that the industrial development is compatible with resources, sea area space, climatic conditions, etc.

Multiple investment channels of marine eco-economic construction with the government as the main body.

Owing to the large scale of investment in the eco-economic construction, slow returns, and smaller direct economic benefits for the investor, the government must be the main investor. The investment areas of the government include environmental observation and monitoring, environmental scientific research, and education and training, environmental technology research and development, construction of eco-environmental demonstration projects, biodiversity conservation, construction of nature reserves and national parks, expenditures of the key pollution controlling projects and the international cooperative projects, etc.

Economic means of eco-economic management: the system of charging for sewage discharge and using the fees (including collecting fees for over-the-standard discharge of sewage, charging more for the new sources of pollution), bringing the fees of sewage discharge into the cost of production, and earmarking the sewage discharge fee for its specified purpose only, mainly for controlling pollution.

Incentive policy for integrated use: The enterprises, which make use of wastes, are given preferential treatment and supplied with three-wastes resources gratis.

Pollution compensation policy: The polluting unit gives the unit which controls the pollution a certain amount of compensation before it gains the right to discharge the pollutants.

8. Integrated Management Plan for Marine Eco-Economic Management

The overall objective of marine eco-economic management plans is to ensure the perpetual use of resources, constant improvement of the environmental quality and sustainable development of the socio-economy. Sustainability of the marine eco-economic system is jointly determined by the marine environment, marine resources, activities of marine development and use, and economic and social development in the coastal zone. Therefore, the work of marine eco-economic management must rely on the coordination and unity among the related sectors in the complex eco-economic system of each region as well as on the coordination and unity of the governmental, market and public behaviors. The marine sector alone cannot manage well the marine eco-economic system, and only through coordination and cooperation between the marine sector and other sectors within the regional framework, such as those of aquatic products, petroleum, communications, tourism, environmental protection, and municipal administration, can the problems of treatment and industrialization of land-based pollutants and scientific management of marine resources of pollution be solved. Therefore, the marine eco-economic construction must be incorporated into the overall plan for socio-economic development. The integrated management plan must bring about a change in the policy of purely preventing and controlling pollution, effect an integrated management of resources and environment, practice the whole-process management of preventing, monitoring and controlling pollution, and strengthen regional and global cooperation. As China's sea area is vast, it is essential to work out regional plans for marine eco-economic management, such as:

- Plan for the integrated development and protection of the Bohai Sea with emphasis laid on the plan for the treatment of land-based sewage, the plan for the control of mariculture and the plan for the environmental protection of oil exploration and development.
- Plan for the integrated development and protection of the Yellow Sea, including participation in the international cooperation on the Yellow Sea large marine ecosystems.
- Plan for the integrated development and protection of the East China Sea, including participation in the international cooperation on the development and protection of the East China Sea area.
- Plan for the integrated development and protection of the Taiwan Straits, including the cross-strait cooperative protection plan.
- Plan for the integrated development and protection of the northern South China Sea, with stress put on the eco-environmental protection and the rational use of important economic fish resources.
- Plan for the integrated development and protection of the Beibu Gulf, including the plan for the protection of the ecological environment of the Beibu Gulf in cooperation with Vietnam.
- Plan for the protection of the Xisha Islands sea area with emphasis on the protection of coral reefs in the island and reef zone as well as the protection of the coral reef ecosystem.
- Plan for the integrated development and protection of the large marine ecosystems in the Nansha Islands sea area, including the plan for the participation in international cooperation.
- Plan for coastal improvement to protect the sea coast from erosion, prevent wind, wave and storm surge disasters and seawater intrusion and create beautiful sea beach environments.
- Plan for waste water treatment with emphasis on the industrialization of waste water treatment at the land point sources and reduction of the discharge of pollutants into the sea as well as recovery of usable water.
- Plan for the conservation and recovery of mangrove, including extension of the mangrove area and protection of the mangrove ecosystem in the old mangrove area and other regions fit for the growth of mangrove.
- Plan for the protection of coral reefs. The coral reefs have been seriously damaged and are hard to be recovered. Therefore, the existing coral reefs must be strictly protected according to plan.
- Plan for the protection of sea-grass beds. This is a problem that has not aroused sufficient attention, for which investigation and scientific research must be made and a protection plan be worked out.